Building Sustainable Futures

Enacting Peace and Development

Building Sustainable Futures

Enacting Peace and Development

Editors
Luc Reychler
Julianne Funk Deckard
Kevin HR Villanueva

2009
University of Deusto
Bilbao

HumanitarianNet

HumanitarianNet is a network linking three types of partners: higher education institutions, research centres, and govern-mental and non-governmental organisations. At present the network consists of over 100 universities, 6 research centres and 9 international organisations across Europe.

This wide membership demonstrates the capacity of the net-work to gather information and mobilize ideas. Humanitarian-Net was created in 1996 to promote research and education projects in five main fields: Human Rights, Poverty and Devel-opment, Humanitarian Assistance, Peace and Conflict Studies, and Migration, Diversity and Identities.

JZ
5538
.B85
2009
GIFT
April 2010

Cover illustration: Javier F. Ferreras.

© University of Deusto
P.O. box 1 - 48080 Bilbao
e-mail: publicaciones@deusto.es

I.S.B.N.: 978-84-9830-236-3
Legal Deposit: BI - 3.252-09

Printed in Spain/Impreso en España

Contents

List of Contributors

Chadwick F. Alger, Mershon Professor of Political Science and Public Policy Emeritus, The Ohio State University; Secretary General, IPRA, 1983-1987; Vice President IPRA Foundation, 1998; President, International Studies Association, 1978-1979. His books and articles focus on peace research, the UN System and the worldwide relations of people and governments in towns and cities around the world.

Iain Atack is coordinator of the M. Phil. programme in International Peace Studies at the Irish School of Ecumenics, Trinity College Dublin. He has postgraduate degrees from the University of Toronto, Trinity College Dublin and the University of Ulster. He is the author of *The Ethics of Peace and War: From State Security to World Community* (Edinburgh University Press, 2005).

Lamiss Azab is an Egyptian teacher, who recently defended her master's thesis in Political Science from the Institut d'Etudes Politiques de Paris (2007). She is interested in the relationship between language, religion sociology and political orientations. She also holds a Master in Translation Studies and is preparing a PhD about «The Translator as a Cultural Mediator.»

Tomas Baum is director of the Flemish Peace Institute. His research interests concern IR theory, ethics and political philosophy with a particular focus on the use of violence by democratic actors. Within the frame of track two diplomacy and people to people programmes he engages as a facilitator in conflict transformation processes.

Roberto Belloni is Associate Professor of International Relations at the University of Trento, Italy. Previously he has held research and teaching positions at the University of Denver, Harvard, Johns Hopkins and Queens University

Belfast. His publications include the volume *State Building and International Intervention in Bosnia* (Routledge, 2007).

Joseph G. Bock, PhD in International Relations (School of International Service, American University, 1985); Special Professional Faculty Member, Kroc Institute for International Peace Studies, University of Notre Dame (2006-); Visiting Professor, Hebrew University (1998-2000). Most recent book: *Sharpening Conflict Management: Religious Leadership and the Double Edged Sword* (Praeger, 2001).

Hans Günter Brauch is chairman of Peace Research and European Security Studies (AFES-PORESS) since 1987, teaches international relations at the Free University of Berlin, is senior fellow at UNU-EHS in Bonn and editor of the Hexagon Book Series on Human and Environmental Security and Peace (HESP) published by Springer.

Anuradha M. Chenoy is Professor in the School of International Studies, Jawaharlal Nehru University, New Delhi. She has held several academic and administrative positions. She has written several books and articles, among which are: *Human Security: Concept and Implications* (with Shahrbanou Tadjbakhsh, Routledge, 2007) and *Demystifying Terrorism* (ARENA, 2006).

Tara Cooper is a Research Officer with the Human Security Report Project. Her main research interests include poverty and conflict in the developing world, with a particular focus on Africa. She is also involved with several Africa-focused non-governmental organizations in Vancouver, Canada.

Wies De Graeve studied classical philology, secondary teacher training and literary studies at the University of Ghent. As communications officer of the Flemish Peace Institute, he is involved with the communication and coordination of the Institute's Scientific Secretariat.

Daniela Dicorrado-Andreoni currently heads the Sector for Peace and Security in the European Commission's Directorate General for Development issues. Her background includes longstanding service in DG RELEX. She has also acted as Representative of the Commission in the boards of the European Institute of Strategic Studies (EISS) and the EU Satellite Centre (EUSC).

Julianne Funk Deckard assisted the IPRA Secretariat in Leuven from 2005-2009, while pursuing her doctoral studies at the KULeuven, Belgium. Her research focuses on the relationship between religion and peacebuilding/ conflict and her field research is with the three religious communities in Bosnia-Herzegovina.

Johan Galtung is currently the director of Transcend, an organization devoted to conflict transformation by peaceful means. He is the founder of the Peace Research Institute in Oslo (PRIO) and the Journal of Peace Research. He has been a professor at Columbia and Princeton universities, and the universities of Oslo and Hawaii. His book, *Peace by Peaceful Means* (Sage, 1996), is used widely.

Annette Giertsen has worked for Save the Children Norway since 1989, as a country director and special advisor. The last ten years she has worked as an adviser on children and young people's participation and lately her special focus has been given to children's and young people's participation in peacebuilding and peace processes.

Linda M. Johnston is the Director of the Master of Science in Conflict Management and the Center for Conflict Management at Kennesaw State University. She also serves as President of the International Peace Research Association Foundation and on the board of Hands Along the Nile and the UN School for Peace On-Line Committee.

Herbert C. Kelman is Richard Clarke Cabot Professor of Social Ethics, Emeritus, and co-chair of the Middle East Seminar at Harvard University. A pioneer in the development of interactive problem solving, he has been engaged for more than 30 years in efforts toward the resolution of the Israeli-Palestinian conflict.

Sabine Kurtenbach, PhD in political science, is a senior research fellow at the GIGA Institute on Latin American Studies (Hamburg, Germany). Her main research interests are peace processes, conflict dynamics, developments in postwar societies and youth. Her regional focus is on Latin America and Southeast Asia. Her current research is on violence and violence control in postwar societies.

Jake Lynch is Director of the Centre for Peace and Conflict Studies at the University of Sydney. He is the author, with Annabel McGoldrick, of the landmark text, *Peace Journalism*, as well as numerous other books, book chapters and articles. He is an Executive member of the Sydney Peace Foundation. Before taking up an academic career, Jake was a professional journalist, having worked as a presenter for BBC World television news, a Political Correspondent for Sky News and the Sydney correspondent for the Independent.

Andrew Mack is Director of the Human Security Report Project at Simon Fraser University, Vancouver, Canada. He was previously Director of the Strategic Planning in the Executive Office of UN Secretary-General Kofi Annan. He held the Chair in International Relations at the Institute of Advanced Study at the Australian National University (ANU) from 1991 to 1998.

Jason MacLeod is based at the Australian Centre for Peace and Conflict Studies (ACPACS) at the University of Queensland in Brisbane, Australia. He is a co-director of the Change Agency, a not-for-profit NGO providing training and education to civil society groups working on campaigns for social and environmental justice.

Zoe Nielsen is the Executive Director of the Human Security Report Project. Prior to joining the Human Security Report Project, she was the Senior Program Officer with the International Peace Academy's Conflict Prevention Program. She is the co-editor, with Chandra Sriram, of *Exploring Subregional Conflict: Opportunities for Conflict Prevention*.

Úrsula Oswald Spring is a full time professor/researcher at the National University of Mexico in the Regional Multidisciplinary Research Centre (CRIM) and first MRF-Chair on Social Vulnerability at United National University Institute for Environment and Human Security (UNU-EHS). She was elected in 1998 President of the International Peace Research Association, and between 2002 and 2006 she was General Secretary of Latin-American Council for Peace Research. She has written 48 books and more than 320 scientific articles.

Ahmedou Ould-Abdallah is currently the UN Secretary General's Special Representative for Somalia. From 1996-2002 he was the Executive Secretary of the Global Coalition for Africa. From 1985-1996 he served at the United Nations in a number of capacities, including Special Representative for Burundi and Special Coordinator for New and Renewable Sources of Energy and Energy Issues. Previously, he held high-level positions in his native country, Mauritania, and as an ambassador to the United States and the European Union.

Thania Paffenholz (PhD) is lecturer for peace, conflict and development at the Graduate Institute of International and Development Studies. She has worked as advisor to the United Nations, the Development Assistance Committee of the Organisation for Economic Co-operation and Development (OECD-DAC) and various governmental and non-governmental organizations, both at headquarters and in different conflict-affected countries. She has authored and edited numerous articles, book chapters and monographs on peacebuilding and on the role of development in conflict settings.

Luc Reychler is professor of international relations at the University of Leuven, and director of its Center of Peace Research and Strategic Studies. From 2004-2008 he served as Secretary General of the International Peace Research Association. His current research focuses on: peacebuilding architecture, leadership and negotiations; the political economy of peacebuilding, evaluating peace negotiations, and peacebuilding in the DR Congo.

Klaus Rudischhauser is Director at the European Commission's Directorate General Development and Relations with African, Caribbean and Pacific States. Previous roles at the European Commission included: Head of Unit at the Directorate General Personnel and Administration and the Directorate General Energy and Transport; assistance to the Newly Independent State; and duties in the Directorate General Environment.

Mila Shah is the data research assistant at the Human Security Report Project. She holds a bachelor's degree in Political Science and International Relations from the University of British Columbia and her research interests include issues of environmental sustainability, climate change and conflict.

Shahrbanou Tadjbakhsh is the Director of Concentration on Human Security, Master's of Public Affairs, Institut d'Etudes Internationales (Sciences

Po), Paris where she founded the Journal of Human Security. She is author of *Human Security: Concepts and Implications* (with Anuradha M. Chenoy, Routledge, 2007) and numerous publications on human security and liberal peace.

Kevin HR Villanueva is the Project Manager of HumanitarianNet. He is also a Visiting Lecturer at the Pedro Arrupe Institute for Human Rights at the Universidad de Deusto in Bilbao, Spain, teaching courses on the International Human Rights Regime and the ASEAN and an introduction to International Politics and Organization at the School of Humanities and Social Science. His areas of interest encompass transnationalism, norms in international relations and the human rights discourse.

Stephen Zunes is a professor of politics at the University of San Francisco. He is the principal co-editor of *Nonviolent Social Movements* (Blackwell, 1999) and chairs the board of academic advisors for the International Center on Nonviolent Conflict (http://www.nonviolent-conflict.org/).

Introduction

Luc Reychler, Julianne Funk Deckard, Kevin HR Villanueva

The IPRA Path

> *The birth of peace studies resulted from the desperate need for a more peaceful world. The Second World War killed between 50 to over 70 million, including the tragedy of the mass killing of Jews by Nazi Germany and many other horrors. This led to the creation of a new science that could prevent a repetition of large scale human made disasters and foster peace. It would counterbalance the sort of "science" that had been used to develop weapons and war* (Kodama, 2004: 1).

The International Peace Research Association (IPRA) was formed in 1964 by a group of scholars of international peace and security, including Kenneth and Elise Boulding, John Burton, Johan Galtung and Bert Röling. Since than, IPRA has sought to improve the quality and quantity of analysis by (a) creating space for competing approaches and schools of thought and (b) fostering worldwide networking among scholars and practitioners. IPRA contributed to the expansion of peace research and to discussions at the cutting edge of rapidly changing global, regional, national and local landscapes.

Sustainable Peace and Development

In recent years, the development aid community has become aware of the vital linkages between conflict and peace building and development and humanitarian interventions. As a consequence, they now try to "do no harm" (Andersen, 1999) and seek to avoid unintended negative effects of aid interventions on conflict dynamics and support local capacities for peace. The example of Rwanda in 1994, for example, displayed the way in which development projects unwittingly played into the conflict and hindered peace between the conflicting parties. On the other hand, peace builders and researchers have come to realize that professionalizing and streamlining their efforts with development interventions is critical to the achievement of sustainable peace (Paffenholz and Reychler, 2007).

In the past, development interventions often worked *around* conflict, or avoided getting involved in conflict areas. Today, however, with many internal, so-called fragile contexts making up nearly 50% of all development aid sites, conflict is a necessary element of development interventions and cannot simply be avoided. Therefore, "peace and conflict sensitive development" seeks to work both *in* and *on* conflict. It concentrates not only on avoiding negative effects upon the conflict, but also on building peace through aid efforts. The development sector's capacity for peacebuilding in three areas is situated at different levels: at the macro political level (through a dialogue between diplomacy and development), at the development sector level (introducing peace and conflict issues addressed to development strategies) and at the operational level (supporting peacebuilding methodologies within development programs and projects).

Given the current relevance of this discussion, the overall theme of IPRA's 2008 Global Conference focused on the interaction between economic development, environmental change and conflict prevention and peacebuilding efforts in the 21st century. The underlying assumption is that improvements to the human climate of our planet (by means of constructive conflict transformation) are necessary for sustainable development and preventing global warming. The challenge is to re-search new futures. Scholars, decision-makers and practitioners must bring intellectual, volitional and emotional functions together. A great many peace interventions do not address the root causes or sources of violence. Peace researchers play a vital role in these processes of constructive transformation. The many facets, conditions and consequences of the interactions between peacebuilding and development will be explored through the articles of this book.

This collaborative book project ultimately reflects the constant evolution of Peace Studies as it is reflected in its expanding areas of research *and* the institutional structures which provide the vertebrae so that the former can develop with greater depth, continuity and sustainability. This is the reason why HumanitarianNet and, in particular, the Peace and Conflict Sub-Group, have teamed up with IPRA to produce this collection of articles.

HumanitarianNet is a thematic network financed by the European Commission, bringing together the work of higher education institutions in the interrelated disciplines of humanitarian development inter-weaving the sciences and humanities, to analyse the underlying causes of humanitarian crises and formulate strategies for rehabilitation and development. In particular, the network has been robustly promoting and developing EDEN — the European Doctorate Enhancement Pro-gramme for Peace and Conflict Studies, consisting of 14 universities from all over Europe and bringing together the diverse disciplinary per-spectives and national traditions on peace and conflict research. EDEN, in the context of the IPRA conference has, therefore, attempted to gen-erate sustained debate and exchange between policy makers, NGOs, media professionals and academics, in order to facilitate mutual under-standing and ongoing feedback between research, knowledge dissemi-nation and policy. It is in this light that the editors hope this project will come to bear significance.

2008 Conference Summary

IPRA, the network for peace researchers, held its 22nd Global Con-ference, *Building Sustainable Futures: Enacting Peace and Develop-ment*, in Leuven, Belgium from 15-19 July 2008. IPRA's interdisciplinary conference provided a space for approximately 400 researchers from all parts of the world to exchange actionable knowledge about the nec-essary but still insufficiently studied and pursued synergies between peace interventions and sustainable development today in order to ad-vance theory, policy, and practice worldwide. Eight plenary sessions, more than 250 presentations on a wide variety of topics, and numer-ous extra highlights facilitated this exchange. In this way, IPRA again sought and met its three objectives for its biennial conferences: (1) communicating the state of peace research, (2) setting the agenda for future research and (3) communicating research findings from the pre-vious two years.

Crucially, IPRA raised funds to ensure the presence of participants from low-income countries and particularly regions of development and all sides of conflict. Participants from all around the world, many differ-ent disciplines, and a diversity of sectors (theory and researchers, prac-titioners, and policy-makers) attended. Sixty-four countries and all con-tinents were represented. A third of participants came from developing and transition countries, most of whom were funded by IPRA grants. These grants and the conference in general were made possible by the generous financial support of: the Belgian Ministry of Foreign Affairs, the Flemish Government, the Norwegian Ministry of Foreign Affairs, the

Plowshares Collaboration and Manchester College, the Swiss Government and the Toda Institute for Global Peace and Policy Research. Additionally, IPRA once again benefited from the essential "in-kind" giving of numerous volunteers (including the Secretary General, Council, and conveners) and sponsors: the KULeuven as well as its Faculty of Social Sciences, Institute of International and European Policy, and Center for Peace Research and Strategic Studies; the City of Leuven and Mayor of Leuven, the Flemish Peace Institute, InBev, Lee Cooper, and Sint-Michielskerk.

Book Overview

The structure of this book reflects the themes of the conference's eight plenary sessions. Additionally, the conference programmed: a "peace pulpit" (Globalization and Environmental Challenges), a short film festival, a video conference with experts in Brussels, Alexandria and Paris (Human rights and responsibilities for a culture of peace and knowledge) and two roundtable events: a day-long session on DR-Congo and a UNESCO Chair on Sustainable Peace (KULeuven) roundtable on the theme of the challenge of an interdisciplinary approach to peace research. For more information, see the IPRA 2008 Conference Report. The compilation of this book has sought to include as many contributions from these highlighted events as possible.

Human Security and the Legitimization of Peacebuilding

Without serious efforts made towards sustainable peacebuilding, the chance of successful sustainable development is jeopardized. The best indicator of successful development and peacebuilding is human security, uniting state and individual security issues into a broad concept of positive peace. What would it take to develop better synergies or integrative approaches between development and peacebuilding? Andrew Mack, Arunradha M. Chenoy and Shahrbanou Tadjbakhsh present their ideas about the links between these activities and perceptions as well as the integrative approaches to achieve coordination and coherence.

Regional Perspectives on Peacebuilding

The section, *African Peacebuilding: A Radical Analysis*, is concerned with the frequent depiction of Africa as the most unstable and underdeveloped region in the world. Despite overall global progress in the direction of human security, Africa is proving a significant exception to this trend of overall good news. Ahmedou Ould-Abdallah and Klaus Rudischhauser consider the frustrations, hopes and peacebuilding potential of the region. Does the outside world further the needs and interests of the African people?

The Middle East in Danger of Peace seeks to contribute to the analysis of this region's persistent conflicts. The policies of the USA and her allies have contributed to the instability and radicalization in the Middle East. Herbert Kelman and Jake Lynch assess the possibility of cooperation within the region and of improvement of relations with the Western World.

Issues in Peace and Conflict Studies

Religions Dealing with their own Violent Extremisms asks how one truly commits to the building of sustainable peace while, at the same time, remaining loyal to one's own religious convictions, even when these run the risk of turning violent. As in the case of political parties relating to their armed wings, this represents a complex challenge involving multiple loyalties. The potential for both violence and peacebuilding in religions already constitutes a sizeable research field. Less explored is how religious peacebuilding actors, caught up in complex networks of loyalties, address the possible violent extremist tendencies in their own religions. Studying the good practices of dealing with religious violent extremisms which threaten the development that sustainable peace demands, becomes crucial in peace research. In this section Joseph Bock and Lamiss Azab share some field experiences and research that they have developed along this theme.

Peacebuilding practice and research has traditionally assumed that civil society has a constructive role to play in peacebuilding. However, we are not sure whether this assumption holds. There has been little empirical analysis of civil society's role in the context of armed conflict, and even less regarding its potential, limitations and critical factors. This section, *Civil and Uncivil Society: Conditions for Supporting Conflict and Peacebuilding*, takes up these questions. Thania Paffenholz presents preliminary results from the international project "Civil Society and Peacebuilding." These results show that civil society has contributed constructively to peacebuilding in many countries, although it often plays a limited role. Based on this, Sabine Kurtenbach and Roberto Belloni therefore discuss enabling and disabling conditions for civil society and the state (respectively) to fulfill a constructive role in peacebuilding.

There is a growing awareness that there are not only limits to growth of, but also to the use violence to manage conflicts. More attention is being paid to policies and methods to transform conflicts in non-violent ways. The EU is depicted as a positive role model. For example, in Georgia and Ukraine nonviolent strategies were recently used to change political regimes. In the section, *Nonviolence in Action: A Global Trend?*, Iain Atack, Jason MacLeod and Stephen Zunes reflect upon how nonviolent policies can be made more attractive and effective to deal with conflicts. To these ends, violence and nonviolence will be broadly defined as well as an assessment of the use of nonviolent policies.

Rejuvenating Conflict Prevention: Confronting the Challenges of Youth and Conflict considers how the plight of children and young people are often sidelined, if not neglected, in the discourse on peace and conflict. The sector is usually portrayed as passive participants (or vulnerable victims of conflict) and does not really paint an accurate picture of where young people really stand in times of conflict: while a good number are passive recipients of the situation, an equal number are also active participants —either as combatants or as peace advocates. Annette Giertsen helps to broaden the understanding and appreciation about youth— who they are, where they are and how they contribute in situations of peace and conflict.

As discussed in *Globalization and Environmental Challenges: Security in the 21st Century*, the end of the Cold War, globalization and global environmental change have triggered a global reconceptualization of security. New security concepts emerged that shifted the referent object from the state to the human being (human security) focusing on environmental challenges (environmental security), on gender issues (gender security) as well as on energy, food, health and water security. Úrsula Oswald Spring and Hans Günter Brauch address the religious, philosophical and ethical dimensions of the thinking on security in eastern, western and southern cultures.

Celebrating the Founders of Peace Research

Many scholars have contributed to the growth of the peace research field. We honour the work of four of them. These people have done excellent scholarly work, were instrumental in the founding and growth of strong academic programs, and were willing to give of their time and talents to develop the next generation of scholars in the field. The scholars we are honouring in this section framed the field and then encouraged younger scholars to expand upon their work. Chadwick

Alger and Herbert Kelman discuss their research in the field while Linda Johnston provides a reflection on the life and work of Elise Boulding. Johan Galtung looking back at his experience, considers what is important for pofessionalism the future of peace research.

Conference Highlights

Finally, the book includes reports on the innovative addition from the Flemish Peace Institute in its popular short film festival, followed by a fascinating discussion and a strategically oriented moral report from the Secretary General to the members of IPRA, reflecting on four years of lessons learned (2004-2008).

References

KODAMA, Katsuya (2004): *The IPRA Path*. At: http://soc.kuleuven.be/iieb/ ipraweb/ documents/iprapath.pdf.

PAFFENHOLZ, Thania and Luc REYCHLER (2007): *Aid for Peace: A Guide to Planning and Evaluation for Conflict Zones*. NOMOS, Baden-Baden.

Peace Research: An Inconvenient Field of Study Address of the IPRA Secretary General

Luc Reychler
University of Leuven

Dear colleagues and friends, welcome to Leuven: one of the hearts of scholarship in the world. Since 1964, researchers and reflecting practitioners have gathered every two years on different continents to assess the state of the conflict and peace in the world and to set the agenda for future research activities. IPRA is a global think-tank or a forum for all researchers who wish to contribute to sustainable peace-building and to intellectual solidarity, which is essential for the transformation of difficult conflicts.

The organization of such a conference is not without challenges, because (1) it implies bringing people from all parts of the world (not just the rich ones), which requires financial resources at a time when flights are becoming more expensive. It also (2) involves cooperative consulates delivering visas on time: this has become more difficult because of the tightened "war on terror" security controls and the Schengen rules of the EU. Additionally, (3) it demands a willingness to invite not only like-minded re-searchers, but also researchers and practitioners who empathize with the so-called spoilers of peace: the political terrorists, extremists, citizens from "evil" countries or people without a country as well as groups which are excluded from the so-called civilized world.

At the IPRA conferences many research questions are raised but three themes stand out: (1) the state of conflict and peace in the world, (2) the obstacles which inhibit peacebuilding, and (3) the agenda of future research.

The State of Conflict and Peace

Has progress been made in the prevention of violence or the building of sustainable peace? Paradoxically, the answer seems to be yes and no. Some annual reports, such as the human security report of Andrew Mack, provide a number of good news indicators, especially about the reduction of armed violence. Other viewpoints are less rosy and point to the high level of unarmed violence and to the confluence of certain threats expected to create havoc if not responded to more effectively. Some of these are: growing competition over resources, the marginalization of the majority world, climate change, global militarization, competition between brutal and sophisticated capitalism and the pressures towards a democratizing the international system. Paradoxically, the latter could be the most destabilizing trend because globalization is not only about trade, the environment, communication, but also about the growing acceptance of the universality of human rights, the awareness of gross inequalities and consequentially the rise of expectations, feelings of relative deprivation and demands for a fair or democratic international system. Equally disturbing is the ongoing march of folly. If Erasmus were alive today, I am sure he would write a second edition of his *Praise of Folly*. Follies are governmental policies that go against national or international interests and are disproportionately expensive. Such follies are not only the work of dictators, such as Mugabe or Saddam Hussein but also of democracies. Democracies are the only countries today that fight international wars and have colonies. Joseph Stiglitz assessed the true costs of the Iraq war at three trillion dollars; these calculations do not even include the impact of negative role modelling this war has brought to the international theatre. A huge folly in the making is the increasing diabolisation and threatening of Iran by the US and its allies. This is no longer a matter of security, but of absolute control over the region and its oil and gas resources.

Obstacles to the Analysis of Peacebuilding

The second question addressed during IPRA conferences concerns the obstacles to sustainable peacebuilding. Probably the biggest obstacle today is the denial of the high level of non-armed violence. The war on terrorism is an exercise in gross denial; it depicts terrorism as the greatest threat on earth and blinds people with a veil of strategic ignorance. A second obstacle is classifying peoples or countries crudely and singularly into good and evil axes, civilized and less civilized cultures, Western and anti-Western groups, just and unjust wars, democratic and undemocratic regimes, etc. The incendiary implications of such classifications can be a sense of encroachment degradation, and humiliation that make it easier to mobilize for rebellion and revolt. Feelings of dignity and humiliation have a great impact on international behaviour. Evelin Lindner calls humiliation the atom bomb of emotions. Another obstacle to the development of coherent peacebuilding policies is approaching complex realities in a reductionistic way, where one threat is singled out and gets all the attention (such as population growth, terrorism, climate, weapons of mass destruction, rogue states) or one approach (such as war or coercive diplomacy) sucks up most of the resources. A last obstacle in peace research relates to data and statistics of conflict and peace. There are not enough reliable, valid and sensitive data on armed and unarmed violence and practically no data about what Carolyn Nordstrom calls the shadows of war: the violence profiteers and their profits. For most people in conflict zones, wars are "total losses" ("*pertes totales*"); for a minority who are conflict profiteers, they are a secure source of income (Naomi Klein calls it disaster capitalism). The war in Iraq, for example, benefits national armies, private security forces, arms and reconstruction industries and those who aspire to control the oil in the region. This war proves that the that world is far from flat.

Strengthening the Impact of Peace Research

The third main question addressed during the IPRA conference relates to what should be done to strengthen the impact of peace research. First of all, researchers and practitioners should take theories more seriously and spend more time to reflecting on the normative, theoretical and epistemological assumptions underlying their opinion-shaping and policy-making. It's also important to do something about the use and misuse of simple concepts which confuse policy-making, such as violence and nonviolence, conflict and post-conflict, war and peace, democracy and non-democracy. More efforts are needed to get a better understanding of sustainable peacebuilding processes, because sustainable development and climate control is doomed to fail without sufficient peacebuilding efforts. If the "human climate" or the way people manage conflicts does not improve, this "weather" will continue to screw up our planet. Peace researchers should also be in the business of evaluating policies, accounting for the costs and benefits, and holding accountable the policy-makers and -shapers of unjust wars or follies. All of this requires not only analytical skills but also courage, which implies a willingness to ask questions that might challenge —and even break— prevailing perceptions and patterns. Research can be risky. In January of this year, a Congolese researcher told me she studied small scale corruption, but abstained from researching large scale corruption because it was not permitted and would be a career and life threatening venture. In America, where freedom of speech and opinion are prime values, few scholars criticized the war in Iraq or the lingering militarization of the Middle East because its not pleasant to be stigmatized as unpatriotic or as anti-American or any other anti-ism, and because this risks the loss of one's promotion or research funding. In order to be politically correct, many colleagues opt for less sensitive political issues or hide behind methodological correctness. Peace research may be an inconvenient science, but it's a vital and hope-raising component of the peacebuilding process.

Three Generations of Peace Researchers

In 1964, IPRA was shaped by a first generation of peace researchers who invented new ways and means for studying and resolving conflicts constructively. It was an exciting and very creative period. This was also the period when a fusion was attempted between researchers and activists: it was called the peace research movement. At the IPRA conference in Groningen in 1990, at the end of the Cold War, a second generation of peace researchers sought to strengthen and institutionalize peace research by sharpening its focus (large scale violence), by using trans-disciplinary approaches, by synthesizing findings and by having a politically detached commitment to peace. It was the end of the peace research movement. Today, in 2008, a third generation of peace research and peace researchers is coming of age. Peace research III is characterized by: (1) an awareness that the assumptions underlying national and international, governmental and non-governmental conflict prevention and peacebuilding activities are strongly biased by Western-generated theories and interests; (2) the conviction that researchers should spend more time in the field and be engaged in planning and evaluating interventions in conflict zones; (3) the belief that a more effective exchange of knowledge and know-how is needed between researchers, practitioners, policy-makers and civil societies[1]; (4) the assumption that world citizenship is no longer a metaphor, but a necessity: peace requires the capacity to transcend boundaries and to develop multiple loyalties; (5) the observation that in the end, peace

---

[1] See the Rhombus Model of peace knowledge and know-how by Elias Lopez and Jacques Haers.

boils down to power relations. Kenneth Boulding has come back, especially his distinction between three types of power: coercive power, market power and integrative power. It has become quite evident that the world cannot afford any more coercive power, and that peaceful sustainable futures will require both economic and integrative power.

Let me end by wishing you all a fruitful and joyful week.

Human Security
and the
Legitimization of Peacebuilding

Human Security and the Legitimization of Peacebuilding

Shahrbanou Tadjbakhsh[1]
Sciences Po

Prelude

The Responsibility to Protect (R2P) doctrine, since its first conception in the 2001 Report of the International Commission on Intervention and State Sovereignty (ICISS), seems to have posed an ethical
responsibility for the international community to act on behalf of individuals in cases where states are unable or unwilling to protect them.
Yet, for critical theorists, the R2P norm has become an instrument for
legitimizing and giving moral authority to new, more direct forms of
Western intervention and regulation (Chandler, 2004). For post-colonial
critics, external intervention, under any name, can hardly create a just
world order for it sustains the existing asymmetry of power in international relations. After all, in conceivable imagination, the South can
never muster the resources or the confidence to intervene in the North,
even though a number of industrialized states, plagued by the down-
turns of economic globalization, are failing in their responsibilities to
protect the jobs, welfare, and social security and healthcare for their
populations. But advocates of utilitarianism and liberal internationalists
counter-claim that the alternative to disengagement, or non-action is
not a viable solution. From a utilitarian viewpoint, a potential relapse to
war could have more negative consequences than the potential side effects of intervention.

Instead of further engaging with the ethical debate about intervention, this essay ponders the aftermath: when interventions do happen,

---

[1] This paper is based on a presentation made at the IPRA conference, July 15, 2008
in Leuven, Belgium. Parts of this article are published in Oliver Richmond, ed. *New Approaches to Peacebuilding*. Palgrave (forthcoming).

whether in the name of the responsibility to protect or for strategic interests and regime changes, what happens afterwards? As Lidén (2009,
abstract) argues, "The damage of imperialistic colonialism is done, and
a postcolonial ethic of non-hegemonic engagement rather than retreat
must follow in its wake." To engage with the ethics of peacebuilding
means channelling the question from whether peacebuilding to how to
do it in a legitimate manner (Lidén, 2006: 102). The question is therefore posed as to whether applying a particular type of a human security
framework can help in the legitimization of the peacebuilding that supposedly comes after interventions and, ultimately, in the development
of this "ethic of non-hegemonic engagement."

I shall present my arguments in three parts. First, a clarification of
definitions of peacebuilding and the broad human security approach is
needed to set the scene. Then, the argument is made that the emancipatory human security approach presents a critical perspective that
addresses theoretical problems of legitimacy in peacebuilding. Finally,
I shall propose a practical solution, the Human Security Integrated
Framework, which is a problem solving approach to addressing legitimacy and efficiency in peacebuilding operations.

The Need to Define Terms

What is Peacebuilding?

Although simply referring to the ensemble of reconstruction efforts after the termination of conflict, the term peacebuilding has many
definitions according to different authors. For Paris (2004: 38), it constitutes "action undertaken at the end of a civil conflict to consolidate
peace and prevent a recurrence of fighting. A peacebuilding mission
involves the deployment of military and civilian personnel from several
international agencies, with a mandate to conduct peacebuilding in a
country that is just emerging from a civil war." Cousens et al. (2001)
refer to peacebuilding as the construction or strengthening of authoritative and, eventually, legitimate mechanisms to resolve internal conflict without violence.

And yet there has been confusion as to what exactly encompasses
the limits and scope of peacebuilding. The 1992 "An Agenda for
Peace" introduced the four phases of the peace process as seen from
the UN point of view as preventive diplomacy, peacemaking, peacekeeping, and peacebuilding. For Boutros-Ghali, peacebuilding includes
"rebuilding the institutions and infrastructures of nations torn by civil

war and strife; and building bonds of peaceful mutual benefit among nations formerly at war." Its aim is "to address the deepest causes of conflict: economic despair, social injustice and political oppression" (Boutros-Ghali, 1992). Peacebuilding is thus the final stage of the peace process. For others, however, particularly NGOs, peacebuilding is an umbrella concept that involves all four of the above stages.

For Kühne (1997) peacebuilding is: first of all a political undertaking, not development or humanitarian aid; second, the priority of peacebuilding is not ending conflict as such, but preventing the resumption of conflict; third, the time dimension of post-conflict peacebuilding is short- and medium-term, whereas development activities and nation-building are long-term pursuits.

There is therefore ambiguity whether the aim of peacebuilding is to fix problems, prevent future conflicts, address structural issues, or transform societies. Ultimately, the scope of peacebuilding is disputed, whether it is simply to end wars (and establish a negative peace) or address the underlying structural root causes to prevent the resumption of conflict. For the purposes of this paper, we shall propose that the purpose of peacebuilding is to attempt to fix core problems underlying conflict in addition to changing patterns of interaction among people and government. Thus, peacebuilding is supposed to have a transformative effect on societies.

This expanded notion of peacebuilding (which Duffield [2001] criticizes as a liberal agenda) is not without its own problems. It remains unclear for example as to who is ultimately responsible for defining the aims of peacebuilding and how these aims are defined, and whether, ultimately, peacebuilding is "demand-driven" or "supply-driven."

There are a number of critiques made to the peacebuilding agenda, but which mostly relate to problems of efficiency. Such literature looks for example at the failure of peacebuilding in practice when wars resume and question the sequencing of interventions or whether there are the resources committed, institutional capacity, and coordination and coherence among international actors as well as whether these are adequate between international and local (Eide et al., 2005; Bellamy and Williams, 2005; Paris, 2004). Among these, Paris (2004) for example focuses on building a liberal democratic state and the role of institutions, rather than on the question of the legitimacy of the model. This essay instead concerns itself around the problematique of legitimacy: whether there is consensus, hence legitimacy, among different actors on the supremacy of the model of liberal peace. The question is how the broad emancipatory approach to human security could potentially contribute to the legitimization of alternative peacebuilding approaches.

What is Human Security After All?

There is also a need to clarify which human security framework is still valid, after the meat grinding debate that the concept has solicited since it made its foray into international relations through the UNDP *Human Development Report* in 1994 by describing it as "freedom from fear" and "freedom from want."[2]

Although there is no widely accepted universal definition of human security, there are two different conceptual precepts that institutions engaging with human security framework operationally follow. A first school insists on limiting it to a narrow definition focusing on "freedom from fear." Such a minimalist approach is adopted by Canada, the Report of the International Commission on Intervention and State Sovereignty *A Responsibility to Protect* (2001), and the EU doctrine for Human Security (2004). It concentrates on factors that perpetuate violence and direct threats to individuals' safety and to their physical integrity: armed conflict, genocide, public insecurity and organized crime. A second approach follows a broad definition, based on "freedom from want, freedom from fear and freedom from indignity" as an essential tool for understanding contemporary crises. The maximalist approach is adopted by the UNDP, by the Government of Japan, and by the Commission on Human Security (2003). It concentrates on threats, both direct and indirect, both objective and subjective, which come from traditional understandings of insecurity, but also from under-development and human rights abuses.

In the academic world, in the meantime, gargantuan debates around human security have saved the *raison d'être* of critical writing. Apart from those, mostly of the realist and neo-realist tradition for whom human security lacks analytical rigor, is not an analytically useful paradigm but a political agenda, and not a new or acceptable paradigm worthy of study, proponents and critiques of human security have curiously both tried to claim terrain within critical theory. Proponents argue that by shifting focus to the individual as the referent object of security, and broadening the range of threats to his or her security, the concept introduces a radical challenge to state-based security theories. Critiques, however, lament that by not engaging enough with deconstructing the politics of securitization, and by simply "grafting on" the need to protect individuals to existing international practices (Kerr

---

[2] See a summary of the variety of definitions used, critiques and counter-critiques in Chapter 1 and 2 of Tadjbakhsh and Chenoy, 2007[a].

et al., 2003), proponents are at best missing opportunities to completely deconstruct or reformat existing security approaches (Peterson, 2009). They act in essence, say the critiques, as collaborators of state-based international organizations and mostly Western powers in keeping the status quo in international relations and reinforcing dominant power relations and structures within the international system (Peterson, 2009). Given the dominant liberal paradigm under which international institutions currently operate, proponents of the human security approach are supposedly reinforcing hegemonic international liberalism. What's more, they have even created a justification for deeper and more invasive forms of interpenetration, as a form of biopower (Duffied, 2007; Richmond, 2007b).

The crosstalk between the various communities seems to stem from whether human security *explains* or at least *identifies* problems or *proposes* solutions, whether it is a framework for description or prescription. The tendency to conflate these, both by proponents and critiques, has arguably added to further conceptual confusion. The underlying misunderstanding, however, is in the different types of human security approaches that proponents and critiques use, mirroring closely the narrow and broad approaches of the operational world. What so far has been agreed is that there is no one human security approach in the singular.³ There are at least two versions: a narrow, liberal approach and a broad emancipatory one.

The narrow conception of the liberal human security approach tends to argue that problems of the developing world of the South can and should be solved through interventions, financial assistance, human rights sanctions, democratization, marketization etc.; all of these are precepts for rendering it liberal. The broad approach argues instead for the universal applicability of the subject, conceived in regards to people's daily concerns —no matter where they live geographically. Relational, objective and subjective perceptions of insecurity persist as much, if differently, among inhabitants of Parisian suburbs as they do in Darfur.⁴ Urban violence, job insecurity, health epidemics, privatiza-

---

³ See parts of the debate in Taylor OWEN (2008): "The Critique that Doesn't Bite: A Response to David Chandler's 'Human Security: The Dog that Didn't Bark'." *Security Dialogue*, vol. 39 (April/June), 445-453; and David CHANDLER (2008b): "Human Security II: Waiting for the Tail to Wag the Dog: A Rejoinder to Ambrosetti, Owen and Wibben." *Security Dialogue*, vol. 39 (April/June), 463-469.

⁴ For Mahbub UL HAQ, writing in the UNDP (1994) *Human Development Report*: "The threats to their security may differ —hunger and disease in poor nations and drugs and crime in rich nations— but these threats are real and growing."

tion of social delivery, militarization of societies, etc. that plague industrialized societies of the North are as much human insecurities as
famine, wars, poverty, and genocides that characterize extreme situations of some countries, notably in the developing or post-colonial
world. That is why the broader approaches may not agree with some
academic attempts to propose a threshold for the severity of threats to
human life (Owen, 2003), which would then fail to recognize the insecurity felt by people in western welfare societies. Contextual analysis
instead of quantitative absolute measurements better reflects the full
meaning attributed to a life worth living. What people consider vital
varies across individuals, societies and cultures (Commission on Human
Security, 2003: 4).

For advocates of the broad human security approach, the mere
recognition of structural violence (Galtung, 1969) and threats to dignity require, de facto, strategic planning, root cause analysis, preventive action, etc. Dignity related threats are certainly not to be dealt with
through short term problem solving approaches. They invite critical assessment of structural causes. In this regard, instead of focusing on
the benefits of R2P, proponents of the broad approach instead prefer a
practice of prior engagement by the international community, long before interventions are supposed to take place in front of *fait accompli* in
the name of responsibility to protect. They also call for a full recognition
of the contributions of negative global politics and power asymmetries
for the development of crisis in post-colonial and developing countries.

Ultimately, the (mis/ab)use of the human security approach by institutions and western powerful states does not deter the viability of
the framework for recognizing alternative perspectives. That is why the
broad emancipatory approach, as opposed to narrow liberal one to human security presents more space for contention and pluralist voices
(Richmond, 2007[b]). As such, it can be a useful framework to engage
with the ethical concerns around the legitimization of contemporary
peacebuilding.

The Critical Approach: Legitimacy, Peacebuilding and Human Security

Theoretical critiques that engage with questions of the legitimacy
of peacebuilding come from a variety of different angles.[5] Similarly,

---

[5] See a full discussion in LIDÉN, 2006.

whether liberal peacebuilding is the best modality for post-conflict reconstruction has been debated at length in the literature.

Peacebuilding in general, because it usually involves external actors, is deemed illegitimate, for example, from a post-colonial perspective. Post colonial critiques contend that external actors violate internal norms and traditions in the name of peace and development. The fact that interventions and external state building always take place by the North in the South reinforces the asymmetry in international relations.

For critical theorists, the uncritical imposition of Western models of governance based on political and economic liberalisation on non-western war torn societies has seen more or less consensus (Paris, 2004; Richmond, 2007[a]; Bellamy et al., 2004; Duffield, 2001). Critiques, however, are split between whether the liberal peace model is legitimate but should be reformed in terms of priorities and timing (Paris, 2004) and those who reject the reformist notion, questioning the underlying assumptions that neo-liberalism is better than welfare in post conflict situations, for example (Pugh, 2005; Pugh et al., 2009; Tadjbakhsh, 2008[a]), or that liberal values are or should be shared by all.

For one set of critical theorists, the liberal model is right but conditions in post-conflict situations are not ripe. To them, liberal, assumedly cosmopolitan principles of universalism, egalitarianism, human rights and democracy form the core of individual moral freedom that are shared by all. Rethinking the mechanisms through which liberal peace is delivered, such as sequencing, prioritization or local participation could in principle provide solutions for the failures.

Others, however, doubt the very essence of the model of liberal peace imposed in post-conflict, non-western societies, questioning, for example, the benefits of neoliberal development models, or competition based democracies as reconstruction strategies after conflicts. Liberalization is not necessarily peace inducing, and may even exacerbate conflict by opening up fragile societies to competition. Democratization, in principle, poses an alternative to violence by encouraging the resolution of disputes through the political process. But in practice, democratic institutions have often failed to resolve conflicts and in some cases have even aggravated them (Luckham et al., 2003; Stewart and O'Sullivan, 1999). Such critiques question the theoretical premises of liberal peacebuilding based on the efficiency of proven record. The model is not bad because it is liberal, but because it is hegemonic, imposed to reinforce international liberalism and used instrumentally. The problem is not the assumption of the values of liberalism, liberty, freedom and human rights, but how and why these are imposed.

A subset of critical voices are increasingly questioning the legitimacy of liberal peacebuilding from the point of view of assumptions made around the universality of norms and values by hegemonic liberalism (Peterson, 2009; Tadjbakhsh et al., 2008[b]). In this regard, they are closer to communitarian critiques who argue that reconstruction efforts destroy indigenous life forms and peacebuilding disregards local politics, informal institutions, values and cultures. Communitarianism concerns itself with the fact that the universalization of liberal values, such as democracy, capitalism and secularism, undermines the traditions and practices of non-Western cultures.

> Because morality is seen as embedded in local culture, this culture itself acquires a moral value to communitarians. It cannot be normatively assessed on outside premises, and the imposition of an international ideological agenda that does not take the local conditions of the host-country as its moral and political point of departure violates the intrinsic moral value of the communities affected (Lidén, 2006: 47-48).

Legitimacy, as opposed to efficiency oriented queries into peacebuilding, ultimately have at their root an engagement with ethics.[6] In the ethical framework, legitimacy matters not from a functional, utilitarian point of view —to improve the efficiency of peacebuilding operations by mustering up to a certain extent local consent for success, such as through heart and mind operations conducted by the military. In such instances, the criticism may be valid that peacebuilding does not treat the subjects of peacebuilding as aims in themselves but as objects or means to the preservation of an international order where the peacebuilders themselves are the primary subjects. Ethics based legitimacy centres instead on discussions of what is right and wrong with reference to norms and values rather than on instrumental calculations for self-seeking purposes (Lidén, 2006: 47-48).

From an ethical perspective, something is considered legitimate if it is considered so by unanimous opinion, or consensus around a common good, presumably that of peace. In peacebuilding settings, the idea of shared norms and values becomes more problematic. The question of ethics in legitimacy is framed by understanding what is such a common goal and who should be defining it (Lidén, 2008).

---

[6] A project of the Peace Research Institute of Oslo (PRIO), *Liberal Peace and the Ethics of Peacebuilding: Towards the Integration of Ethics in Peacebuilding*, focuses on various theoretical and ethical inquiries, including legitimacy, in liberal peacebuilding.

The ethical question is the tension that exists between the answer to these processes: Why peace?; How peace?; Whose peace?; Which peace?

- — *Why peace?* For instrumental, utilitarian reasons (like international security or the security of systems and regimes) or for emancipation of individuals and communities?
- — *How peace?* Through force and coercion, through imposition/ instalment of liberal institutions of the state and the market, or through welfare, participation, inclusion and plurality? Through changing local culture along universal norms or preserving diversity? Through adhering to international law, to domestic norms in the home-country of the peacebuilding practitioners or to the norms of the people affected by these actions?
- — *Whose peace?* That of external actors engaged in peacebuilding or that of local beneficiaries?
- — Which peace? One that responds to local people's understandings of culture or to the culture of hegemony, or for the security of institutions, power etc.? An institutional peace or an emancipatory one?

The Convergence of Legitimacy, Emancipatory Human Security and Communitarianism

From the ethical point of view, the underlying dilemma for a legitimate model of peacebuilding is between a liberal peace that corresponds to internationally recognized norms and principles, and the communitarian peace, which may be embedded in potentially non-liberal cultures and traditions (Lidén, 2008). Communitarianism and pluralism seek to root ethics in local values, culture and traditions, while cosmopolitanism and solidarism emphasise universal norms as a precondition for cultural difference. The dilemma centres around the debate in moral and political theory between liberals or moral universalists and communitarians or moral particularism.

> The former include schools of thought (Kantian, utilitarian, contractarian) that attempt to derive the legitimacy and universal applicability of substantive social, economic and political arrangements from abstract rational (liberal) principles. The latter (communitarians) argue that the principles by which social, economic and political arrangements are legitimized are always grounded in concrete practices, traditions and communities (Lidén, 2006: 47).

For communitarians, morality has to be defined in concrete and particular terms based on local experiences and local responses, sometimes in adoption, sometimes in rejection and sometimes coming up with a hybrid model accepting in part cosmopolitan values.

The debate is similarly echoed in questions surrounding the legitimacy of the ultimate end state assumed in state building exercises. The nation-state is caught between legitimacy from the outside and from the inside.[7] Legitimacy to adhere to international norms and be recognized as a "stable democracy" worthy of its name by the international community of nations requires the state to play by certain criteria: to be open and liberal institutions, over-ruling corruption, monopolizing the use of force and neutralizing deviant non-state actors, defending sovereignty, etc. But legitimacy is also and especially viewed from inside: whether the state can provide, protect and empower its own citizens, how it responds to them and upholds the social contract. Far from the Weberian concept of the state, such a foundation of legitimacy comes from the fulfilment of expectations and needs of the population. The state finds its meaning and moral legitimacy, its *raison d'état,* only in its response to the people. Legitimacy is eroded when a state is highly dependent on foreign aid and answers to the needs of external institutions instead. It is also eroded when the state relinquishes its power to other actors, such as international organizations, NGOs and private companies, out of weakness or force. In an ideal world, the two should coincide, but the challenge of statebuilding in post-conflict situations is precisely the tension that exists around the universal demands upon a centralized, rule creating state with modern institutions, and perceptions from local, traditional and fragmented societies manned by populations with large expectations that the state provide and protect. Making what can be called universal legitimacy coincide with local legitimacy is the challenge.

From an emancipatory human security point of view, the emphasis is on the perceptions of people within a state rather than the existence, power or nature of the state itself. The legitimacy comes, therefore, not from the institutions of leadership, of good governance, or social capital, but from perceptions of justice, the capacity and results of delivering public goods, of the space provided for a diversity of opinions, and to the degree that the population is satisfied in its basic and strategic

---

[7] An argument pursued, albeit in a different format in terms of the clash between tribalism and globalism in the context of terrorism and its threats to democracy, can be found in Barker, 1996.

needs. From such a human security definition, a weak state is one that cannot exercise its primary function of social protection and therefore fails in its duty to protect and care for its citizens (Tadjbakhsh, 2007[b]). A "failed state" therefore is one that is weak primarily in the eyes of its own citizens. Fragility is "dangerous" not because it menaces international security or challenges the institutions of liberal governance and markets, but because it threatens the survival, livelihood and dignity of the population.

As to what type of peace peacebuilders are supposed to build, defenders of the narrow, liberal human security position would argue for a kind of cosmopolitan peace that is recognized externally. The broader emancipatory approach, with its focus on dignity taking meaning at the local level would be more inclined towards a communitarian position. Emancipation, in this sense, is tied to local meaning and values for a moral life, the life worth living. Communitarianism converges with emancipatory human security and the ethical critique of liberal peacebuilding as founded on the premises of external liberal actors rather than on local premises (Lidén, 2006).

In this sense, understanding what peacebuilding means to the persons affected is crucial to ethical reasoning. In post conflict situations, the ethical focus is based on what those who have suffered (individuals) perceive as morally valuable instead of the cost/benefit rationale made by external peacebuilding. The perception of beneficiaries then becomes the legitimizing factor. Legitimacy, from the emancipatory human security point of view, then depends on the consensus around the validity of the models and their content used in peacebuilding by local populations as well as how populations perceive of the success of changes in improving people's everyday lives.

By putting its focus on individual's perceptions of needs, aspirations and opportunities, as opposed to models, states and institutions as referent objects and subjects of peace, emancipatory human security can answer the legitimacy problem of peacebuilding. The more populations and their perceptions of the common good is included, the more difficult it would be to simply impose particular ideals, values, or models deemed universally applicable but proven problematic. But this does not mean a mere adherence to the principles of participation, as utilitarianism would see it, to improve the success of reforms or to prevent inertia at best or a hostile response at worse. Perceptions count not because sentiments of mistrust against imposition or broken promises can result and spark a local backlash that undermines the legitimacy of reforms and may even result in violence (Talentino, 2007). They count because perceptions respond directly to moral judgments by populations of affected countries, whether they are liberal, illiberal or aliberal. The local gains moral ownership by virtue of being the primary subject and object of insecurity, in its broad form.

The emancipatory approach to human security would then answer the ethical questions raised above with a focus on the individuals and communities living the everyday perceptions. Peace becomes a synonym not of the end of violence but a condition that allows for emancipation from insecurities in the broad sense:

— *Whose security/peace?* That of people whose insecurity is at stake and who need to feel secure, as opposed to that of external actors in a peacebuilding situation, or of hegemony, power and institutions (including the state, the international system, and also models and ideas such as liberal democracy, market economy).

— *What type of security/peace?* A peace that responds to emancipation from insecurities in everyday life, be they basic threats to survival and bare life, functional threats that hamper livelihoods, or those concerned with dignity. The emancipatory, everyday peace which has local meaning, as opposed to the cosmopolitan liberal, individualistic peace focused on the validity of institutions or the neo-realist preoccupation with international stability.

— *How to pursue security/peace?* Through empowering people, transforming them into agents of change, protecting them, and providing welfare. A departure from viewing the liberal state as the precondition to peace and international security, by focusing not on the existence or not of such a state, but on its responsibilities.

The Problem Solving Approach: The Human Security Integrated Framework

From a problem solving point of view, the emancipatory human security approach provides three essentially methodological frameworks for principled action: 1) it is an evaluative approach, 2) an agency-driven one, and 3) an integrated tool for the legitimization of peacebuilding practices.

As an evaluative tool, the human security approach identifies the objectives, or ultimate ends, to reach and evaluate outcomes. The success of policies and interventions is therefore judged against the ability to ensure survival, livelihoods and dignity. In practice this means that when the goals of basic security (freedom from violence, conflict prevention, weapons control/disarmament, confidence-building measures); well-being (living standards, economic opportunities, distribution of economic benefits); and justice (rule of law, political rights and freedoms, participatory governance) are achieved, from the point of view of local communities, peacebuilding is deemed as "successful." The most important added value of applying a human security approach is to "evaluate" donor objectives and interventions against the needs and sensitivities of the local population. This requires an understanding of the expectations of the populations concerned by the aid provided, and thus taking into account their needs as well as aspirations.

As an agency tool, the human security approach is not only centred on people as objects of interventions, including of peacebuilding or development. It provides an "agency" to individuals as subjects, as referents of security and ultimately, as providers of security. Thus, the normative objective lies in providing people with the opportunity to develop their own means of coping with human insecurity (Sen, 2000). Local ownership and building the local capacity ensure the legitimization of peacebuilding to the extent to which external actors take into consideration the needs of the populations, their capacities and, ultimately, their judgement. Change is brought about not because it is has been imposed from outside, or is required to adhere to cosmopolitan values of liberalism, but because communities perceive of the benefits of change and assess the trade-offs in terms of local meanings at the everyday level. Community and individual based departure is supposed to make it more difficult to simply impose western ideals, values, or models onto another community, thus answering the communitarian critiques that want to see more locally adapted peacebuilding initiatives. In practice, it means not just "doing" peacebuilding for others (like the Responsibility to Protect would normatively argue), or even engaging local populations in a set of formulaic interventions, but allowing for conditions so that responsibility is brought below to actors that are subjects/objects of interventions for peacebuilding. As an agency tool, the human security framework encourages not just a combination of top-down and bottom-up initiatives in peacebuilding settings, but an empowerment of local communities so that they initiate change.

The Methodological Answer: A Different Type of Integration

The most innovative way that the emancipatory human security approach proposes answers to the practice of peacebuilding is through proposing alternative integration.

The term "integrated approach" to peace operations was mentioned in the 2000 *Report of the Panel on United Nations Peacekeeping* (the so-called "Brahimi report"), although its underlying premises and assumptions are much older. The necessity of a close collaboration between a multiplicity of organizations, institutions and agencies in peace operations has been highlighted by the emergence of so-called complex peacekeeping missions since the beginning of the 1990s. Whereas in traditional peacekeeping missions, the military was an instrument of keeping peace, "complex peacekeeping operations" saw a wide variety of actors being involved at the same time, with the distinction between the civil and the military blurred. Complex operations required a revision of concepts, which the *Agenda for Peace* of Boutros Boutros-Ghali in 1992 attempted to do by delineating the roles and responsibilities of the international community in preventive diplomacy, peace-making, peacekeeping but also peacebuilding and peace-enforcement (Boutros-Ghali, 1992).

The discourse of what in the "Brahimi Report" of the UN was called the "integrated approach" to peace operations is more generally geared towards achieving more efficiency: to avoid duplication, to avoid incoherence and to capitalize on potential complementarities. In other words, the aim is to promote synergies, self-enforcing mechanisms, cross-fertilizations, economies of scale, a more efficient division of tasks, etc.

In other words, "integrated approaches" are all about the efficiency in the achievement of a supposedly common goal. However, whether there is such a common goal and who should be defining it (the "common good" for whom and according to whom?) poses questions of legitimacy, which the Human Security Integrated Framework (HSIF) seeks to answer.

The Human Security Integrated Framework

As an integrated approach, the human security framework tries to address both questions of efficiency and legitimacy. From a perspective of security studies, this means, first, *deepening* security from a focus on the state to a focus on human individuals and communities as the primary security referents (what we shall call vertical integration) and, second, *broadening* or enlarging the agenda of security from the focus on tangible violence to problems like poverty, environmental catastrophes and other "non violent" threats to human lives (referred to here as horizontal integration).

VERTICAL INTEGRATION

Vertical integration deals with the extent to which external actors take into consideration the needs of the populations, their capacities and, ultimately, their judgement. It aims at strengthening linkages between the levels of the individual and the local community to the nation state, but also to international or transnational actors.

At the core of it, vertical integration seeks to bring accountability downwards to the people, from the state, from institutions or from the international community, as well as upwards through feedback mechanisms. Vertical integration is about the coordination and integration of different levels. In practice, vertical integration requires engagement rather than direct intervention. Rather than replacing national governments, peacebuilding should serve to strengthen the links between state and society (Tadjbakhsh and Chenoy, 2007a: 232). Vertical integration therefore recalls not only Hobbes's *Leviathan* in which the state protects citizens through a social contract which defers all power to the ruler of the state, but also how citizens acknowledge the responsibility they have towards ensuring security for themselves and their communities.

HORIZONTAL INTEGRATION

The essence of human security is about the interconnectedness of its components. Horizontal integration thus implies the acknowledgement of an interconnectedness of threats to human security and of responses to such threats. The human security approach recognizes that various threats can spread within a given country (with impoverished areas, for example, threatening the stability of more progressive ones), bleed into other regions (through massive employment migration, export of arms, environmental degradation, health epidemics, etc.), and negatively impact global security (through breeding discontented armed groups, drug exports, etc.). Similarly, the question of the interconnectedness of threats is viewed from the way that these are mutually linked in a domino effect within the human geography: health insecurity could lead to poverty, which could lead to education deficits, etc. Responses to insecurities stemming from environmental degradation could contribute to population movement into other fragile ecological settings, a deteriorating health situation, hunger, loss of livelihoods, and so on. The concept of "mutual vulnerability," coined by Nef (1999), aptly describes the interconnectedness of systematically related security threats: dysfunctionality in one sphere is structurally and sequentially expressed in other sub-systems and leads to a vicious circle of causes and effects. Vertical integration within the Human Security Integrated Framework thus requires peacebuilders to think about these types of interactions and feedback effects, and to analyze how actions in one sector may impact actions in other sectors, a process that seems to have been lacking or deficient in past and current peacebuilding operations.

The core of horizontal integration is best described as intersectorality or an externalities framework. To achieve coherence between various sectors (military, diplomatic, economic, etc.) and to analyze the potential negative and positive externalities, one needs to be aware of the ultimate impact of development or relief interventions upon dynamics of other fields as well as the potential unintended consequences of interventions in one area on the subsequent connected areas.

For instance, when it comes to post conflict state building, the coordination of economic development and the security sector is crucial. For the case of Afghanistan, security itself depends on a wide range of factors that cannot be addressed on the basis of mere military strategies. Food aid, for instance, must be coordinated with rural economic recovery and not carried out in vacuum. Economic strategies for the agricultural sector must in turn match those for mine clearance. Opening up markets may provide new opportunities for the private sector, but if the political system does not have effective accounting or auditing mechanisms in place, or there is an inequitable social system in which one group benefits from economic gains at the cost of the rest of the society, opening the market could potentially refuel competition and tension between parties in conflict (See Tadjbakhsh and Chenoy, 2007ª: Chapter 9).

In practice, vertical integration requires intersectoral and inter-organizational coordination in order to foster mutual learning and trigger positive externalities between one field and another. From a more minimalist point of view, the central point is to avoid the problem of negative externalities and do no harm. From an extended viewpoint, avoiding negative externalities needs correlation with multiplying positive ones. The primary difficulty, however, is to elaborate a comprehensive and coordinated program with a multiplicity of actors so as to meet basic expectations of people, all this within certain organizational and resource constraints as well as turf wars among organizations.

The following table provides an example of how the Human Security Externalities Framework can be employed as an analytical tool, using the seven dimensions of human security identified in the UNDP 1994 report.

	Possible interventions and assistance in a human security field by international donors	Possible effects on other (in)security domains	
		Positive outcomes	Negative outcomes
Economic security	E.g. Micro credit programmes meant for economic security	Increased food production (food security). Communities saved from economic hardship, less bent on fighting (political security) etc.	Competition among receiving and non receiving communities creates conflict (community insecurity). Women targeted for their increased income/power (personal insecurity), etc. State banks not able to cater to savings of rural communities (political insecurity for the state), etc.
Food security	E.g. Relief aid meant to increase food security in communities	Can increase economic security for communities who sell their rations (economic security). Lower rationale for conflict (political security), etc.	State is no longer accountable to the population but to foreign authorities (political insecurity as a result of illegitimacy). Aid is looted (personal insecurity). Aid decreases agriculture production (economic insecurity of farmers) etc.
Health security	E.g. (Re) building the health care system (health security)	Balance (re) attained in mortality/fertility rates (community and personal security). Jobs created (economic security), etc.	Replacement of the state's responsibility in providing healthcare (lack of trust in institutions, political insecurity). Sanitation not taken into account (environmental insecurity), etc.

	Possible interventions and assistance in a human security field by international donors	Possible effects on other (in)security domains	
		Positive outcomes	Negative outcomes
Environmental security	E.g. Installing environmentally sound management practices	Recovering wasted and polluted renewable resources (economic security). Increased agricultural production (food security), etc.	Ignoring agricultural traditions (linked to community insecurity).
Personal security	E.g. Law and order interventions, increased police programs and training (personal security)	Freedom from fear, want and indignity (with impacts on all human security concerns). Job creation (economic security), etc.	Replacement of the state (linked to political insecurity). Increased police presence (personal and community insecurity).
Community security	E.g. Promoting demobilization	Social harmony (leading to the security of all components). Job creation (economic security), etc.	Exacerbated tensions between communities.
Political security	E.g. Support for transition to democratic practices	Reduction of political exclusion phenomena (community security). Participation of communities (community and personal security).	Imposing particular type of governance system (linked to potential community and economic insecurities).

Conclusion

A broad emancipatory approach to human security —by suggesting the articulation of ideas about, as well as cultures and perceptions of peacebuilding, as opposed to the dominance of institutional, state-centric frameworks— contributes yet another type of legitimization for peacebuilding in theory and practice. Such an approach would combine ethical queries, social constructivist openness to ideas, norms, knowledge, and culture (Conteh-Morgan, 2005) and the communitarian imperative to ground and evaluate meanings in local experiences. Local meaning, in both its material and perceptive senses, becomes more important than power or cosmopolitan notions of the "common good" as propagated by realist or liberal approaches to peace. Rather than seeking a common political framework that the agents of peacebuilding should follow, the politics of peacebuilding should spring organically from the agency of the people involved.

From a purely utilitarian, functional position, the "local voice" is supposed to matter because it brings:

1) *legitimacy over the ownership* of the peace process. As Richmond (2009) states: "internal legitimization of perspectives to justify the governance of the unruly other";
2) *effectiveness* by inserting local know how. As Tore Rose (2005) puts it, while the assumption is not that internal actors will always develop better policies than external actors, externally driven peacebuilding, much like externally driven development strategies, often generates resentment, inertia and resistance;
3) *sustainability of reforms.* Critical studies have long argued that the reason peacebuilding does not work is that local content, including culture and informal institutions are not incorporated enough into the institutions to give them local meaning;
4) *appeasement*, for they can spoil the external peace if they do not "buy into" the reforms proposed by the peacebuilding agenda.

The emancipatory human security framework does not stop at local ownership and participation (Chopra and Hohe, 2007; Richmond, 2007[b]). Instead of satisfying itself with the modality of improving peacebuilding (through participation and inclusion), it seeks to open up the more contentious question of compatibility of cultural and value systems. As such, it is not a neo-liberal tool that emphasises individual rights and freedoms for the sake of cosmopolitan values. Instead, and unlike the narrow liberal approach, it seeks to bring meaning down to the local level, to the meaning of everyday life as perceived by communities. In this approach, assumptions are not made about coveting political liberty at the expense of rights to development, as is the case for the liberal view. The inquiry must essentially begin, on the one hand, with a scrutiny of the assumptions made about the value (in both senses of the word) of liberalism and its assumed universality, hence supremacy, and engaging, on the other hand, with the local meanings that values have in those contexts.

In the emancipatory approaches to human security, then, assumptions cannot be made about the legitimacy of liberal politics over socioeconomic well being as a priori. That is why the broad approach puts equal emphasis on development rights as much as political freedoms. What is prioritized comes directly from local experiences. The broad, emancipatory version of human security proposes a communitarian response to the legitimization of peacebuilding.

As to what concerns peacebuilding in practice, by proposing a more holistic, comprehensive and integrated framework, the broad human security approach attempts to propose solutions that are, if not more efficient, decidedly more legitimate in terms of corresponding to the array of interconnected threats in the every day life of individuals and communities.

References

BARBER, Benjamin (1996): *Jihad Vs. McWorld: How Globalism and Tribalism Are Reshaping the World*. Ballantine Books, New York.

BELLAMY, Alex J. and Paul WILLIAMS (2005): *Peace Operations and Global Order*. Routledge, London.

BOUTROS-GHALI, Boutros (1992): *An Agenda for Peace: Preventive Diplomacy, Peacemaking and Peacekeeping*. United Nations, New York.

BRAHIMI, Lahkdar (2000), *Report of the Panel on United Nations Peacekeeping* (UN A/SS/305-S/2000/809). United Nations, New York.

CHANDLER, David (2004): "The Responsibility to Protect? Imposing the Liberal Peace." *International Peacekeeping*, Vol. 11 (Spring), 59-81.

CHOPRA, Jarat and Tanja HOHE (2004): "Participatory Intervention." *Global Governance*, Vol. 10 (July-September), 289-305.

COMMISSION ON HUMAN SECURITY (2003): *Human Security Now: Final Report*. CHS, New York.

CONTEH-MORGAN, Earl (2005): "Peacebuilding and Human Security: A Constructivist Perspective," *International Journal of Peace Studies*, Vol. 10 (Spring/Summer), 9-86.

COUSENS, Elizabeth, M.; Chetan KUMAR and Karin WERMESTER (ed.) (2001): *Peacebuilding as Politics: Cultivating Peace in Fragile Societies*. Lynne Rienner, Boulder.

DUFFIELD, Mark (2007): *Development, Security and Unending War: Governing the World of Peoples*. Cambridge University Press, Cambridge.

— (2001): *Global Governance and the New Wars: The Merging of Development and Security*. Zed Books, London.

EIDE, Espen Barth; Anja Therese KASPERSEN; Randolph KENT; Karen VON HIPPE (2005): *Report on Integrated Missions: Practical Perspectives and Recommendations*. Independent study for the expanded UN ECHA core group (May).

GALTUNG, Johan (1969): "Violence, Peace and Peace Research." *Journal of Peace Research,* Vol. 6, 167-191.

JABRI, Vivienne (2007): *War and the Transformation of Global Politics.* Palgrave MacMillan, London.

JORGE, Nef (2003): "Human Security and Mutual Vulnerability." Ed. Moufida GOUCHA and Francisco ROJAS ARAVENNA: *Human Security, Conflict Prevention and Peace.* UNESCO, Paris.

KERR, Pauline; William T. TOW and Marianne HANSON (2003): "The Utility of Human Security Agenda for Policy-Makers." *Asian Journal of Political Sciences,* Vol. 11, 89-114.

KÜHNE, Winrich (1997): *The Transition from Peacekeeping to Peacebuilding: Planning, Coordination and Funding in the Twilight Zone.* Stiftung Wissenschaft und Politik, Ebenhausen.

LIDÉN, Kristoffer (2009): "Peace, Self-Governance and International Engagement: A Postcolonial Ethic of Pragmatic Peacebuilding." Paper presented at the annual meeting of the International Studies Association, *Exploring The Past, Anticipating The Future* (15 February). New York.

— (2008): "Introduction on the Ethics of Liberal Peacebuilding." Paper presented at the Ethics of Liberal Peacebuilding and the Cyprus Peace Process, PRIO (12 November). Nicosia, Cyprus.

— (2006): *Whose Peace? Which Peace? On the Political Architecture of Liberal Peacebuilding.* MA thesis in Peace and Conflict Studies. University of Oslo, Norway.

LUCKHAM, Robin; Anne Marie GOETZ and Mary KALDOR (2003): "Democratic Institutions and Democratic Politics." Ed. Sunil BASTIAN and Robin LUCKHAM: *Can Democracy be Designed?* Zed Press, London.

OWEN, Taylor (2003): "Measuring Human Security: Overcoming the Paradox." *Human Security Bulletin,* Vol. 2 (October). At: www.taylorowen.com/Articles/ 2003_Paradox.pdf.

PARIS, Roland (2004): *At War's End: Building Peace After Civil Conflict.* Cambridge University Press, Cambridge.

PETERSON, Jenny H. (2009): "Creating Political Spaces to Promote Human Security: A Solution to the Failings of the Liberal Peacebuiding?" Paper presented at the annual meeting of the International Studies Association, *Exploring The Past, Anticipating The Future* (15 February). New York.

PUGH, Michael (2005): "The Political Economy of Peacebuilding: A Critical Theory Perspective." *International Journal of Peace Studies,* Vol. 10 (Autumn/ Winter), 23-42.

—; Neil COOPER and Mandy TURNER (ed.) (2009): *Whose Peace? Critical Perspectives on the Political Economy of Peacebuilding.* Palgrave Macmillan, London.

RICHMOND, Oliver (2009): "The Romanticisation of the Local: Welfare, Culture and Peacebuilding." *International Spectator,* Vol. 44, 149-169.

— (2008): *Peace in International Relations.* Palgrave MacMillan, London.

— (2007a): *The Transformation of Peace.* Palgrave McMillan, New York.

— (2007b): "Emancipatory Forms of Human Security and Liberal Peacebuilding." *International Journal,* Vol. 62, 459-478.

Rose, Tore (2005): "Integrating Conflict Prevention and Peacebuilding into United Nations Development Assistance Frameworks." *International Peacebuilding Assistance, Discussion Paper no. 2* (October). At: http://www.interpeace.org/ pdfs/Publications_(Pdf)/Current_Reports/Integrating_Conflict_Prevention_into_UNDAFS.pdf (accessed 15 June 2009).

Sen, Amartya (2000): "Why Human Security?" Presentation at the International Symposium on Human Security (28 July). Tokyo.

Stewart, Frances and Meghan O'Sullivan (1999): "Democracy, Conflict, and Development: Three Cases." Ed. Gustav Ranis, Sheng-Cheng Hu, Yun-Peng Chu: *The Political Economy of Comparative Development into the 21st Century* (Vol. 1). Edward Elgar, Cheltenham.

Tadjbakhsh, Shahrbanou (2008a): "Economic Woes of Liberal Peace." *Conflict INFOCUS* No. 22. At: http://www.rccp-jid.org/infocus/infocus_22.pdf (accessed 15 June 2009).

—; Hitomi Kubo and Dena Asta (2008b): "Liberal Peace: Value-Based, External Models and Local Alternatives in Peacebuilding." Proceedings of the Conference, *CERI Program for Peace and Human Security at Sciences Po* (16-17 June). Paris. At: http://www.peacecenter.sciences-po.fr/pdf/conf_report_160608.pdf (accessed 15 June 2009).

— and Anuradha M. Chenoy (2007a): *Human Security: Concepts and Implications*. Routledge, London.

— (2007b): "State Failure Through the Human Security Lens." Ed. Jean-Marc Chataigner and Hervé Magro: *Etats et Sociétés Fragiles*. Karthala, Paris.

Talentino, Andrea Kathryn (2007): "Perceptions of Peacebuilding: The Dynamic of Imposer and Imposed Upon." *International Studies Perspective,* Vol. 8, 152-71.

United Nations Development Programme (1994): *Human Development Report*. Oxford University Press, New York.

Towards Sustainable Peacebuilding and Sustainable Development

Anuradha M. Chenoy
Jawaharlal Nehru University

Ninety percent of armed conflicts in recent times are intra-state and conflict sites are civilian arenas. Here mostly civilian casualties occur, rape is a weapon of war, militias represent ethnic and religious groups and the state is party to a conflict with a section of its own people. The lines between the period of conflict and post-conflict blur, since conflict ends for some and continues for others in different forms, such as increased violence against women, violence to keep refugees from returning, and increased marginalization for most people. In these circumstances there is an urgent need to re-think peacebuilding.

There has been a debate between differing paradigms of peace and security and the choice between these is made by states, policy makers, and institutions. The paradigm of national security has dominated the practice of states while an alternate is the human security approach. This paper argues that these models offer radically different conceptualizations of peace, security, democracy and development. The two paradigms offer different explanations of the root causes of conflicts and how peace has to be negotiated. The two paradigms propose different methodologies and envisage different processes and end results. This paper examines these alternate paradigms and then uses a case study of United Nations Peacekeeping and interventions in some regions and argues that adopting a human security approach will strengthen peacebuilding efforts, whereas the national security approach alone will not help human security.

Alternative Concepts

The Idea of Peace

Peacebuilding begins with differences in understanding the idea of peace, security and development. Defining peace as the absence of war has been questioned and the idea of a culture of peace, where violence is rejected and conflicts are resolved by tackling their root causes through dialogue and negotiation (UN, 2000), is more or less universally accepted. This is conceptualized as the liberal peace model that combines peace, democracy and free markets. This mixture however, easily yields a hegemonic peace and this liberal yet hegemonic peace is evident in the way most states deal with armed conflicts: looking for peace as the status quo and stability within markets. A victor's peace does not deny either democracy or markets. Liberal hegemonic peace can be exerted upon another country —for example: US policy in Afghanistan and Iraq, Israeli policy in Palestine— or within a country, such as Indian peace policies in Kashmir, Sri Lankan efforts in its northern civil war with the LTTE (Liberation Tigers of Tamil Eelam), or the situation in Burma. All these states want peace without any significant change in the status quo; they are all comfortable with some elements of democracy and have functioning markets. The insurgents, on the other hand, would like a peace that favours them. The concept of security for a hegemonic peace looks for stability and the status quo, where security trickles down from the state to the individuals.

A liberal hegemonic understanding of peace and security is used by most regimes and voiced by leaders to the extent that it is "normalized" in the consciences of the people. It does not exclude the use of force and accepts non-democratic methods to achieve peace, democracy, and markets. Leaders reiterate militarist solutions: "A strong military is, more than anything, necessary to sustain peace. …We must also consider using military force in circumstances beyond self-defence in order to provide for the common security that underpins global stability" (Obama, 2008). In Sri Lanka, former president Chandrika Kumaratunge's policy of "peace through war" is followed by President Rajapakse: "The ceasefire has failed and peace is not far away" (Rajapakse, 2007[a]). The Burmese military regime calls its main national security council the State Peace and Development Council (SLORC). Israel's policies of collective punishment, like the 2006 blockade on Gaza are legitimized as interventions for Israel's security and Israel's peace. India argues that a military presence in the Kashmir Valley is essential for peace, but it is deeply resented by local people. All these are examples of hegemonic peace.

The problem with the hegemonic approach to peace is that it looks at the peace of one country or community over the other. It looks at intervention as "saving" one community from another. It demands peace for the state without any political change or political negotiation and thus peace as victory over the other. Once this is established, the task of peacebuilding is concluded. In this paradigm, leaders negotiate war and peace at the same time. There is thus little to distinguish between "their war" and "their peace" since these are part of the same discourse. Geo-strategy prevails over the security of local people. In this war/peace people are called "collateral damage" and equated with material damage, treated as objects and part of the infrastructure. People react to this dehumanization and see it as a threat to their communities, identities and honour. In regions (especially the Third World) where there is culture of revenge (like honour killings and retribution in large parts of South Asia, Afghanistan, etc.), this reinforces local solidarity and identification with local fighters regardless of their ideology or method. Such behaviour can be seen in the tribal areas of Pakistan where peace is contested between opposing militaristic aims, one being that of the Pakistan state, which wants an interregnum of peace to extend the writ of the state to its "Tribal Areas", and the other being the Taliban's intention to consolidate its hold on the "Tribal Areas" and then the rest of Pakistan. There are similar parallels in many South Asian regions, where the way to territorial power and control is war, while peace is a time to prepare for conflict. Thus as peacekeepers withdraw (as in Cambodia and Sri Lanka), conflicts take a new turn.

The human security concept of peace and security is a process that is founded on dignity, justice, rights and human development. People are part of the process of decision making. The human security paradigm of peace and security is possible only if states see their own security as inclusive of the security of individuals and communities, even if these communities are in opposition to the state. The process does not end with conducting elections and the creation of a market. It just begins there. The state empowers individuals and decentralizes institutions and is seen to provide a semblance of justice. The state delivers equal rights to dissident minorities, negotiates with their demands, and allows for creative solutions. However, many states and/or political parties see their minorities and dissidents as "national security threats" since they do not conform to the constructed image of a homogenized majority. They work on the presumption that giving those rights or freedoms may put the security and sovereignty of the nation state at risk. One example is Sri Lankan President Rajapakse's statement: "Federalism is out; just don't talk about it. Historically the word is suspect and is linked with separatism" (Rajapakse, 2008[a]). The tendency is to endorse majority sentiment over minorities: "In any peace settlement I have to carry the Sinhala voters with me. I cannot unilaterally impose a settlement" (Rajapakse, 2007[b]). Similarly, the Indian government rejected an "autonomy proposal" that was passed unanimously in the Jammu and Kashmir Assembly in July 2000 by popular vote. The perception of the Indian government was that this was a separatist demand. However, the Kashmir State Assembly saw this proposal as a way to stop the separatist insurgency by granting autonomy within the Indian Union. The attempt to impose the will of a majority is the basis of many ultra-chauvinist political parties, like the Bhartiya Janata Party in India and the JVP in Sri Lanka, that want the majority to prevail over minority citizenship rights. Such domination forms the basis of conflicts between groups and communities. Peace and development that are sustainable are dialectically linked with people at all levels.

The Idea of Development

The idea of development is contested. The dominant paradigm views development as maximizing growth and GDP averages, which "trickles down" to the mass of people. This concept of development wants little state intervention/regulation, and leaves the tasks of development to the market and in private hands. Most states and international financial institutions focus on development around the market, for example, the globalization of capital flow and technology; with big projects where displacement is seen as the unavoidable corollary of development; where aid is linked with conditions and policy advice based on marketization. Human security, on the other hand advocates sustainable human development that emphasizes social sectors with the maximum participation, support, and benefits to local people. They look at the downside of the market-oriented development model and show that an unregulated market excludes those already marginalized. Further, they show that millions remain below the poverty line, inequality increases, and there are more refugees and internally displaced peoples today than ever before. There are over 11.4 million in 2008 (the Iraq War has created two million refugees and there are three million Afghan refugees: mostly in Syria, Jordan and Pakistan). In addition, there are 26 million internally displaced persons worldwide and the OECD has shown that in the last 20 years of globalization, inequalities between people and general disparity has increased in most countries, including those in the West. The deep-rooted financial crises, as well as these examples, show that without regulation by the state, those who are at the margins will suffer most. Further, exclusions lead to economic, social, and political stress and become input for new conflicts. The liberal peace builds market models into peace agreements. The Rambouillet agreement on Kosovo and the Afghan and the Iraqi Constitutions all guarantee that the state will protect private capital and the economy will be based on market principles. There is little scope for alternatives or local considerations and people in post conflict situations that need welfare are instead left at the mercy of the markets. The potential for conflict to recur rises in these circumstances.

Displacement on account of conflict and development leads to: a lack of livelihood, health and education, to unemployment, marginalization and a loss of social networks. Some countries do not have clear resettlement policies or laws for rehabilitation or compensation. Another outcome of growth without human development is that 50 countries decreased on the Human Development Index (HDI) of 2003 as compared with 1990. In many countries, while the GDP grew, the HDI index has not shown a complementary increase and the Millennium Development Goals (MDGs) remain out of reach. Human security theorists warn against imposing particular solutions on other societies and ignoring more viable alternatives (Roland, 1997). This kind of market-oriented growth violates human security and human rights.

Two current examples that showcase the different impacts of development policies are pointed out by Oxfam Director Duncan Green. The recent food crisis impacted two similar countries differently: Haiti saw food shortages followed by rioting, but Botswana, which imports 90% of its food, managed to feed its people. Botswana depends highly on diamonds (that supposedly lead to civil wars), but its GDP per capita has risen a hundred fold. It practices some amount of pluralism as a non-racial democracy, though located in a region with crisis sites. Green shows the reason for this difference. In Botswana, politics plays out through consensus between groups. They have opposed the Washington consensus and instead, have set up state-owned companies, nationalized mineral rights, and implement development planning in addition to free markets. Other states that emulate steps such as redistribution of land and the rule of justice have had good results. Peace, development or aid remain unsustainable; simply increasing GDP and letting the markets decide does not help human development or security. This is because markets look at profits not human development. Sustainable development for peace must have measures of equity that include people in development and policy making processes.

Root Causes of Conflicts: Theory or Problem?

Peacebuilding is engaged in by different actors and has specific contexts and sites where local cultures vary. Peacebuilding and human security are contextual and vary according to the perceived needs of people in different regions. Poverty may be the greatest threat in one third of India's rural districts where there is a Maoist insurgency, while militarization and terrorism is the greatest threat in Kashmir. Both are regions of conflict, but people in the former, Chhattisgarh, see themselves as both neglected by real development and "victims" of development, since growth, mining and industrialization has displaced and marginalized them while enriching the developers. In Kashmir, on the other hand, people are caught in the struggle for self determination and a militarized response. The same peacebuilding or development solution cannot be applied to the two.

The UN Security Council has noted that "the quest for peace requires a comprehensive, concerted and determined approach that addresses root causes of conflicts, including their economic and social dimensions" (2001). There have been several important research projects that attempt to identify the root cause of conflicts. There is a tendency in many studies to homogenize both underdevelopment and root causes of conflicts. For example, researchers like Collier, Sachs and Easterly link underdevelopment and conflict and point to specific "traps." For Sachs, the main traps are: poor nutrition, debilitating disease, terrible infrastructure and high fertility. Collier adds to this list armed conflict, dependence on natural resource extraction, poor governance and isolation from the market. These traps lead to horizontal inequalities, poverty and conflict.

Once the reason for the conflict is narrowed to primarily economic causes, a number of other reasons are neglected, such as: the impact of the international system historically and currently; the role of international trade; social sectors; the role and ethics and policies of multinational corporations; and the privatization of security. Important facts such as perceived historical injustices, citizenship rights, increased inequality, the biases of economic and political institutions, diminishing welfare and social sector benefits and the biased views and policies of states are also part of root causes. Though the role of militias is taken into account, structural violence that impacts communities and the daily militarization of life is a parameter that ought to be included as a cause of conflict. Inadequate governance, which is the technical aspect, is blamed as a reason for conflict whilst politics and political mobilization is not questioned (Tadjbakhsh and Chenoy, 2007). The role of the state is reduced to "failure," which does not give adequate detail. Further, the role of the state as a party in a conflict, like Sudan's role in Darfur, or the failure of states to prevent conflicts and genocide since the regime in power represents one particular community also needs to be noted as part of the root causes of conflicts.

Labelling conflicts as "terrorist" activities takes away from analysis of their root cause. Nelson Mandela, for example, was labelled a "terrorist." In another example, a Maoist underground movement ransacked the Hill Kingdom of Nepal, the poorest country in South Asia, for thirteen years. The Maoists had mobilized people against an oppressive monarchy and for a secular republic, women's, minority and ethnic rights. The Maoists targeted the state using violence and the Nepalese regime hit back, making many ordinary citizens victims. The Maoist movement gathered wide support from rural areas of Nepal. With negotiations and a ceasefire, this Maoist movement gained ground and made major gains in the elections of 2008 for a constituent assembly. The US government labelled them terrorists and pressured the Nepalese state not to negotiate with them. (US ambassador Moriarty supported the king and frequently commented on the Maoists as "the biggest threat" to elections and democracy. But it was the king who proclaimed an emergency, withdrew political rights and clamped down on all political processes.) The political parties in Nepal decided to negotiate after much violence from the side of the Maoists and the state. Nepal is in the process of internal peacebuilding and drafting a constitution through difficult negotiations. The Maoists, once labelled terrorists, are leading the ruling regime. Consequently, it is better to analyze armed conflicts through the ideologies, structures, organizations, demands, mass support, etc., rather than label them as terrorist. Labelling prevents analysis and prevents conflict resolution. A similar case is Afghanistan, where some countries like France would like to talk to the Taliban, whereas others like the US still see them as part of a terrorist coalition.

When the analysis of root causes excludes major reasons for the conflict and depends on labels and military force then solutions to these conflicts also get stunted. Solutions are boiled down to improving infrastructure, governance, accessibility to markets and policy measures. Foreign aid is then based on such parameters. Aid impacts differently when used for geo-strategic purposes and for market reforms as opposed to aid for human security. No wonder then that billions of dollars lead to little change. An example of such an aid policy is the one for Afghanistan, where millions of dollars of aid is not delivering the stability or security for which it is intended.

Most conflicts can be neither explained nor resolved by such paradigms, and more holistic explanations and resolutions are necessary. Two examples show opposing results. The first is in Southeast Asia where there have been instances of successful peacebuilding and the second is in South Asia where peacebuilding has not been successful.

1. In Timor-Leste, a holistic approach involved a sustained engagement by the international community learning from the lessons of Cambodia, where it withdrew after the 1997 elections. The ingredients for the success included a sustained internal process backed by an external one. The two sides —the Indonesian government and the East Timor representatives— agreed "to be helped" and thus facilitated the UN intervention. There was regional involvement and support from the neighbouring countries and by ASEAN. There was a concerted attempt to include all ethnic groups in decision making processes, in the elections and in the making of government institutions. A more equitable sharing of resources between ethnic groups was worked out by parties involved in the peace making process. This holistic strategy focused on human security where the country's social, economic, political and other conditions were taken into account in crafting a peacebuilding agenda. Additionally, the regional approach, which was absent during the earlier part of conflicts was enabled with ASEAN-UN cooperation (ASEAN, 2002).

2. In the conflict/insurgencies of Kashmir, in India's northeast, the Tamil insurgency in Sri Lanka and the civil war in Pakistan's northwest frontier, such an integrated approach is missing. Regional organizations like the South Asian Association for Regional Cooperation (SAARC) are not involved. UN agencies are viewed with hostility. Countries in the region are suspicious of each other, like India and Pakistan or Pakistan and Afghanistan. The local parties in the conflict are not sufficiently engaged in dialogue. Civil society is completely out of the dialogue process. Thus, it becomes difficult to resolve these conflicts even if development funds are poured in. (The US Congress claimed in June 2008 that Pakistan cannot account for two billion US dollars of aid for the Northern Provinces.)

The reality is that each of these conflicts has multiple causes that are rooted in their individual histories, social relations, economic processes and the perceptions and claims of the rights of communities and/or nations. Human rights abuses, denial of justice and a lack of inclusive negotiation become integrated with root causes. This causes "alienation," a collective feeling of "not belonging" or "not being a part" and becomes an element of the root cause that leads people to conflict. Experience has shown that resolving underdevelopment or any one "trap" will not resolve the conflict. The theory that democracy is equal to the market leaves out the root cause for backwardness and oppression. It asks the very forces that sustain markets and caused inequality to actually find solutions. The international causes of internal conflicts need to be identified and addressed (Chimni, 2002). Furthermore, the idea of governance pursues technicalities and leaves out politics. Those who were already excluded from the market and state power remain excluded. This has long term impact where excluded communities and minorities are created. Conflicts, when "managed" but not justly resolved, tend to break out again.

The Human Security Idea

The human security discussion of root causes would address the following issues:

1. Development policies: Have these led to inequalities, marginalization, and displacement or have they helped growth for all sections of society?
2. The impact of the international system on the local situation: Has it led to increased unemployment, inequality and a diminishing welfare and social sector? If not, how can it do so?
3. State policies: Are they discriminatory toward ethnic, religious or other minorities? Do minorities have equal citizenship rights?
4. Identity issues: Are some communities alienated from the state process?
5. Militarization: To what extent is the daily life of people militarized? How many disarmament measures at macro and micro levels have been institutionalized?
6. Violence: What are the forms of violence (physical, gendered and structural) that the community uses and faces? What are the negotiations taking place to resolve such violence?
7. Are the social, economic and political histories of the people and communities reflected in state and party policies? Are local customs and diversities reflected in policy and decision making?

The theory of the market as a democracy ignores the backwardness and oppression of several sectors of the society that require state intervention and regulation. The belief that the market gives equal access to all is misleading, especially in underdeveloped and post conflict societies. Here, it is easier for monopolies to exist and marginalize the rest. When society is broken down, those who are poor are further devalued and forced out of the market. The private sector does not participate in infrastructure rehabilitation especially when they see few profits. Further, when society breaks down, the value of assets declines and distressed sales impoverish large numbers of people, especially the weaker classes, women and communities. There is overwhelming evidence local ownership is necessary for reconstruction (Bojicic-Dzelelovic, 2002). Economic stability is an input to peace but inappropriate economic policies cause conflicts and undermine peacebuilding. The neo-liberal proposals that have been used for post conflict societies have to be replaced by human development.

Force or Empowerment: The Tasks of Peacebuilding

In this section we look at the United Nations peacekeeping and peacebuilding activities, since they form an important component in conflict-torn, underdeveloped societies and show that a human security method should be used for peacekeeping and peacebuilding. In many intractable conflicts there have been different forms of intervention. We take up the case study of UN-backed intervention and the use of UN peacekeepers (UNPK) in this section to bring out the problems of peacekeeping at the ground level and also to show how human security can be used at this level. This section is based on many interviews conducted by the author with UN peacekeepers and force commanders.

The types of operations have accorded with: Chapter VII of the UN Charter for multi-national enforcement actions (Desert Storm); classic inter-state UN peacekeeping operations (Ethiopia/Eritrea, Lebanon, Cyprus); robust UN peacekeeping operations in intra-state conflict, where use of force, if required, is mandated (DR Congo); and stabilization operations by multi-national forces (Afghanistan). Peacekeeping operations get bigger and more expensive; in 2008, fifteen main peacekeeping operations required 7.4 billion US dollars and 90,000 personnel worldwide. This peacekeeping budget is three times higher than non-military expenditures of the UN. Put in perspective, however, it represents just 0.5% of global defence spending or US defence spending in Iraq. But the need for peacekeeping is urgent and out of sixty-three operations since 1948, fifty took place to date since the 1990s. Most of these were intra-state and the belligerents were from para-military groups and armed gangs of warlords. Civilians were the main victims. Hence refugee movements and human suffering drew international attention that prompted intervention in some cases. More recently, intervention has been on the grounds of dealing with terrorism and possible access to weapons of mass destruction (these are incorrectly being termed "peace operations" or "peace support operations").

The use of force for maintaining peace poses a dilemma. Blue helmets were not intended for fire fighting but only to monitor a ceasefire. But this is not happening. Many UN missions involve separation of warring parties, demobilization and enforced disarmament. Lt. General Satish Nambiar (the former head of UN mission to Yugoslavia), stated in an interview to *Outlook Magazine* in 2008: "Since 1991, they [UN military observers] have been increasingly deployed in places where civil wars have just ended, and where there is no agreement between the warring parties" (22).

The United Nations Brahmi report on peacekeeping stated that: "Consent of local parties, impartiality, and the use of minimum force only in self defence must remain bedrock principles" (UN, 2000). This has not happened in several instances, like in the Sudan conflict. In the absence of a peace agreement between warring sides, peacekeepers are seen as an occupying force as in the case of Darfur, where the African Union peacekeepers became (and were perceived as) a part of the conflict. African Union mediators argue that in Darfur "without an agreement on peace, even a force of fifty thousand can't change the situation here radically" (Mamdani, 2007: 10). Mamdani writes that the strength of the mandate in the absence of a political agreement is more likely to deepen than to solve the dilemma. To enforce a ceasefire will mean taking on the role of an invading —not a peacekeeping— force. Thus, without a clear mandate, and often without political will or even a peace agreement, a peacekeeping force runs the risk of becoming an occupation force.

Internal processes are important for peacekeeping and peacebuilding. Mamdani's observations for Darfur, that the UN and the NGOs seem to have little patience with an internal process, could be applicable to several peacebuilding efforts: "For them, the people of Darfur are not citizens in a sovereign political process so much as wards in an international rescue operation with no end in sight. They are there to 'save' Darfur, not 'to empower' it" (Mamdani, 2008: 10). Further, also, "The 'humanitarian' effort is itself based on the conviction that both the crisis and its solution are military, not political; accordingly, there is little appetite for an internal political process designed to strengthen democratic citizenship" (Mamdani, 2008: 11).

Once force is used and militaries intervene, all the problems relating to militaries follow, like excessive use of force, collateral damage, rape and corruption, partisanship and biases, etc. Public investigations have revealed a series of corruption scandals and sexual abuse by members of some peacekeeping missions. For example, a UN investigation has corroborated allegations of serious corruption by the Indian contingent of peacekeepers in the Congo that includes selling arms, food, and buying contraband like ivory and gold from rebels. The experience in conflict areas shows that the very existence of military forces fosters further violence, harms human security, leads to the violations of human rights (called collateral damage) and becomes part of the "root cause" of the conflict. Humanitarian intervention entails other problems, like a large gap in perception and reasons, modalities and intentions between the local population and the interveners. For example, one head of a UN mission said he found himself dealing more with politics and corruption than with peacekeeping: "The mission directive given to me directly conflicted with the interests of not only the warring factions but also of the major players in the diamond racket" (Nambiar, 2008: 22).

Another example is Afghanistan where there are large gaps between the perceptions of the donors and recipients as well as the interveners and the local population on questions pertaining to why intervention is necessary, its modalities, leadership, sequencing, etc. (Human Security Report, Afghanistan, 2006). If the same model of peacebuilding is used in two different places it can lead to unintended results, such as the following example shows. Eight thousand US troops and four thousand peacekeepers were discharged, most of whom never left Kabul. Today the Taliban controls over twenty districts. The peacekeepers and peacebuilders are seen as an occupying force. They lack legitimacy because sustainable and long-term development models are needed that use local institutions and traditions that are comfortable for Afghan society, rather than a "time-bound" modernizing agenda (Tadjbakhsh, 2008). The way of human security is empowerment of communities and gaining their confidence. Isolation of insurgents by their own communities can alone succeed in marginalizing them and changing the vision of peoples. People have different ideas of what peace means to them.

After many peacebuilding efforts, experience shows that for external intervention to work, it must re-enforce an internal process, not substitute for it. With over 27,000 auxiliary posts in UN peacebuilding missions vacant, the UN must call for greater oversight and much more initial rigorous training in human rights, gender sensitization, democratic values and human security. There should be detailed reports by UNPK on systematically analyzing their experience and stating clearly the lessons learned. The lack of such a body of documentation and self-critical analysis is a very serious weakness. In its absence, avoidable mistakes are likely to be repeated, weakening the entire effort. The building of these archives by recalling peacekeeping experiences in earlier missions is indispensable.

Local responsibility is critical in peacebuilding. There can be no real peacebuilding mainly by the force of arms because the moment the military forces depart, conflicts recur. Thus, a balance has to be maintained between force and civil measures. This is possible when there is humanitarian action, rather than a military intervention. The threat of sanctions is not enough, as an Iranian academic told this author: "we have lived with sanctions, they seem normal." Mamdani's argument, that "outsiders can never solve the problem" (2008: 13), has been proven repeatedly though sometimes with a caveat: outsiders can never solve the problem militarily without significant internal negotiation and human security measures.

An example of a successful peacekeeping operation was in Namibia, where UNPK entered after the withdrawal of the superpowers and other regional powers from the region; civilians were a component of peacekeeping and building because of the political nature of resolution. The UN had been involved in the region for some time and so had adequate knowledge of the problems and UNTAG (United Nations Transition Assistance Group: for peacekeeping in Namibia) had a wide mandate and was thus involved in a number of related activities, from return of refugees to voter education and human rights monitoring, etc. Peacekeeping and peacebuilding would gain legitimacy if the UN were brought back into the picture and unilateralism and apathy towards other conflict areas would cease. If a human security model is followed then interventions on humanitarian grounds would regain some legitimacy.

The Peace Table and Forming Peace Committees

In most peace negotiations, those who engage in war participate in peace talks while those who did not take up arms —i.e. civil society actors— are left out. Such an engagement reinforces the hegemonic model of peace. The peace tables in South Asia and Africa have had representations primarily by the warring sides of the conflict. Other communities, ethnic groups and civil society remain largely absent. Despite Security Council Resolution 1325 the role of women in peace accords remains minimal as states and militias reflect the asymmetrical gender relations. The groups that are most impacted by the conflict and are crucial to holding the peace at the grassroots remain outside the negotiations. This exclusion of civil society reinforces a militarized mindset. Talks become a top-down affair or even a "deal" between old and new elites. The new states that emerge are often embedded in structures and ideologies that replicate the old states and retain authoritarian structures and deny women's rights just like the states they came out of. These post conflict formations use similar divide and rule policies, follow the same development models and continue with the same linkages. For example, Bangladesh after it emerged from Pakistan and Turkmenistan from the Soviet Union are not more inclusive of gender than their parent states. The minorities in Bangladesh have similar ethnic problems that the Bangladeshis faced when they were part of Pakistan. Thus the creation of new states does not necessarily lead to citizenship rights for all people. It is therefore important that the peace table be inclusive of all groups and of members of civil society for a sustainable peace.

Peace Committees

Peace talks are successful if preceded by a process of negotiations at different levels. A concrete suggestion that emerges after talks with peacekeepers is the idea of the peace committees at the ground level before, during, and after peacekeeping. These peace committees (PC) are necessary for peacebuilding for the following reasons:

— Peacebuilding missions have been blamed for lack of coordination and coherence between sectors (military, economic, policy, what should come first and what sequence mutually reinforcing). PCs should have direct contact with NGOs and civil society organizations operating in the region like human rights groups, self help, women's, peace groups, etc. UN peacekeepers have stated that that there can be a disconnect and suspicion between peacekeepers and NGOs because NGOs follow the agenda of their funding organizations, are need based and distract from security; do not obey the international mandate; paint peacekeepers black, etc. Peacekeepers cite their experiences in Rwanda to show the difficulty they have with NGOs.

— These PCs with their linkages in civil society should be the building blocks of peacebuilding efforts. The PCs can become a multiple resource for the peacekeepers. These committees counter the rising antagonism and fears in post conflict situations that often leads to an outbreak of hostilities. They could act as a conduit of materials and money to conflict effected areas and family. They would act as early warning signals for the PK in case of incipient tensions or efforts to resume conflict.

— UN peacebuilders should supply PCs with their communiqués on peacebuilding, disarming militant groups and other activities so these committees act as the link between different groups in civil society that are involved or active in conflict situations. Since peacebuilding involves reconstruction of resources of affected communities, the PCs would play a vital role in providing detailed information on losses sustained, family/ sector/ locality wise.

— While peacebuilders must deal with state and state actors one should also recognize that it is often the failure of these actors that has led to these conflicts therefore the complementary role of the peace committee is essential and irreplaceable. Care must be taken to ensure that these PCs are not co-opted by any one faction or the state or by dominant civil society actors who have partisan positions in the conflict or have even been involved in them.

— In almost all societies there are community/ clan/ caste/ tribe leaders who are politically unaffiliated and socially respected. This may include school teachers/ doctors/ community workers and others who can be members of peace committees. In case of resurgence of conflicts the PC would be the best source of information to these UN peacebuilders about the basis and source of these conflicts and the actors involved and their motivation. Only such a committee would be able to negotiate with rival actors to avoid conflicts based on sustained support by the state. Peacekeepers, by working with the PC, would be the best force to help with the peacebuilding because its non-partisan role would not be questioned unlike that of political parties. PC members would generally be more acceptable to militant groups than state actors.

— In the peacebuilding exercise, other UN agencies like the UNDP should help in providing a tabulation and analysis of the real costs of specific conflicts. This should be written in a popular style with illustrations. These booklets, translated into local language, could be distributed by the PCs and other agencies. The ties and bonds of PCs would build in the course of this activity and act as a buffer against renewed conflict after UNPKs departed.

Many area commanders and UNPK officers that I interviewed supported the usefulness of peace committees and cited their experience of such committees in Timor-Leste where these helped restore the confidence of people since there was little trust in the local police or army (UN Peacekeepers, 2008).

Peace negotiations need to be conducted at various levels. In track one talks (between states) or track two talks (between actors close to the state), civil society is excluded, but track three (between civil society groups) is not taken seriously by negotiators. For sustainable and human security peace and development, talks/ policies should not be a top-down affair, but rather include all political and tribal affiliations. This alone can prove to those groups engaged in conflicts that the alternative to armed struggle is dialogue, persuasion and organization. The success of peacekeeping and negotiations can be established if the peacekeepers:

— Work themselves out of job.
— Devolve responsibility back to the local community.
— Maintain legitimacy of intervention.
— Avoid neo-colonial imperialism.
— Ensure gender sensitive/ rights based perceptions.

Structures and Process

A human security outcome of peacebuilding would ensure a process of building peace and security where the multiple needs of citizens are addressed as freedom from fear and freedom from want.

1. Economic dispensation would be one where basic needs of all are addressed; it would be pro-poor, -minorities, -women, etc. Economic processes would have to ensure inclusion of all groups. For such a regime the market would have to have some regulations and rules.

2. The political regime can have legitimacy by becoming participatory; using and empowering local institutions. This is beyond the electoral process and continues into policy making and fi-

nancial control processes; it means de-centralization and transparency in governance; it accommodates dissent and the dissidents and is inclusive of all groups within society.

Such peacebuilding on human security lines alters the structural base of power relations in society and includes social groups that are generally denied power and access. For these mechanisms, such as affirmative action, proportional representation, decentralization of power and transparency, are part of a system that ensures equity and equal access to basic services. This forms the core function of the state, not just conducting elections and governance and then violating every norm or human right.

Conclusion

The failure of the traditional approaches to peace and development has shown the necessity of the human security approach. Many studies on conflict share the conclusion that: "Security in the world is connected to the inclusion of people in gaining voice and access to the basic resources necessary for a peaceful global community" (van Tongeren, et al., 2002). A cost benefit analysis would reveal that the accumulated cost of adhering to existing practices of security and peacebuilding has been too high. There is a high cost to the politics of denial and deception as John Burton writes, and we need to recognize that "we got it wrong."

Regimes that cite national security to create exceptions to the rule of law become arbitrary and disregard human rights. Resolving the security of one community or state at the cost of others makes others insecure. Human security offers a way to harness and broaden national security to bring back people's rights and security. It brings local practices and actors to policy making and peacekeeping. There is an interconnection between insecurities and states elites must be made to see that their security lies with the security of their people. Without this, peacebuilding will remain distant.

References

ASEAN (2002): "Report on the Seminar on Conflict Prevention and Peace Building in Southeast Asia, 19-22 February." Manila. At: http://www.aseansec.org/un_ manila.htm.

BOJICIC-DZELELOVIC, Vesna (2002): "World Bank, NGOs and the Private Sector in Post-War Reconstruction." *International Peacekeeping*, Vol. 9 (Summer), 81-98.

BURTON, J.W. (1990): *Conflict: Resolution and Prevention*. London, Macmillan.

CHIMNI, B.S. (2002): "Refugees and Post-Conflict Reconstruction: A Critical Perspective." In: Edward NEWMAN and Albrecht SCHNABEL: *Recovering from Civil Conflict: Reconciliation, Peace and Development*. Frank Cass, London, 163-180.

COLLIER, Paul (2002): *The Bottom Billion: Why the Poorest Countries are Failing and What Can be Done About it*. Oxford, London.

EDWARDS, Giuliani (2008): "America's Next Foreign Policy." *Foreign Affairs*, Vol. 6 (Sept/Oct), 2-19.

GREEN, Duncan (2008): *From Poverty to Power: How Active Citizens and Effective States Can Change the World*. Oxfam International, London.

— (2008): "Power vs Poverty." *New Statesman*, Vol. 23 (June), 28-30.

MAMDANI, Mahmud (2007): "Blue-Hatting Darfur." *London Review of Books*, Vol. 6 (September), 8-20.

NAMBIAR, Lt. Gen. Satish (2008): Interview. *Outlook Magazine* (2 June), 22-23.

NAKAYA, Sumie (2004): "Women and Gender Equality in Peacebuilding: Somalia and Mozambique." In: Tom KEATING and W. Andy KNIGHT: *Building Sustainable Peace*. UN University Press, Tokyo, 143-163.

OBAMA, Barack (2007): "Renewing American Leadership." *Foreign Affairs*, Vol. 86 (July/August), 2-16.

PARIS, Roland (1997): "Peace Building and the Limits of Liberal Internationalism." *International Security*, Vol. 22, 55.

RAJAPAKSE, Mahinda (2007): Interview, 31 May 2007. At: english.aljazeera.net/ NR/ exeres/654B1090-36E2-4374-AFC9-7EDCE9ACB4C7.htm.

— (2007): Interview, 2 September 2007. At: http://indiainteracts.com/ columnist/2007/09/02/Tamil-aspirations-are-fine-but-Sinhala-votes-are-crucial-Rajapakse.

— (2008): Interview, 19 February 2008. At: http://www. lankanewspapers. com/news/2008/2/24892.html.

SACHS, Jefrey (2007): "The End of Poverty: Economic Possibilities of our Time." Reith Lectures, BBC.

TADJBAKHSH, Shahrbanou (2008a): "What is Fundamentally Aching in Afghanistan?" At: http://www.ceri-sciences-po.org and http://www.ceri-science-spo.com/archive/ juin08/art_st.pdf.

— (2008b): "The Economic Woes of Liberal Peace." At: http://www.rccp-jid. org/infocus/infocus_22.pdf.

— and Anuradha CHENOY (2007): *Human Security, Concept and Implications*. Routledge, London.

UNITED NATIONS (2000): *"A Culture of Peace."* UN Resolution A/Res 52/13.

— (2000): *L. Brahmi, Report on Peace keeping Operations*. At: http://www. un.org/peace/reports/peace_operations/.

UN PEACEKEEPERS (2008): Interviews conducted by author at the UN Peacekeeping Centre, New Delhi, with force commanders and officers of several UN

Peacekeeping missions, including Yugoslavia, Rwanda, East Timor, Lebanon, etc. (3 July).

UN Security Council (2001): SC/7014 (20 February).

Yamaguchi, Hibiki (2008): "Is the military force effective in building peace and forging human rights? The case of war on Afghanistan." Paper for ARENA Conference, Korea and Japan Afghan NGO Network Occasional Papers. At: http://www.jca.apc.org/-jann/occassionalpapers.htm.

Paul van Tongeren; Hans van de Veen; Juliet Verhoeven (2002): "Introduction." In: Paul Van Tongeren; Hans van de Veen; Juliet Verhoeven: *Searching for Peace in Europe and Eurasia, An Overview of Conflict Prevention and Peacebuilding Activities*. Lynne Rienner, Boulder, 2-4.

Global Trends in Organized Violence and Coups d'État[1]

Andrew Mack, Zoe Nielsen, Tara Cooper and Mila Shah

Simon Fraser University

This chapter reviews the global and regional trends in two types of armed conflict: "state-based" conflicts, those in which a state is one of the warring parties, and "non-state" conflicts, those between non-state groups, such as rebel organizations, war-lords or community groups.

The new data from the Uppsala Conflicts Data Program (UCDP) reveal that there has been no change in the aggregate number of state-based conflicts between 2005 and 2006, although there have been significant changes at the regional level between 2002 and 2006.[2] By contrast, the number of non-state conflicts has continued to fall since 2003, though here, too, there are notable differences between the world's six regions. In addition to tracking conflicts trends, we also report on the death tolls from both state-based and non-state conflicts.

The chapter also examines UCDP's data on one-sided violence: or organized political violence against civilians. Globally, the number of campaigns of one-sided violence grew unevenly throughout the 1990s, lending support to the view that targeting civilians had become an increasingly prevalent element of the post-Cold War security landscape. However, after 2004, the number of campaigns of one-sided violence began to decrease.

The chapter ends with a review of global and regional trends in coups d'état. It finds that the average number of coups per decade has halved since the 1980s.

---

[1] Source: Adapted from Human Security Brief 2007 (www.humansecuritybrief.info). Copyright © 2008 by the Human Security Report Project (www.hsrgroup.org). Reprinted with permission.

[2] This five-year period has been chosen because the data on non-state conflicts only go back to 2002.

State-Based Armed Conflict

In 2006 the dramatic decline in state-based armed conflicts that started in 1993 appears to have stalled. The number of state-based conflicts around the world has remained unchanged at 32 for the past three years.[3] Early indications from UCDP suggest that there was little change in 2007.

All of today's conflicts are fought within states —as Figure 1 reveals, there has not been an interstate conflict since 2003. Iraq and Afghanistan, which many people might think of as interstate conflicts, are what UCDP calls "internationalized intrastate conflicts"—i.e., con-

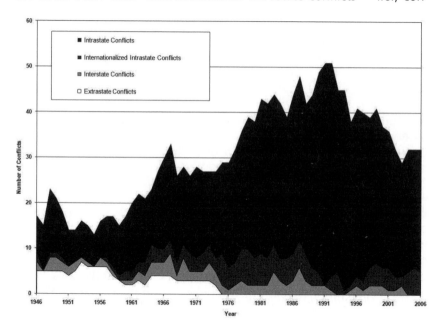

Data Sources: UCDP/PRIO: UCDP/Human Security Report Project Dataset.

Figure 1

After more than a decade of uneven decline, the number of state-based conflicts being fought around the world has levelled off.

---

[3] Note that the UCDP/Human Security Report Project dataset is subject to an annual review and that estimates may change as more information becomes available. The *Human Security Brief 2006* reported that there were 31 state-based armed conflicts in 2005. This number has since been revised upwards to 32.

flicts that take place within a country but which involve foreign military forces. Iraq and Afghanistan would only be interstate conflicts if the US and its allies were fighting against, rather than in support of, the governments of these countries.

With a few exceptions —notably Iraq— conflicts in the post-Cold War period, sometimes called "new wars," have mostly been fought in low-income countries by small, poorly trained and poorly equipped armies that tend to avoid major military engagements.

Recent Changes at the Regional Level

The leveling off of the global state-based conflicts count over the past few years obscures some significant changes at the regional level. The number of state-based conflicts in sub-Saharan Africa declined by 46 percent between 2002 and 2006. In 2002 the region accounted for 40 percent of the world's state-based conflicts; by 2006 it accounted for just 22 percent.

For four years out of the five between 2002 and 2006, Central and South Asia was the most conflict-prone region in the world. It has experienced a net increase in conflicts: going from seven in 2002, to ten in 2006. The number of conflicts in the Middle East and North Africa also increased, rising from four in 2002, to seven in 2006.

There has been just one state-based conflict in Europe since 2002 —that in Russia's Chechnya. Meanwhile, in both the Americas and in East and Southeast Asia and Oceania there were the same number of conflicts in 2006 as in 2002: two in the case of the Americas, and five in the case of East and Southeast Asia and Oceania. However, in both regions the numbers fluctuated slightly in the intervening years.

Deaths from State-Based Conflicts

Figure 2 shows the number of reported battle-deaths from state-based armed conflicts between 1946 and 2006. The overall trend reveals a striking, but very uneven decline in the death toll from the peak caused by the Korean War in 1950 to the present day. The most telling indicator of the changing deadliness of warfare over time is the average number of battle-deaths incurred per conflict per year. Using this metric, we find that in 1950 the average state-based conflict killed some 38,000 people, but by 2006 the toll had shrunk to just over 500, a decline of 99 percent.

Figure 2 also shows the share of battle-deaths by type of conflict. Two things stand out: first, just how large the death toll has been from the relatively small number of interstate conflicts; and second, how the share of interstate deaths has declined over recent decades, while that of intrastate and internationalized intrastate conflicts has increased.

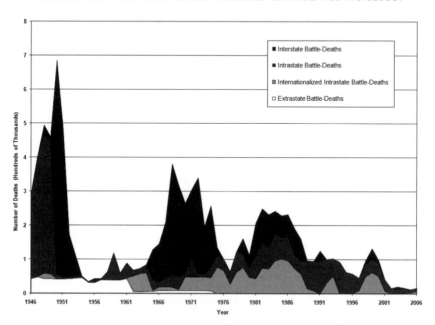

Data Sources: Lacina/Gleditsch. Dataset; UCDP/Human Security Report Project Dataset.

Figure 2

Interstate wars, though relatively few in number, have been by far the deadliest form of armed conflict since the end of World War II.

Intrastate conflicts have been the most common form of conflict over the past 60 years; they have also been the least deadly. Between 1946 and 2006:

— The average interstate conflict killed 34,677 people per year.
— The average internationalized intrastate conflict killed 8,609 people per year.
— The average intrastate conflict killed 2,430 people per year.

In 2006 just five of the conflicts being waged around the world qualified as "wars": i.e., they resulted in 1,000 or more battle-deaths. Two of these were internationalized intrastate conflicts (Afghanistan and Iraq), while three were intrastate conflicts (Chad, Sri Lanka and Sudan).

In the Americas, 2006 saw a sharp reduction in the death toll in Colombia's long-running civil war. Indeed, 2006 is only the second year since 1990 in which the fighting in that country resulted in fewer than 1,000 battle-deaths.[4] Colombia's lower death toll was responsible for the 54 percent drop in battle-deaths across the region from 2005 to 2006.

Battle-deaths in Central and South Asia increased significantly between 2002 and 2006. The 36 percent increase during this period was mostly due to increased fighting in Afghanistan and Sri Lanka. The death toll in the Middle East and North Africa (primarily in Iraq) rose even more sharply (by 93 percent). Together, these two regions accounted for over three-quarters of the world's reported battle-deaths from state-based conflict in 2006.

Europe's sole conflict, that in Chechnya, has been active for 10 of the 12 years between 1994 and 2006, and has resulted in the deaths of almost 100,000 people. However, the number of fatalities has declined sharply since 2004: in 2006 the estimated death toll was less than 300.

In sub-Saharan Africa, the decrease in the number of state-based conflicts between 2002 and 2006 is reflected in the battle-death toll that declined by more than half over this period. In 2002 the region accounted for some 30 percent of global fatalities: by 2006 its share was just 13 percent. However, the trend has not been consistently downwards: increased fighting in Chad and Somalia pushed the region's battle-death toll for 2006 above that for 2005.

The decline in battle-deaths in East and Southeast Asia and Oceania has been uneven, though there has been a small net decline between 2002 and 2006.

State-Based Conflict Onsets and Terminations

The 1990s was an extraordinary decade. On average there were more than twice as many state-based conflict onsets each year as in the 1980s. However, the average number of conflicts ending each year increased even more dramatically. The 1990s was the first decade since the 1950s in which there were more terminations than onsets, which explains the net decline in state-based conflict numbers over the decade.[5]

---

[4] The other year in which the battle-death toll in Colombia dipped below the 1,000 mark was 2003.

[5] Strictly speaking, the UCDP/Human Security Report Project terminations dataset deals with the onset and termination of "conflict episodes." A given conflict can consist of a number of conflict episodes.

In the new millennium, as Figure 3 shows, the average number of conflict onsets per year dropped by 47 percent, although the rate of conflict onsets is still higher than in the 1950s, 1970s, and 1980s. Similarly, while the rate of conflict terminations per year in the new millennium is lower than in the 1990s, it is still higher than every previous decade back to the 1950s.

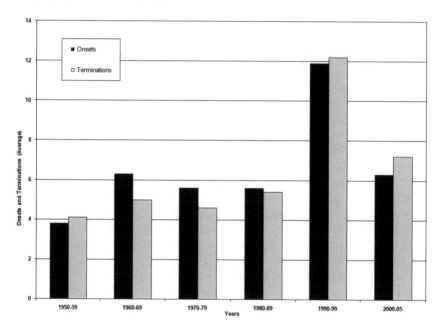

Data Sources: UCDP/Human Security Report Project Dataset.

Figure 3

Following the end of the Cold War, the average number of conflict onsets
per year more than doubled. There was an even greater increase
in the number of terminations.

How Wars End

Figure 3 tells us about the average number of state-based conflicts terminating per year by decade, but it does not tell us *how* those conflicts were terminating —whether by victories, negotiated settlements, or a third catch-all residual category known as "Other." Nor does it tell us anything about the stability of the terminations —i.e., the probability that the conflicts that had stopped would restart.

In every decade from the 1950s to the 1980s there were many more victories than negotiated settlements. But as Figure 4 demonstrates, there was a striking change in this pattern in the 1990s. For the first time there were greater numbers of negotiated settlements than there were victories. The numbers of negotiated settlements in the 1990s also increased in absolute terms —indeed, there were more than three times as many negotiated settlements in the 1990s as in any previous decade.

This pattern appears to have continued into the new millennium, and has become even more pronounced. From 2000 to 2005, there were more than three times as many negotiated settlements as victories.[6] And even though we have data for only six years, there have already been more negotiated settlements in the new millennium than in any previous decade, bar the anomalous 1990s.

Years	VICTORIES			NEGOTIATED SETTLEMENTS			OTHER			TOTAL TERMINATIONS		
	Total No.	No. Restarted in under 5 Years	% Restarted in under 5 Years	Total No.	No. Restarted in under 5 Years	% Restarted in under 5 Years	Total No.	No. Restarted in under 5 Years	% Restarted in under 5 Years	Total No.	No. Restarted in under 5 Years	% Restarted in under 5 Years
1950-59	16	3	18.8	9	0	0.0	16	5	31.3	41	8	19.5
1960-69	23	2	8.7	11	1	9.1	16	3	18.8	50	6	12.0
1970-79	22	7	31.8	13	2	15.4	11	0	0.0	46	9	19.6
1980-89	20	3	15.0	8	1	12.5	26	15	57.7	54	19	35.2
1990-99	23	2	8.7	41	18	43.9	58	32	55.2	122	52	42.6
Total 1950-99	104	17	16.3	82	22	26.8	127	55	43.3	313	94	30.0
2000-05	5*	1	20.0	17*	2	11.8	21*	14	66.7	43*	17	39.5
Total 1950-05	109	18	16.5	99	24	24.2	148	69	46.6	356	111	31.2

Data Source: UCDP/Human Security Report Project Dataset.

* Includes terminations for which it is too early to determine failure rate over the five year period.

Figure 4

In the new millennium, the number of conflicts ending in victory has declined, while the number ending in negotiated settlements has increased.

Both the reduction in the number of victories and the increase in the number of negotiated settlements reflect the sharp increase in peacemaking —the practice of seeking to end wars via negotiation rather than on the battlefield. In the 1990s negotiated settlements

---

6 Attentive readers may expect that, since the *Human Security Brief 2006* published conflict terminations data to 2005, the *Human Security Brief 2007* would update these data to 2006. The data here, however, still end at 2005; this is a result of an adjustment made to coding practices for the conflict terminations data.

were far more likely to restart within five years than conflicts that ended in victories: during this decade, 44 percent of negotiated settlements broke down within five years.

In the new millennium, negotiated settlements seem to be far more stable than was the case previously. Seventeen conflicts were ended by negotiation between 2000 and 2005, and thus far just two of them —12 percent— have broken down. Over the equivalent period in the previous decade (1990 to 1995), 48 percent of the negotiated settlements had failed. The increased stability of these settlements is very likely the result of the international community's increased support for post-conflict peacebuilding in recent years.

While negotiated settlements have become more common and more stable, the reverse appears to be the case with victories, which have become less common and somewhat less stable. The least stable type of conflict termination is that labelled "Other" in Figure 4. This category includes conflicts that terminate because the fighting peters out completely, or because the death toll drops below the 25-battle-deaths-per-year threshold. There were 21 conflict terminations in this category between 2000 and 2005. Fourteen of them —67 percent— have already broken down. "Other" terminations are generally not supported by the international community. Given this, given that neither of the warring parties has been defeated and that there are rarely any negotiations to resolve the disputes that drove the conflict in the first place, it is not surprising that they are so unstable.

Because we only have data on terminations for the first six years of the new millennium, it is impossible to draw any firm conclusions about the stability of the terminations at this point. However, the increase in negotiated settlements and decline in the number breaking down are grounds for modest optimism.

The findings of the terminations' dataset contain important messages for policy-makers: particularly with respect to conflict prevention. Since the point of conflict prevention is to reduce the number of new conflicts breaking out, the huge increase in conflict onsets in the 1990s tells us that if conflict prevention initiatives were being attempted during this period, they were decidedly unsuccessful. Given the huge amount of attention paid to conflict prevention at the UN and elsewhere, this finding is sobering.

In the new millennium, the reduction in the number of conflict onsets could mean that preventive diplomacy activities were having a positive effect, but it could also mean that whatever forces were driving the onset of conflicts in the 1990s have attenuated. The one area in which conflict prevention has clearly had a positive recent impact is in helping to prevent conflicts that have stopped from restarting. There is no doubt that the major increase in post-conflict peacebuilding initiatives has had an important preventive effect.

The sharp increase in the number of conflicts ending in negotiated settlements provides further grounds for cautious optimism. It suggests that what the UN calls "peacemaking" —using third party mediation to help bring conflicts to an end— has been increasingly effective. Given the extremely limited resources that the international community devotes to peacemaking and to conflict resolution more generally, this finding is encouraging.

Non-State Armed Conflict

Until 2002 armed conflicts that did not involve a government were almost completely ignored by the conflict research community, an omission that created a misleading picture of the incidence of conflicts around the world.[7] Five years ago the Human Security Report Project commissioned the UCDP to collect data on a range of non-state conflicts: intercommunal conflicts and conflicts between rebels groups and warlords. The *Human Security Report* published the initial findings of this dataset in 2005. It revealed that in both 2002 and 2003 there were more of these hitherto uncounted "non-state conflicts" than state-based conflicts.

The majority of non-state conflicts have occurred in sub-Saharan Africa. In fact, in each of the five years for which there are data, the number of non-state conflicts in sub-Saharan Africa has been equal to, or greater than, the number of non-state conflicts in all of the other regions of the world combined. However, sub-Saharan Africa experienced a 54 percent decline in non-state conflicts between 2002 and 2006. This decline helped drive the global non-state conflict total down from 36 conflicts in 2002, to 24 in 2006.

The Middle East and North Africa is the second most conflict-prone region and has experienced the greatest increase in the number of non-state conflicts: with numbers more than doubling during the same period.

As Figure 5 reveals, while the trend in non-state conflicts in Central and South Asia has been uneven, the region experienced a mo-

---

[7] One exception is the dataset compiled by Monty G. Marshall at the Center for Systemic Peace in Virginia.

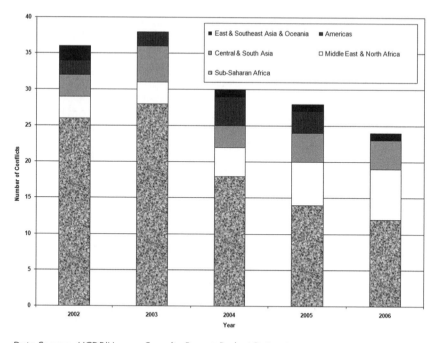

Data Source: UCDP/Human Security Report Project Dataset.

Figure 5

The majority of non-state conflicts have occurred in sub-Saharan Africa,
but even here the numbers have been declining since 2003.

dest increase in the number of these conflicts during the period under
review. The trends in non-state conflicts in the Americas, and East and
Southeast Asia and Oceania have been similarly uneven. However, both
regions experienced a net decline in the number of conflicts between
2002 and 2006. Europe is the only region that has been free of non-
state conflict between 2002 and 2006.

Deaths from Non-State Conflicts

Although non-state conflicts have, on average, been as numerous
as state-based conflicts over the past five years, they are not nearly as
deadly. Between 2002 and 2006, state-based conflicts killed an average of some 17,000 people per year. Non-state conflicts killed less

than a quarter of that number.[8] Figure 6 reveals the 62 percent decline in the number of reported non-state battle-deaths around the world between 2002 and 2006 —notwithstanding the slight increase in the global death toll between 2005 and 2006. This decline is quite remarkable over such a short period of time.

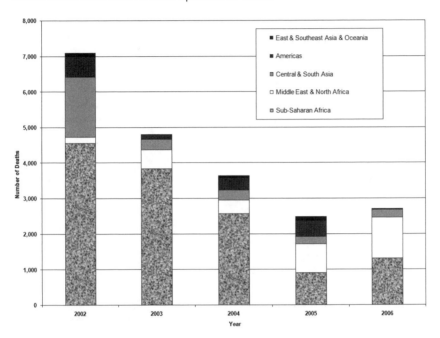

Data Source: UCDP/Human Security Report Project Dataset.

Figure 6

The overall decline in deaths from non-state conflicts has been driven by lower death tolls in sub-Saharan Africa, Central and South Asia, and the Americas.

The Middle East and North Africa is the only region to have experienced a net increase in the number of battle-deaths from non-state conflict between 2002 and 2006. Most of the increase was accounted for by fighting in two countries: Iraq and Sudan.

---

[8] This figure was arrived at by using "best estimates" from the UCDP/Human Security Report Project dataset and rounding to the nearest 1,000.

Despite an increase in the death toll in 2006, sub-Saharan Africa actually experienced a 71 percent decline in the number of deaths from non-state conflict between 2002 and 2006. A reduction in the fighting in the Democratic Republic of the Congo was largely responsible for the long-term decline, while increases in fighting in Somalia, Chad and Senegal drove the modest increase in fatalities in 2006.

Although Central and South Asia experienced a net increase in the number of non-state conflicts between 2002 and 2006, the region experienced an 87 percent decline in the number of battle-deaths over the same period. This was due mainly to a decline in violence in India and, to a lesser degree, Afghanistan.[9]

The trends in the death tolls in the Americas and East and Southeast Asia and Oceania reflect the uneven decline in the number of non-state conflicts in these two regions.

Targeting Civilians

"Terrorism" and "genocide" are both terms used to describe the organized killing of civilians, but each is controversial. At the UN, where the General Assembly has repeatedly failed to agree on a definition of terrorism, there are two main sources of controversy. First, while some believe killing civilians may be acceptable when a people is "resisting occupation," others totally reject the idea. Second, there is no consensus on whether the label "terrorist" should be applied to governments as well as to non-state groups. Were such a comprehensive definition to be accepted, it would have embarrassing consequences for a number of liberal democracies whose governments pursued policies that deliberately targeted civilians in mass bombing raids in World War II.

"Genocide" can also be an intensely contested term, as Turkey's decades-long efforts to reject any attempt to use the term to describe the mass killing of Armenians between 1915 and 1917 attest. More recently there has been a fractious debate over whether the intentional killing of civilians in Darfur constitutes genocide.

Uppsala University's Conflict Data Program (UCDP) avoids both the controversy and politicization associated with the terms "terrorism" and "genocide" by adopting a less emotive term: "one-sided vi-

---

[9] Although the final data are not yet available, it appears that the death toll in Afghanistan increased in 2007.

olence." UCDP describes one-sided violence as the intentional use of armed force against civilians by a government or formally organized group that results in at least 25 deaths within a calendar year. Civilians killed in bombing raids against military targets, or the crossfire of combat are counted in the battle-death tolls, not as victims of one-sided violence.

The 25 deaths that must be perpetrated for a campaign of one-sided violence to be recorded by UCDP can occur at anytime within the calendar year. So both a mass killing of 25 or more civilians in a single day and a series of 25 individual killings spread over the course of a year constitute a campaign of one-sided violence.

A single country can experience more than one campaign of one-sided violence in a calendar year, just as it can experience more than one conflict.[10] In 2006, for example, India and Iraq each experienced four campaigns of one-sided violence; Sudan had three; and Sri Lanka and Nepal each had two. Before UCDP created the one-sided violence dataset at the request of the Human Security Report Project, no government, international organization or research institution had collected data on intentional violence against civilians by both non-state armed groups and governments.[11]

What the Trend Data Reveal

Although not necessarily associated with warfare, one-sided violence most commonly occurs in countries experiencing conflict. In fact, in 2006 only three out of the 16 countries that experienced one-sided violence were not also embroiled in conflict.

Given this association, we might expect that as armed conflicts declined from the early 1990s, campaigns of one-sided violence would have declined as well. This did not happen. Throughout most of the 1990s, the number of campaigns of one-sided violence trended upwards. It is not clear why this should have been the case, but the data clearly lend support to the widely held view that the targeting of civilians has become increasingly prevalent.

---

[10] In a given country in a given year there can only ever be a single campaign of one-sided violence perpetrated by a particular actor —i.e. a government or non-state armed group. However, because there can be more than one non-state armed group in a particular country, it is possible to have two or more campaigns of one-sided violence in any one year.

[11] The genocide and politicide dataset created by Barbara Harff focuses primarily on the killing of civilians but includes deaths of combatants (Harff, 2003).

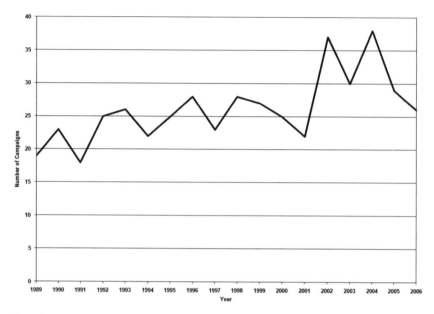

Data Source: UCDP/Human Security Report Project Dataset.

Figure 7

Campaigns of one-sided violence increased in the 1990s then dropped sharply from 2004 to 2006.

The number of campaigns of one-sided violence around the world rose from 19 in 1989 to a high of 38 in 2004. In fact, in 2004 there were more campaigns of one-sided violence than there were state-based armed conflicts. However, as Figure 7 shows, after 2004 things changed —the number of campaigns of one-sided violence began to decrease and by 2006 had dropped to 26— a 32 percent decline.

The Regional Picture

Figure 8 illustrates the extent of the changes in the incidence of campaigns of one-sided violence within the world's regions from 2002 to 2006. Four of the six regions have seen net declines since 2002, one has seen an increase, and one experienced no change.[12]

---

[12] We focus on the 2002-2006 period here for two reasons. First, UCDP's data are more reliable for this period than for the 1989-2001 period. Second, we want to be

Sub-Saharan Africa has seen by far the most dramatic reduction in the number of campaigns of one-sided violence. In 2002 some 40 percent of all campaigns of one-sided violence were in sub-Saharan Africa. By 2006 the region's share had shrunk to just 19 percent. In Central and South Asia the reverse was true. While the number of campaigns fluctuated over the period, there were nearly twice as many campaigns in 2006 as in 2002. The biggest increase was between 2005 and 2006 when the number of campaigns in the region went from four to nine. Most of this increase was accounted for by new campaigns in India, Nepal and Sri Lanka.

As Figure 8 shows, there was no net change in the number of campaigns of one-sided violence in the Middle East and North Africa between 2002 and 2006. However, in the intervening years, the number had increased by 50 percent (from 8 to 12) before declining sharply again in 2006.

Region	2002	2003	2004	2005	2006	Change
Americas	2	1	3	4	1	-1
Central & South Asia	5	3	6	4	9	4
East & Southeast Asia & Oceania	6	4	4	2	3	-3
Europe	1	1	3	0	0	-1
Middle East & North Africa	8	11	11	12	8	0
Sub-Saharan Africa	15	10	11	7	5	-10
Total	37	30	38	29	26	-11

Data Source: UCDP/Human Security Report Project Dataset.

Figure 8

There was a threefold decline in campaigns of one-sided violence
in sub-Saharan Africa between 2002 and 2006; in Central and South Asia
the numbers increased by 44 percent over the same period.

In 2006 Europe was free of one-sided violence for the second year in a row. Although this region has experienced relatively few campaigns of one-sided violence since 1989, some of them have been particularly deadly. The slaughter of 7,500 Muslim civilians by Serb forces in Srebrenica in 1995, for example, killed almost as many people as all of the campaigns of one-sided violence in the Americas during 1989 to 2006 (Eck and Hultman, 2007).

---

able to make comparisons with the non-state conflict trend data and these only extend back to 2002.

Deaths from One-Sided Violence

While we can be reasonably confident about the data on the number of campaigns of one-sided violence, the fatality data are more problematic. Those who kill civilians rarely publicize their actions, so many deaths go unreported and determining the identity of the perpetrators can be very difficult. Knowing who the killers are is important because UCDP will not record a fatality unless it can identify the perpetrators. Without information about the identity of the perpetrators, it is impossible, for example, to distinguish between deaths from political violence and those from criminal violence, or to determine whether the deaths were caused by government or non-state groups.

These coding challenges are compounded by the fact that governments and rebels can —and do— intimidate and sometimes kill those who seek to report the truth about the killings of civilians.

The uncertainties that complicate the coding process are evident in the often much wider variation between UCDP's low and high death toll estimates for one-sided violence than for deaths from armed conflict. For these reasons, and because the challenges of simply counting the civilian deaths in Darfur, Iraq and the Democratic Republic of the Congo are so great, the one-sided violence fatality counts need to be treated with considerable caution. They can indicate broad trends but not much more.

Keeping these reservations in mind, the data suggest that while the number of campaigns of one-sided violence increased unevenly into the new millennium, their death toll has been trending downwards since the catastrophic slaughter in Rwanda in 1994. There was, however, a very slight increase in the reported global fatality toll between 2005 and 2006, though there were no large-scale campaigns —those that kill 1,000 or more people— during this period. The last such campaign was perpetrated by the Sudanese government in 2004.[13]

It is also instructive to look at the regional trends in death tolls. In three regions of the world —Europe, sub-Saharan Africa, and the Middle East and North Africa— there was little or no change in the death toll from one-sided violence between 2005 and 2006, while in the other three regions —the Americas, Central and South Asia, and East and Southeast Asia and Oceania— the changes were quite marked.

Europe, as mentioned earlier, was free of one-sided violence in 2005 and 2006, while in both sub-Saharan Africa, and the Middle East

---

[13] Most of the 200,000 people estimated to have died in Darfur have perished as a result of conflict-exacerbated disease and malnutrition. These deaths are not counted in the one-sided violence —or indeed any other— dataset.

and North Africa, there was a slight decline in the number of reported deaths over the same period.

In the Americas, deaths from one-sided violence dropped by 71 percent between 2005 and 2006, driven by a sharp decline in deaths in Colombia. By contrast, the death toll in Central and South Asia almost doubled, increasing by 91 percent. Much of the change in this latter region can be accounted for by increased death tolls in India and Sri Lanka. East and Southeast Asia and Oceania suffered a 48 percent increase in the civilian death toll from one-sided violence due primarily to escalating violence in Myanmar and Laos. However, it should be borne in mind that these fatality tolls are relatively small and that the estimates have a wide margin of error.

The decline in the number of campaigns of one-sided violence over the past two years, and the longer-term —though uneven— decline in fatality numbers are encouraging. But until we have a much better understanding of what causes violence against civilians to start, as well as to stop, it would be imprudent to assume that the downward trend will necessarily be sustained.

Coups d'Etat

Conflicts and campaigns of one-sided violence are not the only indicators of state instability. Coups d'état are characterized by the swift illegal seizure of state power by part of the state apparatus —almost always the military. They are localized events— usually taking place in the capital. While governments can defend themselves against rebels by increasing the size, firepower, and efficiency of their armed forces, this strategy is quite irrelevant when it comes to protecting against coups. Here, what matters is the loyalty of the armed forces, not their size or effectiveness. Although coups are premised on the potential threat of violence, as the phrase "bloodless coup" suggests, they do not necessarily have to involve the actual use of force (McGowan, 2003).

The University of Heidelberg's Institute for International Conflict Research (HIIK) publishes data that record not only successful coups —those in which there is a change of leadership at the top— but also coup attempts that fail.[14] HIIK researchers stress the difficulties involved in ob-

---

[14] See Conflict Barometer (Heidelberg, Germany: HIIK, various dates). The data for this review were supplied by researchers at HIIK. Although the HIIK data go back to 1945, we have chosen our starting year as 1946. For ease of reference, we refer only to "coups" here, but readers should note that the data are for coups and attempted coups.

taining reliable data, particularly for the early years of the dataset (HIIK, personal communication). Information is not always available, reports may be contradictory, and the veracity of claims questionable —governments, for example, sometimes use the discovery of an alleged coup plot as a pretext for detaining and in some cases executing-political enemies. These caveats aside, the overall trends are not in dispute.

As Figure 9 indicates, from the mid-1950s to the mid-1960s, the number of coups around the world increased rapidly. In the 1960s, 1970s, and 1980s, coup numbers fluctuated unevenly, but averaged about 12 per year. In the 1990s the global average dropped to between eight and nine coups per year, while in the new millennium the annual average has dropped still further —to six.

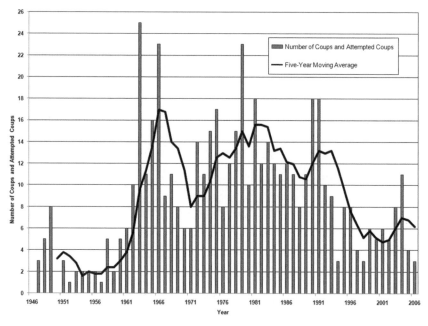

Data Source: HIIK.

Figure 9

Coup numbers rose from the mid-1950s to the mid-1960s
and remained high until the end of the Cold War.

As Figure 10 illustrates, all of the coups between 1946 and 1959 occurred in just three of the world's six regions. In fact, all but one of the 36 coups during this period were in the Americas, and the Middle East and North Africa. The one coup that took place outside of the Americas and the Middle East and North Africa was unsuccessful and was led by three renegade French generals in 1958. Although this coup actually took place in Algeria, because Algeria was still a department of metropolitan France at that time, the coup attempt is coded as having taken place in France.[15]

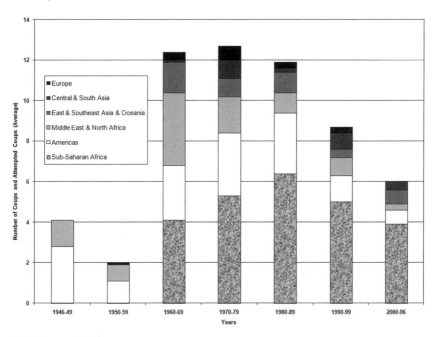

Data Source: HIIK.

Figure 10

Sub-Saharan Africa is the world's most coup-prone region.

By 1969 all six regions of the world had experienced coups, with sub-Saharan Africa experiencing by far the greatest increase in number. The continent had been coup-free during the colonial period, but following independence, coups became a common feature of the intense

---

[15] Any coup or attempted coup in a colony is coded as having taken place in the colonial capital.

struggles for control over the post-colonial state. During the 1960s, sub-Saharan Africa established itself as the world's most coup-prone region, a dubious distinction that remains true today. According to one recent study, only three countries in the region —Botswana, Cape Verde, and Mauritius— have been independent for more than 25 years and have remained completely coup-free to 2001 (McGowan, 2003: 345-346).

The number of coups in the Middle East and North Africa peaked in the 1960s, when there were 36 coups in the region, and then started to decline. In the Americas there were, on average, some three coups per year between 1960 and 1989, but in the 1990s the number dropped significantly and in the new millennium the region has averaged fewer than one coup per year.

Coup numbers peaked in Central and South Asia in the 1970s —reflecting the political instability in Afghanistan, Bangladesh, and Pakistan. Coups in these three countries, as well as in the former Soviet republics of Georgia, Tajikistan, Armenia, and Azerbaijan, pushed the regional total up again in the 1990s.

There is no consistent trend in East and Southeast Asia and Oceania, although it is the only region to have experienced more coups between 2000 and 2006 than in the previous decade. The five coups in the new millennium took place in Fiji (2000 and 2006), the Solomon Islands (2000), the Philippines (2006) and Thailand (2006).

Europe, the region that has been home to the greatest number of consistently democratic states for the longest period of time, is also the region that has experienced the fewest coups. Just eight countries account for Europe's 18 coups (Greece had seven, Albania two, France two, Portugal two, Russia/USSR two, Bulgaria one, Cyprus one, and Spain one). The region's three coups in the 1990s took place in the newly independent Russian Republic (1991), the Russian Federation (1993), and Albania (1998). There have been no coups in Europe in the new millennium.

A history of armed conflict increases the risk of future conflicts. The evidence indicates that the same relationship is true for coups. Seventy-eight percent of countries that experienced a coup between 1946 and 2006 experienced more than one. Sub-Saharan Africa not only accounted for the majority (44 percent) of the world's coups between 1946 and 2006, but was also home to four of the world's eight most coup-prone countries (Nigeria with 15 coups, Comoros with 13, Mauritania with 12 and Benin with 12). The Americas experienced 24 percent of the world's coups, and was home to the world's most coup-prone country —Bolivia— which experienced 22 coups during the period 1946 to 2006. The Middle East and North Africa accounted for 17 percent of the world's coups between 1946 and 2006, and was home to three of the world's eight most coup-prone countries (Syria with 20 coups, Sudan with 18 and Iraq with 15).

Figure 11 provides information on each region's share of the global coup total between 1946 and 2006, but it does not take into account the fact that the number of countries per region varies greatly. While sub-Saharan Africa accounts for 44 percent of the world's coups over the time period in question, it also contains many more states than most other regions. It should be remembered, however, that the number of states in the world increased considerably over the last 60 years as a consequence of the end of colonialism.[16]

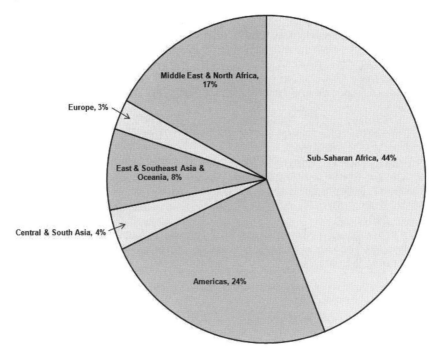

Data Source: HIIK.

Figure 11

Almost half of the world's coups have taken place in sub-Saharan Africa.

---

[16] The HIIK dataset includes a number of countries that have populations of less than 500,000 and are therefore not included in the UCDP/PRIO, UCDP/Human Security Report Project and Lacina/Gleditsch datasets.

The decline in the average number of coups per decade since the 1970s is not only encouraging but is also not accidental. The decline is strongly associated with a range of economic and political changes, including rising incomes; an increasingly entrenched norm against the usurpation of government by the military; and a greater willingness on behalf of the international community and regional organizations to seek to prevent or reverse coups, and to sanction coup leaders. Whether this positive change —and the factors that have driven it— can be sustained remains to be seen.

References

ECK, Kristine and Lisa HULTMAN (2007): "One-Sided Violence Against Civilians in War: Insights from New Fatality Data." *Journal of Peace Research,* Vol. 44, 233-246.

HARFF, Barbara (2003): "No Lessons Learned from the Holocaust? Assessing Risks of Genocide and Political Mass Murder since 1955," *American Political Science Review,* Vol. 97, 57-73.

LACINA, Bethany and Nils Petter GLEDITSCH (2005): "Monitoring Trends in Global Combat: A New Dataset of Battle Deaths," *European Journal of Population,* Vol. 21, 145-166.

MCGOWAN, Patrick J. (2003): "African Military Coups d'État, 1956-2001: Frequency, Trends and Distribution," *Journal of Modern African Studies,* Vol. 41, 339-370.

UPPSALA CONFLICT DATA PROGRAM (UCPD) and HUMAN SECURITY REPORT PROJECT DATASET (2007).

UCDP/PEACE RESEARCH INSTITUTE OSLO (PRIO): Armed Conflict Dataset (2007).

INSTITUTE FOR INTERNATIONAL CONFLICT RESEARCH, University of Heidelberg (2007): unpublished data.

Regional Perspectives
on Peacebuilding

African Peacebuilding:
A Radical Analysis

The Synergy between Lasting Peace and Sustainable Development: Factors in Intervention

Klaus Rudischhauser and Daniela Dicorrado-Andreoni
European Commission

The traditional dividing lines between security and development are no longer useful as an approach to the complex reality of the challenges currently confronting us. It now falls to global actors such as the European Union to comprehend the dynamics and the political and practical implications of the interdependence between security and development.

Reasons

— Globalisation: what began as an economic challenge is also at the root of social and security challenges, and not only in developing countries (for example, the post-Cold War era has coincided with a flood of arms from the Eastern Block to every market in which demand is present);
— The progressive "de-Westernisation" of globalisation has rendered obsolete many of the North-South cleavages, as the Africa-EU Strategic Partnership of last December (2007) demonstrates. New powers are emerging based on a variable and asymmetric geometry of power relationships, in which the military is a component, but which is first and foremost tied to the pairing of demographics and economics (economic critical mass of the overpopulated powers, young vs. aging populations, migratory flows, etc.).

In this context, the impact of our planet's shifting centre of gravity is not limited to the economic sphere with the advantages accruing to emerging and developing countries. Values are affected as well—

the values that form the foundation of democracy, respect for human rights, and all associated freedoms:

— the transition from bi-polarization —or even, to use the triumphalist image of "the end of history" dear to Fukuyama, from a form of mono-polarization— towards multi-polarisation suggests not only the weight of new powers but in particular of non-governmental players (for example, energy industries, financial and IT markets, etc.) whose roles are of even greater consequence as the concept of and the scope of deregulation are extended, leaving them no longer subject to the rules of global governance.

Thus, variable – geometry powers = variable-geometry challenges for security as well as for development.

The Nature of Conflict

— The nature of conflict is an ever greater complexity ranging from internal conflict and heterogeneous internal and external actors with interests which are disparate and complex and which have diverse causes, motivations, objectives and modalities.
— Among the causes are: competition for natural resources, desertification and flooding leading to forced population displacement, famine/lack of food security/pandemics, lack of education and employment opportunities; fragmentation of political authority, delegitimisation of authority; rising power of armed and unarmed non-governmental actors, substitution of legitimate authority by non-governmental actors including those that provide protection and security of populations within weak states; porous borders leading to networks for trafficking of all sorts, in particular arms trafficking, which are enmeshed within familial and cultural/ethnic groups that straddle one or more borders and which are linked to the economics of war, etc.

Evolving Concepts of Security

Evolving concepts of security are based on accelerated diversification of the idea of "threats to security" which, while clearly distinct from threats of a military nature are superimposed over the idea more commonly used in the past of *"stability."* "Security" has become a catch-all term to refer to problems of energy dependence, climate change, a lack of global governance in telecommunications, information technologies, financial products, increasingly radical ideologies and religions, breaches of air, sea, and cyberspace and the like. The first risk is a confusion between the two concepts (security and stability) which, for reasons unrelated to the nature of the problems, risks influencing the analysis as well as the response. The second risk is a confusion between the objectives of development and the objectives of security, which is not, however, the case in the EU's conceptualisation. The third risk is increasing delegation of the protection of what is perceived of as "our security" to non-governmental partners such as private security firms. The fourth risk is confusing our perceptions of and needs for security with those of our partner nations.

Unanimity on a human security doctrine is a long way away, even in the West. Nevertheless, a continent such as Africa is leading the way and uniting around a common definition and agenda[1] through its Common Defence and Security Policy. In turn, neither development nor its doctrine can any longer escape from the new interplay of various actors or the multiple, overlapping factors of instability, such as:

— a world where 21st century policymaking is structured around the challenges of sustainable growth and poverty reduction;
— a world where energy and food crises must be overcome together.[2]

---

[1] In May 2006, the African Union defined human security as follows:

> In line with the Common African Defence and Security Policy, human security is a multi-dimensional notion of security that goes beyond the traditional notion of state security. It encompasses the right to participate fully in the process of governance, the right to equal development as well as the right to have access to resources and the basic necessities of life, the right to protection against poverty, the right to access basic social services such as education and health, the right to protection against marginalisation on the basis of gender; protection against natural disasters, as well as ecological and environmental degradation. The aim of a human security framework is to safeguard the security of individuals, families, communities, and the state/national life, in the economic, political and social dimensions.

[2] As such, in his most recent work ([2008] *Common Wealth. Economics for a Crowded Planet,* Allen Lane, New York), the director of Columbia University's Earth Institute, Jefrey Sachs, notes:

— in 2050 the real income per inhabitant will have multiplied 4.5 times while the world population will have increased by 40%;
— that under these conditions, the achievement of structural objectives such as the elimination of mass poverty and sustainable growth require less than 2% of world income;
— and that even if this cost represents 50% of annual world growth, it is still a "small price to pay" for world stability and the sustainability of our planet.

It is not difficult to draw a connection between sputtering economic growth and unmanageable conflict. Every disastrous impact of economic activities on the environment makes the cost of growth more untenable. The European Union itself has observed that climate change *overlays all of these trends* (including the increasing globalisation of both strategic challenges and the world economy, and the new geopolitics of mining, energy, agricultural and food resources) *and often serves to amplify them.* The current food crisis is illustrative of this, although other more or less related factors are also in play. Developing countries, and not only those of Africa, are already experiencing the effects of global warming, and much more is in store, such as droughts leading to famine and population displacement, massive pollution associated with large-scale flooding, conflicts over increasingly scarce arable land, the increasing fragility of already vulnerable countries, etc. To ensure that the fight against climate change is an integral component of the struggle to reduce poverty, the European Union has proposed its Global Climate Change Alliance in partnership with the poorest of the developing nations.

But all of this is moot unless the other major world powers contribute their share to the colossal effort needed to *create linkages between security, development policy and global governance of global challenges* to ensure that this new process plays an integral role in development cooperation on a global scale.

Two numbers can remind us of the cost of conflict:

— The U.S. Congressional Budget Office estimates that between now and the year 2017, the wars in Iraq and Afghanistan will cost American taxpayers $2.5 trillion. In other words, 2.5 million billion dollars!

[It gives one pause, however, to consider a figure like this when compared with the sums needed to fully achieve the Millennium Development Objectives by 2015. In 2005 in fact, it was announced at the G-8 Summit at Gleneagles and the Millennium +5 Summit of the United Nations that in parallel with other commitments undertaken, aid from the international community would be adjusted upward from $80 billion in 2004 to $130 billion in 2010 (2004 price index). Imbalances of this nature neither create nor sustain the "synergy" we are discussing here.]

— Upon adopting the resolution for UNAMID (UN-African Union Hybrid Operation in Darfur, RES/62/232), the UNGA 62 evaluated its cost at $1.28 billion, not including the funding which until now has supported the AMIS (peace force of the AU) and to which the European Union has contributed over €400 million.

During the Copenhagen Consensus Conference (26-27 May 2008), economic experts identified the most critical issues for our planet, creating a classification system to rate each issue on its "potential for economic destruction." In the first place is civil war, despite the fact that outbreaks have fallen sharply, with 40% fewer conflicts, 40% fewer coups d'état and 80% fewer genocides since 1990.

Clearly, even in strictly economic terms, major investments in the causes of conflicts are a good bet. Furthermore, it seems clear that the tangible reduction in conflicts is attributable to painstaking, quiet development efforts and ongoing dialogue rather than to crisis missions.

Europe's "Enlightened Selfishness"

The founding, distinctive feature of the EU's development and security policies might be characterised as "enlightened selfishness." The internal solidarity which led this continent to its present integrated state is of historic value that extends beyond our borders. The 2003 European Security Strategy (ESS) recognises "distant" threats to be as much a cause for concern to Europe as threats closer to home, but Europeans have also taken stock of the changes taking place worldwide as well as the role played by developing countries, particularly Africa, which is perceived as a "new frontier." Specifically, Africa:

— is no longer seen as a "burden" but as an opportunity;
— is no longer seen as a "challenge" but as a major partner. The joint strategy between Africa and the European Union is simultaneously the expression of and vision of the future.

This strategy marks a turning point in our relations with the African continent and heralds a new era in which our interests go beyond development (trade, the environment, peace and security), beyond bilateral issues (UN, the Middle East, Myanmar, the Balkans, etc.) and beyond the dialogue between institutions (private sector, civil society, parliaments, etc.). Through this strategy, the European Union and Africa have laid the foundation for a long-term, sustainable partnership, based not only on substance but also on an approach which has made its creation possible and which ensures its implementation.

The Approach

For the first time, we have a strategic document drafted jointly by two partners, which constitutes a long-term roadmap for cooperation. The approach is resolutely complex-free and egalitarian. The text encompasses a "traditional" development agenda, but at the same time is grounded in the principle of mutual responsibility and allows adequate leeway for political dialogue and cooperation between partners on the international scene on the major multilateral debates.

Implementation

General political priorities are to be implemented through three-year action plans. The first action plan adopted in Lisbon in December of 2007 identified eight thematic partnerships: Peace and Security; Democratic Governance and Human Rights; Trade, Regional Integration, Infrastructure; the Millennium Development Objectives; Energy; Climate Change; Migration, Mobility and Employment; Science, Information Society and Space. For each of these partnerships, there are dimensions of cooperation and political dialogue, but also implementation of *concrete initiatives with a regional and continental scope*. In short, it is a global approach of political dialogue that promotes the European approach to sectoral policy and collaborates on the international scene and in priority areas of thematic cooperation.

This is an advanced, enriching experiment which should stimulate reflection on a new strategic approach to security in the EU, which will ensure that responses are commensurate to challenges, which metabolises the distinction between security and stability, and which integrates the idea of the "long-term" into human security along with the distinctions from our partners' perceptions and security requirements. A major challenge awaits us: to clarify the definition of concepts and the hierarchy of our priorities.

Building Sustainable Futures in Africa

Ahmedou Ould-Abdallah

United Nations Political Office for Somalia

A Few Remarks

The shared common wisdom is that domestic crises started only with the end of the Cold War and the subsequent expansion and deepening of freedoms within non-democratic states. While this assumption is valid concerning the multiplicity of internal crises, it should not be forgotten that in the 1950, 1960 and 1970 violent conflicts rocked many Asian and Latin American states. Malaysia, Argentina, Brazil, Central American States and many others were home to long and nasty internal armed confrontations.

However, contrary to the 1990's conflicts, those of the 1950-70s were brutally carried out behind closed doors. At that time of East-West struggle, the media, the non-governmental organisations and major powers were not giving them the attention enjoyed today by any minor civil conflict. The Cold War has distorted many values, including reporting on abuses of human rights unless when carried out in the opposing camp. Moreover, as the internet and mobile phones were still undeveloped, victims and their defenders were not able to bring their cases directly to the international public as they do today.

In retrospect, internal conflicts should be seen as part of the modern formation of nation states and of the democratization process. The African crises came after those of Latin American and Asian countries, who gained their independence much earlier in the mid twentieth and twenty-first centuries. Those states went through long domestic conflicts prior to their present stability.

The Case of the African Crises

One primary observation is to recall the diversity of the African continent and thus avoid the overall generalization of such a vast region.

In addition, there is also a diversity of conflicts according to origin, length, nature and the variety of external and regional actors involved. Moreover, globalization has impacted the evolution of conflicts and, in particular, the ways to manage them. In addition to the struggle for survival, political power, resources, etc., this new and additional dimension of conflict is a result of globalization.

New technologies —mobile phones, the internet, websites, FM radios and TV networks— all have made conflict easy to wage, to fund and to pursue. Moreover, they have made crises more difficult to manage and resolve. Mediators and other facilitators have to adapt to the evolution of technology.

Indeed, easy communication within rebel groups as well as between themselves and external media and actors provides a bonus, adding to their capacity to directly reach many segments of the population and the international public. At the same time, central governments, having lost the monopoly on information, are weaker with less influence on their own societies' opinions. This situation has contributed to empowering opposition groups.

Vulnerability

Overall, African states remain more vulnerable to major risks and threats than most countries in other regions of the world. Oil shocks, food scarcity and violent variation in price, as well as environmental issues (water, desertification, soil degradation, etc.) impact brutally and more deeply on this continent than elsewhere. The consequences for rural and outer urban populations are severe and destabilizing at all levels (migration, trafficking).

These new vulnerabilities have weakened most African states, especially their security institutions and financial capacities. The states have become more fragile and prone to crises. Bad governance and especially overt corruption invites people to question and revolt against public authorities.

Underlying Factors

Inefficient leadership and the political culture of winner-take-all had and still have destructive effects on the political and economic management of states. Weak and fragile institutions coupled with inconsistent policies continue to exercise a heavy toll on governments' capacities and credibility. This adds to the known traditional causes of conflicts.

Fast growing urbanization, while having some positive dimensions (for example, national integration), carries destabilizing effects due to the incapacity of central and local authorities to provide jobs and services to an increasingly large number of unemployed youth. Citizens often feel alienated by their elites' behaviour and living styles.

The process of modern nation state formation and the inherent convulsions often paralyze African governments. Democratisation, despite its advantages, has side effects in its early stages: weakening the capacity to run the new states and to implement needed policies in an urgent manner.

Finally, an increasingly large and active diaspora —important for its remittances and calls for freedom— enfeebles government policies when it sides with groups along ethnic or religious lines.

The Role of External Actors

In all conflicts, especially in domestic crises, there is always some external interference. Most conflicts are internal only in principle, not in reality.

First, the neighbours —even when smaller and weaker— play a role in the conflict. They may take sides with one party, host rebel leaders, serve as a base for attacks or provide a channel for the irregular exportations of their unfortunate neighbour's valuable exports. Sometimes, they send troops to support one armed group. In 1997, the Democratic Republic of Congo gave the perfect example of these interferences by its neighbours.

Countries in conflict could also be affected by the competition between their neighbour's support, not one party, but the very continuation of the crisis. This is done by preventing the successful conclusion of peace agreements. Supporting spoiler groups one after the other is a frequent practice. Somalia's conflict is a good example of external players derailing peace processes over and over.

The role of external powers and large corporations have attracted much attention, reports and debate. There is no doubt that external actors often play a negative role by strategizing, through mercantile interests or, worse, by neglect when their role could have been positive. We should, however, avoid generalization and recall that the elites of affected countries bear most of the responsibility in the conflict.

Contrary to the types of Cold War interferences, today interventions by external powers are more discreet but not less effective. Internal and external public opinion could demonize a country, making it much more fragile and prone to conflict. It could also be destabilized by the imposition economic sanctions if not followed by an immediate and firm effective action to resolve the civil conflict.

Observations for Conclusion

Very often a number of African crises are left to academic analyses and humanitarian action. Though needed, these approaches cannot alone bring a lasting solution to a war. Though African conflicts may not constitute an immediate threat to world peace and security, they deserve greater and more focused attention from the UN Security Council to help long term stability and security for the population and the region. The absence of a credible and determined lead country within the Security Council, or in a regional organization, to take effective action is often the cause of a crisis' prolongation. In reality, many African conflicts are orphans, having lost their godfathers since the end of the Cold War.

*The Middle East
in Danger of Peace*

A Declaration of Principles:
Framing an Israeli-Palestinian Peace Agreement

Herbert C. Kelman
Harvard University

The Annapolis conference of November 2007 and the process it initiated have been greeted —for understandable reasons— with pessimism and even cynicism. Still, I believe that the process offers an opportunity to revive the Israeli-Palestinian peace process and advance negotiations toward a two-state solution. My approach is based on what I call strategic optimism: with full awareness of the realities, this approach actively seeks out all realistic possibilities for peace and vigorously pursues them. Since I am convinced that a two-state solution is the only formula for ending the conflict in the foreseeable future, I am eager to grasp whatever opportunities the current process offers and make the most of them.

A central feature of Israeli-Palestinian relations today is the anomalous state of public opinion on both sides. Majorities of both populations have consistently supported a two-state solution —including some of the "painful concessions" it would require. As a matter of fact, in one joint opinion poll, conducted in late 2004, clear majorities on both sides endorsed mutual recognition of the national identities of the two sides after an agreement is reached, accepting Israel as the state of the Jewish people and Palestine as the state of the Palestinian people. And yet the two publics have not given their wholehearted support to negotiations. While supporting a two-state solution, majorities (with fluctuating percentages) have also supported violence against the other side. The two publics have also demonstrated this ambivalence in their electoral choices.

The anomalous findings of the opinion polls can be explained by the profound mutual distrust that has marked the relationship between the two communities since the failure of the Camp David summit and the onset of the second *intifada* in 2000. The prevailing narrative on each side has held that, while "we" have demonstrated our readiness to make the necessary compromises for peace, "they" have refused to do so. Opinion data bear out this conclusion, showing that respondents on the two sides —in mirror-image fashion— underestimated the extent of support for a two-state solution on the other side. The distrust is reinforced by such events as the continuing settlement process on the Israeli side and the electoral victories of Hamas on the Palestinian side. On both sides, there is the feeling that there is no credible negotiating partner on the other side. Hence, the publics have not been prepared to support the painful concessions required for an agreement, since they are not convinced that the other side will reciprocate and follow through on its commitments.

Under the circumstances, it is not just the *terms* of an agreement that are critical, but the way in which the agreement is *framed*. The agreement needs to be framed in a way that *reassures* the two publics —that allays their fears and generates hope— and that elicits their full, enthusiastic support. I want to offer some ideas on how to frame an Israeli-Palestinian peace agreement so that it might achieve these objectives.

Active, quiet negotiations between Israeli and Palestinian leaders have been going on since the Annapolis conference and there are indications that they have made some progress. It is highly unlikely, however, that they will produce a peace agreement by the end of the year (2008). Moreover, the leaderships on both sides are too weak to "sell" such an agreement to their publics in the face of opposition from anti-peace elements on both sides. What has been proposed as a more realistic goal for the coming months is to produce a declaration of principles, rather than a detailed treaty. I want to focus on this possibility because, in my view, it has the potential for a dramatic breakthrough.

To represent a dramatic breakthrough, a declaration would have to go beyond a vague, general commitment to a two-state solution, and lay out the fundamental principles on which such a solution must be based if it is to be perceived as fair and just by the two populations and offer them a positive vision of their future relationship. The statement must address the key final-status issues —notably borders, Jerusalem, settlements and refugees— that a viable two-state agreement would have to resolve. In essence, the statement would *frame* the envisaged final agreement as a principled peace, based on a historic compromise that meets the fundamental needs of both peoples, validates their national identities and declares an end to the conflict and to the occupation consistent with the requirements of fairness and attainable justice.

In my view, a statement of principles that meets these criteria should contain four elements:

1. mutual recognition of the other's national identity and legitimate attachment to the land, leading to a commitment to a historic compromise whereby the two peoples share the land to which both are attached;
2. spelling out the implications of the logic of the historic compromise for dealing with the key final-status issues;
3. highlighting the central features of a peace rooted in this historic compromise; and
4. offering a positive vision of a common future for the two peoples in the shared land.

To concretize the four components of such a framing statement, I composed a hypothetical draft of a joint statement that the two leaderships might issue. I present this draft with all the necessary apologies and disclaimers, because I know very well that such a statement must be produced by the parties themselves. I offer it only in the interest of stimulating thought and discussion.

Draft of an Israeli-Palestinian Joint Statement of Principles

1. *The parties agree that the land that has been in dispute between the Jewish and the Palestinian peoples —the land that includes the State of Israel and the occupied territories (the West Bank and Gaza)— belongs to both peoples: both have historic roots in it, both are deeply attached to it and both claim it as their national homeland. We are convinced that there is no military solution to the conflict resulting from these competing claims.*

   The attempt to impose a solution by violence has caused pain and suffering to both peoples for generations, which we deeply regret. The conflict threatens to destroy the future of both peoples and of the land itself. We are therefore committed to ending the conflict by negotiating a principled peace, based on a historic compromise in the form of a two-state solution. We agree to share the land in a way that allows each people to exercise its right to national self-determination, to express its national identity and to fulfill its national aspirations in its own independent, viable state within the shared land.

2. *The details of a peace agreement that concretizes this historic compromise have to be negotiated, but we are committed to certain basic principles, dictated by the logic of the historic compromise, that must be followed in resolving the key issues in the negotiations. Specifically:*

    a. *The* **borders** *between the two states will follow the 1967 armistice lines, with minor, mutually agreed-upon adjustments, based on an exchange of West Bank territories that contain most of the Israeli settlements for Israeli territories of equal size and value, and with a secure link between the West Bank and Gaza. These borders are necessary in order to enable the Palestinian state to meet the criteria of true independence, viability, governability and contiguity within the West Bank. Palestinians can accept the fairness of these borders because they conform with international legitimacy, as expressed in appropriate UN resolutions.*

    b. **Jerusalem** *will be shared by the two states and contain the national capital of each state, in recognition of the central importance of the city to the national identities of both peoples. Jerusalem's Jewish neighborhoods will be under Israeli sovereignty and its Arab neighborhoods under Palestinian sovereignty, with jointly administered arrangements for security, freedom of movement and municipal services for the entire city and for governance of the Old City. A plan of shared or joint sovereignty will be negotiated for the holy sites, allowing each side control over its own sites and assuring free access to them from both parts of the city.*

    c. *Israeli* **settlements** *with extraterritorial rights and status (including separate roads and protection by Israeli troops) will be removed from the Palestinian state in order to insure the state's independence, viability, governability and contiguity. The right of individual settlers to stay in place as Palestinian citizens or as resident aliens, subject to Palestinian law, will be negotiated.*

    d. *In negotiating solutions to the problem of Palestinian* **refugees,** *Israel recognizes that the refugee problem and the right of return are central to the Palestinian national identity and national narrative, and acknowledges its share of responsibility for the plight of the refugees. Concretely, the refugee problem will be addressed in all its dimensions, with comprehensive plans for financial compensation, reg-*

ularization of the status of refugees in host countries and resettlement when needed or desired. Refugees will be granted citizenship in and the right of return to the Palestinian state. Only a limited number, however, will return to Israel proper, in order to allow Israel to maintain its character as a Jewish-majority state.

3. *The final negotiated agreement, based on a historic compromise as reflected in the above principles, is designed to yield a principled peace, characterized by the following conditions:*

   — *mutual recognition of the national identity of the other people and of each people's right to express this identity in an independent state within the shared land;*
   — *a sense that the agreement is not merely a product of the balance of power, but is consistent with the principle of attainable justice and with international law and the international consensus;*
   — *an end to the occupation and to the conflict; and*
   — *integration of both states in the region and the international community.*

4. *As we commit ourselves to negotiating a final agreement based on the principles of a historic compromise and meeting the conditions of a principled peace, we are enabled to develop and to communicate to our publics a positive vision of a common future for the two peoples in the land they are agreeing to share. Our vision contemplates:*

   — *a secure and prosperous existence for each society;*
   — *mutually beneficial cooperation between the two states and societies in various fields, including economic relations, public health, environmental protection, telecommunications, cultural and educational programs and tourism;*
   — *regional development; and*
   — *stable peace with ultimate reconciliation.*

Our positive vision extends not only to the future of the two peoples in their independent states within the land they are agreeing to share, but to the future of the shared land itself: a land to which both peoples are attached, even though each agrees to claim only part of it for its independent state.

In this spirit, our vision of a common future includes freedom of movement across state borders as well as a range of cooperative activi-

*ties that treat the shared land as a unit and are designed to benefit it in
its entirety.*

Let me add a footnote to the last point in the hypothetical declaration. I have described the vision of the shared land as *a united country with divided sovereignty,* differentiating between country and state.
The future of this country remains open. The parties may move toward
an economic union along the lines of Benelux —perhaps including Jordan as the third member. Over time, they may opt for a confederation,
depending on how the relationship between the two states evolves.
For now, however, the establishment of two separate sovereignties is
responsive to each side's need for an independent national state of its
own.

I believe that a statement of principles along the line proposed
could reassure the two publics about the intentions of the other side
and reestablish trust in the availability of a negotiating partner. What
is particularly reassuring in such a statement is that each side links the
fulfillment of its own identity and achievement of its own rights to the
identity and rights of the other. This is particularly significant in a conflict that has been characterized for generations by systematic denial of
the other's identity.

In sum, the kind of document proposed here —by advocating a
principled peace that acknowledges each side's national identity and
national narrative, that conforms to the dictates of attainable justice,
that provides a rationale for the concessions each side is expected to
make and that offers a positive vision of the future— has the potential
for energizing the two publics and eliciting their full support for the negotiated agreement on a two-state solution.

Given the apparent readiness of the two leaderships to formulate
a declaration of principles, the challenge now is to utilize this moment
as an opportunity to create a visionary document that will reassure and
energize the two publics and elicit their enthusiastic support for negotiating a historic compromise.

The formulation of such a document would be greatly facilitated by
visionary leadership on the two sides —in the mold of a Nelson Mandela or Anwar Sadat. Perhaps such leadership may still emerge. In the
meantime, civil-society efforts based on Israeli-Palestinian dialogue can
be instrumental in generating ideas for a visionary framing document
and conveying them to the political leaderships. Interactive problem
solving —my own form of track-two diplomacy, rooted in the work of
John Burton— may contribute here. Among other things, it can pro-

vide an arena for the "negotiation of identity," which is the underpinning of the proposed document.

Before concluding, I want to stress that the kind of effort proposed here —if it is to be maximally effective— must be accompanied by significant changes on the ground designed to improve the security, economic well-being, quality of life and personal dignity of the two populations. It must also be accompanied by serious efforts to bring at least some of the "extremist" elements in the two societies into the process. I have written, in this connection, about a dual strategy of simultaneously *inching toward* and *looking beyond* negotiations (2007).

The looking-beyond strategy proposed here represents a significant step toward reconciliation between the two communities. We usually think of reconciliation as a process that occurs in the wake of conflict resolution. But it is often the case —and it is certainly the case in the Israeli-Palestinian conflict— that significant steps toward reconciliation are necessary in order to make conflict resolution possible. I propose that this kind of *visionary* approach is the most *realistic* option available to Israeli and Palestinian leaders today.

References

KELMAN, Herbert C. (2007): "Israeli-Palestinian Peace: Inching Toward and Looking Beyond Negotiations." *Middle East Policy*, Vol. 14, 29-40.

International Law and Israel's Assault on Gaza

Jake Lynch

University of Sydney

Was Israel's attack on Gaza illegal under international law? The question was raised, to a position of prominence unusual in the reporting of conflict, in many media which covered the events and aftermath, in the first two months of 2009. It could mark the moment when international law came "in from the cold," as an indispensable analytical factor for the reporting of developments in this conflict. In terms of the agenda-setting model conceived by Daniel Hallin (1989), applying norms and standards from international law to the behaviour of Israel, in particular —as a key US ally— was previously confined to the realm of "deviancy," whereas now it became part of the "legitimate controversy" which forms, Hallin says (116), the majority of news in mainstream media.

Journalists could pick this up from an unprecedented range of senior sources. Complaints about the attack, the weapons used and Israel's targeting policies came from both humanitarian organisations and highly-placed United Nations officials. Richard Falk, the UN Human Rights Rapporteur in the occupied Palestinian territories, underscores, in an article for the English edition of Le Monde Diplomatique, the exceptional nature of the response: "Even the secretary general of the United Nations, Ban Ki-moon, normally so cautious about offending sovereign states —especially those aligned with its most influential member, the United States— has joined the call for an investigation and potential accountability" (15 March 2009, internet edition). Several governments called explicitly for the establishment of some form of tribunal in which the allegations could be tested. These centred on two principles enshrined in the Geneva Conventions on the laws of war: discrimination and proportionality.

Article 3 of the Fourth Geneva Convention of 1949 says "Persons taking no active part in the hostilities" are entitled to specific protections. They "shall in all circumstances be treated humanely," with an absolute prohibition against "violence to life and person." Israel ratified the Conventions straight away, at the start of its life as a state back in 1951, and half a century later, a Conference of the High Contracting Parties to the Fourth Geneva Convention, held in Geneva, affirmed that these provisions did indeed apply to Palestinians "in the occupied Palestinian territories, including East Jerusalem."

The 1977 Additional Protocols to the Geneva Conventions bring further protections. Chapter 1 of Section 1 adds Article 48 to the Conventions, laying down what it says is a "basic rule":

> In order to ensure respect for and protection of the civilian population and civilian objects, the Parties to the conflict shall at all times distinguish between the civilian population and combatants and between civilian objects and military objectives and accordingly shall direct their operations only against military objectives.

This does not oblige parties in conflict to avoid civilian casualties at all costs. As for proportionality, Article 57 specifies that any incidental loss of life should not be "excessive in relation to the concrete and direct military advantage anticipated."[1] It was the sheer disparity in casualty figures that invoked this notion in connection with Gaza: ten years of sporadic, indiscriminate rocket fire aimed at Israeli towns such as Sderot had killed about twenty people, whereas a few days of all-out military assault by Israel caused well over a thousand deaths.

Israeli spokesmen told interviewers that most of those killed were "militants," a claim resting on the dubious classification of 500 or so armed police officers, working for a government run by Hamas, as being in the same category as fighters in the organisation's armed wing. Such distinctions are, surely, intended to be maintained by the provisions of Article 50 of the Conventions (1977): "The presence within the civilian population of individuals who do not come within the definition of civilians does not deprive the population of its civilian character." However, Israel is one of about 30 UN member states to have refused, so far, to sign the Additional Protocols, another being the United States.

These factors form a continuing thread in the reporting by the *New York Times*, for instance. Its coverage in the first two months of 2009

---

[1] Retrieved on 6 May 2009 from *http://deoxy.org/wc/wc-proto.htm*.

was extensive. In the 58 editions of January and February, it published 58 stories in which both the words, "Israel" and "Gaza" appeared at least once each —an average of one per day.[2] In these, the word, "disproportionate" crops up four times, and "indiscriminate" twice, both of the latter referring to Hamas rockets. The phrase, "war crime(s)" occurs 19 times in the articles, and the phrase, "international law" occurs 13 times.

Given that the articles caught in the sample include a smattering from the business pages (concerned with the impact on the price of oil), the domestic section (as then-President Elect Obama attempted to damp down calls for him to respond to the crisis) and even the book reviews, the incidence of these analytical factors in stories explicitly presented as being about the conflict would be higher still. It means that readers who followed the story day by day were highly likely to see it framed in terms of international law.

This is unusual for the *New York Times*. It is supposed to be a paper of record, so Howard Friel and Richard Falk (2004) call their book, criticising aspects of its coverage, *The Record of the Paper*. They survey 70 editorials about the Bush Administration's plans for the invasion of Iraq, finding that none of them so much as mentions international law or the UN Charter. They lament the paper's "persistent refusal to consider international law arguments opposing recourse to and the conduct of war by American political leaders, and by this refusal allowing the citizenry to overlook this essential dimension of controversial foreign-policy decisions" (2).

Over at the *Guardian* in London, similar trends in coverage of the assault on Gaza could be discerned. Counting original articles on the *Guardian Unlimited* website, as well as those which actually appeared in the paper day by day, the number of words is similar to that in the *New York Times*, with a higher number of articles of significantly lesser average length. Here, the word "disproportionate" gets eight mentions, "indiscriminate" two, "war crime(s)" 11 and "international law" 13. Surveys of coverage in Australia's *Sydney Morning Herald* and the *Jakarta Post*, in Indonesia, produce broadly similar results (data for all three collected from the papers' respective websites):

---

[2] Retrieved using the Factiva search engine.

Newspaper	Articles mentioning Israel and Gaza, Jan and Feb '09	Of those, mention "disproportionate"	"Indiscriminate"	"War crimes"	"International law"
New York Times	58	4	2	19	13
Guardian (London)	93	8	2	11	13
Sydney Morning Herald	88	12	1	5	8
Jakarta Post	83	9	6	16	16

The frequent and explicit mentions of international law and war crimes in the *Jakarta Post* were partly attributable to calls from the Indonesian government for their investigation, bearing out the familiar research finding, by Hallin and others, that elite sources generally set the agenda for journalism in mainstream media. The Australian government, on the other hand, resisted calls for discussion of the crisis along such lines, being content, instead, to reiterate statements about "Israel's right to defend itself." The Department of Foreign Affairs and Trade confined itself to media releases about humanitarian aid for Gaza. Even then, the *Herald* went out of its way to compensate for this, as it were, by giving significant space to a feature article discussing the international law aspects of the conflict.

Two frequent themes of the coverage, in all four newspapers, were reporting evidence of the weapons used by Israel —including new variants of white phosphorous— and the targeting of such installations as a UN school and relief centre. Around the fringes of the coverage, and reported more prominently outside mainstream media, were allegations about the use of "Tungsten DIME" —said to truncate peoples' limbs without bleeding— and rumours about the possibility of experimental weapons like "silent bombs" that "vapourise" everything and everyone in the vicinity of where they explode. The inherently indiscriminate nature of such weaponry, if its use is established, would strengthen the case that Israel was in breach of the Geneva Conventions.

Aggressive War?

One key aspect of international law that is less in evidence in the coverage is the concept of aggressive war-making, in contravention of the UN Charter. The two famous clauses of Article 2:

3. All Members shall settle their international disputes by peaceful means in such a manner that international peace and security, and justice, are not endangered.

4. All Members shall refrain in their international relations from the threat or use of force against the territorial integrity or political independence of any state, or in any other manner inconsistent with the Purposes of the United Nations.

As with the Geneva Conventions and the avoidance of civilian casualties, this does not, of course, amount to a blanket ban on the use of force, a topic covered by Chapter VII of the Charter. This ends with Article 51: "Nothing in the present Charter shall impair the inherent right of individual or collective self-defence if an armed attack occurs against a Member of the United Nations, until the Security Council has taken measures necessary to maintain international peace and security."

It was a key part of Israel's narrative for the conflict to establish that "Operation Cast Lead" was an act of self-defence, having sustained a barrage of rockets from Gaza. Interviewed as the military offensive got underway, Israeli Foreign Minister Tzipi Livni told NBC's widely viewed Sunday morning talk show *Meet the Press* (28 December 2008), that: "About a half a year ago, according to the Egyptian Initiative, we decided to enter a kind of a truce and not to attack the Gaza Strip... Hamas violated, on a daily basis, this truce. They targeted Israel, and we didn't answer."

However, a fact sheet produced by the Israeli consulate in New York City, after the Egyptian-brokered ceasefire agreed with Hamas began in June 2008, said the rate of rocket and mortar fire from Gaza dropped to almost zero, and stayed there for four straight months. As Nancy Kanwisher, Johannes Haushofer and Anat Biletzki point out in the *Huffington Post*, the ceasefire ended on 4 November 2008 "when Israel first killed Palestinians, and Palestinians then fired rockets into Israel" (6 January 2009).

This was a story "missed" by most US media, according to an investigation for the Interpress service by Jim Lobe and Ali Gharib. "While the major US news wire Associated Press (AP) reported that the attack, in which six members of Hamas's military wing were killed by Israeli ground forces, threatened the ceasefire, its report was carried by only a handful of small newspapers around the country," they find (8 January 2009).

"The November 4th raid —and the escalation that followed— also went unreported by the major US network and cable television new programmes, according to a search of the Nexis database for all English-language news coverage between November 4th and 7th" (ibid.). Stephen Zunes of the University of San Francisco tells Lobe and Gharib (ibid.): "While neither side ever completely respected the ceasefire terms, the Israeli raid was far and away the biggest violation. It was a huge, huge provocation, and it now appears to me that it was actually intended to get Hamas to break off the ceasefire."

This they did, with a volley of answering rocket fire, which was then used by Israel as justification for escalating the violence, a line accepted by many media, as Israel's newly formed National Information Directorate churned it out. "Israel's air offensive against the Gaza Strip yesterday should not have been a surprise for anyone who has been following the mounting hostilities in the region," the *Washington Post* (December, 2008, internet edition) intoned, in its lead editorial the day after Israel began its aerial pounding of the territory, "least of all the Hamas movement, which invited the conflict by ending a six-month-old ceasefire and launching scores of rockets and mortar shells at Israel during the last 10 days." In the UK, the Media Lens website (12 January 2009) chided the BBC and others for reproducing "key deceptions" over the sequence of events, and for offering coverage in which "context [was] entirely absent or buried out of sight."

Victor Kattan, of the Centre for International Studies and Diplomacy at the School of Oriental and African Studies, University of London, says in a column in *Human Rights Tribune* (19 January 2009, internet edition): "For the purposes of the law of self-defence, it is not always a question of who attacks first." Article 2 of the UN General Assembly's 1974 Definition of Aggression stipulates that: "The first use of armed force by a State in contravention of the Charter shall constitute prima facie evidence of an act of aggression."

However, Professor Yoram Dinstein of Tel Aviv University interprets this to mean "it is not who fired the first shot but who embarked upon an apparently irreversible course of action, thereby crossing the legal Rubicon. The casting of the die, rather than the actual opening of fire, is what starts the armed attack" (2005: 191). "Without doubt —Kattan adds— it was Israel's 27th December attack on Gaza, the biggest air assault on the Strip since 1967, that, to use Dinstein's phrase, constituted the crossing of the 'legal Rubicon.'"

What Happens Next?

Given that world publics have been sensitised, by media reporting, to at least some international law aspects of the attack, is there any prospect that this will be followed by actual legal action against its perpetrators? Francis Boyle (31 December 2008, internet edition), an international law expert from the College of Law at the University of Illinois at Urbana-Champaign, called on the Global Research site for an Israeli War Crimes Tribunal (ICT) and has asked the UN General Assembly to "immediately establish an (ICTI) as a 'subsidiary organ' under UN Charter Article 22" similar to the Security Council's ICTY for Yugoslavia. Its purpose "would be to investigate and prosecute Israeli war crimes, crimes against humanity and genocide against the Peoples of Lebanon and Palestine," Boyle says. Article 22 simply says: "The General Assembly may establish such subsidiary organs as it deems necessary for the performance of its functions."

Any such tribunal would, of course, examine allegations even-handedly, with a mandate, also, to prosecute those responsible for Qassam rockets lobbed into Israel from inside Gaza; indiscriminate weapons, by their very nature. However, the disparity of casualty figures means it would be a travesty of justice if the allegations against Israel were not its main focus. Richard Falk adds:

> These two sides should not be viewed as equally responsible for the recent events. Israel initiated the Gaza campaign without adequate legal foundation or just cause, and was responsible for causing the overwhelming proportion of devastation and the entirety of civilian suffering. Israeli reliance on a military approach to defeat or punish Gaza was intrinsically "criminal," and as such demonstrative of both violations of the law of war and the commission of crimes against humanity (15 March 2009, internet edition).

Phil Shiner, of the UK-based group Public Interest Lawyers, draws attention to the actions governments could have taken in response to an occasion when Israel *was* brought to book, by the International Court of Justice, in 2004, which issued an advisory opinion on Israel's so-called security fence —known to everyone else as "the wall"— which grabbed, divided and reticulated Palestinian territory in the occupied West Bank. He says:

> If the UK and other EU states in particular, had complied with their international obligations, as clearly set out in the advisory opinion of the international court of justice in July 2004, this crisis could have been nipped in the bud at the outset (as could Israel's bombardment of Lebanon and Gaza in August 2006) (*The Guardian*, 14 January 2009, internet edition).

The ICJ's opinion on the wall "could not be clearer," Shiner continues.

It identifies 11 international obligations breached by Israel by the construction of the wall and the maintenance of the system flowing from it of gates, permits, and illegal settlements on Palestinian land. These included non-derogable rules on the Palestinian right to self-determination and the prohibition on the acquisition of land by force (ibid.).

The ICJ judgement spelt out seven separate obligations for other states —in the context of these non-derogable rules— that include two negative obligations that states must not: one, render aid or assistance in maintaining the situation; and, two, recognise the illegal situation. Shiner goes on: "Negative obligations have a lower threshold than positive ones and the burden on the UK and other EU states to meet these negative international obligations from July 2004 has been a high one" (ibid.).

"It is noteworthy," he adds, in the *Guardian* opinion piece (ibid.), "that the UK, as one such state, has done nothing effective to meet these obligations, and has, in fact, increased its aid and assistance in Israel since the ICJ's opinion." Shiner goes on to list some examples of Britain's "positive encouragement" of Israel's actions in the occupied Palestinian territories since July 2004:

— A massive increase in the value of arms-related products licensed to Israel in recent times (a doubling from 2004 to 2005 and a huge increase again in the first quarter of 2008);
— It has resisted all attempts by campaigners that it should apply effective pressure within the EU that the EU-Israel association agreement, which is of great importance to Israel's trading figures, should be suspended as the human rights obligations underpinning it have been breached;
— It has continued to invite Israel's arms companies to exhibit at the biennial London Docklands arms fair;
— It has continued to propagate the myth that the Quartet's Road Map process is the answer to the humanitarian crisis in the occupied Palestinian territories, which has allowed it to resist any positive action.

The Road Map and the Quartet

The last point here, the inefficacy of the Road Map, is connected to both its form and its content. The problem with the latter is the order of the steps it prescribes. Phase one includes an "end to Palestinian violence"; only then will phase two commence, the centrepiece of which is supposed to be an "International Conference to support Palestinian economic recovery and launch a process, leading to establishment of an independent Palestinian state with provisional borders" (2003, "Roadmap For Peace").

There are two problems with this. It makes the prospects of peace a hostage to violence, and it reverses the order of conflict dynamics, observed in so many situations over so many years, and captured in Johan Galtung's comments on the Transcend Media Service website in a column about the conflict in the southern Philippines (16 February 2009):

> Issues of equity and autonomy must be solved to bring about equitable and sustainable peace. The road to DDR (disarmament-demobilization-reintegration), conciliation and development passes through solution, not vice versa. Putting the cart before the horse is pacification, not peace-building, and will fool nobody.

Secondly, in form, the Quartet itself is an unwieldy beast, a pantomime horse of international relations comprising the UN, US, EU and Russia, in which the head and the hindquarters have different priorities and wish to go in different directions. The UN is the sole competent authority to hold the ring in the dispute between Israel and the Palestinians, as Chapter VI of its Charter suggests. The opening article of that chapter, number 33, states:

> The parties to any dispute, the continuance of which is likely to endanger the maintenance of international peace and security, shall, first of all, seek a solution by negotiation, enquiry, mediation, conciliation, arbitration, judicial settlement, resort to regional agencies or arrangements, or other peaceful means of their own choice.

And Article 37 says: "Should the parties to a dispute of the nature referred to in Article 33 fail to settle it by the means indicated in that Article, they shall refer it to the Security Council."

Martin Indyk, an Australian who stepped straight from his role as a pro-Israeli lobbyist in Washington to serve two spells, under President Clinton, as America's ambassador in Tel Aviv, recalls how his career-spanning commitment to the region was inspired by BBC radio broadcasts about Henry Kissinger's attempts to negotiate a ceasefire in the Yom Kippur, or October war of 1973. "I came to understand the pivotal role of the United States as the one party that, through its diplomacy, could help to resolve the Arab-Israeli conflict" (Indyk, 2009: 6).

And, of course, this is the problem. For the US to interpose itself as the mediator of choice has constantly sidelined the proper forum to decide such matters, namely the United Nations, and tilts the playing field in Israel's favour. Indyk admits, in a moment of lucidity, that Washington's "capriciousness" in brokering talks between Ehud Barak and Yasser Arafat, at Camp David in 2000, could be attributed to the "asymmetry" of America's relations with the two parties (ibid.: 308).

Sure enough, when it came to the assault on Gaza, a report in the Israeli newspaper, *Ha'aretz*, revealed how the present US ambassador to the UN, Zalmay Khalilzad, had "received explicit instructions from his superiors at the State Department to torpedo any initiative proposed by the Arab bloc which is designed to grant the Security Council the status of an official arbiter that will have direct involvement with disentangling the Gaza crisis" (6 January 2009, internet edition).

The UN dilutes and weakens its authority, indeed, by entering into such arrangements as the Quartet. An extension of the same logic saw the UN reach a formal understanding with the North Atlantic Treaty Organisation, in a secret agreement between their respective Secretaries General, in September 2008. Hans von Sponeck, the UN's former humanitarian coordinator in Iraq, commented, in a column for the Nuclear Age Peace Foundation website:

> Any evaluation of the UN/NATO pact must take into account that NATO is a relic of the Cold War; that NATO, as a Western alliance, is regarded with considerable mistrust by the other 166 United Nations member states; that a primary NATO aim is to assert, by military means, its energy and power interests in opposition to other United Nations member states and that the United States, a founding member of the NATO community, in the most unscrupulous ways, has disparaged the United Nations and broken international law (17 February 2009).

Two familiar obstacles, then, stand between the now widespread appreciation of a *prima facie* case that Israel broke international law in its assault on Gaza, and any real prospect of holding it to account: namely, the unresponsiveness of institutional frameworks, in particular the reluctance of governments to follow through on their obligations; and the (not unconnected) hegemony, at least in political and diplomatic terms, of the United States, which sees Israel as a key military ally in the region, or, in the words attributed to Caspar Weinberger, "America's unsinkable battleship in the Middle East" (Fisk, 1998).

The prospects for bringing international law to bear on the conflict depend on surmounting those obstacles, or circumventing them.

In any such effort, the media represent a promising field of endeavour. They are, in Michael Schudson's words, "formally disconnected from other ruling agencies because they must attend as much to their own legitimation as to the legitimation of the capitalist system as a whole" (1995: 270). In other words, journalism cannot afford to appear less well-informed, or more credulous, than its readers and audiences. To campaign for a greater prominence of international law issues in media representations of this conflict might be to push at a door that is already at least half open.

References

DINSTEIN, Yoram (2005): *War, Aggression and Self-Defence*. Cambridge University Press, Cambridge.

FISK, Robert (1998): "How America Keeps its Ally Armed to the Teeth," *Independent*. London (13 April), retrieved from Factiva search engine.

FRIEL, Howard and Richard FALK (2004): *The Record of the Paper - How the* New York Times *Misreports US Foreign Policy*. Verso, New York.

HALLIN, Daniel (1989): *The Uncensored War: The Media and Vietnam*. University of California Press, Berkeley.

INDYK, Martin (2009): *Innocent Abroad*. Simon and Schuster: New York.

LOBE, Jim and Ali GHARIB (2009): "US Mainstream Media Ignored a Key Israeli Military Attack." *Noticias Financieras* (8 January), retrieved from Factiva search engine.

"Roadmap For Peace in the Middle East: Israeli/Palestinian Reciprocal Action." (2003): Quartet Support, US Department of State, Bureau of Public Affairs (16 July).

SCHUDSON, Michael (1995) *The Power of News*. Harvard University Press, Cambridge, MA.

Issues in Peace and Conflict Studies

*Religions Dealing
with their Own Violent Extremisms:
Development at Stake*

Overcoming Religious Extremism

Joseph G. Bock

University of Notre Dame

Introduction

My first exposure to religious extremism and its violent consequences was in Ahmedabad, India. I wrote a case study on the work of
St. Xavier's Social Services Society ("St. Xavier's" for short), a humanitarian non-governmental organization (NGO) founded and run by Jes-
uit priests. St. Xavier's had built bridges between people of different
faiths that were considered a foundation upon which to build a violence prevention capacity (Bock, 1999).

There were numerous ways by which this NGO sought to promote
inter-faith good will. They called these "promotive" approaches. They
included: relief and development projects that pulled identity groups
together (mainly Muslims and Hindus living in slums); conducting street
plays that dramatized how people sometimes get manipulated into a
violent frenzy (by politicians, for instance, who exploit ethno-religious
differences as a way of solidifying support of one group); and sponsoring art contests, festivals and songs that enhanced appreciation for
"inter-faith harmony." As a part of these approaches, St. Xavier's also
built local capacity to respond to potentially volatile situations. They encouraged the formation of peace committees in the slums, with officers who undertook training in violence mitigation.

St. Xavier's also used "preemptive" approaches. They were used by
both NGO staff and peace committee members. These included communicating with influential community leaders during tense periods,
advocating for their intervention to persuade the likely attackers that
it was not in their interest to undertake violence. Another approach
was "myth busting" whereby committee members did rapid fact finding in the midst of malicious rumors and then clarified whether a hate-
ful event by members of one group towards those of another had hap-

pened or was about to happen. If it did or was about to occur, then the task was to determine if the act represented a collective animosity by the "aggressors" group *writ large* or, rather, was an isolated, perhaps criminal and not political, occurrence. When violence was imminent, they were trained and encouraged to intervene by, for instance, mediating differences or arguing that aggressors would be arrested. And, finally, they sometimes provided "safe haven" in a neutral location (such as in a convent of Catholic sisters).

It was obvious to me that considerable thought and effort had gone into the NGO's efforts to build inter-faith harmony. I could not imagine a more insightful and deliberate approach to violence prevention. And, indeed, I found that their programming was usually successful. This was consistently so when secular issues were at stake (such as the alleged cheering for the Pakistani cricket team by Muslims in the slums during a match with India). But when tension arose due to religion, and especially religious symbols, the programming was a failure. For example, when the Ayodhya Mosque was destroyed, St. Xavier's staff members were run out (by angry Muslim mobs) of two of the three slums in which they had been working and Hindu shacks were torched.

This was, to say the least, disheartening. St. Xavier's had seemingly done everything right and yet the program had failed when religion and religious symbols were a factor. As aptly stated by Fr. Cedric Prakash, director of St. Xavier's: "We asked ourselves 'what had happened to the community organizations which were so carefully nurtured over the years?' Somewhere, something seriously had gone wrong" (quoted in Bock, 2001).

This chapter offers perspectives on how to effectively prevent violence that is fueled, at least in part, by religion. It covers streams of communication, socio-political patterns that lead to extremism, and peace research implications.

Communication

It is perhaps natural for those of one faith to point a finger at those of another faith when inter-faith aggressive statements or acts have occurred between them. But when one religious group criticizes another, this often causes greater tension.

An opposite way of communicating was offered by the Carnegie Commission on Preventing Deadly Conflict (1999: 118) which stated that "[religious leaders should] take more assertive measures to censure coreligionists who promote violence or give religious justification for violence." Essentially, the Commission advocated that confronting aggression would be most effective if done by those of the same faith, not by those who are recipients of the perceived or actual aggression. And this makes sense in that moderates of the same religion of aggressive extremists are intimately familiar with the sacred texts, doctrines, perceptions and culture of their in-group. As such, they are able to engage in private dialogue with co-religionist aggressors that involve hermeneutic exploration to understand perceived religious imperatives differently. Through intra-faith communication, creating cognitive dissonance in the mind of extremists can be a powerful force (see Steele, 1998). This can be done by pointing out the major thrust of the religion as inconsistent with an extremist interpretation. When private engagement is unsuccessful, public dialogue or debate might be warranted in that it can potentially convince reluctant followers (or simply curious bystanders) that violence is not a moral imperative.

On the other hand, the moderates of the recipients of aggression should know the moderates of the aggressing group so that a concern about aggression is conveyed. This is required in part because aggression, like beauty, is "in the eye of the beholder."

The "architecture" of these streams of intra-faith and inter-faith communication and interaction is depicted in Figure 1, below. Note that religious leaders are only one of three kinds of leaders who can impact in-group and out-group communication and interaction. Civic and political leaders have important roles as well. Their critical attributes are respect and credibility within their respective groups.

One often hears that conflict over religion is really not religious conflict. Rather, it is conflict between groups who are suffering from xenophobia and fear that one group will become violent towards another group. Yes, religion is a factor but the aggression is not an inherent imperative of a given religion. Its moral strictures and social teachings are simply being made to seem that aggression is required. The real struggle, in fact, is not an inter-faith one but rather more aptly viewed as primarily an intra-faith challenge. "Religious conflict" is not, for instance, between Muslims, Hindus and Christians. It is really conflict between moderates and extremists of the involved faith communities.

But we must engage rather than shun orthodox religious leaders, some of whom are knowingly providing rhetorical justification for extremist militancy, and others who are doing so inadvertently (Gopin, 2001). And when moderates confront extremists, skillful use of cognitive dissonance might be a helpful tactic in a context of respect (not as manipulation). The approach should be consistent with the description of dialogue offered by Paulo Freire:

> Dialogue cannot be reduced to the act of one person's "depositing" ideas in another, nor can it become a simple exchange of ideas to be "consumed" by the discussants... it must not serve as a crafty instrument for the domination of one [person] by another. The domination implicit in dialogue is that of the world by the dialoguers; it is conquest of the world for the liberation of [people] (1970: 77).

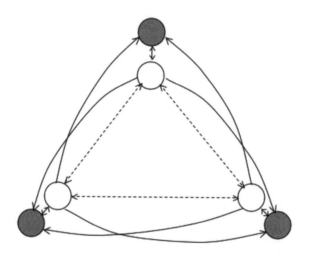

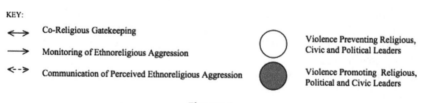

Figure 1

Communication and interaction of religious, civic and political leaders

Socio-Political Patterns that Lead to Aggression

While moderates confronting extremists is one important dimension in understanding the dynamics of religious extremism, another helpful view relates to spirituality, religiosity and secularism. To understand why some societies are more prone to violent religious extremism than others, we need to trace patterns of socio-political states over time. These states are depicted in Figure 2, where celebration of religious diversity (as in appreciating the enrichment of differences) is distinguished from religious tolerance (as in "putting up with"). This can happen where admirable components of a given faith are "envied" by those of another faith—"holy envy" to use the term coined by Krister Stendahl. Examples are as when a Christian envies the discipline of the Muslim fast during Ramadan and where "holy reverence" expresses recognition of the presence of God, such as when a Christian comments on an almost sacramental event —for example, when the Muslim Non-violent Servants of God protected Hindus and Sheiks in Peshawar when British India was being partitioned (Johansen, 1998). This can also happen where inter-spirituality involves a respectful participation of believers from one religion in a sacred ritual of those from another religion (as when a Muslim family participates in a Sukkoth celebration of a Jewish family).

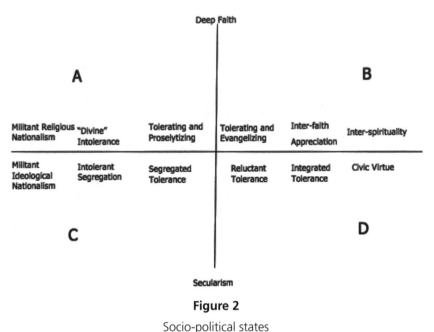

Figure 2

Socio-political states

One pattern that is problematic is when shallow A evolves into shallow D resulting in a double-bind that one has to abandon one's faith in order to get along with (and put up with) those of another faith. Such a double-bind situation constitutes an unstable equilibrium that can be seized upon by extremists who skillfully change the socio-political state to deep A, as depicted in Figure 3.

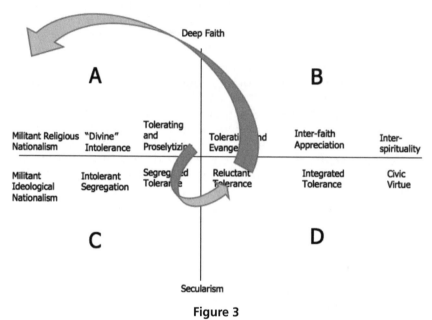

Figure 3

The pattern leading to religious extremism

In contrast, a more desirable pattern for reducing the chances of inter-faith violence is when shallow A moves to deep B, achieving what St. Xavier's staff members called "inter-faith harmony." Deep B involves a pathway whereby celebration of diversity, holy envy, and holy reverence are taken to the point of inter-spirituality, as depicted in Figure 4.

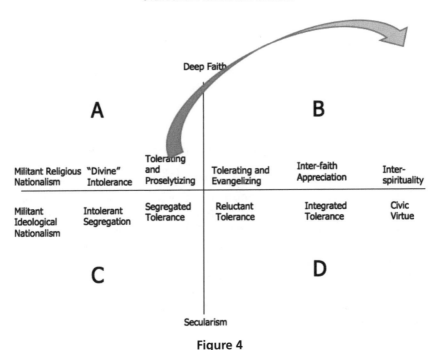

Figure 4

The pattern leading to "inter-faith harmony"

Research Implications

We have not yet empirically tested the Carnegie Commission's recommendation of co-religionist engagement. Because much of this type of communication is conducted privately, research in this area will require a case study approach (as used by Anderson, 1999). They could form the basis of our knowledge of how to best engage in co-religionist dialogue involving hermeneutic windows and symbolic gestures that lead to transformation of understanding. Such a project might yield a comparative reference book similar to the Gospel Parallels (Throckmorton, 1993) but, in this case, sacred passages used to promote violence would be juxtaposed with passages that counteract those isolated interpretations. There might be commentary at the bottom of the page that would provide detail and examples. For instance, it could explain how XYZ case study found that the Croatian Catholic religious leader used this sacred passage to encourage the faithful to attack ABC ethnic Albanian, nominally Muslim, village. But the XYZ case study found that the papal nuncio took immediate action to discredit this Croatian Catholic religious leader...

In contrast to a case study approach, the socio-political states depicted in Figure 2 above could be tracked by assembling and analyzing events data on political and religious discourse. The four states, A-D, and the movement from one to the other, might best be analyzed using Hidden Markov Models (see Bond et al., 2004 for an example). Such research could identify situations that are most prone to religious extremism.

However, Figures 1 and 2 should make us ask some epistemological questions. We must recognize that building relationships and undertaking assertive engagement as depicted in Figure 1 is not an altogether "natural" occurrence. People interact and communicate mostly with those of their own group. And confronting a co-religionist can be as awkward and unpleasant as, for instance, challenging one's brother-in-law who just told a racist joke during a holiday meal. To employ the insights of Simon (1996), the architecture depicted in Figure 1 is "artificial," not "organic." It tends not to occur naturally. It must be created thoughtfully and deliberately. So, whereas identifying the patterns of moving from one quadrant to another as depicted in Figure 2 is "regular" science in that it seeks to understand how religious extremism unfolds, research related to the drawing in Figure 1 is less about how the world works than about how people behave when the conditions for that communication and assertive engagement are created. The question is how to build, how to design, the web of relationships (to use the terminology of Lederach, 2005) and the durability of associations (which is being insightfully analyzed by Varshney, 2001 and 2002), so that people will be inclined to do what is not especially natural. That is a "science of the artificial." Such science can help us understand and design the best intra-faith and inter-faith architecture to overcome religious extremism.

References

ANDERSON, Mary B. (1999): *Do No Harm: How Aid Can Support Peace—Or War.* Lynne Rienner, Boulder.

BOCK, Joseph G. (1999): "The Harmony Project: Peace Building Amid Poverty in India." Adapt., ed. Mary B. ANDERSON: *Do No Harm: How Aid Can Support Peace—Or War.* Lynne Rienner, Boulder. 119-129.

— (2001): *Sharpening Conflict Management: Religious Leadership and the Double-Edged Sword.* Praeger Publishers, Westport, CT.

— and Clark McCauley (2003): "A Call to Lateral Mission: Mobilizing Religious Authority against Ethnic Violence." *Mission Studies*, Vol. 20-2, 9-34.

Bond, Joe; Doug Bond; Sean O'Brien and Vladimir Petroff (2004): "Forecasting Turmoil in Indonesia: An Application of Hidden Markov Models." Paper presented at the International Studies Association Convention (17-20 March). At: http://vranet.com/papers/HMM.pdf.

Carnegie Commission on Preventing Deadly Conflict (1998): *Final Report: Preventing Deadly Conflict*. Carnegie Corporation, New York.

Freire, Paulo (1970): *Pedagogy of the Oppressed*. Continuum, New York.

Gopin, Marc (2001): *Holy War/Holy Peace*. Oxford University Press, New York.

Johansen, Robert C. (1997): "Radical Islam and Nonviolence: A Case Study of Religious Empowerment and Constraint Among Pushtuns." *Journal of Peace Research*, Vol. 34, 1, 53-71.

Lederach, John Paul (2005): *The Moral Imagination: The Art and Soul of Building Peace*. Oxford University Press, New York.

Simon, Herbert (1996): *The Sciences of the Artificial*. MIT Press, Cambridge.

Steele, David (1998): "Conflict Resolution among Religious People in Bosnia and Croatia." Ed. Paul Mojzes. *Religion and the War in Bosnia*. Scholars Press, Atlanta.

Throckmorton, Burton (1993): *Gospel Parallels, NRSV Edition*. Thomas Nelson, Nashville.

Varshney, Ashutosh (2001): "Ethnic Conflict and Civil Society: India and Beyond." *World Politics*, Vol. 53 (April), 362-398.

— (2002): *Ethnic Conflict & Civic Life*. Yale University Press, New Haven.

How Does Islam Deal with its Own Extremism? Provoking Words and Images of Islam: Experiences of Religion in Parisian Banlieues

Lamiss Azab
Université Française d'Egypte

As a Starting Point

A few weeks after 11 September 2001, for my first class at a lycée in the Parisian banlieue, I was teaching the 16-year old girls and boys who were learning Arabic as a third foreign language the word "Salâm," peace, so that we could use it to greet each other at the beginning and at the end of each class. I wrote it on the board —سلام— and started listening to the pronunciation and checking the spelling and writing for each student, while discussing its meaning and putting it in sentences. We started exchanging greetings until I came to Malik, a French teenager with Moroccan origins, who refused to answer my "Salâm." "Do you have a problem with 'peace,' Malik? Why don't you answer my greeting?" I asked. "Well, isn't it true that prophet Muhammad, may prayers and peace be upon him, said that he'd rather have his ears pierced by a burning hot iron bar than greet a woman?" he answered with a smile. Some of his classmates laughed, and waited to see my reaction. Was this my "bullying" session, the trial I had to go through to show what kind of teacher I was and, eventually, be accepted by the community of students?

> Well, I may be a woman, Malik, but first of all I am your teacher and you need grades in this course if you want to pass this year. So, make your choice: either you consider me as a woman and lose a lot of grades, or you think of me as your Arabic professor and prove you understand what I say by answering me. Besides, I would like to have the source from which you learned that Prophet Muhammad said such a Hadîth, please. Do your research and tell me next time... if you decide that you can talk to me! (October 2001, a banlieue northwest of Paris)

While I was preparing my PhD, between 2001 and 2006, I discovered a new face of French Islam, though I have lived most of my life in France and though I have followed with great interest the evolution of this religion as implanted in the specific context of the French banlieues. French Islam is no longer an invisible religion, searching for ways to integrate smoothly, as it was in the 1980s (Kepel, 1987). Today, the youth is explicitly refusing to show their parents' "submission" to many of the French laws concerning the manifestation of their religious beliefs (building mosques, wearing the Islamic veil). They are also showing their own parents, in a flagrant manner, their refusal towards a ritualist Islam and their quest to understand religion, as many French sociologists have explained through the past ten years (Babès, 1997; Cesari, 1998; Khosrokhavar, 1997). Somehow, Islam seems to be more than a component of a complex identity as it used to be. It has become, for those young (15-25) French Muslims of immigrant origins (especially North African ones), an experience (Dubet, 1994), a way of feeling things, of understanding people and events, of constructing reality around oneself. Communication is the central point in this experience, in an attempt to break the stigma that many of these young people feel in the a-religious French context. And communication here has to be understood as Jakobson described it in the early sixties and as Pottier refined it later in the eighties, as a relationship between a "sender" and a "receiver" through the transmission of a "message" in a certain language, through a "channel" and in a "context" that has a crucial importance in determining the meaning and the effect of the discourse. The experience of Islam as built around this communication perspective can sometimes be lived at an extreme point, creating a real dislocation in the socialization process and provoking some people in the public sphere. This particular strategy of self presentation (Goffman, 1957) does not represent the majority. However, as Islamic extremism —and even Islam in its moderate version, is seen as extremism while it is not— has retained attention in France since the end of the 1980s (with the first "affaire du voile" at the banlieue of Creil in 1989) and much more since 11 September 2001, it might be interesting to concentrate on this strategy to understand how this experience helps young Muslims define themselves in the specific context where they live.

In order to do this, I will explain how young French Muslims of immigrant origins, aged 15-25 and living in specific French banlieues, moved from a ritualist Islam to the quest for Islamic discourse, seeking a more active and a more intense experience of religion. This experience of religion, as presented by these young Muslims, seems to be mainly articulated around words and images: affected by the words and images of Islam shown in the French media, young French Muslims look for discourses of Islam produced by different sources and especially by television preachers before they start producing their own discourses of Islam to construct their own image of Islam and to use it to present themselves as Muslims in their banlieue. Through this explanation, I will try to show the impact of the "context" the young Muslims live in on the shaping of the Islamic experience they go through, because the reception of religious discourses in this peculiar context is essential to understanding why it becomes extreme.

The Transformation of the Islamic Quest

To understand the quest for religion that the young Muslims have formulated in France since the beginning of the 2000s, it is essential to insist on the fact that these French young people of immigrant origins are not the grandsons and granddaughters of the migrants Kepel met in his *Banlieues de l'islam*. They are the sons and daughters of another wave of migrants who entered France in the mid-eighties. They are a new "second generation," born in France and bearing the French nationality (most of them). Though the term "second generation" seems to be disqualifying because it dis-integrates those young people from the French society in which they were born (Wihtol de Wenden and Leveau, 1988), it must sometimes be used to situate the transformation of the religious quest which occurred recently in France. Most of the extremist young people I am talking about in this article belong to this generation.

The fact that they are the descendants of first-migrants means that they are still close to the countries of their parents, or at least the cultural elements of these countries, for the parents still bear the habits and customs of their countries. At home, most of the time, there are two coexisting styles, a French one and a North African one. The father and mother speak Arabic (or at least a colloquial language) or Kabyle. And of course, satellite channels transmit Arabic programs, films and series. As children are born in France and start socializing in this country, they have the opportunity (or the curse) of sharing two different cultures. They become able to speak French, while being familiar with an Arabic dialect or with Kabyle (if they are not able to communicate in those languages as well). However, they do not understand literal Arabic, the language of the Koran, but their proximity with dialects makes them feel that they could understand it "if [they] wanted to" as many of them used to tell me from 2001 to 2007 (and until today). In parallel with this crucial characteristic related to language, these young people also have a direct and regular access to different media styles and content, the French one and the Arabic one. For instance, in the aftermath of 11 September events and of the declaration of the American war against Afghanistan and Iraq, they could watch news and programmes both on French channels, such as TF1, France 2, France 3 and Canal + and on satellite channels, mainly Al Jazeerah and Iqra', which became an essential reference during the designated period.

This generation of young Muslims thus entered an experience of Islam that was very special. At the age they started to discover their religion, they started to perceive negative representations of it on an international scale (with the stigmatization of Islam as an extremist and violent religion), as well as on a national one (with the different cases related to wearing the veil in schools and public spheres, the construction of new mosques and "halal" abattoirs). But they also were in contact with sources of Arabic and Islamic discourses through satellite channels and the internet and this contact reinforced the capacity of the young Muslims to react to this stigmatization. No general reaction could be found among those young people living in banlieues, as numerous strategies could be developed by each person, even contradictory ones. Extremism is one of these strategies and it is the one that shows most how Islam is becoming today, more and more, a religion of words and images.

An Islam of Words and Images in a Globalized World

Out of 100 young French Muslims, 80 declare that they are deeply affected by the way Islam is (re)presented in French media (January 2005). And 75 declare that they are very interested in learning more about Islam through discourses produced by different sources (sheikhs at mosques, preachers either physically present in mosques or at conferences, or through cassettes, CDs, satellite channels or the internet). These percentages are high. They reflect how essential religion has become in the eyes of the youth. It is "a central component of the identity," "the main goal [young people] want to achieve in their life," "the only thing that is worth living for, because it shows the principles we need to follow to deserve to be called human."[1] So, we can see that three discourses and images all related to each other prevail in the new

---

[1] I quote the students I knew, the most extremist among different classes, aged 15-17.

quest for Islam. First, the media discourse and images representing Islam in France are considered by many specialists as a major source of stigmatization. Media create an "imaginary Islam" (Deltombe, 2007) that maintains a phobia towards this religion. The extremist idea of Islam that results from this image pushes young Muslims who are really attached to their religion to look for sources in which they would find answers to this discourse and image about Islam. Second are the Islamic discourses and images offered by producers who are recognized by young Muslims as religious references. For the extremists, these sources may be salafi ones (such as local extremist sheikhs or famous foreign preachers like the Egyptians Mohamed Hassan and Mohammed Hussein Ya"qûb or the Saudi Rabî" El Madkhalî) or "normal ones" interpreted in an extremist way (such as the Egyptian Amr Khaled). Third, we see the reformulated Islamic discourses and images produced by young Muslims themselves to express their attachment to religion, to show their rejection of the existing discourses and images about their religion and to explain the "right" meaning of Islam.

The Misunderstood Religion

The editor in chief of Le Monde Diplomatique, Alain Gresh, explained during a conference in 2003 in Paris that the so-called Occidental world discovered after 11 September that it knew little about Islam. In France, for several months, almost all of the media took an interest in this religion, whether in its "original context" (the Middle East) or in new ones, especially France. For example, French magazines (those related to religion, but also history, culture, society, lifestyle, women, psychology and others) focused on Islam, trying to understand its sources, its Book, its message. Muslims of France and of the world were put under a microscope, and journalists, reporters, analysts were trying to get closer and to reveal the truth about them. All kinds of descriptions and analyses were available, and many types of discourse could be read and heard. What Cesari said in an interesting article about the French representation of Islam (1997/1998) seemed to be so true. By the end of the 1990, it was viewed by French as an "étrange étrangeté," a "foreign strangeness," even though their contact with this religion started centuries ago. More precisely, and concerning the vision that the French media presents of Islam, Thomas Deltombe explains in a recent article that since the mid-nineties there is a "repressed islamophobia," especially on television:

> Si les commentaires répètent inlassablement que "l'islam est une religion de paix," la plupart des reportages font rimer "islam" avec

"problème." Une étude statistique montre clairement que ce qui amène la télévision à parler d'islam est toujours lié à ce qui est perçu comme une menace et une agression, à commencer par le voile et le terrorisme. Dès que les crises s'apaisent, la religion musulmane disparaît du petit écran, et les "musulmans modérés" avec elle (2004).

Though the commentary repeats incessantly that "Islam is a religion of peace," most reports equate "Islam" with "problem." A poll clearly demonstrates that the motivation behind the televised media for speaking about Islam is always related to a perception of threat and aggression, starting with the veil and terrorism. As soon as a crisis disappears, Islamic religion also disappears from television, as well as "moderate Muslims" (translation by the author).

The fact is that this vision and (re)presentation of Islam remain today. Many proofs showed this in the period from 2001 to 2006 and a short visit to the INA (Institut National de l'Audiovisuel) in 2007 showed that many of the reportages right after 11 September were based on prejudices and biased visions of this religion, combined with predefined ideas about immigrant populations (as a great number of them are Muslims) and about banlieues in France (which are mainly inhabited by migrants or French people from immigrant origins). This point is essential to understanding the transformation of the quest for religion today. Young French Muslims of immigrant origins living in French banlieues are more sensitive than ever to those three stigmas (related to their origins, to their place of residence and to their religion) in their everyday life, and this sensitivity is being exacerbated by the different discourses and images that are transmitted by the media about those three specific components of their identity.

The stigma concerning religion seems to be the most harmful, which refers to what many Arab writers, such as Amin Maalouf, expressed at the end of the nineties: that religion as a sacred reference seems to be the one that matters the most to many believers. Young Muslims aged 15-20 expressed this idea in many ways between 2001 and 2006:

> Look how they are drawing our Islam on television! We are all "extremists"! We are all Bin Laden! Sometimes, I feel I want to explain how it works. But most of the time, believe me, I feel really hurt, and I feel I don't want to explain anything. And why should I? Did those people try to know my religion or to understand it? Of course not! If they did, there wouldn't have been any 9/11 (Youssouf, 19 years old in 2006).

Concerning words, it is important to understand that French media had —and still have— a real difficulty in finding the proper terminology to label Islam and Muslims, with all their trends, from the most moderate to the most extreme. What is the difference between a "Muslim" and an "Islamist"? Numerous television shows produced in the aftermath of 11 September would use the two as perfect synonyms. We could also try to study the uses of different terms used by media and especially television to designate Islam in general or certain trends (such as "integrism," "fundamentalism," "salafism," among other words). It is clear that some journalists are not always aware of the different significations of these terms and as they use them without understanding them, they perpetuate the misunderstanding and, even worse, the perception of Islam as a "foreign strangeness." What is more dangerous is that this terminological imprecision (Deltombe, 2004) has always been related to an image of Islam that is also very imprecise, which has been diffused by different media until it has become collectively imagined as a religion dominated by extremism. I was very shocked when I realized after a certain while that the majority of the professors I worked with at two different Lycées in the banlieues did not know essential information about this religion (like its five pillars for instance) nor the links between Occidental and Arab civilizations (in Bagdad in the ninth century or in Andalusia in the twelfth century). A teacher told me in January 2003:

> All I know is that I have always lived among Muslim men and women in this banlieue. I have never heard them talking about their religion as the young ones do today. I have never seen a veil on a woman's head. What is going on, now? Why did all these young boys and girls turn into extremists?

Later during the same month, one of the students taught by this teacher told me: "It is becoming very difficult to bear. My veil seems to be the only thing that defines me. It is important, but I am not a veil. I am a Muslim girl who wears a veil! It's not the same thing."

The French media's obsession about the Islamic veil is perhaps an interesting entry to this misunderstood religion, to this distorted image of Islam in the country of "Freedom, Equality, Brotherhood." The veil was —and is still— treated in the context of a wider debate about the possibility of integrating Islam to the French laity system. Numerous debates were organized on different French channels and, sometimes, the television programmes would invite young Muslim girls to talk about the way they think that the veil does not represent a threat to Republican values. The questions that were submitted to these young Muslims and the reactions of the audiences present revealed the predefined vision the majority had of Islam. For many, the veil seemed to be "a symbol of women's repression," of "archaism," "anachronism" and "extremism." And somehow, Islam was represented by a veil. All the other components of this religion were put aside through the reflection on the compatibility of a flagrant sign of religiosity and a context in which religion was supposed be contained in the private sphere. For all my Muslim students, this kind of debate was "a real insult to their identity," "an attack to Islam as a religion and as a culture" and they were outraged to see that these programmes were very popular. So while the French media would present Islam as an extremist religion, young Muslims would see the French media as the extremist party. And though these young Muslims would try to gather into communities to feel stronger and to react to the stigma, they would still be stigmatized by those who considered themselves "normal people." They would be even more stigmatized than they were before their reaction (Goffman, 1963), especially since these young people would base their answers on discourses and images produced by Islamic preahers, which is logical because they build their reactive strategies on stigmatized productions and producers.

Discourses and Images Produced by Islamic Preachers

It has been said earlier that the young French Muslims of immigrant origins living in the banlieues refuse to follow their parents Islamic ritual patterns, and that they always say they want "to know" and "to learn" about their religion so they would not be "practicing a religion without understanding it."[2] This eagerness to "get closer to real Islam" —as they say— becomes even greater as these young people try to answer those who accuse them and their religion of extremism. However, instead of trying to read the sources of Islam directly —the Holy Book and its different interpretations in Arabic and/or French, and the numerous sources of Hadîth— many of the young Muslims look for discourses and images of Islam produced by new preachers who would facilitate access to some of these sources.

> It is very difficult to understand Islam in its real sources. The Koran is written in a very special language and though I started learning Arabic three years ago to be able to read and memorize the Holy Book, I still can't understand most of the verses I read. So, I bought the French translation of the Koran and I try to read it. However, on a daily basis, what I do regularly is listen to sermons and lessons from the most popular preachers (Sarah, 17 years old in 2003).

---

[2] I quote students I taught between 2001 and 2006.

Language is one of the main problems for French Muslims of immigrant origins aged 15-25. However, the paradox is that though they do not master the literal Arabic (fushâ) to be able to read the Koran, the Hadîth and interpretations in their original language, these young Muslims are very interested to listen to sermons in Arabic made by famous preachers of the Arab world such as the moderate Amr Khaled, the salafists Mohamed Hassân, Mohamed Hussein Ya"qûb and Rabî" Al Madkhalî. While it would be more logical that these young people would listen to local preachers such as Hasan Iquioussen or Tariq Ramadan who know more about the context of this generation and who speak a language they understand, they instead turn to ones from different contexts with different problems and in a language they can barely decode. The fact that Khaled, Hassân and others are considered "star" preachers in the whole Arab world is an essential element one has to keep in mind while analyzing this situation. They are well-known and their sermons are distributed in several media (cassettes, CDs, satellite channels, the internet). The appearance of those preaching stars on Arabic satellite channels to which young Muslims have access in France explains why they would rather listen to them. In fact, the far away preachers create a specific charisma between themselves and their "absent" public, "a mediated charismatic relationship" draws itself through new media technologies (Frankl, 1987; Diekema, 1991). The medium helps the receptor feel he is a target, as well as the actual targets present at the channel's studio. It will even make him feel much more important than those direct targets, as the programme is essentially aimed to be transmitted through satellite to him, the indirect receiver. I will come back to this point later, with an analysis of the shift from the globalized context of communication created by new media to the local context of the reception in the Parisian banlieue. What is important to stress here is that young Muslims seem to be happy to receive these discourses and images of Islam, even though they do not understand these discourses and images because of the transmission language. They are even keen to receive it, and they purposefully seek it, as they feel it is the proof somebody is interested in them despite the stigma they live with constantly in their banlieue. Consequently, they would ask an Arab friend to watch the programme with them so he or she would provide them with a translation of the main ideas —this is one of the numerous ways young people have access to the content of the discourses transmitted by satellite channels. Another way would be to search on the internet for French translations of different sermons.

Therefore, the search for these discourses and images of Islam on satellite or on the internet is a search for self-value more than a search for an "objective" answer to stigmatization. It is also possible to consider that a self-valorisation is contained in the answer to disqualification. I said formerly that young Muslims do not have access to the sources of Islam because of the Arabic language they have not mastered —but this is not the main reason since they watch sermons in Arabic on satellite channels. One other essential reason is the fact that young people do not have the patience to look up the information in books, or to constitute their own opinion about different issues treated in those books. In fact, there is a trend amongst young generations of Muslims nowadays that they would rather listen to discourses produced by preachers, some kind of "ready-to-be-consumed" discourses containing references to the main verses, Hadîths and interpretations on each issue. Those sermons also draw profiles of the good Muslim. As Amr Khaled once explained during an interview in 2005, the goal of these discourses and images is to facilitate religion, to help sisters and brothers understand Allah's orders and get closer to him. Through these sermons, young receivers have access to ready-made arguments with selected quotations of the Koran and Hadîth, which corresponds better to what they are looking for in order to answer their own questions or the accusations they have to face in the societies where they live. An interesting analysis of these discursive products is submitted by Olivier Roy (2004) who explains that most of the new preachers have not followed the traditional path of Islamic studies and this distance characterizes their discourses in many ways. First, it made them all draw their arguments from the same "common knowledge, a poor vulgate [that is adapted and adjusted] to help enunciate the logic of the rite, or put a name on this rite" (Roy, 2004: 99). Thus, these discourses simplify the different issues, avoiding a profound analysis of the themes and visions suggested. I would add to these characteristics an essential one that becomes obvious through the numerous discourses I heard from 2001 to 2006. In fact, the producers do not define precise frontiers of common considerations within the Islamic tradition and of what is called by usûl ad-dîn (a specific discipline in religious studies) essential or stable issues (masâ'il asliyya) and what issues are secondary or changing (masâ'il far'iyya, mutaghayyira). This last point is very important and could be considered as a reason why many Islamic discourses have started to sound more extremist. Numerous preachers insist today on presenting secondary issues of religion (such as men's and women's clothing, beards and moustaches) as essential ones. In their quest for religious discourses, young Muslims listen to this kind of message and they become attached to their content, as precious marks on their way to Allah. It becomes thus very difficult to convince them that the words and images presented through these discourses might be extreme or that their own, contextualized interpretations might have transformed their contents into more extreme ones.

Receivers Producing their own Discourses and Images of Islam

Between accusations of being extremists or inferior just because of their adherence to Islam and the search for discourses and images of Islam that could help them answer these accusations, young Muslims start living their experiences of religion and expressing them with their own words. The fact that these young Muslims, who are supposed to be receivers, become producers as soon as they assimilate the discourses of the Islamic preachers —and even before assimilating their contents— is one of the most flagrant characteristics of today's Islamic field. Globalization tools —such as satellite channels and the internet— have largely participated in confusing producer and receiver roles. On the satellite channels, receivers might call or ask questions live or leave a comment during programmes. But it is the web that most reveals this confusion, as internet surfers might easily switch from their role as information seekers to a role of discourse producers on different sites, such as Islamic forums. Anderson stresses this point when he says:

> Islam on the Internet emerges as an intermediate realm of mixed content, mixed intellectual technique, and mixed persons who are not divided into the senders and receivers of mass (or of class) media but instead form a sort of community —commonly called "virtual" (1999: 48).

This confusion of roles is important to point out because it means that receivers who are still in the process of constituting their "religious baggage" and who do not necessarily have all the tools they need to express their ideas may start to become senders. They are senders of messages that correspond to the few ideas they have understood from discourses that already deviate from the traditional norms of religious discourse production. They express themselves on topics that interest them, and most of the time, these topics are not essential or stable ones. They insist on treating secondary or changing issues and giving them a new dimension, "because each point in this religion is worth being discussed and given its weight in daily life" (Malik, 18 years old in 2003). "Everything has to be related to Islam, if we want to deserve the life we live" (Leila, 19 years old in 2005). These arguments have to be linked with what was presented earlier concerning the thirst for religion and the transformation of the religious quest. They have to be understood as reasons for which preachers turn to secondary issues, knowing that they will find a larger public among the young receivers; but they also can be considered as consequences of this trend itself for the abundance of sermons on secondary topics creates a context of poor religious discourse in which receivers can never develop profound reflection on Islam as long as they do not look for other kinds of religious discourse. Finally, these arguments show in which manner young Muslims would talk about Islam and they explain why they would seem so extreme in the eyes of France, the country that asks its citizens to live their religion in the private sphere and not to express their religious ideas in public places or institutions (schools mainly).

However, young receivers who are members of the "virtual internet community" feel empowered because they find a new value for their lives through their quest for religion and through their participation in virtual forums and chatting "majlis" (assembly in Arabic). This phenomenon of "virtual majlis" is very interesting to study. It has become, through the past five years, a context in which young Muslim boys and girls exchange ideas about their religion as well as sources on different topics related to religion. Like real assemblies in which a young audience sit around a preacher or a reference person and listen to him/ her or ask for advice concerning religion, "virtual" ones have become new contexts of producing/receiving Islamic discourses. They represent new "situations" of communication, gathering senders and receivers whose roles start to fade as the traditional criteria defining each role dissipate. As for the senders, they do not have to be qualified by a traditional religious institution such as Al Azhar (Egypt), Zeytouna (Tunisia) or Qarawyin (Morocco) to be considered competent producers. New institutions have arisen (such as some relatively new Saudi religious institutions) but also new ways of qualification (such as oral transmission knowledge, with an oral "idjâza" which is an authorization to transmit knowledge to others given by a sheikh or a religious reference). In this context, receivers get the impression that "religion is closer." It does not become easier, but it is possible to get close to producers who could help them "feel more into it" ("se sentir plus dedans") —as the French youth would say.

By watching television preachers —either moderate or extremist— and attending the Friday sermons and other religious gatherings with local preachers, in parallel with discussions on the internet with other receivers like themselves and exchanging ideas with their peers, some young Muslims start feeling confident about "communicating" Islam. This fact of talking about religion with others must be understood as the most important aspect of the "religious experience" these young people go through. The situation in which they sit in the middle of an assembly of peers, explaining a verse of the Koran or making a presentation of the reasons why a good Muslim should not be in the proximity of the bad ones is a crucial moment in the life of the young-receiver-becoming-producer of Islamic discourse. It is the moment in which he or she stands against the wrong image of Islam drawn by the media, it is then that the whole world could be re-constructed in response to the stigma, using the sources furnished by predicators and it is this moment which will remain alive in the memory of the assembly as a proof that we, young Muslims, are a valuable community. Thus, being producers of religious discourse is another way that helps these young people feel they are important in a context where they otherwise feel disqualified.

The content of these receivers' discourses is essential to analyze to understand what words and images of Islam are circulating among young Muslims. There are different topics that could be treated in the young people's discourses: first of all, there is the interpretation of the Koran; secondly, there are topics —either essential or secondary— related to religion itself or linked to religion in one way or another (such as the prayers, the meaning of fasting, the veil and the beard, the possibility of getting a girl's hair cut and of plucking eyebrows and moustache hairs); thirdly, there are discussions directly concerning the situation of Muslim youth in French society and especially in the French school as a public sphere.

As for the interpretation of the Koran, young Muslims base their discourses on local publications of passages of the Holy Koran, in which the verse is written in Arabic, in transcription and translated into French. They also might listen to a local preacher explaining in French passages of the Holy Book, or to famous television preachers presenting their explanation in Arabic on satellite channels (which must be translated into French by a peer or by a member of the family) or in French on the internet (many preachers translate their important discourses into English, French and other languages on their official sites). The young receiver-producer discourse becomes thus a mixture of all these elements, to which he/she would add his/her own vision of the way the verses could be understood in the local context of the whole assembly. In 2003 I attended a very interesting "*majlis*" that was improvised in a classroom before the teacher arrived, during which the girl-preacher gave her extremist interpretation of the *sourate* called *Al Ikhlâs* (Fidelity), explaining that the only *Ikhlâs* worth dying for was the Fidelity to Allah.

Allahu-s-samad, means that Allah is the One you can lean on, you can depend on, in every step you take in your life. The word *samad* means strong and resisting. Allah is the strong foundation you can depend on. So no matter what people might tell you or do to you... For instance, concerning our veil... We have to remain strong and faithful to Allah, for our strength and faithfulness to Him is much worthier than respect for a law created by vulnerable people (Israa, 17 years in 2003).

When they talk about different issues related to Islam or for which they create a link with religion, young Muslims find their main arguments from the sermons they listen to. As shown earlier, they would mix the different ideas together and use them in their own context to convince their interlocutor of their point of view. There are many examples of topics that could be submitted here, but I"ll stick to one example only —the Islamic veil— since it was discussed by the French media for years and it seemed to be a critical issue in which Islam was going through the trial of modernity. Concerning this issue, the majority of the young girls had learned by heart each of the twelve arguments presented by Amr Khaled in his famous sermon about "*Al hayâ'*" in Islam. They might add to these arguments other ones presented by other more extremist producers, so that they would make Khaled's ideas even more extreme and present them as their own. However, the problem with this technique of borrowing arguments from other producers and especially non-local ones is not only that the reflection is not authentically the young Muslims'. It is essentially that, even if the arguments are not extreme ones at the beginning or in their original context, the discourse does not always fit within the specific context of use, so it may sound "strange," "extremist" and "violent." So, while Amr Khaled's discourse about the veil sounds very moderate in Egypt —some Egyptians who do not belong to the specific social category the preacher aims at even find it too "loose," "not strict enough" and "not well structured"— it becomes a "threat" in the French banlieue, a "source of fear" and a "potential menace to the local social order" as many French teachers described it themselves.

While treating the third issue (i.e. the Muslims' situation in France), young Muslims also use discourses they listen to or they read on the internet. However, the representation these students give of themselves is even more complicated in the eyes of their peers and teachers when they adopt extremist discourses from the beginning. The words they use and the images of Islam they draw in this case are not at all understandable for the people surrounding them. For instance, when they borrow what the *salafi* preachers preach (such as the Saudi sheikhs Djazâ'irî or Rabî' Al Madkhalî, or the Egyptians Mohamed Hassân and Mohamed Hussein Ya"qûb), they sound totally contradictory. As an example, it seems very difficult for some of the French youth to understand why their Muslim peers defend the necessity of "staying away from non-Muslims to keep their purity" while "they could have stayed in countries where most of the people are Muslim." What is even more striking is that, most of the time, the migrant parents themselves do not agree with their sons and daughters who choose the path of salafism. However, they feel helpless as their children's quest for religion cannot be satisfied by the limited information they have about religion and the rites they find essential in the definition of being a good Muslim. Thus, the experience of Islam that these young Muslims build upon the extremist discourses and images produced by salafi preachers is not only a de-contextualized one. It is also rejected by everyone in the context, even those who should be the closest ones to the young Muslims. Thus, instead of helping them to be accepted by the society in which they live, the discourses they produce isolate them in the restricted area of an imagined purity that becomes their only experience of religion. Dialogue with them is almost impossible, for the one language they listen to is their own and the only images they accept are the ones transmitted by their privileged preachers. However, being accepted by others is not the aim of these young people. They are "contented with the feeling of being accepted by Allah," as they say:

> I feel I don't need people's opinion. I know Allah is protecting me, and I am sure He knows I am right, for my intention is not bad. I refuse the judgment of others, as I don't judge them. The good Muslim is an example. He is an example for others to follow and this has nothing to do with the context we live in. The Muslim is the one who thinks of Allah in each step he takes, every day, every minute and every second. He is the one who is proud to be different, even if this difference causes some troubles. Somehow, yes, I feel I am better because I am Muslim, because this religion satisfies me. It is all I need to feel good. I do not need others (Sarah, 19 years old in 2005).

Provoke the Provoker as an Answer to Extremism

Dealing with extremism in some of the Parisian banlieues has sometimes been very complicated as the young Muslims refuse to listen or to consider what they listen to. I tried to have conversations with them, but it was not always easy to do. Even when they would accept a discussion with me, I could feel sometimes that they would look at me as if I was an outsider, a non-Muslim myself, as I agree to deal with non-Muslims or to discuss issues they see as essential. Therefore, one of the strategies I followed to get to know these young extremists was to provoke them. At the beginning, I did not know where this strategy was taking me, I did not even know that I was provoking them (as in the situation I described at the beginning of this article). However, it turned out to be a way of getting some young people to (re)think about their positions concerning religion. They never changed their opinions about the different issues we talked about together, but at least they spent some time reading or thinking about them. I will present one example of provocation I developed during my presence in the banlieues. During a discussion with young Muslims, they told me that the Koran itself contains proofs of the superiority of Islam. One of the verses that was used frequently says *"'inna ad-dîna 'ind Allah al'islâm"* ("For God, the religion is submission") (Al Imrân: 19). This verse is usually interpreted by these young Muslims as a proof that God considers the only valuable religion is Islam. I responded that the same Koran contained another verse that said *"Lâ 'ikrâha fid-dîn"* ("There is no compulsion in religion") (The Cow: 256). Moreover, the Koran has defined the community of Islam as the *"'ummatan wasata"* ("medium [just] nation") (The Cow: 143), a nation that not only does not leave its religion but also does not make of it an obsession. If the only religion recognized by God was Islam, how would he ask us to accept other religions and to not impose Islam upon others, since we are a "medium nation." However, for the young people with whom I spoke, these verses did not prove that Islam was not the only religion accepted by God. When I tried to explain that many verses in the Koran insisted on the importance of being different to learn tolerance and to get to know each other, they answered that, as Muslims, they would still be superior while living among people from different religions. Consequently, they would not use other verses and they would not analyze the ones I cited. Discussions were thus very difficult with these young people. First of all, they knew little about the Koran as a whole and they used to make selections of verses with specific interpretations. Secondly, they had not read much about interpretations of the Koran and they were not convinced that one verse could have many readings. Thirdly, they would stick to the arguments they heard from their preachers and they would refuse to consider different arguments, from other producers.

As a Conclusion

In a context marked by islamophobia or at least by the feeling that Islam is stigmatized, young Muslims who look for religious discourses turn to new sources of knowledge. Islamic preachers offer them new, valorising religious discourses and images, but while doing so, they also provide them with elements that become arguments and components of a new, extreme religious discourse, presented by young Muslims as their own experience of religion. If not consolidated by regular reading and learning about religion, these arguments and components do not help these young actors to develop their religious experience in a mature way that corresponds to their context. The extremist young Muslims living in the French banlieues need to attend gatherings in which they would meet other young people interested in Islam and in religion generally, so that a true discussion would be started, and the will to get closer to others in order to understand them and to be understood by them might be fostered. Contented by the little they know about Islam, they refuse to go further. Standing on the frontier of their relationship with people and with God, they think they are at the core of this relationship, though the link is very fragile because of the lack of knowledge and openness. In many French private schools, a very successful experience has shown great results: interreligious meetings on a weekly basis are an opportunity to talk and to exchange, to read and to think, to try to understand and to help the other understand too. This experience could be spread through general intercultural meetings as public schools may not provide religious meetings. Until journalists and reporters of the French media agree to consider Islam as a religion that is not fundamentally extremist and obscurantist, schools and municipal institutions might start by aiming to restrict the impact of de-contextualized religious discourse. It might be an invitation to re-consider the methods of reading religious sources and to analyze them in the context where people live and use them.

References

ANDERSON, Jon W. (1999): "The Internet and Islam's New Interpreters." Ed. Jon ANDERSON and Dale F. EICKELMAN: New Media in the Muslim World: The Emerging Public Sphere. Indiana University Press, Bloomington, 45-60.

ANDERSON, Jon W. and Dale EICKELMAN (ed.) (1999): New Media in the Muslim World: The Emerging Public Sphere. Indiana University Press, Bloomington.

BABÈS, Leïla (1997): *L'islam positif. La religion des jeunes musulmans de France* (Les éditions de l'Atelier). Collection Débattre, Paris.

CESARI, Jocelyne (1998): *Musulmans et Républicains*. Complexes, Bruxelles.

— (1997/1998): "'Cette étrange étrangeté': les représentations françaises de l'islam." *Confluences en Méditerranée*, Vol. 24 (Winter), 43-59.

DELTOMBE, Thomas (2004): "Un 'islamisme' télégénique. A propos de l'islamophobie refoulée des chaînes de télévision françaises" (September). At: http://lmsi.net/spip.php?_article306.

DIEKEMA, David A. (1991): "Televangelism and the Mediated Charismatic Relationship." *The Social Science Journal*, Vol. 28, 143-162.

FRANKL, Razelle (1987): *Televangelism. The Marketing of Popular Religion*. Southern Illinois University Press, Carbondale, IL.

GAFFNEY, Patrick D. (1994): *The Prophet's Pulpit. Islamic Preaching in Contemporary Egypt*. University of California Press, Berkley.

HAENNI, Patrick (2002): "Les nouveaux prêcheurs égyptiens et la modernisation paradoxale de l'islam." *Religio Scope* (November), 15.

JAKOBSON, Roman (1963): *Essais de linguistique générale —Tome 1— Les fondations du langage*. Transl. Nicolas Ruwet. Les éditions de minuit, Paris.

KEPEL, Gilles (2004): *Fitna. Guerre au cœur de l'islam*. Gallimard, Paris.

— (1991): *Les banlieues de l'islam. Naissance d'une religion en France*. Editions du Seuil, Paris.

KHOSROKHAVAR, Farhad (2006): "L'islam et occident: le choc des representations." *Philosophie Magazine*, No. 4 (January).

— (1997): *L'islam des jeunes*. Flammarion, Paris.

LOTFY, Wael (2005): *Zâhirat ad-du'â al-djudud. Tahlîl, Idjtimâ'î. Ad-da'wa, aththarwa, ach-chuhra*. Maktabat al-'usra, Cairo.

POTTIER, Bernard (1987): *Théorie et analyse en linguistique*. Hachette Classiques, Paris.

ROY, Olivier (2004): *L'islam mondialisé*. Editions du Seuil, Paris.

TERNISIEN, Xavier (2004): "L'islam de France et les medias" (Nouveaux regards sur l'islam de France, L'islam institutionalise). *Les Cahiers de l'Orient, Revue d'étude et de réflexion sur le monde arabe et musulman*, Vol. 76, 131-139.

*Civil Society
and Peacebuilding*

Civil and Uncivil Society:
Conditions for Supporting Conflict and Peacebuilding

Thania Paffenholz
The Graduate Institute of International and Development Studies

With the proliferation of armed conflicts in the 1990s and the rising complexity of peacebuilding efforts confronting the international community, the attention of the peacebuilding research and practitioner communities has increasingly turned to the role of civil society. Civil society is seen as a key actor in peacebuilding. However, we still know very little about what civil society can actually do for peacebuilding and how effective it is for ending armed conflicts and sustaining of the peace thereafter. An international three-year research project under the direction of Thania Paffenholz at the Geneva-based Centre on Conflict, Development and Peacebuilding (CCDP) at the Graduate Institute of International and Development Studies has researched this pertinent question in a comparative manner across 13 countries.

The overall objective of the project is to contribute to a better understanding of the role of civil society in support of peacebuilding —during and in the aftermath of armed conflict. The key research questions are: What are the constructive roles/functions of civil society in support of peacebuilding? What are the main supporting factors, and what are the main obstacles that hinder civil society to fulfill these functions?

The first phase of the project (2006) provided an overview of the concept of civil society, its history and understanding in different contexts. It elaborated an analytical framework of civil society functions derived from democracy, development and peacebuilding theory and practice, as well as from existing case study knowledge. This process was accompanied by an international expert panel, the results of which were published in a research study (Paffenholz and Spurk, 2006).

During the second phase of the project (2007-2008), the analytical framework was applied to 13 case studies (Bosnia-Herzegovina, Northern Ireland, Nigeria, Somalia, Democratic Republic of Congo, Afghanistan, Israel and Palestine, the Kurdish conflict in Turkey, Cyprus, Sri Lanka, Nepal, Guatemala and Tadzhikistan). A series of workshops were organized for all the researchers involved and a number of external experts were invited to discuss the analytical framework, the case studies and the conclusions. The entire project comprised 30 researchers and 25 external experts.

The case studies analysis focused on:

— The context of the conflicts and the understanding of peace-building in each case;
— The status and composition of civil society in each case;
— Other relevant factors, such as the state, the media, and gender issues;
— The seven core functions of civil society in peacebuilding:

1. *Protection* of citizens from violence from all parties;
2. *Monitoring* of human rights violations, the implementation of peace agreements, etc.;
3. *Advocacy;*
4. *Socialization* for democratic values and a culture of peace, and for in-group identity of marginalized groups;
5. *Inter-group social cohesion,* i.e. bringing people together from adversary groups;
6. *Facilitation* on the local and national level between different types of actors;
7. *Service delivery* to create entry points for peacebuilding, i.e. for other functions.

— The main supporting and hindering factors for civil society to fulfill these roles in each of the case studies.

The effectiveness of each function was assessed against the objective for peacebuilding in four phases of conflict/peacebuilding (war, armed conflict, windows of opportunity for peace, post-war), i.e. a contribution to the reduction in violence, a negotiated agreement or medium to long term sustainability of the peace agreement, as well as a reduction of violence or establishing conditions for treating the conflict constructively in society at large. Within each function different methodologies were applied, such as: content analysis of peace agreements to verify whether themes advocated or discussed by civil society groups or conflict resolution workshops have been taken into account;

evaluation studies or results from public opinion polls that assess attitude change of groups at particular times of an initiative or processes; or interviews conducted specifically for our project.

The results of all cases were then subject to comparative quantitative coding as well as qualitative analysis identifying and analyzing common patterns throughout cases and isolating them from context-specific trends.

The results of the project are to be presented both in the form of an academic book (Paffenholz 2009 forthcoming), and a policy paper (Paffenholz 2009: http://www.graduateinstitute.ch/ccdp/home/publications.html) to support donors, agencies and local organizations in their work. A number of launching events are to be held in Europe and the US, and in many of the countries studied by the project.

The project applies a very broad understanding of civil society, including a wide range of actors from professional associations, clubs, unions, faith-based organizations like churches or Islamic charities, NGOs, traditional and clan groups or even user groups and communities. Excluded are: media, business and political parties with the exception of media or business associations. The foci of analysis have been local and national civil society groups. The project has neither explicitly looked at global civil society campaigns, nor at international NGOs or other civil society groups that are not part of the national or local arena. However, it has explored the links between national civil society and their international partners.

The following chapter gives an overview of theoretical considerations, presents the analytical framework of the project and summarizes the main results of the project.

Understanding Civil Society

"Civil society" is a complex concept. Although the term has become widely used, seeming to be "the big idea on everyone's lips" (Edwards, 2004: 2), there is no commonly agreed upon definition. Most do not question, however, that civil society is the arena of voluntary, uncoerced collective action around shared interests, purposes and values (Merkel and Lauth, 1998: 7). To define civil society further, many authors proceed in describing its position in relation to other sectors of society and then attribute specific actors to these sectors. Thus, the Centre for Civil Society, London, considers civil society as a sector on its own vis-à-vis the three other main sectors: state, business and family (see Figure 1a). This sectored understanding is fairly agreed upon in the literature; however, the attribution of actors to each of these sectors is contested. For example, some authors state that "family" is not a separate sector but belongs to civil society, and others prefer to consider business as part of civil society rather than being a sector on its own (Glasius, 2004: 1). Some researchers use a different and more sophisticated segmentation of socio-political space, distinguishing between overlapping "spheres," rather than separate sectors. They designate a "political sphere" (state apparatus, political parties and parliamentarians), "economic sphere" (companies and markets) and "private sphere," and define spaces where these spheres overlap. Thus, some actors do not belong just to one sector but to various spheres (Croissant, 2003: 240).

A slightly different approach stresses that civil society is not (only) a sector on its own but "the space in between societal sectors" (Merkel and Lauth, 1998: 7). Thus, actors are attributed to specific sectors but do also occasionally act in "civil society" (see Figure 1b). Entrepreneurs, for example, usually part of the business sector, act as part of civil society when demanding a new law on tax exemption. This approach also allows one to "see" other potential civil society actors, like traditional groups in Africa, based on an assessment of what actions they take (Croissant et al., 2000: 18).

a) Civil society as a sector   b) Civil society as an intermediate sphere

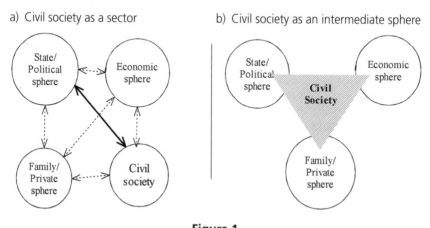

Figure 1

Civil society as a sector and an intermediate sphere

Both approaches can be summarized in the following definition or understanding: civil society is the sector of voluntary action within institutional forms that are distinct from those of the state, family and market, keeping in mind that in practice the boundaries between these sectors are often complex and blurred. It consists of a large diversity of voluntary organizations, often competitive with each other and oriented to specific interests. It is comprised of non-state actors and associations that are not purely driven by private or economic interests, are autonomously organized, and interact in the public sphere. Additionally, civil society is independent from the state, but not completely, since civil society is oriented towards and interacts closely with the state and the political sphere.

Civil society has been an almost purely Western concept, historically tied to the political emancipation of European citizens from former "feudalistic" ties, the monarchy and the state during the 18th and 19th centuries. Other civil societies that might have existed in other countries or continents (Asia, the Middle East, Latin America) or different times (pre-colonial, middle ages) are hardly reflected in the international debate about civil society (Appiagyei-Atua, 2005: 2-3; Pouligny, 2005: 498). The early European civil society debates go back to the Greek political philosophers such as Aristotle, but mostly to modern political theorists like John Locke (1632-1704), who was the first to stress that civil society is a body in its own right, separate from the state, or Charles Montesquieu (1689-1755), who elaborated his model of a separation of powers (*De l'Esprit des Lois*, 1748). Equally important is the contribution of Alexis de Tocqueville (1805-1859), who stressed the role of independent associations in civil society (*De la Democratize en Amérique*, 1835) and also Antonio Gramsci (1891-1937) who analyzed civil society from a Marxist theoretical angle. Gramsci stresses the potentially oppositional roles of civil society as a "public room," separate from the state and the market, in which ideological hegemony is contested. Similarly, Jürgen Habermas (*1929) also focuses on civil society's role within the public sphere, arguing that the political system needs interests to be articulated in the public space in order to put different concerns on the political agenda. This function cannot be left to established institutions (e.g. political parties); rather, it is necessary to build organizations, especially for marginalized groups, to articulate public interests, as parties and parliaments are "in need [...] to get informal public opinion beyond the established power structures" (Habermas, 1992: 374).

These are clearly Western concepts of civil society and there still is debate as to whether these concepts are transferable to non-Western countries or other historical contexts with different conditions for democracy and economy (Lewis, 2002; Harneit-Sievers, 2005: 1). Despite such debates, research demonstrates that civil society *has* taken a variety of forms in different times and geographical contexts.

Understanding Civil Society Peacebuilding

Civil society has emerged from being a marginal actor in peacebuilding during the Cold War period (with exceptions), to an accepted key actor in almost all peacebuilding theories, and even more so in peacebuilding policy discourse and practice (see chapter 3 in Paffenholz, 2009 forthcoming). One has seen a rapid growth in civil society peacebuilding initiatives from the mid-1990s onwards; yet this has not been matched by an accompanying research agenda. Only a few publications explicitly deal with the topic. One finds an actor oriented type of studies that aims to understand who is doing what (e.g. van Tongeren et al., 2005); single-actor oriented studies that analyze the role of particular civil society actors (mostly NGOs) in peacebuilding (e.g. Aall, 2001; Barnes, 2005; Pouligny, 2005; Richmond and Carey, 2006; Goodhand, 2006); studies that analyze civil society as an actor within the framework of the liberal peace (Bendaña, 2003; Paris, 2004: 179-211; Richmond, 2005: 127-148; Heathershaw, 2008: 607-609 and 616-618); studies assessing the effectiveness of NGO peace work in general (Anderson and Olson, 2003) or evaluate the impact of specific (mostly conflict resolution) civil society initiatives (D'Estrée et al., 2001; Çuhadar, 2004; Ohanyan with Lewis, 2005; Athieh et al., 2005); and country case studies (e.g. Foley, 1996 on El Salvador; Paffenholz, 2003 on Somalia; Belloni, 2001 on Bosnia-Herzegovina; Patrick, 2001 on Timor-Leste; Orjuela, 2003 and 2004 on Sri Lanka; Challand, 2005 on Palestine).

The existing studies, however, address different research questions and methodologies, something that then complicates any attempt to conduct a meaningful comparative analysis, to draw substantial conclusions on the role of civil society in peacebuilding, or even to determine to what kind of peacebuilding civil society can contribute.

Next to some specific achievements of civil society in peacebuilding, we also see many critical findings about the effectiveness of specifically NGO peacebuilding. However, what is missing is a coherent and more systematic picture of how exactly civil society actors (beyond and including NGOs) can contribute to peacebuilding and what main supporting and limiting factors exist. The systematic analysis of civil society's role in peacebuilding along the comprehensive analytical framework of our project is therefore a helpful analytical instrument that can be —and is already— used by researchers beyond our project.

The Comprehensive Analytical Framework

At the end of the first phase of the project, a *Comprehensive Framework for the Analysis of Civil Society Peacebuilding* was developed by Thania Paffenholz and Christoph Spurk and subsequently applied in a series of case studies. Please find the graphical overview of the framework below. The elaborated framework can be found as a separate chapter (see chapter 4 in Paffenholz, 2009 forthcoming).

CONTEXT ANALYSIS		Identifying civil society functions in peacebuilding	Assessing relevance of functions in context along phases of conflict	Identifying activities by actors incl. non-civil society actors along phases of conflict	Analyzing effectiveness of implementation along phases of conflict	CONCLUSIONS FROM SINGLE CASE STUDIES: LINKING FUNCTIONS WITH CONTEXT
	1. Protection					
	2. Monitoring and early warning					
	3. Advocacy and public communication					
	4. In-group socialization					
	5. Inter-group social cohesion					
	6. Facilitation					
	7. Service delivery					
	CONCLUSIONS					

Source: Paffenholz and Spurk, files 2008.

Figure 2

Comprehensive framework for the analysis of civil society peacebuilding

The Project's Main Findings

Summarizing the main findings of the project, we can see that civil society can play an important and often effective role in peacebuilding in all stages of conflict. However, if one looks carefully at civil society's engagement in peacebuilding, compared to the involvement of other actors, it becomes clear that while civil society's role is constructive, it is not necessarily decisive. Rather, it is supportive. The central impetus for peacebuilding comes in most cases from political actors —above all from the conflict parties themselves. This impetus is often reinforced by strong regional actors like the European Union in Europe and the Mediterranean, or India in South Asia. Such efforts were sometimes combined with international involvement. For instance, during the conflict in Nepal the Indian government supported the king and the ruling government both politically and militarily against the Maoist movement. When India changed position, froze military aid and political support to the government/king, a strong window of opportunity for peace opened that was embraced also by civil society actors and led to the end of authoritarian rule and armed conflict. In Northern Ireland, the main impulse for the peace process came from an escalating level of violence that motivated the main political/military elites to undertake a credible peace process. In Sri Lanka, the business community supporting the election campaign of the pro-negotiation opposition party was essential in creating the conditions that led to the ceasefire agreement in 2001.

Nevertheless, civil society have played important supportive roles in reducing violence, contributing to negotiated settlements, and the sustaining of peace after large-scale violence ended.

During armed conflicts and war, civil society groups monitored human rights violations, used this information for advocacy, and as a result managed to protect people from violence. Next to many small local or national protection initiatives in many countries, civil society groups in Nepal, for example, in concert with international partners, triggered the biggest UN human rights monitoring mission that contributed to the speedier termination of the armed conflict.

During windows of opportunity, civil society movements successfully have advocated for the signing of peace agreements as happened with the "YES" campaign in Northern Ireland, or the end of authoritarian rule as was the case with the April 2006 people's movement in Nepal. Civil society is also very effective in local facilitation: between the conflict parties and the people, communities and returning refugees, aid agencies and the conflict parties or the communities. In a few cases successful informal and formal facilitation between the major parties was done by eminent persons from established civil society institutions (such as church leaders in Guatemala, Sri Lanka and Northern Ireland).

After large-scale violence ended, civil society movements in general have dissolved and regrouped in smaller organizations that focused on specific initiatives depending on their interests and mandates. There were successful (advocacy) initiatives —but overall the influence on the implementation of peace agreements was limited. On the local level, however, civil society continued to contribute to community reconciliation and other tasks.

The cases or phases where civil society was less successful in supporting peacebuilding could be explained by:

— The strong counteractive forces outside civil society like a coercive state, an extreme level of violence, insufficient media support and the lack of funding for necessary initiatives. For the functions of socialization and social cohesion, additionally we see strong socialization institutions like schools, families, or military that work against peace as they preach segregation, intolerance and enemy images about the "others." One finds such institutions also within civil society, for instance religious schools, sport and other clubs, tribal associations etc.;

— The focus of many civil society initiatives on dominant conflict lines only, i.e. Israelis versus Palestinians, while mostly ignoring other divides in the two societies, such as that between moderates and religious fundamentalists;

— The ineffectiveness of many initiatives that are not relevant at a given time, not effective on their own or too scattered in nature;

— Civil society organizations not using their potential or else being run in an unprofessional way;

— The power and gender relations, hierarchies and lack of democratic structures within civil society organizations themselves.

A deeper look at the seven civil society functions reveals the following results.

Protection is always of high relevance during armed conflict and war, and decreases in importance in most cases after large-scale violence has ended. However, as cases like Cyprus and Guatemala demonstrate, it is the level of violence that determines the impotence of protection, rather than the existence of a peace agreement. In Cyprus, the presence of a UN peacekeeping force has lead to a frozen conflict situation with no violence, and in Guatemala the level of violence in the form of general insecurity due to crime, political and household violence still makes protection very needed ten years after the peace agreement.

Interestingly, the high relevance of the function during violent phases is not matched with the actual level of activities. Only in one third of the cases was protection conducted, either by local (often traditional and religious) actors, or by professional protection NGOs. When combined with monitoring and advocacy campaigns that were picked up by the media and international networks, protection was in some cases very successful as mentioned above for the Nepal case. Many people also fled the country and chose migration as a form of protection. The main limiting factors for protection are: a high level of violence, a coercive state and a lack of funding for professional initiatives.

Monitoring is always relevant, however the issues to be monitored change according to the phases and context of a conflict situation. The main focus of monitoring during armed conflicts and wars is on human rights violations. The main actors involved are local and national professional (human rights) organizations and research institutions that are often linked to international human rights organizations. The high relevance again did not correlate with the actual level of activities. Monitoring was not performed in all cases or only to a limited extent mainly due to restrictions set up by either a coercive state, extreme levels of violence or lack of funding. The effectiveness of monitoring —when performed— was fairly high in most cases; however, this was never the case as a stand-alone function. Monitoring became the precondition for protection and advocacy. The main limiting factors for effective monitoring are —as for protection— the restriction of the space for civil society action by the state or by other conflict parties, as well as extreme levels of violence.

Advocacy is of high relevance in all phases of conflict/peacebuilding. Advocacy is also conducted throughout all phases of conflict/peacebuilding. Overall, civil society advocacy was one of the most effective functions in all phases of conflict. Next to advocacy for protection-related issues, civil society groups advocated for the inclusion of relevant issues into peace agreements, i.e. land reform in Guatemala, human rights provisions in Northern Ireland, or legal issues around the recognition or implementation of the rights of marginalized groups (e.g. Majas in Guatemala, Kurdish minorities in Turkey, Muslims in Sri Lanka). Otherwise, they advocated for issues around the implementation of peace agreements (e.g. refugee return in Bosnia-Herzegovina, Truth and Reconciliation Commissions). Women's groups are often successful in bringing minority and gender issues to the agenda.

In general, if targeted advocacy campaigns are combined with monitoring, media attention and support of international networks, their effectiveness is highest. Advocacy initiatives for protection could achieve good results both in their local and national contexts. Many local initiatives by community groups, local NGOs or traditional leaders were also effective. In Somalia, clan leaders are in particular sensitive to protecting their interests and aggressively lobby political figures and aid agencies to ensure they are accorded a fair share of resources and positions. In some cases, clans have effectively used affiliated civil society groups to advance their claims. Women's groups in Nigeria, for instance, in many cases played a successful advocacy role for the protection of women and ethnic minorities. In Afghanistan under the Taliban, an NGO anti-landmine campaign convinced Mullah Omar to issue a fatwa banning the use of mines. Specialized NGOs were in some cases also very successful in lobbying for protection or legal issues. The main limiting factors for advocacy are again linked to: the shrinking space for civil society to act; a highly restricted media; the lack of specialized knowledge; and the incapacity to manage successful campaigns.

Socialization of the population at large with generic democratic and peace values is relevant in most phases; however, it had little effect in times of armed conflict and war due to the high level of violence and the radicalization in society. We found that in all cases, the existing socialization institutions in society are the **key** influences for how people learn democratic and conflict behavior, i.e. schools, religious and secular associations, clubs, work, families. In all cases, not only in group identity conflicts with two or more key adversary groups like Northern Ireland, Sri Lanka or Israel/Palestine, but also in conflicts with more differentiated divides like Guatemala, Nepal, Afghanistan, DR Congo or Nigeria, existing socialization institutions tend to re-enforce existing divides often to an extent that fosters radicalization. In Cyprus, for example, youth in each community have been educated along nationalist lines and in a way that disregarded the needs and fears of the other side. The Greek-Cypriot children were socialized with the idea that the island was and "will always be Greek" and Turkish Cypriots learned that "the island is Turkish and should go back to Turkey." We also found radical movements within civil society that openly foster an enemy image of the other group, e.g. settler movements in Israel, veteran associations in Bosnia-Herzegovina, ethnic community associations in Nigeria, Sinhala nationalist organizations in Sri Lanka or the Orange Order in Northern Ireland, where members are expelled when they marry a member of the other group. Interestingly, peace agreements in adversarial, multi-group settings often foster these very divides, as power-sharing mechanisms have become popular practices. While this seems to be good for transitional mechanisms, it seems that there should be an understanding of when such arrangements will come to an end such that society and politics can be constituted according to other values than group identity.

These findings stand in stark contrast to the actual activities performed by civil society organizations and external funding flows to counteract these negative trends. The main activities within this function were NGO peace education initiatives in the form of workshops, trainings, public seminars, peace media like soap operas or news features, distribution of books and brochures. More events and courses took place in conflict situations, which were either framed as group identity conflicts or were high on the international agenda, or a combination of both. Overall, the majority of work has not been effective at all because the deeply permeated notion of radical in-group socialization within existing socialization spaces in conflict societies cannot be counterbalanced by a few local or national NGO initiatives that also take place outside of these spaces.

The specific in-group socialization of particular groups in a conflict situation, i.e. empowering of underprivileged groups in asymmetric conflict situations, has proven to be in many instances effective, as a generation of civic leaders has been empowered through training and capacity building (like Maya activists in Guatemala or Dalit organizations in Nepal). However, the strengthening of group identity has also had negative effects, such as reinforcing exiting conflict lines and sometimes even radicalization, as demonstrated by some ethnic groups in DR Congo.

Inter-group social cohesion is also mostly relevant at all times. However, it depends a lot on the specific understanding of the function, i.e. what bridges need to be made with whom. At first glance, in-group identity conflicts like those in Northern Ireland, Bosnia-Herzegovina or Sri Lanka, it seems clear that it is about bridging the divides between the main groups (e.g. Protestants/Catholics, Singhalese/Tamils). However, in societies with less clear divides like Guatemala or Afghanistan, there seems to be only limited need for this function. A deeper analysis, however, reveals that societies are facing deep divides between all sorts of groups that go beyond the main/obvious adversary groups even in group-identity conflicts. In Israel there are deep divides between the religious orthodox and the secular Israelis; in Afghanistan the cleavages exist strongly between religious and secular groups, between different religious schools and doctrines, between tribal and modern parts of society, and between various ethnic identities. When violent, i.e. destructive, ways of dealing with conflict have entered a society, there is a high risk that other conflict divisions also turn into violence. It thus becomes a matter of violence prevention to address these cleavages. We found many such examples in our case studies. The uprising of violence in the Southern Nepali Terrai region immediately after the signature of the Comprehensive Peace Agreement in 2006 is a case in point. The focus on the main conflict between the Maoist movement and the government seems to have neglected other tensions and —perhaps— even reinforced ethnic divides.

These findings, interestingly, do not correspond to the actual activities of civil society groups performed in the social cohesion function. Besides a few exceptions, attention focuses exclusively on the main visible conflict lines, as well as on the well- known group identity conflicts. Social cohesion initiatives are, however, quantitatively (beyond general service delivery) the most performed civil society initiatives. Most of these initiatives take place in group-identity conflicts, i.e. Israel/Palestine, Cyprus, Bosnia-Herzegovina, Sri Lanka. Activities reached their peak in the mentioned cases (i.e. an actual mushrooming of initiatives) during windows of opportunity or immediately after a peace or ceasefire agreement, for example after the Oslo peace agreement between Israel and Palestine, during the ceasefire agreement in Sri Lanka, and after the Dayton peace accord in Bosnia-Herzegovina. This was due to the high level of external funding for these activities.

The effectiveness of conflict resolution workshops, dialogue projects, and exchange programs is very low for a number of reasons (to be found within initiatives themselves and in the context in which they operate). The primary ones are:

— the radicalization within society hinders counteractive peace work;
— the main focus of most initiatives is on the main conflict lines only;
— the scattered, short term and fragmented nature of most initiatives;
— the selection of participants in many initiatives that are English-speaking, elite-based representatives that are often already "converted" to the idea of positive images of the other group;
— people-to-people programs do not reach the society at large as they only focus on the individual level;
— the a-political nature of most initiatives, i.e. framing a deeply political problem as a relationship problem only is often misleading and receives little acceptance and ownership within society;

there is a danger that social cohesion initiatives are funded as a scapegoat to political inactivity, since it is easier for donors to fund such initiatives than to put pressure on the respective government or political actors in the country;

— many initiatives aim at changing attitudes, yet this does not seem to work even over a long period of time; in Bosnia-Herzegovina there is strong resistance against any project that is labeled "bridging." Initiatives have therefore changed their labels and tried to bring people together for other reasons than reconciliation and dialogue. Interestingly, these initiatives showed better results, i.e. people had positive experiences in working with the other group, often even producing concrete outcomes or common work initiatives. Existing evidence from Cyprus and Israel/Palestine insinuates that attitude change might not be necessary for behavior change.

On the positive side, however, it was noted that participation in such initiatives was an act of empowerment in most cases for the marginalized groups. Moreover, those activities that were not directly related to peacebuilding, like professional initiatives that brought together people from different groups, were more successful than the peace-related work.

Local facilitation by civil society groups is highly relevant in all phases of conflict/peacebuilding. We find facilitation on the local level performed by community leaders (e.g. traditional, religious and others) or local NGOs and associations. They facilitate between the conflict parties and the community, between aid agencies and the conflict parties or between communities and returning refugees. It seems that facilitation on the local level has been one of the most performed functions by civil society (even if we can not fully underline this judgment with adequate data as it is difficult to gather data on this level and the availability of data across our case studies varied considerably for local facilitation). Its effectiveness is contingent upon the context and we saw many successful initiatives. In Afghanistan during the Taliban, traditional mediation was the only resource for facilitating between the Taliban and the communities. Local civil society groups also successfully negotiated between the Taliban and aid agencies. In recent years, the Tribal Liaison office helps to organize local peace "jirgas" with religious and local leaders to explore options for peacebuilding. In Nepal during the armed conflict, local groups successfully facilitated the release of prisoners in many villages. Their success was in many cases greatly helped by the monitoring and advocacy work of Nepali NGOs. In general, a high level of violence and coercive conflict parties are the main limiting factors. Cooperation between traditional and "modern" forces has in many instances enhanced effectiveness.

National facilitation between the main conflict parties is less of a civil society task. On this level primarily political actors and, sometimes, business people are involved. When we find eminent civil society persons, often religious or other leaders, they can be very effective in paving the way to official negotiations and supporting the official mediators in times of deadlocks. Church leaders have been involved in facilitation in Guatemala, Northern Ireland and Sri Lanka and paved the way to the official negotiation process. These initiatives have been particularly important during windows of opportunity of peace or when the official negotiations broke down and no other channels were available. In the case of Nigeria, the government nominated a Catholic priest as chief mediator between different Ogoni groups.

Service delivery proved to be a function in peacebuilding only when actually used as an entry point for other functions. Service delivery was by far the most executed activity that also received most of the external funds. However, if we count only those projects that managed to create entry points for peacebuilding, they were not that many. This came a bit of a surprise after years of conflict sensitive aid and "do no harm" awareness. If aid initiatives are, however, systematically used for peacebuilding, they have often created good entry points for protection, monitoring and social cohesion. The relevance of the function is dependent on the degree of entry points it can create for other functions as well as on the state's ability to provided services for the population —i.e. the more service delivery creates entry points for peacebuilding, the higher its relevance during war and armed conflict as well as in times immediately after large scale violence has ended. The cases of Cyprus and Somalia demonstrate this impressively. In Cyprus, service delivery by civil society was almost absent due to the presence of a functioning state and the absence of violence. Therefore service delivery was not a function for peacebuilding in that case. On the contrary, in Somalia the total absence of a state for almost two decades has made service delivery the main activity performed by civil society. Islamic charities and local NGOs were in many instances successful in creating entry points for peacebuilding through extending their network across clan and regional lines. Service delivery is the civil society activity that receives most resources. As a consequence it diverts energy and resources from other civil society activities. Moreover, aid projects can also have a conflict-exacerbating effect when increasing social and geographical cleavages in society through allocation of resources and staff recruitment.

Enabling and Disenabling Factors for Civil Society Peacebuilding

In addition to the findings of functions, our project found that the context in which civil society operates is crucial for its ability to act and fulfill a constructive role in peacebuilding. We found that the level of violence and the behavior of the state, mainly its government, are the two main factors that determine the space for civil society to act (see the two following chapters by Belloni and Kurtenbach for more details on these aspects). The higher the level of violence and the more repressively the state performs, the more civil society's space is reduced. Whereas democratic forms of governance generally create enabling conditions for civil society, in most conflict countries, either only formal democratic structures exist, or often neo-patrimonial ones, which tend to oppose or co-opt civil society in a way that weakens its ability to act. On the other hand, high levels of violence and authoritarian rule are often main reasons for civil society to start mobilizing for change.

The media play also a crucial role for civil society. Through professional media reporting and coverage, the effectiveness of many civil society activities, especially for protection, monitoring and advocacy, are strengthened. The media also suffer from violence and a repressive state, as freedom of the press is often dramatically reduced in conflict situations. The media and civil society are thus closely interlinked. Press freedom can thereby even serve as an indicator for civil society space, i.e. the more the freedom of the press is limited, the more the space for civil society is also reduced. The composition and characteristics of civil society itself also influences its effectiveness, i.e. the more civil society is polarized and radical tendencies are dominant, the more difficult it becomes to act for a common cause for peacebuilding. External actors including donors can also have positive or negative influences on the political situation in the country in general and thus influence the suitability of conditions for civil society to act.

References

AALL, Pamela. (2001): "What Do NGOs Bring to Peacemaking?" Ed. Chester CROCKER, Fen Osler HAMPSON and Pamela AALL: *Turbulent Peace*. United States Institute of Peace Press, Washington D.C., 365-383.

ANDERSON, Mary; Lara OLSON and Kristin DOUGHTY (2003): *Confronting War: Critical Lessons for Peace Practitioners*. The Collaborative for Development Action, Cambridge, MA.

APPIAGYEI-ATUA, Kwadwo (2005): *Civil Society, Human Rights and Development in Africa: A Critical Analysis*. At: http://www.peacestudiesjournal.org.uk/ (accessed 10 January 2006).

ATIEH, Adel; Gilad BEN-NUN; Gasser EL SHAHED; Rana TAHA and Steve TULLIU (2004): *Peace in the Middle East: P2P and the Israeli-Palestinian Conflict.* United Nations Publications (UNIDIR), Geneva.

BARNES, Catherine (2005): "Weaving the Web: Civil-Society Roles in Working with Conflict and Building Peace." Ed. Paul VAN TONGEREN; Malin BRENK and Marte HELLEMA: *People Building Peace II, Successful Stories of Civil Society.* Lynne Rienner, Boulder, 7-24.

BELLONI, Roberto (2001): "Civil Society and Peacebuilding in Bosnia and Herzegovina." *Journal of Peace Research,* Vol. 38, 163-180.

BENDAÑA, Alejandro (2003): "What Kind of Peace is Being Built? Critical Assessments from the South." Paper Prepared for the International Development Research Council (IDRC) on the 10th Anniversary of An Agenda for Peace. Ottawa, Canada.

CHALLAND, Benoît (2005): *The Power to Promote and to Exclude: External Support to Palestinian Civil Society.* European University Institute, Florence.

CROCKER, Chester; Fen Osler HAMPSON and Pamela AALL (ed.) (2001): *Turbulent Peace. The Challenges of Managing International Conflict.* United States Institute of Peace Press, Washington D.C.

CROISSANT, Aurel (2003): "Demokratie und Zivilgesellschaft in Ostasien." *Nord-Süd Aktuell,* Vol. 2, 239-260.

—; Hans-Joachim LAUTH and Wolfgang MERKEL (2000): "Zivilgesellschaft und Transformation. Ein internationaler Vergleich." Ed. Wolfgang MERKEL. *Systemwechsel 5. Zivilgesellschaft und Transformation.* Leske+Budrich, Opladen, 9-49.

ÇUHADAR, Esra (2004): *Evaluating Track Two Diplomacy in Pre-Negotiation: A Comparative Assessment of Track two Initiatives on Water and Jerusalem in the Israeli-Palestinian Conflict.* Syracuse University, Syracuse.

CURLE, Adam (1971): *Making Peace.* Tavisstock Publications, London.

DE TOCQUEVILLE, Alexis (1835): *De la Démocratie en Amérique.* Louis Hauman et Comp Libraries, Brussels.

D'ESTRÉE, Tamra Pearson; Larissa FAST; Joshua WEISS and Monica JAKOBSEN (2001): "Changing the Debate about 'Success' in Conflict Resolution Efforts." *Negotiation Journal,* Vol. 17, 101-113.

EDWARDS, Michael (2004): *Civil Society.* Polity, Cambridge.

FOLEY, Michael W. (1996): "Laying the Groundwork: The Struggle of Civil Society in El Salvador." *Journal of Interamercian Studies and World Affairs,* Vol. 38, 67-104.

GLASIUS, Marlies (2004): *Civil Society.* At: www.fathom.com (accessed 10 January 2006).

GOODHAND, Jonathan (2006): *Aiding Peace. NGOs in Armed Conflict.* Lynne Rienner, Boulder.

HABERMAS, Jürgen (1992): "Zur Rolle von Zivilgesellschaft und politischer Öffentlichkeit." Ed. Jürgen Habermas. *Faktizität und Geltung.* Suhrkamp, Frankfurt a.M., 399-467.

HARNEIT-SIEVERS, Axel (2005): "'Zivilgesellschaft' in Afrika: Anmerkungen aus historischer Perspektive." Vortragsmanuskript. Humboldt-Universität, Berlin (2 December).

Heaterhsaw, John (2008): "Unpacking the Liberal Peace: The Dividing and Merging of Peacebuilding Discourses." *Millennium: Journal of International Studies*, Vol. 36, 597-621.

Lewis, David (2002): "Civil Society in African Contexts. Reflections on the Usefulness of a Concept." *Development and Change*, Vol. 33, 4, 569-586.

Merkel, Wolfgang and Hans-Joachim Lauth (1998): "Systemwechsel und Zivilgesellschaft. Welche Zivilgesellschaft braucht die Demokratie?" *Aus Politik und Zeitgeschichte*, Vol. 6, 3-12.

Montesqieu, Charles (1748): *De l'Esprit des Lois* (Ed. Roger Caillois). Gallimard, Paris 1951.

Ohanyan, Anna and John Lewis (2005): "Politics of Peacebuilding: Critical Evaluation of Interethnic Contact and Peace Education in Georgia-Abkhaz Peace Camp, 1998-2002." *Peace and Change*, Vol. 30, 1, 57-84.

Orjuela, Camilla (2003): "Building Peace in Sri Lanka: A Role for Civil Society." *Journal of Peace Research*, Vol. 40, 195-212.

— (2004): "Civil Society in Civil War, Peace Work and Identity Politics in Sri Lanka." PhD Dissertation. Department of Peace and Development Research, University Göteborg.

Paffenholz, Thania (2003): *Community-based Bottom-up Peacebuilding. The Development of the Life and Peace Institute's Approach to Peacebuilding and Lessons Learned from the Somalia Experience (1990-2000)*. Life and Peace Institute, Uppsala.

— (2009): "Civil Society and Peacebuilding." *CCDP Working Paper*, Number 4. Centre on Conflict, Development and Peacebuilding, Geneva. At: *http:// graduateinstitute.ch/ccdp/home/publications.html* (accessed 14 May 2009).

— (2009 forthcoming): *Civil Society and Peacebuilding: A Critical Assessment*. Lynne Rienner, Boulder.

— and Christoph Spurk (2006): "Civil Society, Civic Engagement and Peacebuilding." Social Development Papers, Conflict Prevention and Reconstruction Paper, No. 36. World Bank, Washington D.C.

Paris, Roland (2004): *At War's End. Building Peace After Civil Conflict*. Cambridge University Press, Cambridge.

Patrick, Ian (2001): "East Timor Emerging from Conflicts: The Role of Local NGOs and International Assistance." *Disasters*, Vol. 25, 48-66.

Pouligny, Beatrice (2005): "Civil Society and Post-Conflict Peacebuilding: Ambiguities of International Programmes Aimed at Building 'New' Societies." *Security Dialogue*, Vol. 36, 495-510.

Richmond, Oliver (2005): *The Transformation of Peace*. Palgrave Macmillan, London.

Richmond, Oliver and Henry Carey (2006): *Subcontracting Peace. NGOs and Peacebuilding in a Dangerous World*. Ashgate, Aldershot.

van Tongeren, Paul; Malin Brenk and Marte Hellema (ed.) (2005): *People Building Peace II, Successful Stories of Civil Society*. Lynne Rienner, Boulder.

Civil Society, the State and Peacebuilding

Roberto Belloni
University of Trento

This chapter presents some results from a three-year international research project on civil society and peacebuilding. This project investigated seven core functions that civil society can play in furthering peace in conflict areas: protection of citizens from violence, monitoring of human rights violations and of the implementation of peace agreements, advocacy for peace and human rights, socialization for democratic and peace values as well as for in-group identity, facilitation between all actors, and service delivery as an entry point for other peacebuilding functions. A number of factors influence civil society's ability to carry out these functions and play a constructive role in peacebuilding, including the behaviour of the state, the level of violence, the influence of the media, the composition of civil society itself, and the role played by external political actors and donors (Paffenholz, 2010). Here I discuss some conclusions emerging from this project with regard to two of these factors. First, I review the relationship between civil society and the state, highlighting how state institutions are often the major source of contention among social groups. Second, I assess the problem known as "dark social capital," or "uncivil civil society," that is, the presence within civil society of divisive and even violent groups. These two issues are discussed within the context of Bosnia-Herzegovina and Northern Ireland, respectively.

Civil Society and the State

The state plays a vital role vis-à-vis civil society in regions plagued by communal conflict. To begin with, the state can be one of or even the most important source of conflict. Often the state is closely controlled by one community or group at the expense of other societal groups. In cases as different as Guatemala, Turkey, Sri Lanka, Israel/Palestine, Nigeria, Northern Ireland and Nepal, the lack of access to domestic political institutions by marginalized groups has motivated and sustained armed insurgencies demanding some degree of self-governing autonomy and/or a share in decision-making power and national wealth. In response, the state has undertaken various forms of military action to quash demands of political and economic inclusion.

Where the state is considered illegitimate by at least a significant section of the population, collective action within civil society is likely to take place along the existing major dividing lines. Common national/ethnic/religious background provides the basis for cooperation within civil society groups. At the same time, in such polarized contexts, groups reaching out across the communal divide will face significant criticism and may even be denounced as "unpatriotic." Truly multi-ethnic and multi-national groups will be a rarity. Moreover, the domestic form of governance could further complicate civil society activism. As a rule, the less democratic a state, the more limited the space for civil society. And even when institutions are formally democratic, they might be controlled by one group —as in Northern Ireland from 1921 to 1972 (when domestic institutions were finally suspended by the government in London amid escalating chaos and violence) and in Turkey since the creation of the modern Turkish Republic after World War I. In such cases, extensive gerrymandering and tailored-made election laws prevented the inclusion of significant sections of society. In turn, not only does exclusion favour the creation of mono-ethnic civil society groups but it can also convince some members of these groups that armed confrontation is the best way to express their grievances.

In addition to being repressive and only partially democratic, institutions in conflict areas are often based on a system of patronage and clan-based politics, which is strongly de-mobilizing for civil society. The patrimonial system is based on the patron's ability to deliver material benefits in return for political support. Civil society and the state become intertwined in a complex network of relationships, which is used by all parties to gain access to various degrees of resources and wealth. In a patrimonial state dominated by clientelistic and often criminal interests, the autonomy of civil society groups is undermined. Civil society organizations may become a reservoir of political support for the ruling party (or parties), as in Congo and Nigeria. Furthermore, clientelistic relationships can lead to the subordination of citizenship rights to patron-client relationships, as in Guatemala, Nepal and Turkey. In these and similar cases, many organizations, including sport and youth groups, veterans groups and associations of displaced persons, may quiet their opposition to the political establishment in exchange for access to resources, and even maintain a strong uncompromising stance vis-à-vis outsiders in order to preserve such access.

The consolidation of a patrimonial system can also be favoured by the post-war creation of consociational institutions —as in Bosnia-Herzegovina. These institutions allow each group to govern itself autonomously, while bringing together decision-makers from all main groups to govern issues of common concern. In so doing, the ruling parties in each group may use patrimonial and clientelistic relationships to preserve the dominance over their respective communities. Moreover, consociational institutions may be further demobilizing for civil society groups because of their focus on elite collusion. In such a system, political elites govern their own communities exclusively and have little or no interest in the development of cross-ethnic ties at the communal level. Arguably, inter-ethnic moderation would actually undermine their political power which is legitimated by the key consociational principle that "high fences make good neighbours."

An Illustration: Bosnia-Herzegovina

The fear among Bosnian Serbs that the state could be dominated by Croats and Muslims contributed to the outbreak of the Bosnian war in April 1992. After Slovenia and Croatia declared independence in 1991, Bosnia-Herzegovina faced a stark choice between remaining in a much-reduced and Serb-dominated Yugoslavia and attempting to undertake the road to independence. A referendum in late February 1992 overwhelmingly confirmed support for independence among both Croats and Muslims, but was boycotted en masse by the local Serb population. A last-ditch effort to avoid war came on 5 April, when thousands of citizens occupied the Parliament building in Sarajevo demanding peace, the resignation of nationalist politicians, the banning of ethnic parties and new elections. Serb paramilitary units fired on marching peace demonstrators, marking the beginning of the war. The armed confrontation was brutal and led to the mass displacement of the population. In this context, very little civil society activity was possible, although activists in urban centres such as Tuzla (and, to some extent, Sarajevo) attempted to preserve at least a semblance of civil coexistence.

During the war, paramilitary units were often responsible for the atrocities that made this conflict infamous worldwide. The war also presented countless opportunities for trading and smuggling across the front lines. The signing of the Dayton Peace Agreement in November

1995 provided a further opportunity for enrichment. Criminal groups, in collusion with parts of the political class, could continue their practices from war to peacetime, while taking advantage of the influx of foreign aid. Tellingly, the ruling nationalist parties declared a post-war amnesty for a number of crimes committed during the war, including economic ones. The period covered by the amnesty went back to January 1991, 15 months before the outbreak of the conflict, when the three main nationalist parties were voted into office (Andreas, 2004).

In the post-Dayton period, domestic politicians shrewdly took advantage of the reconstruction aid to bolster their positions and to hand out resources to their constituencies. For example, international donor agencies typically made aid conditional on the fulfilment to one or more aspects of the peace agreement. Once aid was allocated, however, it was directed to the nationalist parties' own respective constituencies. The process of privatization provided a further opportunity to entrench clientelistic and neo-patrimonial practices. Citizens were given certificates enabling them to invest in small/medium-sized companies. The managers of these companies forced down their values while war profiteers and well-connected private businessmen bought certificates at a sell-out price. In some cases, state assets were sold directly to members of the dominant political/ethnic group in a given area, thus reinforcing the links between the political elite (which supervised the selling of assets) and local patrons (which took advantage of bargain basement prices) (Belloni, 2007). Overall, privatization cemented the control of a class of ethnic oligarchs which thrives through a corrupt ethnic-based patronage system. Local civil society organizations (particularly veterans groups, associations of displaced persons and sport and youth clubs) are frequently part of this system. In this neo-patrimonial structure, local organizations are in danger of being, or becoming, extensions of the state, legitimising rather than transforming the status quo.

Consociational institutions contributed further to the consolidation of a neo-patrimonial system of governance and complicated the (re) building of local civil society. Consociationalism requires political elites to share power at the centre, while prescribing proportionality in government and guaranteeing mutual veto rights and communal autonomy (Belloni, 2007). Needless to say, communal autonomy in the case of Bosnia-Herzegovina shielded ethnic politicians from outside scrutiny, and favoured the consolidation of the kind of neo-patrimonial system briefly described above. In addition, decentralization, which is common to all consociational institutions but taken to an extreme in the Bosnian case, creates further obstacles to the work of civil society organizations.

First, these organizations are prevented from working freely in the entire Bosnian territory by registration rules which are different in the two entities which form the Bosnian state, i.e. the Croat-Muslim Federation and the Serb Republic. Second, the Bosnian constitution gives the central government very limited powers (which are further limited by the presence in the country of an interventionist international community). In this context, civil society's advocacy and monitoring campaigns are hampered by the weakness of state institutions. Local organizations are often better off pressuring the international community —which ultimately holds the key to political power— than the government in Sarajevo. Third, the key principles of consociationalism, those of a group's autonomy and elite collusion, are at odds with the attempt to rebuild inter-communal ties at the social level. Ethnic political leaders would see their power diminished or undermined in a context of a mass thawing of ethnic relations. Unsurprisingly, they provide little or no support to civil society's reconciliation efforts.

Civil Society and its Potential for Radicalization

At least since the publication of Robert Putnam's influential *Making Democracy Work: Civic Traditions in Modern Italy* (1993), a view persists among scholars and practitioners alike that civil society plays a fundamental, positive role in promoting political and economic development, social cohesion, and general individual and collective well-being. This perspective has stimulated civil society building programs in various part of the world, including both developed and established liberal democracies (such as the United States) and states recovering from domestic conflicts (such as Bosnia-Herzegovina, Kosovo, Guatemala, El Salvador and Sri Lanka, to name a few). In all cases, the attempts at reviving and developing civil society are based on the conviction that civil society contains positive human, social and political resources that can be mobilized to monitor a state's behaviour and limit its excesses, while creating and supporting a participatory and democratic ethos among civil society members.

There are countless examples to confirm this view. At the same time, however, civil society can also be the incubator of sectarian, xenophobic, and violent ideas. Occasionally these ideas are turned into action. Examples from Eastern Europe, Colombia, Honduras and Russia, among other cases, suggest that unsocial and dark capital or uncivil civil society, as variously labelled in such instances, may constitute an important reason for political instability (see, for example, Cox, 2009).

In the most extreme cases, as in Rwanda during the 1994 genocide, civil society has been directly involved in waging a ruthless campaign of violence aimed at preventing power-sharing and democratization. In other cases, as for example in Nigeria (Niger Delta), Sri Lanka and Turkey, state and military repression can lead to the radicalization of civil society actors and their transformation into armed militant groups.

More commonly, civil society in conflict areas is neither a force supportive of peace and democracy nor one responsible for mass violence or armed insurgencies. Rather, civil society reflects and incorporates society at large. Most civil society organizations are divided along ethnic/national/religious lines, reflecting the main dividing lines that characterize a given conflict. Accordingly, they reflect the ups and downs of a peace process. In periods of escalating tensions, civil society organizations may contribute to diffidence and hostility vis-à-vis the "other side." In periods of thawing of political tensions, civil society organizations may also be more open to reaching out across the communal divide. Thus civil society does not inherently represent a force for peace or for conflict, but mirrors and often sustains the broader cleavages present in society at large.

In this context, a considerable number of organizations might be working to sustain cooperation between opposing groups and to promote a democratic politics of inclusion and mutual accommodation. Often these organizations are NGOs with weak social roots supported by international donors. Alongside these organizations, however, there exist at least two other broad categories of civil society groups (Belloni, 2008). First, mafia-like organizations thrive in a context dominated by communal divisions and often by the absence of a functioning state providing public goods to the population. Where the state is unable or unwilling to guarantee the benefits of citizenship, such as security, political participation and public services, patrimonial (and often patriarchical) relations intrude into the public sphere, and can even lead to the replacement of the rule of law with the rule of the strongest. Under such conditions, civil society is liable to succumb to illegal and violent interests. In Northern Ireland, Colombia, Honduras and several post-Yugoslav states, to name just a few examples, paramilitary organizations and criminal groups prosper in a context of inter-communal divisions, and often maintain close ties with the political establishment.

Second, and more commonly, individuals group themselves into mono-ethnic and mono-religious organizations. Membership in these organizations is often regulated according to ascriptive criteria, such as religion or race or by having fulfilled patriotic duties, such as military service. Membership can have negative effects on both insiders and on inter-community relations. Internally, individual freedom may be restricted in the name of group solidarity, while critical views are silenced or marginalized. Externally, the very existence of these organizations can exacerbate the differences between insiders and outsiders and even intensify inter-group competition. In other words, social capital created by in-group membership reinforces existing societal divisions and promotes a fertile ground for divisiveness. In the most extreme cases, mono-ethnic and mono-national organizations can serve as recruiting tools for extremists —as in Rwanda, where the 1994 genocide was supported and even carried out by members of these organizations.

An Illustration: Northern Ireland

Northern Ireland is rich with associational life. Thousands of organizations have contributed decisively to the furthering of the peace process that culminated with the signing of the Belfast Peace Agreement in April 1998. Even in the post-agreement phase, they have provided Northern Irish citizens with countless opportunities for political, economic and social empowerment. Yet this lively civic sector represents only part of the civil society landscape.

To begin with, paramilitary organizations have been a dominant force at least since the outbreak of the "Troubles" (as the conflict between Protestants and Catholics is known in Northern Ireland) in the late 1960s. Paramilitary groups have enforced tight control over their respective communities and have prospered through their control of illegal activities such as drug dealing, smuggling and prostitution. Although they have justified their existence by pointing to the need for providing the protection of their respective communities from external dangers, the negative consequences of their actions are often borne by the very communities they claim to represent. Ironically, these organizations possess high degrees of social capital, of the dark or uncivil kind, that allows them to perform their activities quite efficiently. Even in the post-agreement phase, they have continued to be a source of insecurity and fear, and generally a barrier to the consolidation of democratic politics.

In addition to these violent and illegal groups, there exists a majority of organizations which may abide by the law, but remain divided along national/communal lines. Over a quarter of civil society organizations are either wholly Protestant or Catholic, while three quarters of them have management committees entirely or primarily from one community. In large measure, participation in these organizations tends

to reinforce the members' views, perpetuating sectarianism and an everyday reluctance to engage with the "other side." In addition, the two
communities remain divided in most aspects of socialization, including
work, recreation and education, allowing individuals to live a life dis-
jointed from the members of the other community. Perhaps counter-in-
tuitively, even housing has become more segregated in the post-agreement phase.

In this context, participation in civil society activities is an expression
of one's membership in his/her community (Belloni, 2009). The most
popular organizations have a clear political affiliation, whether formal
or informal. On the Protestant side, the Orange Order is the most significant organization representing cultural/political Protestantism. This
association proclaims itself "primarily a religious organization" which is
"Christ-centred, Bible-based, and Church-grounded." Although it declares itself a bastion of civil and religious liberty, it is resolutely sectarian. Its members must be Protestant from Protestant parents and must
leave if they marry a Catholic. The Order's activities have been a lasting
source of inter-community tension and even conflict. Among these activities the Order commemorates the 1690 Battle of the Boyne when
King William III, Prince of Orange, defeated the Catholic King James.
Orange lodges hold regular parades from their Orange Hall to a local
church. Many Catholics perceive these marches as a symbolic claim to
the territory of Northern Ireland and a means to assert Protestant dominance over it. Of the thousands of parades held every year, a few are
particularly contentious. Since the mid-1990s, the Drumcree Orange
Church parade in Portadown has emerged as a serious symbolic/cul-
tural/political problem in the relationship between the two communities. The dispute over this parade has involved paramilitaries, necessi-
tated high-level political attention, and eventually split the Protestant
community between those willing to negotiate with the Catholics and
hardliners who maintain an uncompromising stance. Ultimately, the Orange Order has sided explicitly with the hardliners. It has expressed no
confidence on the Belfast Agreement and provided no encouragement
whatsoever to its implementation.

On the Catholic side it is difficult to find an equally contentious organization, but the reality of a civil society divided along communal
lines remain. The most popular Catholic Organization is the Gaelic Ath-
letic Association (GAA), which is firmly nationalist, although not sectarian. Since its foundation, the Association has condemned British
control of Northern Ireland and frequently advocated for the reunifi-
cation of the island under the government in Dublin. As with the Orange Order, the GAA expresses the popular sentiment, and socializes

its members into the norms and values of Irish and/or Catholic identity. Moreover, as with the Orange Order, throughout the peace process the organization became entangled in the ups and downs between the two communities. Rule 21 of its rulebook prohibited members of the British Army and of the Protestant-dominated police force from playing Gaelic games. Although in practice this rule had limited impact, it represented an important symbolic statement which sparked considerable controversy between the two communities. Only in 2001, three years after the signing of the Belfast Agreement, did the GAA repeal Rule 21. Both the cases of the Orange Order and the GAA suggest that civil society in regions divided along ethnic/national/religious lines reflects and reproduces the larger political context in which it is embedded. Both organizations confirm and recreate the identity, historical traditions, and cultural and political aspirations of their members. By so doing, the effectively mark the boundary between insiders and outsiders and quietly reinforce the divisions between the two groups. Unsurprisingly, disputes about these organizations' activities occur at times of high political tensions, and reflect the difficulties faced by the political process.

References

ANDREAS, Peter (2004): "The Clandestine Political Economy of War and Peace in Bosnia." *International Studies Quarterly*, Vol. 48, 29-51.

BELLONI, Roberto (2007): *State Building and International Intervention in Bosnia*. Routledge, London.

— (2008): "Civil Society in War-to-Democracy Transitions." Ed. Anna J. JARSTAD and Timothy D. SISK: *From War to Democracy: Dilemmas of Peacebuilding*. Cambridge University Press, Cambridge, 182-210.

— (2009): "Shades of Orange and Green: Civil Society and the Peace Process in Northern Ireland." Ed. Michaelene COX: *Social Capital and Peace-Building: Creating and Resolving Conflict Through Trust and Social Networks*. Routledge, London, 5-21.

COX, Michaelene (ed.) (2009): *Social Capital and Peace-Building: Creating and Resolving Conflict with Trust and Social Networks*. Routledge, London.

PAFFENHOLZ, Thania (ed.) (2010): *Civil Society and Peacebuilding: A Critical Assessment*. Lynne Rienner, Boulder (forthcoming).

PUTNAM, Robert (1993): *Making Democracy Work: Civic Traditions in Modern Italy*. Princeton University Press, Princeton.

Violence and Civil Society Peacebuilding

Sabine Kurtenbach

University of Duisburg-Essen

The use of direct physical violence or the threat to use it lies at the core of civil wars. Only recently have some scholars begun to study the concrete dynamics and consequences of violence on society[1]; its effects on civil society peacebuilding however have not been studied systematically. Here, two issues are relevant: first, the consequences of violence on civil society and on civil society peacebuilding abilities and, second, the changing forms of violence in the transformation process from war to non-war situations.

To address these issues, it is important to distinguish between different forms of violence in conflict. A rough distinction can be made between:

— lethal forms of violence and non-lethal forms (rape, kidnapping, forced recruitment, etc.);
— symmetrical and asymmetrical forms of violence that depend on power relations between the armed actors but do have serious implications for civilians, e.g., if civil society is held hostage by armed actors;
— indiscriminate and selective forms of violence that are used in different phases of conflict.

Another important distinction must be made between different motivations or purposes for violence. War-related violence is mostly perceived as political, although during the last years there has been an intensive discussion on economic motivations for armed violence. Research has shown that in most wars a grey zone exists between economic violence in armed conflict[2] and organized forms of criminality

---

[1] See Kalyvas, 2006; Geneva Declaration, 2008; on sexual violence Bastick et al., 2007.
[2] See the discussion on lootable resources.

(drug trade being the most prominent example). At the same time it is difficult to make a clear distinction between political violence against the real or perceived adversary and social violence directed against, e.g., beggars, street children or other marginalized groups. The distinction between different forms of violence is not just an academic exercise but is important for the control and containment of violence as different forms of violence need to be addressed by different mechanisms. While political violence can have certain forms of legitimacy (e.g. if conducted against authoritarian regimes), criminal or economic violence is mostly regarded as unlawful behaviour. Thus one may be able to negotiate with actors using political violence but (at least under a rule of law approach) one cannot (or only under certain exceptional circumstances) negotiate with criminals. The importance of these distinctions can be seen in many conflict countries when governments and civil society organisations have to develop strategies against actors operating in the grey zone between political and economic violence.

Consequences of Violence for Civil Society Peacebuilding

Independent of its motivations, violence is the most important limiting and disabling factor for civil society peacebuilding because direct physical violence and/or the threat to use violence in armed conflict does not exclusively aim at combatants, but is directed against a wide range of non-combatants and civilians.[3] This has serious implications for civil society beyond the death toll.

First of all, violence, displacement as well as forced or "voluntary" migration disrupt and/or destroy existing forms of social organisations and of social networks. This weakens independent organisation because many civilians seek survival and protection from the different armed actors (e.g. in so-called liberated territories or through the establishment of armed militias). Civil society organisations themselves are mostly unable to protect themselves or their constituencies. It is important to note that these violence-induced changes affect the possibilities of civil society peacebuilding not just momentarily, but may change the very structure of civil society. Sri Lanka is just one case study that shows how violence increases polarisation between ethnic groups.

---

[3] Although reliable data are difficult to get, civilian deaths as well as indirect conflict deaths outnumber direct combat related deaths three to four times (see Geneva Declaration, 2008).

A second feature limiting the possibilities of civil society actors is the fact that they are the main targets of selective as well as indiscriminate violence in most wars (e.g. Guatemala, Colombia, El Salvador, Sri Lanka). The reports of international NGOs like Amnesty International, Human Rights Watch or the International Crisis Group document the victimization of human rights activists, members and representatives of social organisations and peace movements every year. The experiences of communities that declare themselves neutral in armed conflict are another case in point as these are frequently attacked by the armed actors.

Both the above —violence directed against organized actors of civil society and against civilians— affect the overall possibilities for civil society peacebuilding negatively and influence the relative strength of single actors or segments of civil society. Not even indiscriminate violence is omnipresent. In some countries, the risk of victimization for leaders of modern segments of civil society —like social movements, unions or political parties— is considerably higher than for representatives of traditional civil society organisations, like churches. Latin American countries are a case in point as well as Afghanistan. This can have consequences for the composition of civil society as traditional organisations may be strengthened while modern actors are weakened. At the same time violence against civil society organisations reduces independent public action not only through regulations reducing civil rights and liberties but also through the prevalence of a climate of fear and terror that can result in the development of a culture of violence characterised by a diffusion of the violence into everyday life as is the case in Guatemala, Sri Lanka and other longstanding armed conflicts.

As a consequence, violence and civil society peacebuilding functions are intimately related. During conflict phases, a high level of violence protection would be the most important function for civil society peacebuilding. As this cannot be provided by most civil society organisations, they have to look for protection from other actors. As in most armed conflicts, if the state is a party to the conflict the only alternative is cooperation or at least coexistence with the armed actors. Migration either to territories not affected by war, to the country's capital or out of the country can be another way to look for protection. All of these strategies seriously limit the possibilities of civil society peacebuilding either through the dependency on armed actors or because those most likely to seek refuge or migrate are those opposing armed conflict. Thus in many conflicts violence enhances the polarisation and militarization of civil society making mediation and facilitation difficult for civil society actors.

But besides these negative influences of violence on civil society, violence can at the same time be a central motif for civil society organisation to become active. The escalation and spill over of violence to everyday life in armed conflict has initiated the organisation of human rights groups, victim's organisations and peace movements all over the world. Combat against high levels of violence have been a uniting factor in Guatemala and other places, where civil society established local mechanisms of monitoring and advocacy to raise awareness inside and outside the war affected countries. This can lead to alliances and networks between internal and external actors in favour of peacebuilding. Cooperation between local human rights organisations and international NGOs or UN-missions has been important for peacebuilding in many wars, providing new opportunities and some political space for civil society peacebuilding and the termination of armed conflict.

Violence and the Transformation from War to Non-War Contexts

Violence determines the relative strength of the armed actors and is thus a central feature shaping the substance of peace accords as well as the possibilities and options for civil society's engagement. The relations (access as well as distance or closeness) between armed actors and specific civil society actors are important for their influence (or the lack of it) on the peace accords.

Peace accords aim at ending armed violence, but there is rarely a clear cut end of violence with a ceasefire or the signature of a peace accord. Even in cases where the armed conflict comes to an end, other forms of violence may influence the implementation of the accords as well as civil society's peacebuilding abilities. Different actors and purposes of violence can be distinguished in post-war transformations.

Most attention is given to so-called spoiler violence that is used by actors aiming either to undermine or change peace accords or to obstruct the process of transformation towards peace and democracy. The motivation of most spoilers is the fear that the end of war might endanger their relative strength in relation to other actors or that certain provisions of the peace accords are perceived as unfavourable. Other forms of post-war violence are more indirectly linked to the armed conflict. Darby (2006: 4ff) identifies two sources of violence beyond spoilers: violence exerted by state actors and violence "on the ground" which consists of unorganised conflicts, riots or increasing criminality of paramilitary actors that transform into criminal networks.

Both issues are related to the basic problems of transitioning out of war (see Kurtenbach, 2008ª) and influence the capabilities of civil society in peacebuilding. A core issue in these processes is the containment and control of violence and the establishment of at least minimal standards of public security. The specific problems resulting in these processes are closely related to the experience of war and to the deficits in the process of disarming, demobilizing and reintegrating of ex-combatants and the entire population. Post-war societies are characterised by a high level of fire arms circulation. This does not necessarily pose a problem per se but is often so, given the lack of a functioning state and non-state mechanisms to control and/or sanction violence. The result is a high level of privatisation and diffusion of violence. At the same time, violence shifts from the political sphere into society. The main actors are not merely the gangs of former ex-combatants who secure their daily survival with their gun because they lack other options (and capabilities). Actors can also be criminal groups that might not have been directly involved in the war but have benefited from the post-war power vacuum.

Another important legacy of violence and armed conflict are war economy structures not only providing financial resources and economic opportunities, but also serving as a basis for (mostly asymmetric) power relations and as a means of social control. These structures are an important basis not only for many spoilers but also for other un-civil actors. The Dayton agreement on Bosnia-Herzegovina was the first to have a specific provision on the problem of the war economy, but has not led to a dismantlement of criminal organisations up to today. Most peace accords do not address this issue at all. External as well as local actors have serious problems to address the resulting forms of economic and social violence. They rarely make the connection but perceive these forms of violence as a problem to be dealt with by the justice and criminal systems. As the majority of post-war states are fragile and characterized by serious deficits of the judiciary, the result is a diffusion and change of violence rather than its containment. Guatemala is an illustrative case for the above-mentioned developments.

An Illustration: Guatemala[4]

Guatemala's internal war (1962-1996) belonged to the category of protracted and long lasting as well as a very violent war. Four phases

---

4 On violence in postwar Guatemala see Kurtenbach 2008ᵇ.

of war can be distinguished that were shaped by different dynamics and by different levels of violence and schemes of victimization. While during the 1960s the main battleground was in the country's east, the most violent phase happened between 1981 and 1984 in the Maya populated western highlands. Maya communities had few possibilities for coping with violence: they could either collaborate with the military, getting a certain form of physical protection, or they could migrate, in both cases destroying the traditional forms of social organization and community life. Leaders of civil society were the main targets of selective violence during most of the war whenever mobilization seemed to endanger the existing social status quo. Violence was at the same time the main driving force for organisation in civil society. Under the umbrella of the Catholic Church, widows and victims began to monitor as well as to advocate for an end to violence.

Guatemala's war ended in 1996 with the signature of the peace accords, but violence did not. While the number of violent deaths significantly declined until 1999, it has more than doubled since then and developed into a violent order embedded in the basic structures of the state. The main actors are the so called hidden powers —networks of organized crime, military structures and status quo oriented actors— that undermine democratic reforms and governance. Guatemala not only shows a high level, but also a variety of forms of violence, leading to a highly complex situation.

While political violence has declined since the war's end, it is still used by the different actors against the political opposition, non-corrupt lawyers and prosecutors, human rights activists and defenders, and leaders of different social organisations (indigenous, *campesino*, etc.). Social violence (*social cleansing*) is another constant phenomenon in Guatemala's history. It is mostly directed against street children and youth, beggars and other marginalised people. Individual and organised forms of criminal violence are responsible for the largest share of violence in post-war Guatemala. They are closely related to the dismantlement of the repressive state apparatus and the deficits in the construction of new, functioning and democratically legitimated forms of public security. At the same time they show an increasing pattern of transnationalisation. Violence, again, is the main disabling factor for civil society peacebuilding in post-war Guatemala. Although there are various punctual initiatives by the more professional think tanks and NGOs addressing the need to control the circulation of fire arms or advocating police and justice reforms, these are undermined by the "hidden powers." As in other post-war societies living through a process of regime change, public security and the control of violence are a condition for medium and long term peacebuilding beyond the formal termination of war. The central question —unresolved up to today— is how the escalation and diffusion of violence can be contained in the short run without impeding long term peacebuilding goals. The political regime is an important factor here as it has implications for the possibilities and limits of violence control. While most authoritarian regimes can suppress individual as well as collective forms of violence (at least for some time), democratic regimes are at least formally bound to do so by the limits of the rule of law. In most post-war societies, the establishment of stable and functioning mechanisms of violence control and of civil forms of conflict management is a historic task and long term endeavour. Civil society organisations need to engage in this process to cope with violent structures and actors and to prevent the resurgence of violence in its various forms.

References

BASTICK, Megan; Karen GRIMM and Rahel KUNZ (2007): *Sexual Violence in Armed Conflict. A Global Overview and Implications for the Security Sector*. Geneva Centre for the Democratic Control of Armed Forces, Geneva.

DARBY, John (ed.) (2006): *Violence and Reconstruction*. University of Notre Dame Press, Notre Dame, IN.

GENEVA DECLARATION (2008): *The Global Burden of Armed Violence*. Geneva Declaration Secretariat, Geneva.

KALYVAS, Stathis (2006): *The Logic of Violence in Civil Wars*. Cambridge University Press, Cambridge.

KURTENBACH, Sabine (2008a): "Youth Violence in Post-War Societies. Conceptual Considerations on Continuity and Change of Violence" (Project Working Paper No. 1). In: *Social and Political Fractures after Wars: Youth Violence in Cambodia and Guatemala*. INEF, Duisburg.

— (2008b): "Guatemala's Postwar Development: The Structural Failure of Low Intensity Peace" (Project Working Paper No. 3). In: *Social and Political Fractures after Wars: Youth Violence in Cambodia and Guatemala*. INEF, Duisburg.

Nonviolence in Action:
A Global Trend?

Nonviolent Action, Pro-Democracy Struggles and Western Interventionism

Stephen Zunes
University of San Francisco

The United States has done for the cause of democracy what the Soviet Union did for the cause of socialism. Not only has the Bush administration given democracy a bad name in much of the world, but its high-profile and highly suspect "democracy promotion" agenda has provided repressive regimes and their apologists an excuse to label any popular pro-democracy movement that challenges them as foreign agents, even when led by independent grassroots nonviolent activists.

In recent months, the governments of Zimbabwe, Iran, Belarus and Burma, among others, have disingenuously claimed that popular nonviolent civil insurrections of the kind that toppled the corrupt and autocratic regimes in Serbia, Georgia and Ukraine in recent years —and that could eventually threaten them as well— are somehow part of an effort by the United States and its allies to instigate "soft coups" against governments deemed hostile to American interests and replace them by more compliant regimes.

This confuses two very different phenomena. The U.S. government has undeniably provided small amounts of money to various opposition groups and political parties through the National Endowment for Democracy (NED), the International Republican Institute (IRI) and other organs. Such funding has at times helped a number of opposition groups cover some of the costs of their operations, better enabling them to afford computers, internet access, fax machines, printing costs, office space and other materials. Assistance from foreign governments has also helped provide for poll watchers and other logistical support to help insure free and fair elections. In addition, the United States, through the NED, the IRI and other U.S.-funded projects, has also provided seminars and other training for opposition leaders in campaign strategies.

What is controversial about these endeavors is that they have been directed primarily at helping conservative, pro-Western parties with a free-market orientation and generally not parties of the democratic left. Nor are they aimed solely at pro-democracy struggles challenging autocratic regimes. Indeed, U.S. agencies have also backed opposition parties in countries such as Venezuela, despite the government allowing for democratic elections.

Some opposition groups in some countries have welcomed U.S. assistance while others have rejected such aid on principle. There is no evidence, however, to suggest —even in cases where this kind of limited U.S. support for opposition organizations has taken place— that the U.S. government or any U.S.-funded entity has ever provided training, advice or strategic assistance for the kind of mass popular nonviolent action campaigns that have toppled governments or threatened the survival of incumbent regimes.

How Democratic Change Occurs

The United States remains the world's number one supplier of armaments and security assistance to the world's dictatorships. There is little reason to take seriously the idea that U.S. foreign policy, under either Republican or Democratic administrations, has been based upon a sincere belief in advancing freedom and democracy as a matter of principle. History has shown repeatedly that the U.S. government, like most Western powers, supports democratic rule only if it is seen to promote perceived economic and strategic interests. Conversely, the U.S. government has frequently opposed democratic rule if it is seen to be contrary to perceived economic and strategic interests. Since the vast majority of Americans, according to public opinion polls, do support democracy as a matter of principle, however, support for "democracy" has long been used as a rationalization for various U.S. foreign policy initiatives, even when these policies end up supporting authoritarianism and repression. As a result, though support for democratic change in countries ruled by autocratic regimes is certainly a worthwhile goal, skepticism over the pro-democracy rhetoric of U.S. government officials is indeed warranted.

In any case, true democratic change comes from within. Recent years have witnessed the emergence of a series of broadly based nonviolent social movements that have succeeded in toppling dictatorships and forcing democratic reforms in such diverse countries as the Philippines, Chile, Bolivia, Nepal, Czechoslovakia, Indonesia, Serbia, Mali and

Ukraine. Even the relatively conservative Washington-based Freedom House, after examining the 67 countries that have moved from authoritarianism to varying degrees of democratic governance over the past few decades, published a study (Karantnycky and Ackerman, 2005) concluding that these transitions almost never came as a result of foreign intervention and only rarely through armed revolt or voluntary elite-driven reforms. In the overwhelming majority of cases, according to this report, change came through democratic civil society organizations engaging in massive nonviolent demonstrations and other forms of civil resistance, such as strikes, boycotts, tax refusal, occupations of public space, and other forms of non-cooperation.

Whenever governments are challenged by their own people, they tend to claim that those struggling for freedom and justice are traitors to the nation and agents of foreign enemies. In previous decades, opposition activists challenging U.S.-backed dictatorships in Latin America, Southeast Asia and elsewhere were routinely labeled as "communist agents" and "Soviet sympathizers." Today, pro-democracy movements within U.S. client states in the Middle East are depicted as "Islamic fundamentalists" and "Iranian agents." Similarly, opposition activists in Iran, Belarus, Burma and Zimbabwe have been labeled as "supporters of Western imperialism" and "American agents."

In reality, the limited amount of financial support provided to opposition groups by the United States and other Western governments in recent years cannot cause a nonviolent liberal democratic revolution to take place any more than the limited Soviet financial and material support for leftist movements in previous decades could cause an armed socialist revolution to take place. As Marxists and others familiar with popular movements have long recognized, revolutions are the result of certain objective conditions. Indeed, no amount of money could force hundreds of thousands of people to leave their jobs, homes, schools and families to face down heavily armed police and tanks and put their bodies on the line unless they had a sincere motivation to do so.

Conspiracy Theories

A number of regimes facing popular opposition have gone so far as to claim that certain small independent non-profit organizations and supporters of nonviolent action from Europe and the United States who have provided seminars and workshops for opposition activists on the history and dynamics of nonviolent resistance were somehow working as agents of the Bush administration. Some Western bloggers and other writers critical of the Bush administration and understand-ably concerned about U.S. intervention in the name of "democracy," actually bought into some of the claims by these governments. These conspiracy theories were turn picked up by some progressive websites and periodicals and even by some in the mainstream press, which then repeat them as fact.

Virtually all of these seminars and workshops, however, come at the direct request of opposition organizers themselves. And at least as many of them have been on behalf of pro-democracy activists strug-gling against right-wing dictatorships as there have been on behalf of pro-democracy activists struggling against left-leaning dictator-ships. Over just this past three years, for example, my colleagues and I worked with Egyptians, Maldivians, Palestinians, West Papuans, Sah-rawis, Azerbaijanis and Guatemalan Indians struggling against repres-sive U.S.-backed governments. In addition, virtually all of these groups have a strict policy of refusing support from the NED or any other government-funded entities. As a result of my own involvement in a number of these groups and personally knowing most of their princi-pal workshop leaders, I recognize charges that such individuals as Gene Sharp, Jack DuVall, Bob Helvey, Ivan Marović and such organizations as the Albert Einstein Institution, the International Center on Nonvio-lent Conflict (ICNC), and the Center on Applied Nonviolent Action and Strategies (CANVAS) are somehow in cahoots with the CIA or are serv-ing as agents of U.S. imperialism are totally unfounded.

Unfortunately, even Venezuelan President Hugo Chavez —ech-oed by some of his North American supporters— has apparently fallen for these false charges and has accused some of these individuals and groups of plotting with his opponents to overthrow him. Chavez has every right to be a bit paranoid, given the very real U.S. govern-ment efforts to subvert his regime, including support for a short-lived coup in 2002. In reality, however, the only visit to Venezuela that has taken place on behalf of any of these non-profit groups engaged in educational efforts on strategic nonviolence was in early 2006 when I —along with David Hartsough, the radical pacifist director of Peace-workers— led a series of workshops at the World Social Forum in Ca-racas. There we lectured and led discussions on the power of nonvio-lent resistance as well as offered a series of screenings of a film ICNC helped develop on the pro-democracy movement in Chile against the former U.S.-backed dictator Augusto Pinochet. The only reference to Venezuela during those workshops was how massive nonviolent ac-tion could be used to resist a possible coup against Chavez, not fo-ment one. In fact, Hartsough and I met with some Venezuelan officials regarding proposals that the government train the population in various methods of nonviolent civil defense to resist any possible future attempts to overthrow Chavez.

Workshops on Strategic Nonviolence

The American and European groups that share generic information on the history and dynamics of strategic nonviolence with civil society organizations in foreign countries are not unlike the Western private voluntary organizations that share environmentally sustainable technologies and agricultural techniques to farmers in developing nations. Both offer useful tools that, if applied consistently and effectively, could improve the quality of life for millions of people. There is nothing "imperialistic" about it.

Just as sustainable agricultural technologies and methods are more effective in meeting human needs and preserving the planet than the conventional development strategies promoted by Western governments, nonviolent action has been shown to be more effective in advancing democratic change than threats of foreign military intervention, backing coup plotters, imposing punitive sanctions, supporting armed rebel groups and other methods traditionally instigated by the United States and its allies. And just as the application of appropriate technologies can also be a means of countering the damage caused by unsustainable neo-liberal economic models pushed by Western governments and international financial institutions, the use of massive nonviolent action can counter some of the damage resulting from the arms trade, military intervention and other harmful manifestations of Western militarism.

Development based on Western models usually means that multinational corporations and the governments of wealthy capitalist countries end up exerting a large degree of control over these societies, whereas appropriate technologies allow for genuine independence and self-sufficiency. Similarly, unlike fomenting a military coup or establishing a military occupation —which relies on asserting control over the population and potential political opponents— successful nonviolent civil insurrections are necessarily based on a broad coalition of popular movements and are therefore virtually impossible for an outside power to control.

It is ironic, then, that some elements of the left are attacking those very individuals and groups who are trying to disseminate these tools of popular empowerment against the forces of oppression and imperialism.

People Power

Another difference between these people-to-people educational efforts and U.S. intervention is that, unlike the NED and other government-backed "pro-democracy" efforts, which often focus on developing conventional political initiatives led by pro-Western elites, these workshops on strategic nonviolence are primarily designed for grass-roots activists unaffiliated with established political parties who seek to make change from below.

Historically, individuals and groups with experience in effective non-violent action campaigns tend to come from leftist and pacifist traditions which carry a skeptical view of government power, particularly governments with a history of militarism and conquest. For example, my own background in strategic nonviolent action is rooted in my involvement in the late 1970s as a nonviolence trainer for the anti-nuclear Clamshell Alliance and the nonviolent revolutionary group Movement for a New Society, both of which were radically decentralist in structure and decidedly anti-capitalist and anti-imperialist in orientation. More recently, my fellow workshop leaders have included a South African veteran of the anti-apartheid United Democratic Front, a leading Palestinian activist from the first intifada, and former student leaders from the left-wing Serbian opposition to Milošević.

Conversely, large bureaucratic governments accustomed to projecting political power through military force or elite diplomatic channels have little understanding or appreciation of nonviolent action or any other kind of mass popular struggle. Indeed, what would CIA operatives know about nonviolence, much less grassroots organizing?

In short, not only is it naïve to assume than an external power could provoke a revolution of any kind, it should be apparent that the U.S. government does not know the first thing about fomenting a nonviolent civil insurrection. As a result, the dilemma for U.S. policy-makers —and the hope for all of us who support democracy as a matter of principle and not political expediency— is that the most realistic way to overthrow the world's remaining autocratic regimes is through a process the U.S. government cannot control.

The U.S. government has historically promoted regime change through military invasions, coup d'etats and other kinds of violent seizures of power that install an undemocratic minority. Nonviolent "people power" movements, by contrast, make regime change possible through empowering pro-democratic majorities. As a result, the best hope for advancing freedom and democracy in the world's remaining autocratic states comes from civil society, not the U.S. government, which deserves neither the credit nor the blame for the growing phenomenon of nonviolent democratic revolutions.

Strengthening the Bush Agenda

The emergence of civil society organizations and the growing awareness of the power of nonviolent action in recent years have been among the most positive political developments in what has otherwise been largely depressing political times. It is most unfortunate, then, that supposedly "progressive" voices have chosen to attack this populist grass roots phenomenon as some kind of Bush administration conspiracy.

It is also ironic that so many in the Western left —after years of romanticizing armed struggle as the only way to defeat dictatorships, disparaging the potential of nonviolent action to overthrow repressive governments and dismissing the notion of a nonviolent revolution— are now expressing their alarm at how successful popular nonviolent insurrections can be, even to the point of naively thinking that it is so easy to pull off that it could somehow be organized from foreign capitals. In reality, every successful popular nonviolent insurrection has been a home grown movement rooted in the realization by the masses that their rulers were illegitimate and the current political system was incapable of redressing injustice. By contrast, no nonviolent insurrection has succeeded when the movement's leadership and agenda did not have the backing of the majority of the population. This is why the 2002-2003 "strike" in Venezuela's oil industry failed to bring down Chavez while comparable disruptions to economies elsewhere have often forced out less popular leaders.

"Leftist" critics of nonviolent pro-democracy movements parallel right-wing supporters of U.S. intervention in that both denigrate the power of individuals to take their destiny into their own hands and overthrow oppressive leaders and institutions. Instead, both appear to believe that people are passive victims and that social and political change can only come through the manipulation of foreign powers.

Reagan Redux

For example, despite President Ronald Reagan's insistence during the 1980s that the popular armed insurgencies that challenged repressive U.S.-backed regimes in Central America were the result of a Soviet "hit list," the reality was that the revolutions in Nicaragua, El Salvador and Guatemala were homegrown popular movements. The Soviets provided a limited amount of assistance and obviously wanted to take political advantage of the possible overthrow of pro-American oligarchs by having them replaced with leftist revolutionaries who would be friendlier to their interests. But the oppressed peasants and workers of those Central American countries were not following the dictates of Moscow. They were struggling for basic rights and an end to repression.

Similar claims heard today that the United States is somehow a major force behind contemporary popular movements against dictatorships in Burma, Iran, Zimbabwe and Belarus or that the United States was somehow responsible for the successes of previous movements in Serbia, Georgia or Ukraine are equally ludicrous. This attitude parallels claims by those on the right who disingenuously credited Reagan's dangerous and militaristic Cold War policies for the fall of Communism in Eastern Europe and tried to depict the union activists, peasants, students, priests and others martyred in the course of popular struggles in Central America as Soviet agents.

In addition, it is important to remember that the vast majority of successful nonviolent civil insurrections have not been against dictatorships opposed by the U.S. government, but dictatorships supported by the U.S. government. Right-wing autocrats toppled by such "people power" movements have included Marcos in the Philippines, Suharto in Indonesia, the Shah of Iran, Duvalier in Haiti, Pinochet in Chile, Chun in South Korea and Numeiry in Sudan, to name only a few.

Another problem with this kind of simplistic reductionism is that when nonviolent civil insurrections do succeed in bringing democrats to power in countries previously under anti-American dictatorships, the new often-inexperienced leaders are faced with plaudits from conservative Western political leaders and suspicion from the European and North American left. This could lead them to wonder who their friends really are and reinforce the myth that those of the right, rather than the left, are the real champions of freedom.

The conspiratorial thinking and denigration of genuine popular movements appearing increasingly in some leftist circles serves to strengthen the hand of repressive regimes, weaken democratic forces, and bolster the argument of American neo-conservatives that only U.S. militarism and intervention —and not nonviolent struggle by oppressed peoples themselves— is capable of freeing those suffering under repressive rule.

How Change Occurs

Successful nonviolent revolutions, like successful armed revolutions, often take years or decades to develop as part of an organic process within the body politic of a given country. There is no standardized formula for success that a foreign government or a foreign non-governmental organization could put together, since the history, culture and political alignments of each country are unique. No foreign government or NGO can recruit or mobilize the large numbers of ordinary civilians necessary to build a movement capable of effectively challenging the established political leadership, much less of toppling a government.

Trainers and workshop leaders like me and my colleagues emphasize certain strategies and tactics that have been successful elsewhere in applying pressure on governments to change their policies and undermining the support and loyalty required for governments to successfully suppress the opposition. In some cases, local activists may try to emulate some of them. However, a regime will lose power only if it tries to forcibly maintain a system that the people oppose, not because a foreign workshop leader described to a small group of opposition activists certain tactics that had been used successfully in another country at another time.

In maintaining our steadfast opposition to U.S. interventionism and exposing the hypocrisy and double-standards of the rhetoric from certain Western leaders in support of democracy, we must also challenge those who denigrate popular indigenous movements as creations of Washington or slander reputable non-profit groups that share their generic knowledge of nonviolent strategies and tactics with like-minded organizations overseas.

Finally, both to maintain our credibility and because it is the right thing to do, progressives should recognize the moral imperative of opposing repressive regimes regardless of their ideology or their relationship with Western governments. Progressives should also embrace strategic nonviolent action in the cause of freedom as an ethical and realistic alternative to Western interventionism.

References

KARATNYCKY, Adrian and Peter ACKERMAN (2005): *How Freedom is Won. From Civic Resistance to Durable Democracy*. Freedom House. At: http://www.freedomhouse.org/uploads/special_report/29.pdf.

The Role of Strategy
in Advancing Nonviolent Resistance in West Papua[1]

Jason MacLeod
University of Queensland

Introduction

A nonviolent struggle for self-determination has been occurring in West Papua. Located on the Western rim of the Pacific, West Papua is a previous Dutch colonial outpost that Indonesia took control of on the 1st of May 1963. The territory has been the scene of one of the most protracted, complex and volatile conflicts in the Pacific. Although acts of state violence or the activities of the armed struggle occasionally get reported by the mainstream press, nonviolent resistance in West Papua has rarely been noticed or analysed in depth. Most analysts of West Papuan politics have focused on conventional politicking and armed resistance. Nor has nonviolent struggle in West Papua been investigated by those conducting research into the dynamics of nonviolent action.

In addition to the political and social context affecting movement trajectories and outcomes, the nonviolent struggle in West Papua also faces substantial internal challenges. There is an important role for strategy in addressing these. This chapter analyses the West Papuan struggle from the perspective of the theory and dynamics of nonviolent resistance and the strategic principles of nonviolent conflict. I begin by discussing the historical background, root causes of the conflict and the sources of Indonesia's power in the territory. Historical resistance to Indonesian rule is discussed and contemporary nonviolent struggle against the Indonesian state examined. The main section of the paper analyses some of the possible ways forward for nonviolent resistance in

---

[1] Thanks to Ralph Summy, Dale Hess, Brian Martin and Maria Stephan for helpful comments on an earlier draft of this chapter.

West Papua from the standpoint of theory and strategic insights into nonviolent resistance.

Historical Background

In 1848, The Netherlands Government in agreement with the Germans and the British partitioned the island of New Guinea in two, along the 141st meridian east of Greenwich. After the Indonesians gained independence in 1949, the Dutch retained control of the territory, arguing that West Papua (or "Netherlands New Guinea" and later "Nieuw Guinea" as it was then called by the Dutch) was a distinct political entity from other parts of the Indonesian Republic with no significant administrative, historical or cultural connection to the rest of the Indonesian archipelago. This claim was vehemently rejected by Indonesian representatives to the United Nations who insisted that West Irian (as it was then called by the Indonesians) was part and parcel of a united Indonesia that included all the former Dutch East Indies (Permanent Mission of the Republic of Indonesia to the United Nations, 2003).

Few West Papuans, however, advocated integration with Indonesia. Encouraged and supported by the Dutch government's belated support for self-government, a small but fervent indigenous pro-independence nationalist movement took root. In 1961 Papuans were inducted into a national legislature. On 1st December 1961, national symbols of an embryonic state were formally adopted. *Hai Tanahku Papua* (Oh my Land of Papua) became the national anthem, the name *Papua Barat* (West Papua) was agreed upon, and the West Papuan national flag, known as the Morning Star, was unveiled. Although West Papuans stopped short of declaring independence, many West Papuans regard the 1st of December as their national day.

The Indonesian government, however, maintained that these were just holding actions, feeble attempts by the Dutch to fan the embers of a dying colonial empire. In response, and with financial support from the Russians, Indonesian President Sukarno launched a sustained diplomatic campaign backed up by small scale military operations. For Indonesian nationalists West Papua was part and parcel of the Indonesian republic. Nationalists argued that the struggle against colonialism and for independence would not be completed until all territory formerly under Dutch control —from Sabang in Aceh to Merauke in West Papua— was returned to the Motherland. It did not matter to the newly founded Indonesian government that the Papuans were Melanesian. The majority of Indonesian nationalists held that the new state of Indonesia was multi-ethnic and multi-religious. Many Indonesians also believed that the West Papuans themselves greatly desired to join the republic (Singh, 2008: 60; Chauvel, 2005).

It was the height of the Cold War and, anxious about the left leaning Sukarno's relationship with the Soviet Union, U.S. President John F. Kennedy's administration stepped into the fray to broker a deal between the Indonesian and Dutch governments. The subsequent 1962 New York Agreement stipulated that Netherlands New Guinea would be handed over to the United Nations to administer. Eight months later on the 1st of May 1963 the U.N. transferred administration to the government of Indonesia. In doing so, the U.N. was following the successor state principle *Uti possidetis juris* —that is, the understanding that decolonization would not change the borders established by the colonial power— which, for better or worse, guided much of the post-war decolonization process.

Although fundamentally undemocratic, the New York Agreement did give the West Papuans certain rights. These included freedom of movement, freedom of assembly, and freedom of association. Most importantly, the Agreement required that an act of self-determination "in accordance with international practice" would occur no later than six years after Indonesia took control. While "in accordance with international practice" was not defined in the New York Agreement, West Papuan activists at the time believed that it meant a referendum carried out in accordance with the principles of universal suffrage (Saltford, 2003). Leading up to the "Act of Free Choice," as the act of self-determination was known, the government of Indonesia, according to Saltford (2003) —in full knowledge of the international community— bombed West Papuan villages from the air, strafed West Papuans with machine-gun fire, detained dissidents without trial, and tortured, executed or managed the disappearance of those who dissented against Indonesian control.

The "consultation" that followed was an orchestrated affair. Indonesian authorities handpicked participants with one late addition (less than 0.2% of the population), and interned them in camps. The process of selecting participants for the Act of Free Choice was not observed by the United Nations, the independent observers or the international press. In a series of "consultations" spanning over a couple of months, 100% of the 1022 Papuans (4 were sick and did not participate) who participated in the Act of Free Choice indicated their desire to remain with Indonesia. But there was no vote. Instead, after a presentation by an Indonesian military official and a few rehearsed speeches by West Papuans, those selected were simply asked to raise their hands if they wanted to remain with Indonesia. On the 19ᵗʰ of November 1969, the United Nations General Assembly "took note" of the results of the Act of Free Choice and West Papua was formally integrated into the territory of Indonesia and removed from the list of non-self-governing territories awaiting decolonization. As Saltford (2003) observed, it was cold war politics. The actual wishes of the Papuans were immaterial.

Root Causes of the Conflict in West Papua

Since the Act of Free Choice, conflict and violence in West Papua has persisted. These causes are multiple and varied. They include not only ongoing dispute over the transfer on sovereignty but also direct violence caused by a history and continuation of state-sanctioned human rights violations, military operations, and a culture of impunity. In addition there is chronic indigenous disadvantage in the areas of health, education and welfare caused by a combination of state neglect and socially, culturally and environmentally destructive large-scale development projects.

Conflict caused by economic exploitation is made worse by the Indonesian military's predatory role in the economy. Some seventy to eighty percent of the Indonesian military's (or TNI: *Tentara Nasional Indonesia*) budget comes from the TNI's involvement in legal and illegal business, including the provision of security to transnational corporations, giving the military a vested interest in maintaining conflict (King, 2004). Since the TNI's partial withdrawal from Aceh (another province in Indonesia where there has been a secessionist movement) following the Helsinki peace agreement, West Papua has become even more important to the TNI as a source of income.

West Papua's abundant natural resources and an Indonesian state's transmigration program designed to foster national unity and development has also altered the demography of West Papua. Far from helping, however, to realize the Indonesian state's modernization agenda, increased migration has intensified conflict and competition over land and economic opportunity (McGibbon, 2004). Institutional racism further exacerbates indigenous exclusion from widespread participation in the structures of the society, and it functions to help justify direct violence. These prevailing historical causes and the direct, structural and cultural forms of violence in West Papua are mutually reinforcing, making the conflict extremely resistant to resolution.

The Sources of the Indonesian Government's Power in West Papua

The Indonesian government maintains power in West Papua in eight key ways. Firstly, and most importantly, the Indonesian government would not be able to maintain control of the territory without the Indonesian security forces —the police, intelligence services and the military— whose presence in West Papua is ubiquitous. The security forces' willingness to use violence and harsh legal penalties to quell what has mostly been nonviolent dissent has functioned to simultaneously increase indigenous resistance to Indonesian rule and repress movements for change.

Secondly, the internalised beliefs of West Papuans themselves help maintain Indonesian rule. As a result of a combination of factors, particularly disunity, Melanesian "big men" politics, internalised racism, tribal divisions, state neglect of education and indigenous leadership and a type of conservative Christian evangelism that has focused on the hereafter rather than working for "heaven" on earth, West Papuan efforts for change have faltered. Many Papuans have nurtured the erroneous belief that they are not able to create the change they long for. There is a need for Papuans to decolonise beliefs that they are incapable of being successful agents of liberation.

Thirdly, violence and exploitation of the indigenous population in West Papua has been kept largely hidden from the outside world due to the fact that the Indonesian government has closed the territory off to sustained international scrutiny. Foreign journalists, humanitarian organizations and even international diplomats are routinely denied permission to visit the territory, particularly areas where there are military operations.

Fourthly, as described above, West Papua occupies a central place in Indonesia's national imagination. West Papua was the site of what Indonesians view as a culmination of a long and ultimately successful struggle against Dutch colonialism. Still smarting from the "loss" of East Timor and fearful of a foreign conspiracy that covets West Papua's natural resource wealth, the overwhelming majority of ordinary Indonesians believe that West Papua is a rightful part of Indonesia. Determination to retain West Papua "at all costs" unifies Indonesian opposition to West Papuan claims for independence.

Fifthly, the Indonesian government controls large-scale economic development in the province, particularly in the mining sector. The Freeport Rio Tinto gold and copper mine for instance, the worlds largest open cut mine and worlds largest gold deposit, is the Indonesian government's largest tax payer.

Sixthly, in addition to the use of repression as a tool of control, the Indonesian government maintains its authority through a montage of confusing and contradictory policies that have functioned to undermine opposition by generating elite competition and by playing West Papuans against one another. The key central government institutions that formulate policy in West Papua include not only key ministers, cabinet, senior members of the security forces and the various committees of national parliament (based in Jakarta, Indonesia's capital), but also the State Intelligence Agency (BIN: *Badan Intel Nasional*) and the National Resilience Institute (Lemhannas).

However, it is not just those in Jakarta who determine policy and carry out the function of the state. West Papuans themselves are in key positions of authority in West Papua. Papuan elites vie for favour from Jakarta and compete against each other for position and power. Richard Chauvel (2008) observes that two distinct political realms exist in Papua (overlapping like a Venn Diagram): the formal official government structure that works with Jakarta to maintain Indonesian government policy and rule in West Papua, even when that contradicts popular aspirations, and a clandestine sphere, often invisible and regularly repressed that strives for independence. Ruling through local political structures run by indigenous West Papuans is the sixth way the Indonesian government maintains control of the territory.

Finally, and critically, the Indonesian government's legitimacy and ability to rule in West Papua is heavily dependent on external sources of power: political, economic and military support willingly provided by the Indonesian government's elite allies and the domestic constituencies in the societies of Indonesia's elite allies. Unlike the British occupation of India, where the British depended on Indian consent and cooperation to govern India, for instance, the Indonesian government, the Indonesian state's security forces and the large multinational corporations operating in West Papua simply do not need the skills and knowledge of ordinary West Papuans to run the day-to-day affairs of the territory.

Although an invader may not be dependent on the people they dominate to run the day-to-day affairs of a territory, they are always dependent (Summy, 1993). In the case of West Papua the Indonesian government is heavily dependent, firstly, on domestic support and, secondly, on the diplomatic, economic and military support of its elite allies. These international and national elite allies operate in ways that mutually reinforce one another's actions. Diplomatically, Indonesia relies on member states of the United Nations to maintain the fiction that the transfer of sovereignty in West Papua was free and fair. Economically, Indonesia depends on the continued investment of multinational corporations as well as the continued economic support of the IMF and World Bank through the Consultative Group on Indonesia. Militarily, Indonesia depends upon countries like the United States to arm and train the TNI, legitimize the role of the TNI in protecting the territorial integrity of Indonesia, and to secure a stable environment for investment. In turn, the Indonesian government's elite allies (like the governments of the United States, Australia, members of the European Union and Japan) depend on the active and passive consent of local constituencies such as voters, bureaucrats, workers, intellectuals, public opinion makers, shareholders, superannuants and unions, to maintain support for Indonesia's occupation of West Papua.

The Indonesian government's dependence on national opinion inside Indonesia and the ongoing support of international allies and their domestic constituencies means that even if the overwhelming majority of indigenous West Papuans were able to organize and sustain a mass withdrawl of their consent and cooperation, by itself such action would not be sufficient to leverage Jakarta to make political concessions. This insight has important implications for developing an effective nonviolent strategy.

Contemporary Nonviolent Resistance in West Papua

Contemporary nonviolent resistance in West Papua dates back to oppositional movements against colonial rule by the Dutch and Japanese. These localised rebellions, often known as cargo cults or millenarian movements emerged in both the highlands and lowlands, often fusing with popular interpretations of Christianity and expectations of the second coming of Jesus Christ. West Papuan theologian Benny Giay (1995) argues that these popular mobilisations and messianic movements represented Papuan aspirations for peace, freedom, justice and prosperity. Many were explicitly nationalist. One of the most well known was a largely unarmed movement led by Angganita Menufandu in Biak during the 1930s and 1940s (de Brujin, 1951; Worsley, 1970; Kamma, 1952). At its height, Menufandu and her followers numbered over 30,000. Together with Stephanus Simiopiaref and other leaders, they engaged in mass tax resistance, a defiance of bans on traditional singing, dancing and cultural practices, and non-cooperation with forced labour programs, all designed to herald a new age of peace and freedom. The movement, argued de Brujin (1951: 10) was "far less a religion than self-conscious Papuan cultural nationalism." It paralysed Dutch rule in Biak. Papuan euphoria over the Japanese defeat of the Dutch in 1942 soon descended into guerrilla warfare by the Papuans against the Japanese. Heavy handed reprisals continued until the United States liberated Biak in 1944.

Hopes vested in a new age precipitated by U.S intervention, however, were short-lived. By the 1st of May 1963, the Dutch were gone and the Indonesian government was in control of the capital and slowly extending their rule throughout the territory. Armed resistance by the OPM (*Organisasi Papua Merdeka*-The Free Papua Movement) began almost immediately. Local groups armed with little more than bows and arrows clashed with the Indonesian military. The origins of the OPM which date back to the Kebar uprising led by Ferry Awom in 1965, later became re-organized and known as the TPN-PB (*Tentara Pembebasan Nasional —Papua Barat*— The National Liberation Army of West Papua). However, the TPN-PB remains a loose network of decentralized commands throughout West Papua. It has a combined estimated active fighting force of fewer than one thousand men with even fewer modern weapons and poor communication and coordination amongst fighting forces. These troops sustain themselves through hunting, gathering forest produce and subsistence farming. For the most part, full-time jungle based guerrilla fighters are unplugged from the global economy. Except from incursions by the Indonesian military and forays into the surrounding cities and towns many fighters also live in virtual political and administrative isolation from the Indonesian state.

Between 2002 and 2008, the TPN-PB has continued to conduct low-level attacks against Indonesian military personnel, launched raids on weapons and ammunition depots, and has attacked resource extractive industries. Never posing a serious military threat to Indonesian rule, the TPN-PB has also been severely hampered by rivalry, factionalism, lack of coordination and communication systems across the territory, personality disputes, poor discipline and a history of collaboration with Indonesian security forces. Coupled with a Melanesian culture of authoritarian "big men" politics, the TPN-PB has to date been unable to develop a unified command structure or pose a serious threat to Indonesian rule.

Despite the popular story of Papuans resisting the might of the Indonesian army with bows and arrows, overwhelmingly resistance to Indonesian rule in West Papua has been through the cultural sphere and popular nonviolent civilian based struggle. One of the antecedents for nonviolent resistance is the work of the cultural music group *Mambesak* established by West Papuan anthropologist and musician Arnold Ap in the 1970s and 1980s.

Ap's project of cultural revitalization and cognitive liberation was far reaching. It came at a time when to refer to oneself as Melanesian or West Papuan was considered politically subversive. Through collecting and performing traditional Papuan songs and dances, *Mambesak* helped create the consciousness of a shared national identity that was other than Indonesian. In the end, Ap's enormous popularity posed too great a threat to the Indonesian state. On 30th November 1983, Arnold Ap and his colleague Eddie Mofu were arrested and jailed. On the 26th of April 1984 the pair was extra-judicially executed by Indonesian Special Forces, ostensibly while trying to escape from jail. However, Ap, Mofu and *Mambesak's* legacy continues. Through song, music and dance Papuans continue to reweave the cultural and psychological fabric of nationalism, communicating grievances, sharing stories, inspiring resistance and strengthening indigenous determination to resist.

The most popular expression of nonviolent resistance to Indonesian rule has been the raising of the Morning Star flag, the banned symbol of the West Papuan independence movement and a symbol of national and cultural identity. There have been countless actions of this type since the 1960s, many of which have resulted in harsh repression by the security forces. In 1980, for example, six West Papuan women, led by Priscilla Jakadewa raised the flag outside the governor's office in Port Numbay/Jayapura. More recently, Filep Karma and Yusak Pakage peacefully raised the Morning Star flag on 1st December 2004, receiving sentences of 15 and 10 years jail respectively. In 2008 Jack Wainggai and ten others received jail sentences of 3.5 and 3 years, also for displaying the flag at a series of nonviolent demonstrations.

Millenarian movements, armed resistance, the work of *Mambesak* and nonviolent actions such as raising the Morning Star Flag have all helped develop oppositional consciousness in West Papua. They have helped reframe the private trials and tribulations of ordinary West Papuans as a national concern. In the process, these actions and movements laid the foundations for later more extensive political actions.

Following the fall of Indonesian dictator Suharto in May 1998, the popular struggle for self-determination in West Papua entered a new phase of openness and intensity. Resistance was transformed from a low-level armed struggle in the mountains and jungles to a popular nonviolent movement waged in the cities and towns of West Papua characterized by the formation of new political and civil society organizations and the mass participation of ordinary West Papuans. A team of 100 prominent Papuans met with the Indonesian President Habibie in February 1999 and demanded independence. In 1999 and 2000 two large political meetings then took place, the Musyuwarah Besar -

Mubes or large consultation and the Papuan Congress. These meetings openly declared the goal of independence from Indonesia and pledged to realise this through nonviolent means.

However, by late November 2000, the political space in West Papua that had been opened by Indonesia's transition to democracy began to close again. Key congress leaders were arrested and jailed. Then a year later Theys Eluay —the elected leader of the Papuan Presidium Council formed at the Congress meeting— was assassinated. From this point an organised national movement for independence began to collapse. From the high point of the "Papuan Spring" (Chauvel, 2005) when the Indonesian President Wahid sponsored the Congress meeting and permitted the Morning Star to fly free, expressions of Papuan aspirations for self-determination have been forced underground while a new generation of Papuan elites compete for positions and resources. Meanwhile the original root causes of the conflict remain.

However, despite a renewal of repression there have been partial successes. Papuans have survived as a people and despite ongoing repression and military operations many indigenous communities have maintained their identity, cultural practices and continued to meet their needs through subsistence based agriculture, gathering forest produce, fishing and hunting. Those communities not straddling coveted resource wealth —timber, oil and mineral resources— have also been able to ensure partial control of land and resources. The Special Autonomy Law introduced in 2001, while considered a failure to the overwhelmingly majority of Papuans, has allowed for greater Papuan involvement in running the affairs of the territory and redistributed income from resource extraction back to the province.

Papuans have also continued to organise. The Dewan Adat Papua —DAP, a network of National Papuan Customary Councils and Leaders— has filled some of the vacuum left by the Presidium Dewan Papua. DAP has attempted to avoid repression by limiting its activities to the cultural sphere. Over time, however, it has become increasingly political, organising a rally of 10,000 people in 2005 to "hand back" Special Autonomy.

Resistance groups have also been quietly working underground. In November and December 2005, activists met in Lae, Papua New Guinea to form the West Papua Coalition for National Liberation (*Koalisi Nasional Papua Barat untuk Pembebasan*). In a clear departure from the PDP, whose hierarchical structure made it vulnerable to repression by Indonesian security forces, the WPNCL attempted to re-organize the resistance movement as a coordinated network of autonomous groups unified more by a shared vision, shared political goals and strategy to achieve them than by charismatic leadership. Twenty-eight resistance organizations drawn from civil society, political organizations and the TPN-PB are members of the Coalition. The WPNCL is a coalition of coalitions. The Coalition went on to meet again in Madang, PNG in 2006, Ipoh, Malaysia and the PNG/West Papua border region in 2007 and Port Vila, Vanuatu in 2008 (WPNCL, 2008). Factionalism, however, continues to hamper unity. Several key groups including the remnants of the PDP, the DAP and the West Papua National Authority as well as some leaders are involved in organising competing resistance alliances.

In the absence of a coordinated civilian based movement for independence that has the capacity to mobilise resistance across the territory, some groups have engaged in more localised campaigns for social and environmental justice and economic and cultural rights in ways that are delinked from independence. Many of these campaigns have been successful. They include Tongoi Papua's campaign for labour rights in 2007, a campaign organised by West Papua's first independent workers union. The campaign brought together indigenous workers from the giant Freeport mine —both highlanders and islanders— under the one organisation. Eschewing the demand for independence, Tongoi also successfully sought out and won the support of migrant workers and their families. Using the tactics of strike drawn out over several days, Tongoi won major concessions —a 100% wage increase for a number of workers, the reinstatement of workers who were unfairly dismissed and the sacking of several supervisors for alleged racism. There have been other campaigns as well. Primary school teachers from all 196 primary schools in Nabire striked in 2007 and successfully won a series of key demands —including the payment of wages which had not been forthcoming for several months. The group Catholic Peace and Justice have launched a campaign to protect the rights of Papuan women market sellers in Jayapura. While still ongoing there is every indication that the campaign to secure a permanent site for market sellers that have been economically marginalised and discriminated against by both municipal authorities and the police will succeed. And when this happens it will have implications for other Papuan market sellers in every city and town in West Papua.

Although the movement has not yet achieved its goal of independence it has achieved partial success. Most importantly indigenous people in West Papua have survived successive periods of colonial rule by the Dutch, Japanese and the Indonesian governments which have oscillated between neglect and savagery. In 2001 Papuans also secured wide ranging autonomy from Jakarta on the back of popular nonviolent mobilisation. Special Autonomy has made a difference to the nature of political rule in West Papua and virtually all political leaders in the territory are now Papuans directly elected by the people. However, significant elements of the autonomy proposal have not been implemented. Campaigns by Tongoi, teachers in Nabire and other communities have also won varying degrees of success. These successes, however, have been partly obscured by the insistence that Special Autonomy has been "a total failure" as well as a renewal of low level repression, intimidation by the Indonesian government's security forces and a lack of interest in the plight of Papuans inside Indonesia and internationally. Internal disunity, factionalism, a range of internal movement problems and a lack of strategy have also been to blame.

The Role of Strategy in Advancing Nonviolent Resistance in West Papua

The history of nonviolent resistance for self-determination in West Papua reveals some important lessons. There are a number of insights from the theory and practice of strategic nonviolent action that, if applied, could maximise the effectiveness of nonviolent resistance in West Papua. Firstly, it is clear that there is not yet a widespread shared understanding of what nonviolent action is —a misunderstanding that restricts its potential application. The popular perception held by many West Papuans and even by some scholars is that nonviolent struggle can be equated to peaceful dialogue, human rights advocacy or efforts to make West Papua "a Land of Peace." Although nonviolent action encompasses these things, it is not limited to them.

Nonviolent action is a third sphere of action. It has its own logic and dynamics that are distinctly different from armed struggle and conventional political action like lobbying and electoral politics (Summy, 1993). Kurt Schock (2005) and Gene Sharp (1973 and 2005) describe strategic nonviolent action as methods of collective *action* that do not involve physical violence or the threat of physical violence towards other human beings and are designed according to a plan to achieve social or political goals. Nonviolent action includes acts of omission (not doing something), commission (doing something) or a combination of both (Sharp, 1973). Nonviolent action encompasses four distinct classes of tactics: protest and persuasion (such as marches and demonstrations), non-cooperation (such as strikes and boycotts), disruptive nonviolent intervention (such as blockades and occupations) and creative nonviolent intervention (such as the creation of parallel social, political and economic structures designed to meet the human needs of the resisting population) (Burrowes, 1996).

In the case of West Papua, the social political context continues to be dominated by a stark power asymmetry between West Papuans and the Indonesian state and is characterised by entrenched structural violence (Galtung, 1969). One of the main reasons Jakarta will not enter into political dialogue with the West Papuan leadership is because there has not been a credible civilian-based movement with unity of purpose and organisation able to back up West Papuan demands and compel Jakarta to sit at the negotiating table. It is my view that a powerful civilian based movement in West Papua supported by the active participation of West Papuans at the grassroots, together with coordinated campaigns inside Indonesia and in the international community is necessary to persuade Jakarta to negotiate. And if the movement is unable to alter Jakarta's willingness to dialogue then the central government may need to be compelled to sit at the table by campaigns designed to undermine its sources of its power. Creating the context for problem solving political talks will require the mobilisation of organised and sustained civilian based power.

Secondly, it appears that nonviolent action in West Papua is not yet one unified national movement but, rather, exists more as five distinct inter-related and overlapping struggles:

1. a political struggle for independence waged against the Indonesian state;
2. a struggle waged against resource extractive industries (such as the giant Freeport gold and copper mine and logging and palm oil companies) for a more equitable distribution of wealth, indigenous control of land and resources, and greater environmental protection;
3. a cultural struggle to defend and promote indigenous identity/ies;
4. a struggle for the protection of civil and political rights, an end to impunity by the security forces and demilitarization, and
5. local struggles for economic, social and cultural rights.

The effectiveness of the nonviolent struggle for self-determination will be enhanced by finding ways these separate struggles can be unified into a single movement with a shared vision and unity of purpose. Unless these disparate movements can unite under a shared goal and shared strategy, it is likely that national indigenous demands and aspirations for self-determination will remain elusive.

The need for a shared vision is the third point. The project of clearly articulating, communicating and having the resisting population embrace a shared vision of the future is yet to be realized. Certainly a number of West Papuans have emphasized the need for West Papuans to clearly articulate what they mean by "freedom" and "independence" (McLeod, 2007: 40-44). However, a concrete, positive and inclusive vision of a free Papua is as yet still ill-defined. A powerful West Papuan vision for freedom that can mobilize discontent and galvanize opposition needs to be based on a widespread and concrete understanding of what *merdeka* (freedom) actually means for ordinary people in West Papua. An inclusive and positive vision of tomorrow will make it easier to unify resistance.

Fourthly, out of a shared vision, clear and achievable political goals can be developed. These goals will need to move beyond the rhetoric of "full independence." These goals well need to be:

— specific;
— have local and national dimensions;
— immediate: they reflect the day-to-day grievances of ordinary Papuans;
— expose the illegitimacy of Indonesian rule;
— within the capacity of local activists to organize around;
— planned with a clear timeframe in mind, and;
— winnable.

Political goals can in turn be realised through a series of short-term strategically focused campaigns designed to build movement power. This is the fifth point. Each campaign will also need to have its own short-term objectives. Seasoned campaigners recommend designing objectives that are SMART (specific and strategic, measurable, achievable —theoretically winnable—, realisable —that is, within the capacity of the campaigning organisation— and time bound). By campaigns I mean a series of sequenced tactical manoeuvres applied over time designed to achieve a specific objective. In the context of West Papua, campaigns should also bring the movement closer to political goals and a shared vision of self-determination. Daniel Hunter (2003) says that campaigns work because they use tactics that can be applied in different contexts that get taken up by local groups. The replication of tactics and campaigns in other contexts helps build the movement and win broader movement goals. Powerful campaigns are also proactive. In other words, movements that organise campaigns don't just protest an injustice; they seize the initiative and redefine the agenda for change. Campaigns also bring in new energy and help form new allies which are essential to winning many campaigns.

Campaigns can be developed by finding issues that resonate with the resisting population. The most potent issues are ones that are immediate, specific and winnable (Beckwith and Lopez, 1997). By immediate I mean some kind of grievance that is experienced daily by the people, that they are passionate about changing. By specific I mean something that is concrete, something you can touch, smell and feel. Powerful campaigns also need issues that are winnable.

Gandhi's most successful campaign, the *salt Satyagraha* did not organise people around independence. Instead Gandhi mobilised discontent around the British Raj's tax on salt —an issue that touched the lives of India's impoverished masses. Likewise in Poland, Lech Walesa eschewed demands for independence and first focused on mobilising ship workers around the desire for independent trade unions. After winning that campaign it was easier to build the Solidarity movement for a democratic Poland. In the United States, Martin Luther King Jr. prepared to attack the bastions of racism and inequality by first mobilising people around desegregating buses in Montgomery and then lunch counters in Nashville, before tackling the bigger issues of voter rights (Ackerman and Duvall, 2000). These big movements all built strength through smaller campaigns created around local issues that were immediate, specific and winnable.

In West Papua, gross state neglect in the areas of education and health together with the destruction of Papua's forests (the largest tropical forest outside the Amazon and the Congo)[2] all have the potential to become issues that can be developed into campaigns designed to mobilise a national nonviolent movement that builds real civilian based power. These are just examples. West Papuans themselves will need to choose their own strategic objectives and campaigns based on issues that can be used to mobilise discontent on a Papua-wide scale. Some of these strategic objectives may reflect more modest aims but they give direction to nonviolent action that will bring West Papuans closer to their ultimate vision: *merdeka* (freedom).

Sixth, Papuans will need to think about how campaigns and political goals are framed. Since taking control of West Papua, the Indonesian state has brutally repressed previous armed and unarmed movements for independence. The Indonesian military has engaged in military operations against localised rebellions, mostly armed with bows

---

[2] Forests cover some 75% of the territory. Forest communities are dependent on forest products for subsistence and to sustain cultural practices. Forest destruction also cuts to the core of the explosive issue of community based land rights.

and arrows, and popular leaders of previous nonviolent movements in West Papua like Arnold Ap and Theys Eluay have either been assassinated or, as in the case of Thomas Wainggai, jailed for long periods (Wainggai later died in jail). In addition there is currently little international or domestic Indonesian support for independence. Given this, it may be prudent in the short to medium term for West Papuans to find issues, develop campaigns and frame their aspirations in ways that are delinked from independence and at the same time appeal to cherished Indonesian values. Doing so will expand the amount of political space available for organising.

Seventh, the nonviolent movement in West Papua needs to continue to develop resilient organizational structures. There is strong evidence to suggest that the development of coordinated networks of decentralized organizations such as federations, umbrella groups and coalitions increases a movement's resilience to repression and enhances strategic coordination. Certainly this was the case for unarmed insurrections in both the Philippines and South Africa. It is important to emphasize that while these organizational structures may be decentralized they still facilitate unity. However, it is unity around long-term political goals, short to mid-term strategic objectives and strategy and tactics rather than unity contained by a single hierarchical organizational form. Kurt Schock (2005) says there are five factors that help explain why coordinated networks of decentralized organizations in repressive contexts are more effective than hierarchical and bureaucratic organizations:

1. A decentralized movement structure is more likely to withstand state repression because one organization or leader cannot be targeted. This was a major weakness of the PDP's structure.
2. A devolution of leadership means that the movement can continue to function when movement leaders are imprisoned or murdered by the state or state-backed militia groups. When the leadership of the PDP was arrested and Theys Eluay was assassinated the PDP virtually collapsed. Failure to develop a decentralized (but coordinated) leadership structure was a factor in the failure of the 1989 Chinese Pro-democracy movement and the first (unarmed) Palestinian Intifada.
3. Decentralized movements are likely to be more democratic, which increases the commitment of the activists involved, makes the leadership more accountable, decreases the likelihood of co-option and lays the foundations for a new democratic society.

4. Decentralized movement structures are more likely to help develop an oppositional consciousness which enhances the ability of diverse groups to work together toward a common goal despite a lack of ideological consensus.
5. Because of their flexibility and capacity to distribute information horizontally, decentralized movements are likely to be more creative and develop innovative tactics than more hierarchical and rigid organizational forms.

West Papuans have started to move down the path of developing a coalition of resistance groups (McLeod, 2007; Singh, 2008). However, a coalition does not exist for itself. Successful campaigns are needed to develop and strengthen effective coalitions.

Eighth, the movement will need to continue to expand its repertoire of tactics beyond the tactics of oppositional consciousness and everyday resistance. In particular the powerful tactics of political, economic and social non-cooperation will need to be developed if the movement is to pose a substantial threat to the Indonesian government's sources of power. Non-cooperation needs to target the West Papuan, Indonesian and international "pillars of support" (Helvey, 2004) that prop up Jakarta's rule in West Papua (point twelve below). One effective example of non-cooperation is the Kingmi Church's determination to withdraw its membership from the Indonesian wide Indonesian Tabernacle Gospel Church (*Gereja Kemah Injil Indonesia*) and establish an independent Synod in West Papua. Another is mass non-cooperation undertaken by Tongoi —the first independent West Papuan labour union that emerged in 2007 to win labour rights for Freeport mine workers through strike action. This class of tactics —mass non-cooperation— is the most powerful tactic in the nonviolent armoury. It needs to be used more often in the pursuit of carefully defined strategic goals. The movement will also need to develop what Robert Burrowes (1996) calls the creative class of nonviolent intervention, particularly parallel political and economic structures that function independently of the Indonesian state.

Ninth, inside West Papua itself it is important that there is a critical discussion about the viability of a strategy of mixed defence (a strategy that simultaneously employs violent and nonviolent means to achieve political objectives). There is substantial evidence to suggest that a strategy of mixing violent and nonviolent strategies often reduces the political space and leverage available to the nonviolent movement (Helvey, 2004; Schock, 2005). Guerrilla action by the TPN-PB has justified indiscriminate repression and criminalization of an entire people by the TNI, particularly in the rural regions where 80% of the population live. A quantitative study by Karantnycky, Ackerman and Rosenberg (2005: 8) and published by Freedom House provides evidence that transition from non-democratic rule to democratic rule is "significantly enhanced when there is no violence from the opposition." Another large N study by Stephan and Chenoweth (2008: 8) provides evidence that nonviolent resistance has achieved success 53 percent of the time, compared with 26 percent for violent campaigns.

The evidence from other struggles suggests that what is particularly needed in the case of West Papua is greater discipline among the activists, particularly by the student and youth activists and coalitions that commit themselves to resistance through nonviolent means. Nonviolent discipline will be assisted by a comprehensive program of training, beginning with less risky actions that focus on achieving more limited objectives in the building of movement strength; the development of a code of ethics to guide activist behaviour; the use of peacekeepers or marshals during political action; and the undertaking of advance preparation, which includes the development of contingency plans (Burrowes, 1996).

Tenth, West Papuan activists in general and leaders in particular, will need to prepare the movement for repression. Paraphrasing the German philosopher Arthur Schopenhauer, repression can increase resistance: "First they ignore you, then they ridicule you, then they fight you, then you win."[3] Viewed like this, repression is not a sign of failure but something to be expected. Repression can even foretell success. It can be an indication that movements are having an impact, a sign that they threaten the interests of the power holders. And that is why the state uses repression: to make movements stop. As a political tool wielded by those in power, the purpose of repression is to inflict a combination of physical, psychological, social, political and economic costs so that activists give up. There is no question that increased repression can destroy a movement. However, an increase in repression does not necessarily have to result in decreased mobilisation of people power. In fact it can lead to the radicalisation of activists and an increase in mobilisation (Tilly, 2005).

There are things activists and movements can do to build resilience and increase the likelihood of success, even in the face of brutal repression. Firstly, individual activists can prepare for repression, meeting in small groups to support one another and develop capacities for sustained struggle. Secondly, as mentioned above, movements can de-

---

[3] This quote is often and possibly misattributed to Gandhi.

velop organisational resilience through the development of active and effective federations, coalitions, alliances or umbrella organisations. Thirdly, activists can develop tactical resilience by: organising peace-keepers, protective accompaniment and international observation; preparing contingency plans and discerning when to utilise tactics that concentrate activists in one place and when to use tactics that emphasise dispersal (Burrowes, 1996: 238-245). Fourthly, movement strategists can ensure that the movement is targeting the opponent's sources of power, altering their willingness to conduct aggression and/or eroding their opponent's legitimacy and ability to carry out acts of aggression (Burrowes, 1996). Finally, activists can develop plans to activate "backfire" in the event that repression occurs (Martin, 2006). Backfire involves sequencing tactics that promote outrage over acts of injustice. These classes of tactics include: exposing the injustice; validating the activists and their actions and challenging attempts to devalue them; framing communication in ways that emphasise the injustice; keeping the issue in the public arena; avoiding efforts by the opponents to use formal procedures to give the appearance of justice; and, resisting attempts by the power-holders to engage in threats, intimidation and further repression.

The eleventh point —also related to framing— is the need for media exposure and a communication strategy that appeals to universal values such as human rights and democracy. Different communication strategies will be required to mobilise different audiences: in West Papua, in other parts of the Indonesian archipelago and in the societies of the Indonesian government's elite allies. Theys Eluay was able to mobilise Papuan dissent by appealing to traditional values and indigenous identity. Different strategies will be needed to mobilise support from ordinary Indonesians in other parts of the archipelago. It will be difficult —if not impossible— for West Papuans to mobilise domestic Indonesian support by invoking a frame that challenges core Indonesian identities. Mobilising on the basis of indigenous identity, historical grievances and a demand for self-determination is useful in West Papua but not inside greater Indonesia. A frame of democracy or the environment or equal rights may resonate more with Indonesian audiences in places like Java. Creative communication strategies that make both repression by the Indonesian government and nonviolent resistance by West Papuans visible to both a domestic and international audience are needed in order to circumvent the Indonesian government's attempt to close the province to external scrutiny.

Finally, the movement's effectiveness will be dramatically enhanced by continuing to develop a strategy that challenges the sources of the

Indonesian government's power not just within West Papua itself but inside Indonesia and internationally. Because the Indonesian government depends largely on the political, economic and military support of third parties to maintain its rule in West Papua, West Papuan activists will need to develop a strategy that engages external third parties in all three sites of struggle in order to increase the movement's leverage. Third parties include not only the Indonesian government's elite allies but also the key constituencies in the societies of Indonesia's elite allies upon which the government of Indonesia indirectly depends. For example, in the case of the giant Freeport gold and copper mine, this includes those who finance Freeport's mining operations, such as pension (superannuation) funds.

In embarking on a strategy of internationalisation, West Papuans also need to be aware of the dangers of external support. The movement could become dependent on third parties. Third parties could try to channel dissent into less disruptive channels. West Papuans could become dependent on institutional funding and movement leaders could become co-opted. Therefore while it is critical that West Papuans understand the need for solidarity inside Indonesia and abroad, ultimately it is West Papuans alone who are the primary agents of liberation.

Conclusion

In the face of enormous obstacles, West Papuans have been able to transform resistance from armed to nonviolent struggle. Despite a renewal of repression West Papuans have continued to find creative nonviolent ways to resist violence and oppression and survive as indigenous people. Nonviolent resistance in West Papua has already achieved partial success, securing Special Autonomy in 2001 —a significant concession from the central government— despite the fact that the promises of Special Autonomy have been incompletely realised. The goal of genuine self-determination, whether that results in full independence or not, however, is not guaranteed and the movement faces significant challenges from within and without. It is critical that the movement develops a shared vision, clear and achievable political goals, and intermediate campaigns based on issues that are immediate, specific, winnable and have a national (West Papua wide) dimension. These campaigns of nonviolent action need to target the sources of Jakarta's power in West Papua —not just inside the territory but in Indonesia and in the societies of Jakarta's elite allies as well. Most importantly

West Papuans need a shared strategy for realizing their objectives and goals. Given the transnational nature of the Indonesian government's sources of power, any successful strategy will require an enhanced level of strategic coordination and an international dimension. What is clear, however, is that Jakarta cannot maintain its rule without a combination of cooperation from Papuan elites and heavy handed control by the security forces. Yet each act of repression only stokes the fires of dissent and deepens feelings of alienation towards the Indonesian government among West Papuans. Nonviolent struggle for self-determination in West Papua will most likely be more difficult than a conventional nonviolent struggle against a dictator (which is challenging enough!). The struggle against occupation has been ongoing for over forty years. But Papuans have already been successful. Further success is possible. West Papuans have the creativity, determination, intelligence and commitment needed to realise their aspirations for genuine self-determination, whether that is within the framework of the Indonesian state, as an independent country or utilising some other creative framework that satisfies the parties' needs.

References

ACKERMAN, Peter and Jack DuVALL (2000): *A Force More Powerful: A Century of Nonviolent Conflict*. Palgrave, New York.
— and Christopher KRUEGLER (1994): *Strategic Nonviolent Conflict: The Dynamics of People Power in the Twentieth Century*. Praeger, Westport, CT.
BECKWITH, David and Cristina LOPEZ (1997): *Community Organizing: People Power from the Grassroots*. Conference presentation, Center for Community Change. At: http://comm-org.wisc.edu/papers97/beckwith.htm.
BUDIARDJO, Carmel and Liem Soei LIONG (1988): *West Papua: The Obliteration of a People*. The Indonesian Human Rights Campaign, Tapol.
BURROWES. Robert. J. (1996): *The Strategy of Nonviolent Defense: A Gandhian Approach*. State University of New York Press, Albany.
CHAUVEL, Richard (2008): "Rulers in Their Own Country? Inside Indonesia," Vol 94: *West Papua: Inside Indonesia?* At: www.insideindonesia.org/content/view/1128/47.
— (2005): *Constructing Papuan Nationalism: History, Ethnicity, and Adaptation* (Policy Studies 14). East-West Center, Washington D.C.
— and Ikrar Nusa BHAKTI (2004): *The Papua Conflict: Jakarta's Perceptions and Policies* (Policy Studies 5). East-West Center, Washington D.C.
DE BRUJIN, Jan. V. (1951): "The Mansren Cult of Biak." *South Pacific*, Vol. 5, 1-10.
KARANTNYCKY, Adrian; Peter ACKERMAN and Mark ROSENBERG (2005): *How Freedom is Won: From Civic Resistance to Durable Democracy*. Freedom House, New York.

GALTUNG, Johan (1969): "Violence, Peace and Peace Research." *Journal of Peace Research*, Vol. 6, 167-191.

GIAY, Benny (2000): *Menuju Papua Baru: Beberapa Pokok Pikiran Sekitar Emansipasi Orang Papua*. Deiyai/ELSHAM Papua, Jakarta.

— (1995): *Hai: Motif Pengharapan "Jaman Bahagia" di Balik Protes Orang Amungme di Timika, Irian Jaya dan Isu HAM*. Deyai, West Papua.

HELVEY, Robert (2004): *On Strategic Nonviolent Conflict: Thinking about the Fundamentals*. The Albert Einstein Institution, Boston.

HUNTER, Daniel (2003): "Campaigning for Social Change: beyond just protesting for it!" Unpublished article (1 October).

INTERNATIONAL CRISIS GROUP (2006): *Papua: The Dangers of Shutting Down Dialogue* (Asia Briefing No. 27). International Crisis Group, Jakarta/Brussels.

— (2003): *How Not to Divide Papua*. International Crisis Group, Jakarta/Brussels.

KAMMA, Freerk C. (1952): "Messianic Movements in Western New Guinea." *International Review of Missions*, Vol. 41, 148-160.

PERMANENT MISSION OF THE REPUBLIC OF INDONESIA TO THE UNITED NATIONS (2003): *Questioning the Unquestionable: An Overview of the Restoration of Papua into the Republic of Indonesia*. United Nations, New York.

KECK, Margaret and Kathryn SIKKINK (1998): *Activists Beyond Borders: Advocacy Networks in International Politics*. Cornell University Press, Ithaca and London.

KING, Peter (2004): "West Papua and Indonesia since Suharto: Independence, Autonomy or Chaos?" UNSW Press, Sydney.

MARTIN, Brian (2006): *Justice Ignited: The Dynamics of Backfire*. Rowman and Littlefield, Lanham, MA.

MACLEOD, Jason (2007): "Self-Determination and Autonomy: the Meanings of Freedom in West Papua." Ed. M. Anne BROWN: *Security and Development in the Pacific Islands: Social Resilience in Emerging States*. Lynne Rienner, Boulder, 139-167.

MCGIBBON, Rodd (2004): *Plural Society in Peril: Migration, Economic Change, and the Papua Conflict*. East West Centre, Washington D.C.

OSBORNE, Robin (1985): *Indonesia's Secret War: The Guerrilla Struggle in Irian Jaya*. Allen and Unwin, Sydney.

SALTFORD, John (2003): *The United Nations and the Indonesian Takeover of West Papua, 1962-1969: The Anatomy of Betrayal*. Routledge Curzon, London.

SCHOCK, Kurt (2005): *Unarmed Insurrections: People Power in Nondemocracies*. University of Minnesota Press, Minneapolis.

SHARP, Gene (1973): *The Politics of Nonviolent Action*. Porter Sargent, Boston.

— (2005): *Waging Nonviolent Struggle: 20th Century Practice and 21st Century Potential*. Extending Horizons Books, Porter Sargent, Boston.

SINGH, Bilveer (2008): *Papua: Geopolitics and the Quest for Nationhood*. Transaction Publishers, New Brunswick.

STEPHAN, Maria J. (2005): *Nonviolent Insurgency: the Role of Civilian-Based Resistance in the East Timorese, Palestinian, and Kosovo Albanian Self-Determination Movements.* PhD Thesis. Fletcher School of Law and Diplomacy.
— and E. CHENOWETH (2008): "Why Civil Resistance Works: the Strategic Logic of Nonviolent Conflict." *International Security,* Vol. 33 (Summer), 7-44.
SUMMY, Ralph (1993): "Nonviolence and Democracy." *Social Alternatives,* Vol. 12, 15-19.
TILLY, Charles (2005): "Repression, Mobilisation and Explanation." Ed. Christian DAVENPORT; Hank JOHNSTON and Carol MUELLER: *Repression and Mobilization.* University of Minnesota, Minneapolis.
WEST PAPUA NATIONAL COALITION FOR LIBERATION-KELOMPOK KERJA PERDAMAIAN PAPUA BARAT (2008): *Laporan Sosialisasi: "Let's work together to end the suffering of our peoples."* Unpublished report. Port Numbay, West Papua.
WORSLEY, Peter (1970): *The Trumpet Shall Sound: A Study of "Cargo" Cults in Melanesia.* Paladin, London.

Some Reflections on Transformative Nonviolence

Iain Atack
Trinity College Dublin

Introduction

A distinction is sometimes made between tactical and strategic uses of nonviolent political action, depending upon the objectives of a particular campaign and the extent of the political and social changes sought. Thus, it is suggested tactical nonviolence seeks changes to a specific government policy, for example, or modification to a particular instance of corporate or business behaviour. Strategic nonviolence aims to achieve much broader, and perhaps even revolutionary objectives, such as regime change (from an undemocratic to a democratic government, for example) or national independence.

The division between these two types of nonviolence is somewhat artificial in practice, of course, since the two types of objectives often co-exist within particular examples of nonviolent action or nonviolent campaigns, at least partly because such campaigns often consist of broad coalitions of different groups or movements with divergent goals. Also, the tactical use of nonviolence around a specific issue can be used quite deliberately in conjunction with or as a prelude to much larger strategic objectives. Gandhi's salt march and his use of the salt tax and salt monopoly to illustrate the inequities and failures of British rule in India is a classic example of this.

Nonetheless, this distinction between the tactical and the strategic dimensions of nonviolence is a useful analytical device, if only because it helps us identify the range of purposes for which nonviolent political action can be used. My suggestion, however, is that this distinction is incomplete or not fully adequate because it does not capture fully the transformative potential of nonviolent political action, including strategic nonviolence. In order to do this, we need to examine more closely whether or not the purpose of even strategic nonviolence is to establish or rectify conventional political structures, such as state sovereignty or democracy, or to transform conventional political, economic and social institutions through releasing or liberating popular power. We also need to understand the sources of power behind effective uses of strategic nonviolence, sometimes known as the consent theory of power.

The Consent Theory of Power

According to the consent theory of power, the power of the ruler or the ruling group within a society depends ultimately upon the compliance, obedience or consent of those they rule or govern. Once this consent is withdrawn, and a suffcient number of people or institutions within a society refuse to cooperate with the ruler or the ruling group, their power begins to evaporate and they can no longer govern. They must change their behaviour and their policies or else be replaced by a new government or a new regime.

This understanding of power helps explain the effectiveness of nonviolent political action. The withdrawal of popular consent from the existing regime or the status quo can be organised nonviolently through strikes, boycotts, mass demonstrations and so on, methods that do not rely upon and can deliberately avoid the use of political violence to achieve their objectives. Furthermore, this view of power is prevalent throughout the history of nonviolent action and those who reflect upon or try to explain its effectiveness. This includes both those who have a more principled or normative view of the reasons for employing nonviolence, such as Gandhi, and those whose support for nonviolence is much more explicitly pragmatic, or concerned primarily with its effectiveness in achieving its political objectives, such as Gene Sharp.

The focus of this theory of power is often on its capacity to explain the ability of popular mobilisation or nonviolent civil resistance to achieve significant political change, even in the face of highly oppressive and brutal regimes. In other words, the emphasis is often upon the sources of power of the ruling group and how the removal of consent, compliance and obedience can undermine this. We also need to look at the flip side of this, however, and understand its significance for understanding the power of the people themselves, and their capacity to mobilise and organise to achieve strategic political objectives.

Related to this is a need to assess the ultimate purpose or goal of such nonviolent civil resistance or nonviolent political action. The aim often seems to be to replace one ruling group with another, at the top of the social or political pyramid, consistent with the standard diagram used to illustrate the dynamics of the consent theory of power. The significance of this achievement cannot be overestimated, of course, if we are replacing a brutal military dictatorship with a democratically elected government that respects human rights and observes the rule of law.

On the other hand, if we look at nonviolent civil resistance not only as a method for undermining the power of the ruling regime, but also as a mechanism for releasing or liberating popular power, then perhaps we can see its transformative potential more clearly. In other words, rather than aiming only at regime change, perhaps it can aim at a more profound structural transformation of society, in which we eliminate or at least level out conventional hierarchical social and political structures. The aim of nonviolent action is not merely to change those who are at the top of the social and political pyramid, but to dismantle the pyramid altogether.

Strategic versus Transformative Nonviolence

Thus, just as we can begin to distinguish between tactical and strategic objectives of nonviolence, we can also begin to distinguish between its strategic uses and its transformative potential. Again, the separation between these is by no means absolute or exclusive. These three aspects or dimensions of nonviolent action often work in tandem or in a mutually supportive role. The transformative vision requires the support of clear strategic thinking, and both must be embodied by discrete, achievable and more immediate tactical goals. Nonetheless, the transformative potential of nonviolent action is often overshadowed or neglected because of the difficulties, obstacles and challenges confronting its effective strategic and tactical use, and the euphoria we quite rightly feel when we succeed in achieving some of these objectives.

The distinction between strategic and transformative nonviolence is important because it cuts to the heart of our understanding of the nature and purpose of nonviolent action. We can view nonviolence as an "exceptional" form of political activity, for instance, required and justified only when conventional political institutions fail. In other words, in a fully democratic society, in which political institutions and political decisions fully reflect the will of the people, there would be no need for nonviolent political action. Citizens could express themselves fully and freely and contribute to decision-making by means of conventional democratic processes. Various forms of nonviolent action, such as petitions, protests and marches, are required only because no democracy is ever complete or fully realised. This conforms to one of the conventional definitions of nonviolent action as providing some sort of "third way" between political violence and established political structures, as a method of expressing the popular will and putting pressure on unrepresentative governments.

On the other hand, we can view nonviolent civil resistance as more than a collection of methods, techniques, tactics and strategies that deliberately avoids the use of violence but also operates outside conventional political structures such as the state or government. On this view, the "civil" component is equally important to the "nonviolent" component in understanding the dynamics of nonviolent civil resistance or nonviolent political action. There are new forms of political power and political expression inherent in the organisations and groups formed to engage in popular mobilisation and nonviolent civil resistance. Such organisations have more than instrumental significance. In other words, they can be more than alternative vehicles for achieving strategic objectives such as regime change or national liberation within conventional state structures. They can also represent new and creative forms of political organisation that can provide a permanent or institutionalised mechanism for ordinary citizens to engage in direct political action and to continue to express their views politically outside (or perhaps even replacing) conventional hierarchical political structures such as the state.

There are many recent examples of strategic uses of nonviolent political action achieving siginficant and even revolutionary change within countries or soieties. These range from the rather abrupt end to Soviet-sponsored communist regimes in Eastern Europe, to the end of apartheid in South Africa, to the removal of Milošević from power in Serbia and the so-called colour revolutions in Georgia and the Ukraine. Success in each of these instances depended upon sustained popular nonviolent mobilisation against existing regimes and in support of democratic forces. The end result was to replace an undemocratic regime with a liberal democratic and pro-Western government. In many cases, the groups sponsoring or organising nonviolent civil resistance (such as Solidarity in Poland) became or were absorbed into conventional political parties or acted in support of or in coalition with such political parties, and satisfied themselves with access to the conventional mechanisms of government and state power.

These are hugely important achievements and demonstrate quite clearly the capacity of popular mobilisation and nonviolent political action to achieve change where poltical violence and the use (or threat) of military force have failed. On the other hand, we can ask whether the ultimate aim of nonviolence is to replace Milošević with Kostunica in Serbia, or to replace a pro-Russian government with a pro-Western government in the Ukraine. Nonviolent political action can then be subsumed into the margins of political acitivity, to resurface perhaps around specific issues or complaints, but not to form the basis of a new type of society or a new way of doing politics, not merely "in extremis" but as a more systematic or permanent feature of political and social life.

It is perhaps much more difficult to find examples of transformative nonviolent political action which really have achieved fundamental structural change. This may well be because such change is utopian and not fully realisable. It may be due to a failure of political imagination or because of the very real difficulties in achieving the tactical and strategic objectives of nonviolence when confronting highly oppressive and repressive regimes, never mind aiming at more ambitious goals. It may demonstrate the limits of the consent theory of power, and the inevitability of some element of coercion and hierarchy in political structures, however representative and bound by the rule of law they may be. Perhaps we need to look for examples of the transformative power of nonviolence on a smaller-scale, at the local level or in the context of social change organisations themselves. Nonetheless, I think the transformative potential of nonviolence is an important complement or supplement to its tactical and strategic uses. It provides the critical vision we need to go beyond a compilation of successful techniques, methods and case studies of nonviolent political action, to an assessment of its ultimate aims and objectives.

Conclusion

I began this reflection with the conventional distinction between tactical and strategic uses of nonviolence. My suggestion is that we need to move beyond such instrumental categories of nonviolent political action, as important as they are, to include its transformative dimension. The consent theory of power has been used to explain the effectiveness of nonviolent political action in both tactical and strategic terms, or how popular nonviolent mobilisation can achieve both behavioural change on the part of governments or private businesses and also regime change or the replacement of one ruling group by another. This theory of power also suggests, however, that such popular mobilisation can initiate new non-hierarchical political structures, for example, that provide the basis for a deeper and more fundamental structural transformation of society. While there are many recent examples of both the tactical and the strategic use of nonviolence, including some spectacular successes (as well as failures), it is perhaps more difficult to find examples of its transformative use. Nonetheless, this transformative vision allows us to move beyond an instrumental assessment of nonviolent political action to an examination of its ultimate political and social objectives.

Rejuvenating Conflict Prevention:
Confronting the Challenges
of Youth and Conflict

Adults' War and Young Generations' Peace: Experiences from Children and Youth Taking Part in Peacebuilding

Annette Giertsen
Save the Children Norway

Introduction

This article builds on Save the Children Norway's "thematic evaluation" on children's participation in armed conflict, post conflict and peacebuilding, and also on work and written material by the external consultants Clare Feinstein and Claire O'Kane.

The term *children* refers to children and young people up to 18 years. The evaluation includes research and documentation of children's experiences from armed conflicts as well as their reflections, opinions and proposals. It addresses children's experiences from and their visions and planning for peace and in this way it gives children and young people an opportunity to go beyond the situation of violence and despair, to creating hopes and making plans for a better future. While evaluating and documenting, children have also been supported in their peacebuilding initiatives.

Evaluating Children and Young People's Participation in Armed Conflict, Post Conflict and Peacebuilding

The evaluation has gone on for two years and finished in January 2009 with a global launch and closing workshop. Save the Children Norway decided to do a more thorough evaluation on this area, opening up for a longer period of work, which allowed for involving children and young people in a more comprehensive way. They have taken on different tasks and responsibilities, such as advisers during planning to ensure focus of the evaluation; as active respondents in exploring and documenting information; as peer-researchers when applying tools and taking part in analysing and assessing information; as development workers when strengthening and developing their activities and clubs; and as peace agents when preparing and disseminating their messages for peace. In addition, the process itself has served to empower them and give them self-confidence also in handling contradictions and conflicts. In addition, this way of evaluating has allowed children to take initiatives in peacebuilding, and has consequently been a way of responding to most children's deeply expressed longing for peace.

The Formative Dialogue research method has been applied. It combines elements from process evaluation and action research and allows for "forming" or modifying projects and methods while the evaluation takes place. This opens the "beneficiaries" to improving their activities and projects while they are in the process of documenting and identifying findings and recommendations. It applies dialogue as a special way of gathering information and uses "why" questions for that purpose. Dialogue is also a way of making people meet, start talking and in this way achieve change. A children's club in Nepal presented this example: the club members took part in a campaign on Compulsory School Enrollment and

> hung a banner with the name of the campaign in the middle of the village. After one day the Maoists took the banner away. The children's club organized a three-party meeting involving parents, the Maoist area commander and children's club members. Children said that the school enrollment campaign is part of their work as education is a child's right. They negotiated with the Maoists and explained that 100 children's clubs in the district are part of the campaign. They day after, the Maoists put the banner back in the same place and promised that they would cooperate in more positive ways in the future. (*Adults' War and Young Generation's Peace*, 2009).

This shows how children are using dialogue and achieve changes.

The children and young people who took part in the evaluation come from four countries: Guatemala, Bosnia-Herzegovina, Uganda and Nepal. Two of the countries have been in a post conflict phase, while the two others have gone from violent conflict to post conflict phase during the evaluation period. They were all members of children's groups, clubs or associations run by organisations which are supported by Save the Children Norway. All together 683 children and young people have been actively involved, while 2740 have been consulted. They were from 8 to 18 years old and from rural and urban areas; the majority was attending school; there were children with ethnic minority backgrounds and children with disabilities, children and young people who lived in camps for internally displaced people and those who have been associated with armed groups.

The evaluation raises several examples about sufferings such as feeling hunger and "crying lots of tears"; family separation and loss of culture; sadness caused by disappearances and deaths; having bad feelings and thinking of revenge —and forgiveness; being exposed to sexual harassment, early pregnancy and having to function as midwives; being threatened and maimed, witnessing killing, ordering people to kill and being obliged to kill. They tell about land disputes and struggles, ethnic and religious grouping, about a culture of fear and silence and that parents and children do not trust each other.

Children's experiences from war are well documented; here issues related to peace and peacebuilding will be addressed.

Children and Young People's Understanding of Peace and Peacebuilding

Children have a multifaceted understanding of peace. It includes issues such as no discrimination against girls, children with disabilities, low caste and class and different ethnic groups, no violence, no poverty or corruption. They also said what peace *is,* such as: equality between men and women, justice and freedom; faithfulness, forgiveness and reconciliation; protection and safety; access to education, health and recreation and job opportunities for their parents; and included children's involvement in peacebuilding. A young person from Guatemala gave his understanding of peace:

> A war per se does not end when both parties stop confronting each other, nor with the signing of an accord. A war ends when conflicts are solved and justice is made. ... The present of Guatemala is being forged and we cannot be excluded from it. Peace is something that is being built, and not something that is signed (*Adult's War and Young Generation's Peace*, 2009).

Gathering children's understandings is the result of various tools, among them *"visioning exercises,"* which enable children to reflect on and develop concrete ideas about peace, which has been particularly important for those who have lived all their life in a situation of armed conflict.

Children demonstrated a rich and holistic understanding of the complexity of peacebuilding and took into account: social factors such as attitude and behaviour; values, cultural and religious aspects, as well as structural, economic and political factors. They have included elements such as the need to work for peace talks, peace agreements and reconciliation among different groups; working for political stability, democracy and good governance, addressing corruption and transparency; working for unity, equity and sharing of resources as well as non-discrimination and respect for human, women's and children's rights. Of these, they have given special emphasis to inclusive participation, non-discrimination, respect for human and children's rights and equal and fair distribution of resources as fundamental for establishing and sustaining peace. They have also underlined the importance of broader political and social development initiatives in order to address poverty, discrimination and the unfair distribution of resources.

Children and young people highlighted how peacebuilding starts at an individual level among family and friends and moves outward. A boy from a peace club in Uganda put it this way: "Peace begins with you; then it extends to the surroundings. If you don't love yourself then you will not find peace in you." In Guatemala children and young people addressed social dividedness:

> We want it to be gender equity, equity among social classes or groups, equity among students from different universities. The society is divided not only by classes or groups, but also in small social groups; there is no common goal, everybody only minds their own business, trying to subsist without paying attention to others. We should get together, it is important to get out of this individualist awareness (*Adult's War and Young Generation's Peace*, 2009).

In the four countries, children recognised that various forms of discrimination and exclusion based on religion, ethnicity, caste or low income have been instrumental in conflicts. They identified violations of children's and human rights as a root cause and also as a negative impact of conflict. In order to establish and sustain peace, they emphasized: inclusive participation, non-discrimination, respect for human and children's rights, equality and fair distribution of resources. Broader political and social development initiatives were also underlined, as well as structural changes which addressed poverty, discrimination, unfair distribution of resources and violation of human rights. They described political processes through which peace may be agreed upon, justice secured and structural changes promoted, according to the specific socio-political context. For example:

— In Nepal, they highlighted the importance of the peace agreement and the constitutional assembly process to get more inclusive forms of governance, address poverty and discrimination and to ensure fair distribution of resources.

— In Uganda, they advocated to be included in the formal peace talks taking place in Juba (South Sudan) and they emphasized forgiveness and reconciliation and making use of traditional forms of justice.

— In Bosnia-Herzegovina, delegates of children had met with the Prime Minister to advocate for their recommendations on the provision of quality education.

— In Guatemala, children had reflected on the presidential elections and efforts for greater attention to monitoring of the peace accords and implementation of children's rights.

They have identified factors that hinder their participation in peacebuilding, factors that are equally relevant for their participation in general, such as traditional views that children should not express their opinions, lack of awareness about children's participation, lack of trust in children's capacities, disrespect of children's views and violations of their rights. There are politicians who express that peace agreements have to be in place before children can be listened to; thus ignoring both their potential contributions as well as their right to be heard in matters that affect them.

Children highlighted what enhances their participation, such as: sensitising key adults in their lives to recognise the importance of listening to their views and encouraging them to take part in peacebuilding and having access to child friendly information about government policies and processes so that they can engage meaningfully in policy developments and formal peace talks, for example the constitutional assembly in Nepal, the election process in Guatemala and the formal peace talks in Uganda. They also underlined the importance of receiving support to form children's clubs, associations and networks at different levels and have the opportunities for training in peacebuilding and child rights.

They also recognise risks they may face, such as abuse, insults, torture and abduction, trauma, hindered education, lack of respect for their views and support from adults.

Children's Contributions to Peace in Situations of Violent Conflict and Post Conflict Situations

At the Individual Level

— Children have produced pamphlets, posters and publications on peace and child rights and have shared them with local communities.

— They have shown great capacities for change. A boy in Uganda recalls:

> One day in 1991 my father was killed by the LRA (Lord's Resistance Army) rebels whereby I was having feelings of revenge. But when I joined the peace club and attended some workshops, I realised that revenge is very bad. I have changed from the spirit of revenge to reconciliation and forgiveness. Now there is peace in my heart (*Adult's War and Young Generation's Peace*, 2009).

— They also showed capacities for forgiveness. Children and young people from Srebrenica in Bosnia-Herzegovina build peace by socialising with and respecting other children and by not discriminating against each other.

> We need to respect everyone's rights regardless of their ethnicity, and we should all be united and respect each other. We need to give a second chance to others in order for everyone to be united again. So don't hate each other, don't hurt each other. Let's build peace, let our future be better and happier, full of love and respect (*Adult's War and Young Generation's Peace*, 2009).

Another boy from Uganda tells this story:

> I was traumatised when I saw in the newspaper how people were being cooked by the LRA. I wanted the LRA to be slaughtered. However, when I became involved in the thematic evaluation I learnt about dialogue, reconciliation and peace. I now want the LRA to return to their land and serve God and my country (*Adult's War and Young Generation's Peace*, 2009).

Social Emotional Rehabilitation

They supported each other and helped improve everyday life:

— Young people in Guatemala involved in a mental health project received guidance and supervision to give psycho-social counselling to peers, including orphans.
— Children supported each other when joining the same group; a young girl in Uganda experienced this:

> Before joining the association I could really [not] be thinking throughout the day and night because I lost my parents and I thought I was the only one having this kind of problem and difficult

condition. When I joined the association we started sharing problems and we are coming out with the solution (Research team in Uganda, 2008).

Contributions to Increased Security at School and in the Local Community

— In Nepal, in areas where children's clubs have been working on issues such as children's rights for a time, the number of abducted children was much lower than in other areas.
— With support from adults, children in Nepal negotiated with armed groups to release their abducted peer.
— Children's clubs in Nepal managed to prevent Maoists, government army and police from entering schools and interfering with their studies. They were supported by adults when negotiating and pressuring both parties in the conflict, and used the concept of "School as a Zone of Peace" as a support.

Support for Reconciliation and Reintegration in the Local Community

— They contributed to the reintegration of formerly abducted children into their local communities through weekly radio programmes on *Radio King* in Gulu, Uganda, where they present and encourage discussions on issues raised about peace and broadcast songs and poetry on peace. The issues had been identified based on key findings, messages and recommendations from the evaluation and presented in a *Children's Memorandum*. It also outlined key issues to enhance their participation in peacebuilding and those issues they wanted to bring to the attention of decision-makers.
— In Bosnia-Herzegovina, children and young people organised a round table conference with community and religious leaders and local stakeholders. This led to changes in adults' views on them as the adults started to recognise that the massacre of thousands of male Bosniak habitants had deeply affected the young people and that they had opinions and reflections on it. One of the adults was surprised by this, and said: "I had not expected that children thought about those issues and that they have ideas for its improvement..." (Research team in Bosnia-Herzegovina, 2006).

Initiatives on Education

— Children's clubs in Nepal identified children who were directly af-fected by the conflict, assessed their situation and decided to set up a fund to support their enrollment in school, thus enabling them to continue their education.
— Children and young people in Nepal, Bosnia-Herzegovina and Guatemala highlighted their role in improving quality education and as active participants in developing the curricula. In this way they want to influence education reforms to make schools more inclusive, non-discriminatory and promoting a culture of peace rather than violence.
— Guatemalan and Bosnia-Herzegovinian children have empha-sised the importance of including the history of conflict in the school curricula.
— Nepal and Uganda called for including children's clubs in the general curriculum so that other children recognize the impor-tance of the clubs.
— Bosnia-Herzegovina called for establishing student councils to ensure children's participation and representation in school man-agement as well as broader district and national level education policy and practice developments. This would also be a way for them to promote peace and address discrimination based on ethnicity and religion.

Influencing Local Policy

Children made a risk map that identified dangers in the city, and presented it to the Municipal Mayor of Konjic in Bosnia-Herzegovina. Having listened to the children, he promised the necessary funding for the reparations to eliminate the dangers; in addition he invited the chil-dren to be part of creating a developmental strategy for Konjic munici-pality for 2008-2012.

Influencing National Policy

Children in Nepal were involved in the Constitutional Election proc-ess: representatives from children's clubs in 48 districts participated in a national children's conference in December 2007 where they developed a declaration, which was presented to various political parties. In April 2008, prior to the constitutional election, representatives from different political parties signed a joint declaration of commitment to children.

Influencing Peace Agreements

Children participated in consultations on agenda three of the Juba talks in Uganda dealing with reconciliation and accountability. Their views have contributed to a broader report and have been presented to the government and the LRA, the rebel group. In the emerging agreement there is a special section on children that includes the need to:

— consider the experiences and concerns of *all* children;
— protect the dignity and security of children in any reconciliation proceedings;
— ensure that children are not subject to criminal justice proceedings —but participate in reconciliation processes;
— facilitate children's participation in implementing the agreement.

This is probably the first time that children have been included in peace talks at this level, and it is interesting to see how their views have contributed to more comprehensive and inclusive agreements.

Considerations about the Future: Who Are the Children Affected by War and Taking Part in Peacebuilding?

These are the children who happened to live in a country at the time of a violent conflict or after; some have been associated with armed groups: those who happened to be abducted, or who took the initiative to join an armed group. All of them are children.

They are portrayed as —and they might also be— passive participants, for example, those confronted with situations beyond their capacity for coping. They are also vulnerable victims of conflicts, risking one or more of their developmental needs; and that very psychological distress hampers their ability to develop and thrive. Some of them have been active combatants or in other ways associated with armed groups. Sometimes children are described one-dimensionally, as passive recipients, as especially vulnerable victims or active combatants. And this may be the reality for some of them. But at the same time children also combine different roles: they have been passive, are vulnerable and have been associated with armed groups —and later on they become agents of peace. For example, one boy in Nepal was an active member of the Maoist group and later became the leader of a children's club; former abducted children in Uganda (associated with armed groups) have later become active members of the peace club.

This shows that children may enter very different roles in different situations.

When young people are both victims and perpetrators, it creates difficulties, and they become anxious about reactions and punishment. Children in Uganda had opinions on this; some mentioned they wanted to be ensured that they would not be subject to criminal justice proceedings. Instead they emphasized the use of traditional accountability mechanisms —a system related to restorative justice. They wanted to contribute in reconciliation processes and they see themselves as active participants in the implementation processes of the peace agreement.

Why Document Children's Experiences from Armed Conflict and Their Contributions to Peace?

Much has been done to document children's experiences in conflict situations. It is also important that children and young people's history is brought into the common history of a country; this should include children's opinions, proposals and initiatives as well. Giving such documentation an official status is a way for marginalised groups to receive recognition and acceptance for who they are and for their culture, for their experiences and sufferings, and also for their contributions. The documentation of children's experiences, opinions and contributions in armed conflict would also mean such recognition. It would be a way to recognize children and young people as part of civil society. Often they make up 40% of the population, but rarely are they acknowledged as a group with their own rights. Such documentation would also be a way to recognise them as citizens, in accordance with the UN Convention on the Right of the Child, which was signed about 20 years ago and has been ratified by all nation states but two. In addition it would be a way of increasing children's opportunities to talk directly with decision-makers and hold them accountable, as well as to tell them about their initiatives for survival and protection, for peace and reconciliation. Save the Children has seen that it makes a difference when children address decision-makers directly and also use the media.

Participatory Research and Change Making

If the purpose of the research is to grasp children's experiences and opinions as well as inspiring them for further action, the use of participatory methods will be more appropriate.

In this evaluation the "beneficiaries" —children, young people and adults— were trained in applying a set of participatory tools (see *Kit of Tools for Participatory Research and Evaluation for Children, Young People and Adults*); they analysed and assessed the material. They were included in the process and thus had ownership of the results, which motivated the children to improve the functioning of their clubs and develop peacebuilding initiatives. They gained new knowledge and recognition, empowerment and insight and took on new roles and identities. Some of these are:

Knowledge and Recognition

> Before participating in the research, I thought that only my district and community were affected by the conflict. Now I came to know that the whole nation is affected. … Participating in workshops brought positive changes and treatment of community people; they have started to listen to us (boy in Nepal) (Research Team in Nepal, 2007).

> Participating in this process improved our skills, knowledge on the tools and the subject, but also built our confidence in children's potentials and role in peacebuilding. Besides, we learnt about significant achievements made by children, e.g., to stop child marriages in the community (adults in Nepal) (*Adult's War and Young Generation's Peace*, 2009).

Feeling Empowered

> Through our activities we discovered that we can influence peacebuilding and peace-keeping in our country. We also learned that we are the ones who have to give their best in order to succeed and stick with our goals (primary school children in Bosnia-Herzegovina) (*Adult's War and Young Generation's Peace*, 2009).

Gaining Insight

> Our experiences of peacebuilding has given us new ideas, for example, more skills are needed for guidance and counselling in peacebuilding; we know that people do not have the same problems, but our differences are what disrupt our peace —so we should sit together and talk about them; we should seek advice from elders… We are all part of the peacebuilding process no matter our age or status (*I Painted Peace*, 2009).

Visions about Identity

> Our goal is to be agents of peace, and I think we will be able to make it (boy from Guatemala) (*I Painted Peace*, 2009).

Commitment to Peacebuilding

> We would like to be part of the process of building peace, to participate in different organisations, events that seek alternatives and actions that contribute to a different Guatemala (boy from Guatemala) (*Adult's War and Young Generation's Peace*, 2009).

Experiences from the Evaluation Revealed New Proposals

The children were asked: if you want to plan future activities, would you do the same thing or would you make any changes? Overall, they wanted to continue with their existing activities but with greater support: more funding and increased adult support. They wanted to reach out to more children, young people and adults, to new schools, communities and towns with more and different activities; they wanted more technical training, also on peacebuilding and a guarantee of follow-up to their activities; they recognised that they need to be well prepared to carry out their activities and to involve parents in the work that they do. They set up some concrete proposals such as: organising public tribunals on peacebuilding (Bosnia-Herzegovina); establishing a national Child Forum (Nepal); creating peace guidance and counselling centres, and supporting interaction between children and peace talk representatives, the government and rebel army (Uganda); more preparations for the International Peace Day, and to establish an International Year of Peace.

Children's proposals have implications for our future work and we, Save the Children, will follow up on this. In cooperation with the children, young people and adults participating in the evaluation we have prepared supporting material such as *A Handbook in Peacebuilding with and for Children and Young People; Ethical Guidelines*, including protection issues; a children's *Peace Album* as well as the *Kit of Tools for Participatory Research and Evaluation for Children, Young People and Adults,* as mentioned above.

We are also identifying issues for follow-up, one of them is to further explore children and young people's roles in peacebuilding, including peace processes. How should their voices be heard? Through written documents presented by adults and/or by their direct presence, such as the young people in Uganda are proposing? If they should join a peace process, in what moments and in which ways should they be involved and how should it be arranged? What do we see as the political impacts of children's participation and how are political decisions influencing their situation and peacebuilding initiatives?

Considering such issues is a way of recognising children and young people as a way of ensuring children's rights in peace processes and children and young people also as citizens in peace processes. It is a way of responding to their yearning for peace; and a way of supporting them in the task given to them, that of building a lasting peace.

References

ADULTS' WAR AND YOUNG GENERATION'S PEACE: CHILDREN'S PARTICIPATION IN ARMED CONFLICT, POST CONFLICT AND PEACE BUILDING. GLOBAL REPORT (2009): Save the Children Norway.

I PAINTED PEACE: HANDBOOK ON PEACE BUILDING WITH AND FOR CHILDREN AND YOUNG PEOPLE (2009): Save the Children.

RESEARCH TEAM IN BOSNIA-HERZEGOVINA (2006): "History from Srebrenica." *Save the Children Norway's Child Participation Web Group*. At: www.reddbarna.no/chp.

RESEARCH TEAM IN NEPAL (2007): "A Summary Report of National Capacity Building Workshop in Nepal." *Save the Children Norway in Nepal*.

RESEARCH TEAM IN UGANDA (2008): "Stories of Most Significant Changes, Girls' Stories of Change." Internal note. *Save the Children in Uganda*.

See also Save the Children Norway's website on children's participation (www.reddbarna.no/chp) and sub-areas:

— The thematic evaluation on children's participation in armed conflict, post conflict and peacebuilding (http://www.reddbarna.no/default.asp?V_ ITEM_ ID=11746).

— publications (http://www.reddbarna.no/default.asp?V_ITEM_ID=19028).

Globalization and Environmental Challenges:
Security in the 21st Century

Three Cosmovisions: Oriental, Indigenous and Occidental Thinking on Peace

Úrsula Oswald Spring

National University of Mexico, CRIM

Introduction

Religions have played a crucial role in the history of civilizations and are still doing so to surmount dangerous threats such as wars, terrorism and global injustice. However, the expansion of West European culture in the world and its imposition on non-European cultural behaviours transformed the pluralistic nature of human cultures and thinking into a monolithic Eurocentric and later Occidental imposition, due to global ideological drivers (Preiswerk, 1984; Syamsuddin, 2005), dominant military security thinking, conquest and an economic globalization based on free-market ideology. Potential clashes among civilizations could emerge, e.g. between Islam and the West and between Western civil rights fundamentalism and Chinese socialists. But there is also a new process of Eastern spirituality renewing Western society and its spiritual loss. These processes are visible in yoga and meditation groups, Buddhist churches and socialization of Eastern values such as *ahimsa*, *satyagraha* and self-discipline and control. The economic achievements in China and India reflected in a substantial reduction of poverty are other indicators of different values providing hope for a different globalization with a human face.

India's Nonviolence

Peace in Hinduism[1] is related to religious beliefs. During the past 5,000 years, it grew in syncretism creating numerous sects, integrating

---

[1] Hinduism is the world's third largest religion, representing 13% of the world's population. The "Veda —the liturgy and interpretation of the sacrifice— and Upan-

dissidents, new gods and different religious practices. Within the doctrine of "*karma*" the individual reaps the results of his actions through
different lives. The liberation from suffering and the compulsion of re-
birth is attainable through the elimination of passions, the comprehen-
sion and respect of the other and the union with god. Hinduism has
no single founder or central religious organization and this syncretism
stresses tolerance and mutual co-existence with permanent renovation.
The core element of violence, linked to exclusive doctrines, is absent.
Security is interlinked with the safety of authorities, who guarantee the
security of the people. Hinduism anchored social differences to birth
through the caste system and created conflicts for resource appropria-
tion and numerous poor people.

Jainism conciliates the inner world with freedom, transmigration
and relativism as spiritual and moral guiding principles. God is not crea-
tor and protector, but living in society with nonviolence (*ahimsa*), truth
(*satya*), non-stealing (*achaurya*), celibacy (*brahmacharya*) and non-pos-
sessiveness (*aparigraha*), which opens an infinite potential in humans in
perception, knowledge, power and bliss for freedom and spiritual joy
of soul. Jainians propose a perfect system of democracy and an emphasis on equality of opportunities to achieve freedom and spiritual
perfection. Their ethic practises signifies religious tolerance, moral purity, spiritual contentment and harmony among self, others and the environment through perception, knowledge and conduct (Majumdar,
1968; Shree Chand Rampuria, 1947). Jainism recognizes the natural
phenomena as symbioses of mutual interdependence, which has created the bases for modern ecology and nonviolence or "*ahimsa*" (Radhakrishnan, 1952; Radhakrishnan and Moore, 1957; Radhakrishnan
and Muirhead, 1958).

Buddhism[2] developed a "way of the middle" (*Bodh-Gaya*) through
meditation. Buddha transmitted his maxims within monks (*bhikkhu*),
nuns (*bhikkhuni*), and male (*Upasaka*) and female laypersons (*Up-
asika*). His teachings were based on tolerance for other religions,
races, social groups and a peaceful life together. Buddha did not
recognize a god, a soul, a caste or any other discrimination against
humans and nature. He taught with his life how to find freedom and
peace on earth.

---

ishad," which contain the Brahman doctrine, are sacred scriptures. Later theistic elements were developed in the *Bhagavad-Gita*.

  [2] As a 35 year old prince, Siddhartha Gautama (563-483 B.C.) was illuminated and
renamed "Buddha": the illuminated.

Mohandas K. Gandhi's thinking was deeply influenced by these Indian religious and moral traditions. By learning through mistakes he understood that people are resistant to change and he worked on himself to find the truth (*satya*). The concept of *ahimsa* or active non-resistance, represented by the little voice inside guiding oneself to do the right things, is at the same time the guiding force for the eternal universal forces. His exercises with truth challenged his personal life, but also the British colonial forces (Gandhi, 1982 and 1996). *Ahimsa* offered also a new model of conflict resolution and nonviolent struggle for independence.

Chinese Thinking on Peace

Kongfuzi (551-479 BCE), born as a poor villager, consolidated political theories and institutions and created a value system for living in peace within an organized society. Human behaviour depends on five virtues: humanism, uprightness, morals, wisdom and sincerity as well as three social obligations: loyalty, respect for parents and ancestors, and courtesy substituting violence, conquest and exploitation.

Lao Tse (around the 6th century BCE) developed the "*tao*" (way), representing the origin of the world order and the knowledge for guiding society through moral behaviour by peaceful means. "*Ren*" (humanity, love for others) and learning during life represents the second pillar of his metaphysics. His ideal was a small country where the king knew his people who lived in small peasant communities, away from power and ambitions (Waley, 1953: 102). He promoted the abolition of army and war, not precisely for moral reasons, but because any conquest was always insignificant compared with the unlimited internal resources of a person.

General Tzun Tzu integrated social concerns in his book *The Art of War*. He postulated that "the supreme art of war is to subject the enemy without fighting" (6th century BCE, 2000). Moral thinking may become concrete only through congruent acting. The common well-being among subjects and rulers is mutually dependant and the political stability favoured scientific and cultural progress that has influenced the Occident and America (García, 1988). In peace terms, the small countries learnt through *shih-ta* to serve the big one and to find in this dependency protection and security. There, love and integration with nature spread over all of Asia and is one of the core principles of harmony with other human beings and with the environment.

Latin America's Search for Peace

Two powerful empires emerged during the 14ᵗʰ century in Mexico and Peru (Pizarro, 1978): the Aztec and the Inca. The key idea of indigenous religions was *equilibrium*. The intimate relationship between caring for and fearing nature established a harmony between humans, nature and divinities. Values of cooperation, dignity, freedom, love, solidarity, respect and peace were taught, together with a hierarchical system of power. Military force, science and technology improved livelihoods and were able to maintain a growing population in very different and difficult ecosystems. Crime, mismanagement of communal land and other behaviours against the social code had to be confessed. Sacrifices of animals and, in severe cases, of humans were offered for re-establishing the harmony between divinities, humans and nature. Pestilence, earthquakes, volcano eruptions, famine and defeat were understood as a failure in the observation of the ceremonies, giving priests a parallel power to the emperor. People were educated to respect this intimate relationship, together with respect for the political system.

Within their cosmogonist genesis of the Earth in both empires, humans established a system of communication with divinities creating a dynamic process of control, obedience and negotiation to achieve equilibrium. The priests and military induced fear and death in the subjugated regions. The hierarchical rule of power and the exploitation through tributes of large parts of the empire introduced suffering among the subjugated people, reducing their capacity for preventive peacebuilding and conflict resolution, but also developed science, astronomy, medicine, urbanization and technologies of irrigation.

Spain and Portugal conquered these empires and the Catholic Church imposed an ideological control that fostered economic underdevelopment and subordination to European power interests. Natural resources —food, gold, silver, minerals, medicinal plants and later, oil and gas— were looted. Forced labour and new diseases decimated the indigenous population. To replace the native work force in mines and agriculture, the colonial powers brought African slaves to the Americas. This violent displacement created social fragmentation in Africa and America. Global European interests were imposed by authoritarian colonial, religious and military regimes, reinforced by a rape capitalism and occidental patriarchal dominance. After independence struggles and revolutions, most Latin America countries suffered from the U.S. neo-imperial interests, based on the Monroe Doctrine.

Conquest, post-colonial exploitation and foreign interventions created in Latin-America a highly stratified social structure, dependency and a few political, military, religious and economic elites. The accumulation of capital in only a few hands institutionalized the impoverishment of majorities, limited the creation of a middle class and created permanent tensions, rebellions, revolutions, guerrillas and military coups (Valenzuela, 1991). Therefore, Latin-America is the region with the highest income gap and, after two centuries of independence, with a dramatic situation of poverty in almost half of the population as well as the a rapid growth of urban slums.

Peace and violence characterizes the history of the subcontinent, where local and regional violence created empires with high cultural achievements (Inca, Maya and Aztec). Science, technology and food innovations spread from the subcontinent globally, and European colonization and independence reinforced the highly stratified society. However, the history of Latin-American invasions, exploitation, ethnocide and neo-colonial threats resulted in the legal principle of non-intervention in the United Nations Charter. Many Latin-American states proposed mechanisms for conflict resolution within regional bodies prior to involving the UN Security Council, such as the Organization of American States. As neighbours of the new superpower, the subcontinent tried to protect the rest of the world from interventions it had experienced and which were justified with the Monroe Doctrine (1823).

Greek, Roman and Christian Thinking on Peace

In Europe, peace thinking emerged from early Greeks' *"eirene"* and Roman concepts of democracy, citizens' rights and *Pax Romana* and was linked with internal security, well-being and prosperity. It mediated between private and public goods and among citizens and states. Socrates' dialectical method transformed human beings into moral ones through education. Plato's "transcendental idealism" sought eternal "forms." In the Platonic tradition, peace is an act of will and a superior value, justifying all means to attain it. Aristotle's *"eirene"* understood virtue between two vices, cowardice and rashness, and peace as a process between different vices and virtues.

The Roman Empire consolidated its civilization with *"Pax Romana"* and offered the "king's peace" once the ruled submitted to the will of the ruler. *"Pax Augusta"* was a desideratum of thinkers and writers (Cicero, Livi, Virgil), determining that there is no just war and peace is the highest value for humans. Augustine's Neo-Platonism facilitated the acceptance of the Christian doctrine. The purification of the soul by self-control, moral education and submission to the "divine will" consolidated the hierarchical male-dominated structure of the church with a power beyond the Roman Empire ("*pax Augustana*"). Saint Thomas Aquinas linked peace with joy (*gaudium*) and related it to love (*caritas*). His inner peace represented the rule of God on the world and in the soul, similar to oriental beliefs. These cross-cultural connections linked physical acts with intentional spirituality for peaceful behaviour.

Nevertheless, the Christian church persecuted other religions, organized Crusades and genocides and killed millions through the inquisition. Their peace understanding reinforced the military logic of "an eye for an eye" pragmatism. Peace was understood in its negative sense as the "absence of war." With the adoption of non-intervention into the internal affairs of established states (Westphalia Peace, 1648), a legal system emerged, able to secure goods beyond military protection: the paradigm of the legal protection of private property (Richards, 2000). The "state of law" from ancient Greece offered society the peaceful use of conquered goods and territories and a system of legal inheritance along the patrilineal line.

Thus, a second paradigm against peace was consolidated: *patriarchy*.[3] Its mythological origin goes back to the irrigation societies and incipient social differentiation. The Christian church, Islam and Judaism based their ideological control of power on gender and social classes' discrimination, subjection and exploitation. The division of labour resulted in a division of power legitimizing the exercise of power, war and violence, until the American Declaration of Independence (1776) and the French Revolution (1789) reclaimed sovereignty for the people. Independence movements in prosperous colonies combined with the disintegration of great empires (e.g. Napoleonic, Ottoman, Austro-Hungarian, etc.) consolidated capitalism with wealth in metropolitan powers and increased poverty in colonized countries, but never questioned the patriarchal power exercise.

During the Enlightenment, Grotius, Montesquieu, Rousseau and Kant developed a cooperative paradigm to challenge the bellicose pragmatism of Machiavelli and Hobbes. Liberal thinkers (Locke, Hume) questioned hegemonic interests, but could not avoid wars, torture, concentration camps, genocide and the concentration of wealth. They

---

[3] A mythological justification emerged when the male half-god Zeus controlled lightening and thunder and took power over earth and the sky, justifying a hierarchical, violent and patriarchal dominance.

established the legal bases for an idealist world based on human rights and personal responsibility within the capitalist system. Kant proposed in his "eternal peace," peace equality for all citizens, and a republican constitution with democratic and representative organs. Within a "League of Nations," the danger of wars should be reduced and the rights of a world citizen is granted by the hospitality principle. The difference between morale and policy made him transfer to the people the adoption of laws for controlling violence of powerful monarchs and statesmen.

Industrialization pushed peasants off their land, and the new social class configuration (Marx and Engels, 1945) caused insecurities for workers through an intensive process of exploitation of their work force. Men were transformed into breadwinners and women into housewives. Marx denounced the inhuman reality of British capitalism. Together with Engels (1902) he created the First International, a movement for economic and intellectual liberation through a united struggle of the working classes. Intellectuals and workers fought together for securing new rights and social struggles increased. In her humanitarian Marxism, Rosa Luxemburg stressed the need for democracy. She believed that only through revolutionary mass action of the proletariat was it possible to achieve international socialism and peace. A permanent tension remained and Keynes' (1935) welfare state provided temporary support for needy citizens, when economic circumstances avoided caring for them.

Neoliberalism substituted this paradigm, arguing that benefits will automatically trickle-down from the free-market. The outcome is a regressive globalization process with a relatively wealthy northern and a poor southern society, where only elites can link up to the modern system of consumerism. In the early 21st century, more than three billion human beings live in poverty, similar to the situation in the 18th century when rape capitalism (McGregor, 1984) created an exploited and peace-less society.

In the international arena and after five centuries of colonialism and two World Wars, the founding members of the United Nations agreed in its Charter on the goal "to maintain international peace and security… to take effective collective measures for the prevention and removal of threats to peace, and for the suppression of acts of aggression or other breaches of the peace" (UN Charter, Preamble). Nevertheless, since 1945, the UN was unable to promote an era of development and well-being for the whole world, due to the longstanding Cold War. Scientific and technological progress promoted a globalized world, but with improvement only for minorities.

In terms of conceptual development, the idea of peace changed from a static no-war and negative peace to a more dynamic process of enabling social change with sustainability, equity and equality in terms of freedom from want and freedom from fear. In the South, the basic idea of Freire's *Pedagogy of the Oppressed* (1998) admitted that the marginalized have been deprived of their voices and therefore, denied their role as active co-creators of culture and the future. By changing this process, the marginalized could themselves transform the situation of oppression into cultural liberation.

Comparison of the Thinking on Peace in Diverse Traditions

In theoretical terms, Confucius, Lao Tse and Tzun Tzu could somewhere stand for the ideal-types of three traditions. Confucius represents the oriental rationalist or pragmatist, similar to Grotius. Lao Tse is more representative of an Eastern idealism or radicalism. Similar to Kant, he tried, through laws and agreements with smaller countries, to establish peaceful co-existence and mutual interdependence. Finally, Tzun Tzu's thinking on war could be initially compared with Hobbes and classified as realism. However, his vision to avoid wars at any cost and his interpretation of armed struggle as a primary defeat also makes him a pragmatist. While this comparison of Chinese and Occidental philosophical and political thinking and praxis is perhaps overdrawn, it allows one to see that 2000 years earlier, Eastern cultures have developed philosophical concepts which were taken up again in the Occident from the 16th century AD onwards. The Chinese integration of humankind and nature and their educational processes converted all three masters into forerunners of their societies, such that they were able to overcome the evolutionary constraints of rational or idealistic cultures of peace that have existed in other cultures and religions.

Colonial conquest, globalization and exclusion brought both challenges to and opportunities for peacebuilding for philosophy, religions, UN institutions, governments, social movements and individuals. At the same time, the present stage of world development and globalization uses the accumulation of knowledge to concentrate wealth in a few hands, contributing to new insecurities, violence, environmental destruction and also terrorism. Gaps in internal wealth and extreme exploitation often foster opposition by the excluded such that even those in power are affected. Thus, a new peace thinking is emerging, which goes beyond the regressive globalization paradigm.

Finally, new threats linked to global and climate changes are affecting both hemispheres, although more threatening to the South, and preventive behaviour and remediation requires global cooperation for mitigation and adaptation, affecting present productive processes and scientific-technological development. In addition, as world society is closely linked, peace efforts, violence or war in one part of the world often systemically affects wider regions (see: the effects of the wars in Afghanistan and Iraq on increased terrorism; the links of forced migration; or the global learning process from Gandhi's *ahimsa*).

In synthesis, the tensions among individual responsibility, free-market ideology and socio-political domination have created social tensions and a geographical division of the world into North and South. The social stratification of rich and poor inside countries and between them has increased social vulnerability and marginalization that have been aggravated by racial, ethnic and gender discrimination. These things have created four basic contradictions: physical violence and terrorism; structural violence and social inequity; gender violence and inequality and environmental threats. These four oppositions simultaneously open up the following challenges for peaceful behaviour: 1) cooperation with solidarity and equality vs. isolationism and elite behaviour; 2) cultural diversity and equity vs. economic monopoly; 3) nonviolent peacebuilding or *ahimsa* vs. *himsa* and physical violence; and 4) spirituality and integration with nature vs. secularity and global environmental changes.

The world's population dreams of stability and equal livelihoods, a green and healthy world where humans live in harmony and cooperate to mitigate the threats posed by global environmental change and a social organization able to prevent physical and natural threats. A world with increasingly scarce and polluted resources requires new models of dialogue, negotiation and sharing. Tolerance, mutual understanding, respect for diversity, co-existence and cooperation among world civilizations and development strategies based on equality create ethical and practical concerns, where different traditions contribute to the wisdom of peaceful co-existence and peacebuilding for nonviolent conflict resolution and global human progress without discrimination and violence.

References

ENGELS, Friedrich (1902): *The Origin of the Familiy, Private Propety and the State*. University Press of Chicago, Chicago.
FREIRE, Paulo (1998): *The Pedagogy of the Oppressed*. Continuum, New York.

GANDHI, Mohandas K. (1982): *An Autobiography: The Story of My Experiments with Truth*. Penguin Books, London.
— (1996): *Non-violence in Peace and War*. Penguin Books, London.
GARCÍA, Víctor (1988): *La Sabiduría Oriental: Taoismo, Budismo, Confucianismo*. Ed. Cincel Kapelusz, Bogotá.
HUNTINGTON, Samuel P. (1996): *The Clash of Civilizations and the Remaking of World Order*. Simon & Schuster, New York.
KEYNES, John Maynard (1935): *The General Theory of Employment, Interest and Money*. King's College, Cambridge.
MCGREGOR, Douglas (1984): *Mando y Motivación*. Diana, México.
MAJUMDAR, Ramesh Chandra (ed.) (1951, 1968): *The History and Culture of the Indian People*, Vol 2. G. Allen, London & Unwin, Bombay.
MARX, Karl and Friedrich ENGELS (1844-1845, 1945): *The Holy Family* and *The Condition of Working Class*. Lawrence & Wishart, London.
PIZARRO, Francisco (1541, 1978): *Historia del Perú*. Universidad Católica, Lima.
PREISWERK, Roy A. (1984): *À contre-courants. L'enjeu des relations interculturelles*. Ed. d' en bas, Lausanne.
RADHAKRISHNAN, Sarvepalli (ed.) (1952): *History of Philosphy: Eastern and Western*. Macmillan, New York.
— and Charles A. MOORE (ed.) (1957): *Contemporary Indian Philosophy*. Princeton University Press, Princeton.
— and John H. MUIRHEAD (1958): *Indian Philosophy*. Macmillan, New York.
RICHARDS, Howard (2000): *Understanding the Global Economy*. Maadhyam Book Services, New Delhi.
SHREE, Chand Rampuria (1947): *The Cult of Ahimsa: A Jain View-Point*. Sri Jain Setamber Terapanthi Mahasabha, Calcutta.
SYAMSUDDIN, Din (2005): "The Role of Religions in Promoting Intercultural Understanding Towards Sustainable Peace." Paper presented at the Conference on Interfaith Cooperation for Peace (22 June). United Nations Headquarters, New York.
TZUN TZU (2000): *El Arte de la Guerra*. Ed. Gestión, Barcelona.
VALENZUELA, María Elena (1991): "Women under Dictatorship and Military Regime: The Case of Chile." Ed. Elise BOULDING; Clovis BRIGAGAO and Kevin CLEMENTS: *Peace Culture and Society. Transnational Research and Dialogue*. Westview, Boulder, 229-240.
WALEY, Arthur (1953): *Three Ways of Thought in Ancient China*. Travel Sciences' Longitude, Ford Lauderdale.

Reconceptualizing Security in the 21st Century: The End of the Cold War, Globalization and Global Environmental Change in the Anthropocene

Hans Günter Brauch[1]

Introductory Remark

The *reconceptualization of security in the 21st century* has gradually evolved since the end of the East-West conflict (1989-1991) and has been influenced by processes of globalization and global environmental change.[2]

This chapter: (1) introduces the security concept, (2) discusses the relationship between context, concept and action, (3) examines the links between contextual change and conceptual innovation, (4) reviews drivers and centres of conceptual innovation and (5) the discussions on the security concept in history, the social sciences, philosophy and in international law as well as (6) the debate within the UN on regional security focusing on conceptual history and conceptual mapping. In conclusion, the article (7) discusses the relevance of conceptual mapping for the analysis of security in the early 21st century.

---

[1] This chapter is based on a text in Turkish, "Güvenliğin Yeniden Kavramsallaştırılması: Bariş, Güvenlik, Kalkinma ve Çevre Kavramsal Dörtlüsü" (Brauch 2008e), which relies on two chapters by Brauch (2008, 2008a), where a detailed research bibliography is available.

[2] This chapter outlines the scientific context for a *Security Handbook for the Anthropocene* that bring together about 275 peer reviewed book chapters written by about 300 authors from more than 80 countries from all parts of the world and many disciplines in an effort to conceptually map the rethinking on security in the early 21st century. This handbook is presented in detail at: http://www.afes-press-books.de/html/hexagon.htm and http://www.springer.com/series/8090.

The Concept of Security

Security is a key *concept* in the social sciences that refers to frameworks and dimensions and applies to individuals, issue areas, societal conventions and changing historical conditions and circumstances. The security concept is closely related to peace and is a value and goal of the activities of nation states and supra- and sub-state actors that require "extraordinary measures." Security has been used to legitimize major public spending. As an individual or societal political value, security has no independent meaning and is always related to a context and a specific individual or societal value system and its realization.

In the Western tradition, the term "security" was coined by Cicero and Lucretius as *securitas*, referring initially to a philosophical and psychological status of mind, and it was used since the 1st century as a key political concept in the context of "Pax Romana." But there is another origin, starting with Thomas Hobbes (1651), where ""security" became associated with the genesis of the authoritarian "super state" —Hobbes' *Leviathan*— committed to the prevention of civil war" (Arends, 2008: 263), that was influenced by Thucydides. Arends (2008: 263) argues that "the contemporary concept of 'security' therefore proves to be a 'chimeric' combination of a) the ancient Athenians' intention to prevent the destruction of their empire, b) the religious connotations of Roman *securitas*, and c) the Hobbesian intention to prevent civil war."

The modern security concept evolved since the 17th century with the dynastic state when internal security was distinguished from external security that became a key concept of foreign and military policy and of international law. Internal security was stressed by Hobbes and Pufendorf as the main task of the sovereign for the people. In the American constitution safety is linked to liberty. During the French Revolution the declaration of citizens' rights declared security as one of its four basic human rights. For Wilhelm von Humboldt, the state became a major actor to guarantee internal and external security while Fichte stressed the concept of mutuality where the state, as the granter of security, and the citizen interact. Influenced by Kant, Humboldt, and Fichte the concepts of the "*Rechtsstaat*" (a legally based and constituted state) and "*Rechtssicherheit*" (the legal predictability of the state) became key features of the thinking on security in the early 19th century (Conze, 1984).

Influenced by Kant's second definitive article in his *Eternal Peace* (1795), Woodrow Wilson based the security concept of the League of Nations (1919) on "collective security." This was first contained in its Covenant and it was developed further in the UN Charter (1945). But during the interwar period (1919-1939), the security concept was hardly used, while references to defence, national survival, national interests and sovereignty or power (Carr, 1939) prevailed.

The concept of "social security" gradually evolved in the 19th and 20th centuries as a key goal to advance the security of citizens. The "social security" concept became a *terminus technicus* during F.D. Roosevelt's New Deal when he addressed (on 8 June 1934) advancing the security of citizens as a key goal of his administration: "the security of the home, the security of the livelihood, and the security of the social insurance." This goal is contained in the *Atlantic Charter* of 1941 as "securing, for all, improved labour standards, economic advancement and social security" (Brauch, 2008: 34). In 1948, social security became a key human right in Article 22 of the General Declaration on Human Rights.

The "national security" concept emerged during World War II in the United States "to explain America's relationship to the rest of the world" (Yergin, 1977: 193). "National security" became a key post-war concept with the evolution of the American security system (Czempiel, 1966) or the national security state (Yergin, 1977). This concept was used to legitimize the major shift in the mindset between the interwar and post-war years from a fundamental criticism of military armaments during the 1930s to support of an unprecedented military and arms build-up and militarization of the prevailing mindset of the foreign policy elites. While the Democratic US Presidents (Roosevelt, Truman, Kennedy, Johnson) pleaded for a big state to deal with both security tasks, the Republicans in the 1940s first opposed both security agendas. At the end of the Cold War and in the post-Cold War period, US Republican presidents (Reagan, G. Bush, G.W. Bush) maintained and strengthened the big security apparatus with a strong industrial and economic base, a powerful intelligence and police force.

As a societal value (Kaufmann, 1970, 1973) security is used in relation to protection, lack of risks, certainty, reliability, trust and confidence, predictability in contrast with danger, risk, disorder and fear. As a social-scientific concept, "*security* is ambiguous and elastic in its meaning" (Art, 1993: 821). Arnold Wolfers (1952, 1962: 150) pointed to two sides of the security concept: "Security, in an *objective* sense, measures the absence of threats to acquired values, in a *subjective* sense, the absence of fear that such values will be attacked." For Art (1993: 820-822) its subjective aspect implies: "to feel free from threats, anxiety or danger. Security is therefore a state of the mind in which an individual … feels safe from harm [done] by others." Due to the anarchic nature of international relations, "a concern for survival breeds a preoccupation for security." For a state to feel secure requires "either that it can dissuade others from attacking it or that it can successfully defend itself if attacked." Thus, security demands sufficient military power but also many "non-military elements ... to generate effective military power." Art (1993: 821) noted a widening of security that involves "protection of the environment from irreversible degradation by combating among other things, acid rain, desertification, forest destruction, ozone pollution, and global warming. ... Environmental security has impelled states to find cooperative rather than competitive solutions."

For the constructivists, security is *intersubjective*, referring to "what actors make of it" (Wendt, 1992, 1999). Thus, security depends on a normative core that cannot simply be taken for granted. Political constructions of security have real world effects, because they guide the action of policymakers, thereby exerting constitutive effects on political order (Wæver, 2008; Baylis 2008; Hintermeier 2008).

For Wæver (1995, 1997, 2008, 2008ᵃ), security is the result of a speech act (*"securitization"*), according to which an issue is treated as: "an existential threat to a valued referent object" to allow "urgent and exceptional measures to deal with the threat." Thus, the "securitizing actor" points "to an existential threat" and thereby legitimizes "extraordinary measures" (Wæver 2008: 582). With the end of the Cold War, not only the scope of "*securitization*" has changed, but also the referent object has shifted from a sole "national" to also a "human-centred" security concept, both within the UN system (UNDP, 1994; 2008), and in the academic security community.

Since the late 1970s, an expanded security concept has been discussed in academia (Krell, 1981; Buzan, 1983; Møller, 2001, 2003). In the policy debate, the "security concept" has gradually widened since the late 1980s.[3] Ullman (1983), Mathews (1989) and Myers (1989, 1994) put environmental concerns on the US national security agenda. Since the early 1990s, many European governments adopted an extended security concept. Based thereon, Buzan, Wæver and de Wilde (1998) have distinguished between the *wideners*,[4] which include an economic[5] and environmental dimension, and the *traditionalists*, focus-

---

[3] See Krell, 1981; Wæver, Lemaitre and Tromer, 1989; Buzan, Wæver and de Wilde, 1995, 1998; Albrecht and Brauch, 2008.
[4] Proponents of a widened security concept are: Ullman, 1983; Jahn, Lemaitre and Wæver, 1987; Nye and Lynn-Jones, 1988; Mathews, 1989, 1991, 1992, 1997; N. Brown, 1989, 2001; Nye, 1989; Haftendorn, 1991; Buzan, 1983, 1987, 1991, 1997; Tickner, 1992.
[5] Economic security issues were discussed by Gilpin, 1981; Luciani, 1989; Crawford, 1993, 1995; Gowa, 1994; Mansfield, 1994.

ing on the primacy of a narrow military security concept (Walt, 1991; Chipman, 1992; Gray, 1992, 1994; Dorff, 1994).

The Copenhagen School (Buzan and Wæver, 1997; Wæver, 1997; Buzan et al., 1998), distinguished five dimensions (*widening*: military, political, economic, societal and environmental) and five referent objects ("whose security?"), or levels of interaction or analysis (*deepening*: international, regional, national, domestic groups, individual). But they did not review the *sectorialization* of security from the perspective of *national* (international, regional) and *human security* (Table 1).

They also distinguished five levels of analysis of: *international systems, international subsystems, units, subunits* and *individuals*. Others referred to five vertical levels (Møller, 2003) of security analysis: a) global or planetary (Steinbruner, 2000), b) regional (Mouritzen, 1997; Buzan and Wæver, 2003), c) national (Tickner, 1995), d) societal (Møller, 2003) and e) human security (UNDP, 1994; Newman, 2001; CHS, 2003). Some suggested expanding the human security discourse to the environmental dimension, especially to interactions between the individual and humankind as the cause and victim of global environmental change (Bogardi/Brauch, 2005; Brauch, 2003, 2005, 2005ª, 2008ᵈ).

Table 1

Vertical levels and horizontal dimensions of security in North and South

Security dimension ⇒ Level of interaction ⇓ (referent objects)	Military	Political	Economic	Environmental ↓	Societal
Human →				Social, energy, food, health, livelihood threats, challenges and risks may pose a *survival dilemma* in areas with high vulnerability	
Village/Community/Society				↓↑	
National	"Security dilemma of competing states" (*National Security Concept*)			"Securing energy, food, health, livelihood etc." (*Human Security Concept*) combining all levels of analysis & interaction	
International/Regional				↓↑	
Global/Planetary →					

"Security in an objective sense" refers to specific *security dangers* —i.e. to "threats, challenges, vulnerabilities and risks" (Brauch, 2005)— to specific *security dimensions* and *referent objectives* (international, national, human) as well as *sectors* (social, energy, food, water), while "security in a subjective sense" refers to *security concerns* that are expressed by government officials (civil servants, military officers), media representatives, scientists or "the people" in a speech act or in written statements by those who securitize "dangers" as security "concerns" being existential for the survival of the referent object and that require and legitimize extraordinary measures and means to face and cope with these dangers and concerns. Thus, *security concepts* have always been the product of orally articulated or written statements by those who use them as tools to analyse, interpret and assess past actions or to request or legitimize present or future activities in meeting specific security dangers.

The *perception* of security threats, challenges, vulnerabilities and risks depends on the worldviews or traditions of the analyst and on the mindset of policy-makers. The English School (Bull, 1977; Wight, 1991) distinguished three approaches to security where the *realist* (e.g. Thucydides, Machiavelli, Hobbes, Morgenthau) points to the interests and power of his own state, while the *rationalist* or *pragmatist* (Grotius, [1625] 1975) points to an international society where the subjects are states as the decisive units that by cooperation can build institutions, norms, diplomacy and international law, and thus build "a society of states, an international society." The *idealist* (e.g. Kant, [1795] 1965, 1992) believes that the "ultimate solutions only exist when we get the states and their state system off the scene and allow for the unfolding of dynamics based on individuals and a community of mankind, world society (where the subjects in contrast to international society are individuals, not states)" (Brauch 2008[a]: 78).

These three European traditions stand for three "ideal type" approaches to international relations and security that also exist in non-Western cultures and philosophies (Oswald, 2008). Booth (1979, 1987: 39-66) argued that old mindsets often have distorted the assessment of new challenges, and that they "freeze international relations into crude images, portray its processes as mechanistic responses of power and characterize other nations as stereotypes" (1987: 44). The perception of security is a key concept of: a) *war, military, strategic* or *security studies* from a Hobbesian perspective and b) *peace and conflict research* from a Grotian or Kantian view that has focused on war prevention or positive peace (Albrecht and Brauch, 2008).

Since the 1990s, in European security debates an "extended" security concept has been used by governments and in scientific debates. Møller (2001, 2003) distinguished a "national" and three expanded security concepts of "societal, human, and environmental security." Oswald (2001, 2007, 2009) introduced a combined "human, gender and environmental" (HUGE) security concept (Table 2).

Table 2

Expanded concepts of security (Møller, 2001, 2003; Oswald, 2001)

Concepts of security	Reference object (security of whom?)	Value at risk (security of what?)	Source(s) of threat (security from whom/ what?)
National security [political, military dimension]	The state	Sovereignty, territorial integrity	Other states, terrorism (sub-state actors)
Societal security [dimension]	Nations, societal groups	National unity, identity	(States) Nations, migrants, alien cultures
Human security	Individuals humankind	Survival, quality of life	State, globalization, GEC, nature, terrorism
Environmental security [dimension]	Ecosystem	Sustainability	Humankind
Gender security	Gender relations, indigenous people, minorities	Equality, identity, solidarity	Patriarchy, totalitarian institutions (governments, religions, elites, culture), intolerance

Within the UN, NATO and the EU, different security concepts co-exist: a state-centred political and military concept and an extended security concept with economic, societal, and environmental dimensions. A widening and deepening of the security concept prevailed in OECD countries, while some countries adhered to a narrow national security concept that emphasizes the military dimension (Aydin, 2003; Selim, 2003; Kam, 2008).

Although, since the 19th century the key "actor" has been the state, it has not necessarily been a major "referent object" of security which is often referred to as "the people" or "our people," whose very survival is at stake. A major debate (Wiberg, 1987: 340, 1988; Walker, 1990, 1993; Shaw, 1994) has evolved since the late 1980s whether the state as the key referent object ("national security") should be extended to the people (individuals and humankind as "human security"). Walker (1988) pointed to the complexity of a non-state centred redefinition of security towards "individual" or "global peoples" security while Buzan (1991) following Waltz's (1959, 2001) man, state and war, distinguished between the international, state and individual levels of analysis and the inherent tension among the latter two, but he remained critical of the human security approach (Buzan, 2004).

From 1947 to 1989, national and military security issues became a matter of means (armaments), instruments (intelligence) and strategies (deterrence). Whether a threat, challenge, vulnerability or risk becomes an "objective security danger" or a "subjective security concern" also depends on the political context. Müller (2002: 369) argued that the traditional understanding of security "as the absence of existential threats to the state emerging from another state" (Baldwin, 1995; Betts, 1997; Gray, 1992; Kolodziej, 2005; Prins, 1998; Walt, 1991) was challenged both with regard to the key subject (the state), and carrier of security needs, and its exclusive focus on the "physical —or political— dimension of security of territorial entities" that are behind the suggestions for a horizontal and vertical (Suhrke, 1999; Klare, 1994, 1996; Klare and Thomas, 1991, 1994, 1998) widening and deepening of the security concept. The meaning of security was also interpreted as a reaction to globalization (Cha, 2000; Mesjasz, 2003). Müller (2002: 369) opted for a "conventional understanding of security: security between states, and related mainly to the organized instruments for applying force —the military in the first instance (Betts 1997; Buzan 1987)".

The security concept also combines its domestic roots and politics (lobbies, strategic doctrines) with international affairs (Gourevitch, 2002: 315). Security is examined for security "communities" (Deutsch, 1957; Herrmann, 2002: 131-132), "regimes" (Rittberger and Mayer, 1993), "cultures" (Katzenstein, 1996) or "complexes" (Kostecki, 1996) and as a "security dilemma" (Herz, 1959).

New methodological approaches and inter-paradigm debates relevant for security have emerged:

a. prevailing *traditional* methodological approaches (e.g. geopolitics, English School);

b. *critical security studies* (Klein, 1994; Jones,1999; Ralph, 2001);
c. *constructivist* and *deconstructivist* approaches.[6]

While the "collective" security system (Wolfrum, 1995) is the basis of the UN Charter, since the 1980s, different cooperative security concepts have emerged from a *traditional* approach: a) *common security* (Palme, 1982; Väyrynen, 1985; Butfoy, 1997); b) *mutual security* (McGwire, 1988; Smoke and Kortunov, 1991); c) *cooperative security* (Carter et al., 1992; Nolan, 1994; Zartman and Kremenuk, 1995; Carter and Perry, 1999; Steinbruner, 2000; Cohen and Mihalka, 2001); d) *security partnership*; a *"comprehensive"* (Westing, 1986, 1989) or *"equal"* (NATO, 1999) security.

With regard to its "spatial" context, the classical goals of security policy to defend national sovereignty, in terms of its territory, people, and system of rule has also been changing due to the trends of globalization and regional integration. In Europe, close economic interdependence, sometimes competing trans-Atlantic and European political goals, but also changes in technology have replaced these classical security goals. Since the 1990s two processes (Brauch, 2001: 109-110) have co-existed:

— A process of *globalization* in finance, production and trade, in information and media, resulted in a *deborderization* of exchanges for people, capital and goods (e.g. within the EU among its member states) and a *deterritorialization* of international relations.

— A process of *territorial disintegration* and *fragmentation* of multi-ethnic states combined with a *reborderization* of space along ethnic and religious lines and disputes on territorial control of areas.

In the discourses on territory (Brauch, 2008[c]), two schools coexist: a) on *geopolitique* and *critical geopolitics* (Amineh and Grin, 2003) and b) on *globalization* (Mesjasz, 2003). In some countries in the North, national security has been supplemented with *alliance security*, while in the South, security has often remained nation-oriented with the strong role of military thinking for the security and political elites.

In the security discourses, different concepts for security dangers are used: *threats, vulnerabilities, challenges, uncertainties* and *risks*

---

[6] Representatives of constructivist approaches to international relations are: Adler, 2002; Berger and Luckmann, 1966; Buzan, Wæver and de Wilde, 1998; Checkel, 1998; Fearon and Wendt, 2002; Krell, 2000; Müller, 1994, 1994[a]; Ruggie, 1998; Wendt, 1999; Møller, 2003 and Mesjasz, 2003.

dealing with both *hard* (military) and *soft* security issues (drugs, human trafficking, migration). Within the EU, *national* and *internal security* issues (justice and home affairs dealing with issues of asylum, migration and citizenship) are distinguished. The deborderization has been supplemented with two securitization strategies based on *intergovernmental* structures in contrast to the *communitization* of other issues.

While the classical means and instruments of a narrow security policy have remained the military and diplomacy, in the EU this classical *domaine réservé* of the nation state has entered a process of fundamental transformation with close consultations, common policies and strategies, and increased common voting in international institutions (UN, OSCE). In many international regimes (food, climate, desertification), the EU is a full member aside from its 27 member states. Its evolving common *European Foreign and Security* (CFSP) and *Security and Defence Policy* (ESDP) has affected the traditional national military and diplomatic leverage.

Within international organizations (UN, FAO, UNDP, UNEP, OECD, IEA), sector-specific security concepts are widely used, such as "environmental security" (Brauch, 2003, 2009), "food security" (FAO, 1996; Collomb, 2003; Oswald, 2009[a]; Salih, 2009; Kapur et al., 2009), "global health security" (WHO, 2002; Rodier and Kindhauser, 2009; Leaning, 2009), "energy security" (Jacoby, 2009) and "livelihood security" (OECD, 2002; Bohle, 2009).

The political and scientific concept of security has changed with the international order. With the Covenant (1919), the concept of "collective security" was introduced; after World War II the concept of "national security" was launched to legitimize the global US role and after 1990 the security concept widened and deepened and new concepts such as "human," "environmental," and sectoral security concepts were added to the policy agenda.

Events-Structures-Concepts-Action

Political and scientific concepts like security are used within a complex context (Koselleck, 2006). Concepts have a temporal and systematic structure, they embody and reflect the time when they were used and they are thus historical documents reflective of the persistent change in the history of events (*histoire des événements*) and structures (Braudel's [1949, 1972] *histoire de la longue durée*). Concepts are influenced by perceptions and interpretations of events that rarely change the structures of international politics and of international relations.

The analysis of terms and concepts requires a combined methodological approach of etymology, concept formation, conceptual history and a systematic conceptual mapping. Etymology uses methods of historical and comparative linguistics. A concept describes an object not in its totality but focuses on its characteristics with regard to its content and scope. Thus, a concept requires a mental effort that separates essential from irrelevant features. For Kant, the interaction between concept and contemplation produces cognition and knowledge. He distinguished between empirical concepts and categories based on reason. The modern logic of concepts analyses primarily the extentional relations between concepts.

Concept formation refers to "the process of sorting specific experiences into general rules or classes" where "a person identifies important characteristics and ... identifies how the characteristics are logically linked" (Brauch 2008ª: 66). This refers to a psychological process where the essence and function of an object or situation are covered. Charles E. Osgood distinguished between perceptive, integrative and representative concepts that involve three cognitive processes of discrimination, abstraction and generalization.

Concept history was first used by Hegel for historical and critical research of the development of philosophical concepts. The history of concepts or conceptual history according to Koselleck (1979, 2002, 2006) addresses the complex linkages between the temporal features of events, structures, and concepts in human (societal) history but also the dualism between experience and concepts. A major focus of Koselleck's (2006: 86-98) work on historical concepts dealt with the temporal structures of conceptual change. In his last book, *Begriffsgeschichten* (histories of concepts), Koselleck (2006: 529-540) argued that it is essential for conceptual history to develop hypotheses with the goal of showing their internal semantic structure, to develop hierarchies of conceptual fields to point to the power of some concepts to structure the context. At the same time, on the semantic level concepts reflect experiences and expectations in different scientific disciplines. Thus, the language (or "speech act") becomes an important tool to document conceptual changes as they are perceived, articulated, and documented at a certain moment or over a period of time. The semantic documentation of experiences is scientifically linked to contexts.

A methodological challenge is to understand the specific semantic contribution of nonverbal phenomena (facts) as well as the challenge of nonverbal predispositions that require a semantic or conceptual response. Conceptual history, Koselleck (2006: 525-540) argued, "opens a way to empirically check these differentiations." He pointed to the contextual nature of concepts that gain in precision from their relationship to neighbouring and opposite concepts. Furthermore, he argued that conceptual history looks for key and corner points that illustrate an innovative strength that can only be observed from a longer-term perspective.

Influenced by Koselleck, Wæver (2006) drafted a conceptual history of security for international relations relying primarily on the Western intellectual tradition from its Greek and Roman origins to the present time in which he also documented the different reconceptualizations with a special focus on launching the "national security" concept in the 1940s that was later taken up by Russia, Japan, Brazil (as a doctrine) and other countries. Both the temporal evolution and systematic analysis of concepts has been a major task of philosophy, and especially of political philosophy and of the history of ideas that links one subfield of political science with broader philosophical endeavours and trends.

"Conceptual mapping" focuses on the use of the security concept in different countries, political systems, cultures and religions and scientific disciplines, in national political processes, within civil society and social movements, but also as a guiding and legitimating instrument within international organizations. Any conceptual mapping has to reflect the specific context in time and space that influence the meaning and the use of concepts. In the social sciences, especially in the debate in security studies, the security concept is theory-driven.

The political events of 1989 toppled the Communist governments in all East European countries, and thus were instrumental for the collapse of the Soviet Union and the dissolution of the Warsaw Treaty Organization and Comecon (1991). The Cold War bipolar order of two highly armed political systems became obsolete and with it the traditional security legitimizations. This structural change of the international order influenced the security policy agendas and provoked a global political and scientific debate on the reconceptualization of security. This debate was stimulated by many policy actors, scientists and intellectuals. The results are documented in the national security doctrines and strategies and in the defence white papers of many countries. They have also been the object of analysis for the scientific community that gradually emancipated itself from the US dominance.

But these Northern discourses on security have often ignored the thinking of the philosophical traditions in Asia, Africa, Latin America and in the Arab world (Brauch et al., 2008). While Huntington in his "clash of civilization" (1993, 1996) succeeded to "securitize culture" from the vantage point of US national security interests and strategies, the critical responses reflected the cultural and religious diversity of the rest of the world. The perception of global environmental change (GEC) as a "threat" to the survival of humankind has contributed to a widened, deepened and sectorialized security concept that increasingly reflects the existing cultural and religious diversity also in the debates and discourses on security (Brauch, 2009a).

Thus, reconceptualizing security and defining the manifold security interests and preferences structures the public policy discourse and legitimates the allocation of scarce financial resources to "face" and "cope" with major security dangers and concerns that threaten the survival of states, human beings or humankind and thus require "extraordinary" political action.

Contextual Change and Conceptual Innovation

After the independence of the United States (1776), the French Revolution (1789) and the wars of liberation in Latin America (1809-1824) and the emergence of new independent states (1817-1839), four global contextual changes can be distinguished in Europe that resulted in new international orders:

— The *Peace Settlement of Vienna* (1815) and the European order of a balance of power based on a Concert of Europe (1815-1914) in an era of imperialism (Africa, Asia) and the post-colonial liberation in Latin America.

— The *Peace of Versailles* (1919) with a collapse of the European world order, a declining imperialism and the emergence of two new power centres in the US and in the USSR with competing political, social, economic and cultural designs and a new global world order based on the security system of the *League of Nations* (1919-1939).

— The *Political Settlement of Yalta* (February 1945) and the system of the United Nations discussed at the conferences in Dumbarton Oaks (1944), *Chapultepec* (January/February 1945), and adopted at *San Francisco* (April/June 1945).

With these turning points during the European dominance of world history, the thinking on security changed. After the French Revolution, the thinking about "*Rechtssicherheit*" (legal predictability guaranteed by a state based on laws) gradually evolved. With the Covenant of the League of Nations "*collective security*" became a key concept in international law and relations (IR).

Since 1945, this "national security" concept has become a major focus of the IR discipline. During the Cold War, the modern "security concept" emerged as a political and a scientific concept in the social sciences that were dominated by the American and Soviet strategic cultures. With the end of the Cold War, its prevailing security concepts had to be adjusted to the new political conditions, security dangers and concerns. The process of a "reconceptualization of security" and "redefinition of security interests" that was triggered by the global turn and slightly modified by the events of 11 September 2001 and the subsequent US-led "war on terror," has become a truly global process. The dominance of the two superpowers has been replaced by an intellectual pluralism representing the manifold traditions but also the cultural and religious diversity.

Drivers and Centres of Conceptual Innovation

The drivers of the theoretical discourse on security and the intellectual centres of conceptual innovation have shifted away from Russia (after 1989) but also from the United States. During the 1980s, conceptual thinking on "alternative security" in Europe searched for alternatives to mainstream deterrence doctrines and nuclear policies (Weizsäcker, 1972; Afheldt, 1976; SAS 1984, 1989; Brauch and Kennedy, 1990, 1992, 1993; Møller, 1991, 1992, 1995).

In 2008, the discourses on security are no longer a primarily American social science (Crawford and Jarvis, 2001; Hoffmann, 2001; Nossal, 2001; Zürn, 2003). The critiques of alternative security experts in Europe during the 1970s and 1980s, but also new national perspectives during the 1990s, e.g. in France (Lacoste, Bigo, Badie), in the UK (Buzan, Booth, Smith, Rogers), Canada and Germany (Albrecht, Czempiel, Senghaas) challenged American conceptualizations of national security. Since the 1990s in Southern Europe a re-emergence of geopolitics (France, Italy, Spain) can be observed. In other parts of the world a new geopolitics school has emerged (O'Tuathhail, 1996, 2000, 2004; Dalby, 2002, 2002ª, 2008; Dalby et. al., 2009).

Groom and Mandaville (2001: 151) noted an "increasingly influential European set of influences that have historically, and more recently, informed the disciplinary concerns and character of IR" that have been stimulated by the writings of Foucault, Bourdieu, Luhmann and Habermas and from peace research by Galtung, Burton, Bouthoul, Albrecht, Czempiel, Rittberger, Senghaas and Väyrynen.

Since 1990, new centres of conceptual innovation emerged when new journals on IR and security problems were launched and pan-European Conferences on International Relations (ECPR) were held in Heidelberg (1992), Paris (1995), Vienna (1998), Canterbury (2001), The Hague (2004) and Turin (2007), where intellectual debates on security, peace, the environment and development have been taking place. In August 2005, the first world conference on international relations took place in Istanbul and the second in Slovenia in 2008. New centres of intellectual and conceptual innovation have emerged in the security realm:

— In Europe, Aberystwyth, Paris and Copenhagen are associated with critical "schools" on security theory (Wæver, 2004; Albrecht and Brauch, 2008).

— The human security concept was promoted by Mahub ul Haq (Pakistan) with the UNDP report of 1994 and developed further by the Human Security Commission (CHS, 2003) and promoted by both globally.

— Civil society organizations in South Asia developed the concept of livelihood security.

— International organizations introduced the sectoral concepts of energy (IEA, OECD), food (FAO, WFP), water (UNEP) and health (WHO) security (see Brauch et. al., 2009).

— In the US, Canada, Switzerland and Norway the concept of environmental security emerged during the 1980s and 1990s.

— The Earth System Science Partnership (ESSP) and its four programmes: IHDP (International Human Dimensions Programme), IGBP (International Geosphere-Biosphere Programme), WCRP (World Climate Research Programme) and Diversitas resulted in global scientific networks that indirectly address new security dangers and concerns (Brauch et al., 2010).

Trends in the reconceptulization of security have been: a) a widening, deepening, and sectorialization of security concepts; b) a shift of the referent object from the state to human beings or humankind (human security); c) a perception of new security dangers (threats, challenges, vulnerabilities and risks) and securitization of new security concerns; and d) a search for new non-military strategies to face and cope with newly perceived security dangers and concerns and new environmental dangers, hazards and disasters that pose a "survival dilemma" (Brauch, 2008[b]) for affected and vulnerable people. These new drivers and centres of conceptual innovation have fundamentally challenged the narrow state-focused security concept of the traditionalists and realists in the Cold War.

History, Social Sciences, Philosophy, International Law

Contextual Change and Conceptual History

The history of concepts was instrumental for a major editorial project (Brunner et al., 1972-1997). Koselleck (1979, 1989, 1994, 1996, 2000, 2002, 2006) addressed the complex interlinkages between the temporal features of events, structures and concepts in human (societal) history but also the dualism between experience and concepts.

The changes in the thinking on security and their embodiment in security concepts are also a semantic reflection of the fundamental changes as they have been perceived in different parts of the world and conceptually articulated in alternative or new and totally different security concepts. Competing securitization efforts of terrorism or climate change are behind the transatlantic and global security policy debate and the global scientific conceptual discourse (Brauch, 2009[a]; Cerutti, 2007; Sunstein, 2007).

Conceptual Mapping in the Social Sciences

In the social sciences, the security concept has been widely used in political science (Baylis, 2008), sociology (Bonß, 1995) and economics (Mursheed, 2008; Mesjasz, 2008) that focus on different actors: on the political realm (governments, parliaments, public, media, citizens); on society and on the business community. In political science, the security concept has been used in its threefold context: of policy (the field of security policy), politics (process on security, military and arms issues) and polity (legal norms, laws and institutions on the national and international level). The US National Security Act of 1947 (Czempiel, 1966; Brauch, 1977) and its adjustments have created the legal and institutional framework for the evolution of the "national security state," sometimes also referred to as a military-industrial complex (Eisenhower, 1960, 1972). This evolution has been encapsulated in the US debate on the concepts of "national" and, since 2001, also "homeland" security.

Analysis of Concepts and their Linkages in Philosophy

The evolution and systematic analysis of concepts has been a major task of political philosophy and of the history of ideas. From a philosophical perspective after the end of the Cold War, Makropoulos (1995: 745-750) analysed the evolution of the German concept *"Sicherheit"* from its Latin and Greek origins and its evolution and transformation during the medieval period, after the reformation as a concept in theology, philosophy, politics and law, with a special focus on Hobbes, Locke, Wolff, Rousseau and Kant. In the 20th century he reviewed the prevention and compensation of genuinely social and technical insecurity as well as new social risks. While this article briefly noted "social security," the key concept of "national security" or the more recent concept of "human security" were not mentioned.

Security Concepts in National Public and International Law

Since the 18th century, the security concept was widely used in the context of constitutional or public law for the legal system providing *"Rechtssicherheit"* (security based on law) for the citizens in their engagement with the state. The concepts of "international peace and security" are used in the Covenant and in the UN Charter. Wolfrum (1994: 51) points to the subjective and objective elements of "international security," the pursuit of which "implies a transformation of international relations so that every state is assured that peace will not be broken, or at least that any breach of the peace will be limited in its impact." He also referred to the "defining characteristic of the concept of collective security [as] the protection of the members of the system against a possible attack on the part of any other member of the same system," and he noted that "the distinction drawn between the concepts of collective security and collective self-defence has been blurred to some extent in practice, and it also has lost relevance with respect to the United Nations" because due to the universal nature of the UN system "any distinction based upon external or internal acts of aggression [have been rendered] meaningless."

Debate on Security Concepts within the United Nations

In a report of the Secretary General on *Concepts of Security* (UN, 1986: 2), Pérez de Cuéllar noted that these concepts "are the different bases on which States and the international community as a whole rely for their security" and he observed that the participating state representatives "recognized the different security concepts [that] have evolved in response to the need for national security and as a result of changing political, military, economic and other circumstances." Since 1990, Secretaries General Boutros Ghali (1992, 1995) and Annan (2005) have conceptualized "security" and "human security."

For the post-Cold War (1990-2006) years, Bothe (2008) analysed the changes in the use of the concept of security in UNSC decisions on activities that have been considered as threats to "international peace and security" or as "breaches of peace." Dedring (2008) reviewed the introduction of the "human security" concept in the deliberations of the Security Council as a result of the activities of Canada on the protection of civilians in armed conflicts while Fuentes (2002; Fuentes and Brauch, 2009) analysed the activities of the Human Security Network in the promotion of a common human security agenda. The reconceptualizing of security can also be observed in statements of international organizations.

The Reconceptualization of Regional Security

New security concepts have been adopted with the *Declaration of the Organization of American States* in October 2003 in Mexico (Rojas, 2008), with the *European Security Strategy* of 2003 by the European Union (Hintermeier, 2008), by the United Nations with Annan's (2005) report *In Larger Freedom* (Einsiedel, Nitschke and Chhabra, 2008), as well as by NATO (Dunay, 2008; Bin, 2008).

With the ongoing globalization process, new, transnational, non-state actors (from transnational corporations to terrorist and criminal networks) have directly affected objective security dangers and subjective concerns. Not only has "international terrorism" become a major new security danger in many national security policy statements and in UN and other resolutions by IGOs, but threats to "human security" are also posed by the impact of global climate change through an increase in the number and intensity of natural hazards and disasters (storms, cyclones, hurricanes, drought) that are caused by anthropogenic activities, which are partly responsible for the misery of those affected most by extreme weather events (e.g. cyclones in Bangladesh or drought in the Sahel). These events have contributed to internal displacement and migration and have thus reached the North as new "soft" security problems. The developments caused by global environmental change (GEC) have contributed to the emergence of a new phase in earth history, the "Anthropocene" (Crutzen, 2002; Crutzen and Stoermer, 2000; Clark et al., 2004, 2005) that poses new security dangers and concerns for many people in the South.

Besides the global turn of 1990, several regional and national structural changes, the impacts of globalization and with GEC, new dangers and concerns for the security and survival of humankind are evolving. The perception or the securitization of these new security dangers as threats for international, regional, national and human security have all contributed to a reconceptualization of security.

Conclusion: The Relevance of the Four Pillars for the Analysis of Security

From a European perspective, this chapter introduced the discourse on the reconceptualization of security (first six sections) by combining three scientific methods of etymology, conceptual history and systematic conceptual mapping. Analyses from other cultural backgrounds, intellectual traditions and disciplines and in other languages are needed to diversify this Euro-centred perspective.

The underlying epistemological interest and research question has been to conceptually map the extent to which the global contextual change at the end of the Cold War triggered conceptual innovations primarily for the security concept and its three related concepts of the quartet. They were analysed by the four research programmes and can be observed for six dyadic conceptual linkages and for four conceptual pillars (Brauch 2008[a]).

This analysis does not offer simple answers but provides a framework for a multi-disciplinary and multicultural mapping of the rethinking of security since 1989-1990. The changes have been significant as the widening, deepening, and the sectorialization of the security concept illustrate. This is an ongoing process, where the securitization has shifted from the narrow military focus of the Cold War to many newly perceived security concerns posed by global environmental change and most particularly by climate change.

Awarding the Nobel peace prize of 2005 to Wangari Matthai and in 2007 to the IPCC and Al Gore, as well as putting "human security" and "climate change" on the agenda of the UNSC are all indications of an ongoing change in the thinking on and use of the "security" concept in its relationship to peace, development and the environment. With the securitization of climate change and water (Oswald and Brauch, 2009) the threat is posed not by "them" (the other, the enemy) but by "us" (humankind), by those who have posed the threat through the consumption of fossil fuels that have contributed to anthropogenic climate change (Oswald et al., 2009).

This requires a fundamental new policy of peace and security where sustainable development and sustainable peace are two strategic components to deal both with the "security dilemma" among nations (top-down perspective) and with the "survival dilemma" posed for the most vulnerable and poor people (bottom-up perspective) in developing countries (Brauch and Oswald, 2009).

References

ADLER, Emanuel (2002): "Constructivism and International Relations." Ed. Walter CARLSNAES; Thomas RISSE and Beth A. SIMMONS: *Handbook of International Relations*. Sage, London, 95-118.

AFHELDT, Horst (1976): *Verteidigung und Frieden: Politik mit militärischen Mitteln*. Hanser: München.

ALBRECHT, Ulrich and Hans Günter BRAUCH (2008): "Security in Peace Research and Security Studies." Ed. Hans Günter BRAUCH *et al.*: *Globalization and Environmental Challenges*. Springer, Berlin, 503-525.

AMINEH, Mehdi Parvizi and John GRIN (2003): "Globalisation, States, and Regionalisation: Analysing Post-Cold War Security in the Mediterranean Region." Ed. Hans Günter BRAUCH *et al.*: *Security and Environment in the Mediterranean*. Springer, Berlin, 267-276.

ANNAN, Kofi (2005): *In Larger Freedom: Towards Development, Security and Human Rights for All*. UN, New York (21 March).

ARENDS, J. Frederik M. (2008): "From Homer to Hobbes and Beyond —Aspects of 'Security' in the European Tradition." Ed. Hans Günter BRAUCH *et al.*: *Globalization and Environmental Challenges*. Springer, Berlin, 263-278.

ART, Robert (1993): "Security." Ed. Joel KRIEGER: *The Oxford Companion to Politics of the World*. Oxford University Press, Oxford, 820-822.

AYDIN, Mustafa (2003): "Security Conceptualization in Turkey." Ed. Hans Günter BRAUCH *et al.*: *Security and Environment in the Mediterranean*. Springer, Berlin, 345-355.

BALDWIN, David A. (1995): "Security Studies and the End of the Cold War." *World Politics*, Vol. 48, 117-141.

BAYLIS, John (2008): "The Concept of Security in International Relations." Ed. Hans Günter BRAUCH *et al.*: *Globalization and Environmental Challenges*. Springer, Berlin, 495-502.

BERGER, Peter L. and Thomas LUCKMANN (1966): *The Social Construction of Reality*. Anchor, New York.

BETTS, Richard, K. (1997): "Should Strategic Studies Survive." *World Politics*, Vol. 50, 7-33.

BIN, Alberto (2008): "NATO's Role in the Mediterranean and Broader Middle East Region." Ed. Hans Günter BRAUCH *et al.*: *Globalization and Environmental Challenges*. Springer, Berlin, 725-732.

BOGARDI, Janos and Hans Günter BRAUCH (2005): "Global Environmental Change: A Challenge for Human Security —Defining and Conceptualising the Environmental Dimension of Human Security." Ed. Andreas RECHKEMMER: *UNEO —Towards an International Environment Organization— Approaches to a Sustainable Reform of Global Environmental Governance*. Nomos, Baden-Baden, 85-109.

BOHLE, Hans-Georg (2009): "Sustainable Livelihood Security. Evolution and Application." Ed. Hans Günter BRAUCH *et al.*: *Facing Global Environmental Change*. Springer, Berlin, 521-528.

BONSS, Wolfgang (1995): *Vom Risiko. Unsicherheit und Ungewißheit in der Moderne*. Hamburger Edition HIS Verlag, Hamburg.

BOOTH, Ken (1979): *Strategy and Ethnocentrism*. Croom Helm, London.

— (1987): "New Challenges and Old Mind-Sets: Ten Rules for Empirical Realists." Ed. Carl G. JACOBSEN: *The Uncertain Course. New Weapons, Strategies and Mind-sets*. Oxford University Press, Oxford, 39-66.

BOTHE, Michael (2008): "Security in International Law Since 1990." Ed. Hans Günter BRAUCH et al.: *Globalization and Environmental Challenges*. Springer, Berlin, 475-485.

BOUTROS-GHALI, Boutros (1992): *An Agenda for Peace. Preventive Diplomacy, Peacemaking and Peace-keeping. Report of the Secretary-General*. UN, New York (17 June).

— (1995): *An Agenda for Peace 1995*. United Nations, New York.

BRAUCH, Hans Günter (1977): *Struktureller Wandel und Rüstungspolitik der USA (1940-1950). Zur Weltführungsrolle und ihren innenpolitischen Bedingungen* University Microfilms, Ann Arbor-London.

— (2001): "The Mediterranean 'Space' Beyond *Geopolitique* and *Globalization*. Common Space —Divided Region." Ed. Antonio MARQUINA and Hans Günter BRAUCH: *The Mediterranean Space and its Borders. Geography, Politics, Economics and Environment*. UNISCI, Madrid and AFES-PRESS, Mosbach, 109-144.

— (2003): "Security and Environment Linkages in the Mediterranean: Three Phases of Research on Human and Environmental Security and Peace." Ed. Hans Günter BRAUCH et al.: *Security and Environment in the Mediterranean*. Springer, Berlin, 35-143.

— (2005): *Environment and Human Security*, InterSecTions, 2/2005 (Bonn: UNU-EHS).

— (2005a): *Threats, Challenges, Vulnerabilities and Risks in Environmental Human Security*. UNU-EHS, Bonn.

— (2008): "Introduction: Globalization and Environmental Challenges: Reconceptualizing Security in the 21st Century." Ed. Hans Günter BRAUCH et al.: *Globalization and Environmental Challenges*. Springer, Berlin, 27-43.

— (2008a): "Conceptual Quartet: Security and its Linkages with Peace, Development and Environment." Ed. Hans Günter BRAUCH et al.: *Globalization and Environmental Challenges*. Springer, Berlin, 65-98.

— (2008b): "From a Security towards a Survival Dilemma." Ed. Hans Günter BRAUCH et al.: *Globalization and Environmental Challenges*. Springer, Berlin, 537-552.

— (2008c): "Securitization of Space and Referent Objects." Ed. Hans Günter BRAUCH et al.: *Globalization and Environmental Challenges*. Springer, Berlin, 323-344.

— (2008d): "Conceptualising the Environmental Dimension of Human Security in the UN." Ed. Moufida GOUCHA and John CROWLEY: *International Social Science Journal*, Vol. 57 (Special issue on *Rethinking Human Security*). Wiley-Blackwell, Chichester and UNESCO, Paris, 19-48.

— (2008ᵉ): "Güvenliğin Yeniden Kavramsallaştirilması: Bariş, Güvenlik, Kalkinma ve Çevre Kavramsal Dörtlüsü" (Reconceptualizing Security: Conceptual Quartet of Peace, Security, Development and Environment). Ed. Hans Günter BRAUCH; Mustafa AYDIN and Ursula Oswald SPRING: *ULUSLARARASI İLİŞKİLER (International Relations)*, Vol. 5 (Summer), 1-48.

— (2009): "Introduction; Facing Global Environmental Change and Sectorialization of Security." Ed. Hans Günter BRAUCH et al.: *Facing Global Environmental Change.* Springer, Berlin, 21-42.

— (2009ᵃ): "Securitizing Global Environmental Change." Ed. Hans Günter BRAUCH et al.: *Facing Global Environmental Change.* Springer, Berlin, 65-102.

— and Robert KENNEDY (ed.) (1990): *Alternative Conventional Defense Postures for the European Theater. Vol. 1: The Military Balance and Domestic Constraints.* Crane Russak, London.

— and Robert KENNEDY (ed.) (1992): *Alternative Conventional Defense Postures for the European Theater. Vol. 2: The Impact of Political Change on Strategy, Technology and Arms Control.* Crane Russak, London.

— and Robert KENNEDY (ed.) (1993): *Alternative Conventional Defense Postures for the European Theater. Vol. 3: Force Posture Alternatives for Europe After the Cold War.* Crane Russak, London.

—; P.H. LIOTTA; Antonio MARQUINA; Paul ROGERS and Mohammed E-Sayed SELIM (ed.) (2003): *Security and Environment in the Mediterranean. Conceptualising Security and Environmental Conflicts.* Springer, Berlin.

— and Úrsula Oswald SPRING (2009): "Towards Sustainable Peace for the 21ˢᵗ Century." Ed. Hans Günter BRAUCH et al.: *Facing Global Environmental Change.* Springer, Berlin, 1295-1310.

—; Úrsula Oswald SPRING; Czeslaw MESJASZ; John GRIN; Pal DUNAY; Navnita Chadha BEHERA; Béchir CHOUROU; Patricia KAMERI-MBOTE and P.H. LIOTTA (ed.) (2008): *Globalization and Environmental Challenges: Reconceptualizing Security in the 21ˢᵗ Century.* Springer, Berlin.

—; Úrsula Oswald SPRING; John GRIN; Czeslaw MESJASZ; Patricia KAMERI-MBOTE; Navnita Chadha BEHERA; Béchir CHOUROU and Heinz KRUMMENACHER (ed.) (2009): *Facing Global Environmental Change: Environmental, Human, Energy, Food, Health and Water Security Concepts.* Springer, Berlin.

—; Úrsula Oswald SPRING; Czeslaw MESJASZ; John GRIN; Patricia KAMERI-MBOTE; Béchir CHOUROU; Pal DUNAY and Jörn BIRKMANN (ed.) (2010): *Coping with Global Environmental Change, Disasters and Security —Threats, Challenges, Vulnerabilities and Risks.* Springer, Berlin.

BRAUDEL, Fernand (1949): *La Méditerranée et le monde méditerranéen s l'époque de Philippe II.* Armand Colin, Paris.

— (1972): *The Mediterranean and the Mediterranean World in the Age of Philip II* (2 volumes). Harper & Row, New York.

BROWN, Neville (1989): "Climate, Ecology and International Security." *Survival,* Vol. 31, 519-532.

— (2001): *History and Climate Change. A Eurocentric Perspective.* Routledge, London.

BRUNNER, Otto; Werner CONZE and Reinhart KOSELLECK (ed.) (1972-1997): *Geschichtliche Grundbegriffe. Historische Lexikon zur politisch-sozialen Sprache in Deutschland*. Ernst Klett Verlag, Stuttgart.

BULL, Hedley (1977): *The Anarchical Society. A Study of Order in World Politics*. Columbia University Press, New York and Macmillan, London.

BUTFOY, Andrew (1997): *Common Security and Strategic Reform*. Macmillan, Basingstoke.

BUZAN, Barry (1983): *People, States & Fear. The National Security Problem in International Relations*. Harvester Books, Brighton.

— (1987): *An Introduction to Strategic Studies. Military Technology and International Relations*. Macmillan, London.

— (1991): *People, States and Fear. An Agenda for International Security Studies in the Post-Cold War Era* (Second Edition). Harvester Wheatsheaf, London and Lynne Rienner, Boulder.

— (1997): "Rethinking Security after the Cold War." *Cooperation & Conflict*, Vol. 32 (March), 5-28.

— (2004): "A Reductionist, Idealistic Notion that Adds Little Analytical Value." *Security Dialogue*, Vol. 35 (September), 369-370.

— and Ole WÆVER (1997): "Slippery? Contradictory? Sociologically Unstable? The Copenhagen School Replies." *Review of International Studies*, Vol. 23, 143-52.

— and Ole WÆVER (2003): *Regions and Powers: The Structure of International Security*. Cambridge University Press, Cambridge.

—; Ole WÆVER and Jaap DE WILDE (1995): "Environmental, Economic and Societal Security." *Working Papers* No. 10. Centre for Peace and Conflict Research, Copenhagen.

—; Ole WÆVER and Jaap DE WILDE (1998): *Security. A New Framework for Analysis*. Lynne Rienner, Boulder.

CARR, Edward Hallet (1939): *The Twenty Years' Crisis, 1919-1939*. Macmillan, London.

CARTER, Ashton B. and William J. PERRY (1999): *Preventive Defense. A New Security Strategy for America*. The Brookings Institution, Washington D.C.

—; Williams J. PERRY and John D. STEINBRUNER (1992): *A New Concept of Cooperative Security* (Brookings Occasional Papers). The Brookings Institution, Washington D.C.

CERUTTI, Furio (2007): *Global Challenges for Leviathan. A Political Philosophy of Nuclear Weapons and Global Warming*. Rowman & Littlefield, New York.

CHA, Victor D. (2000): "Globalization and the Study of International Security." *Journal of Peace Research*, Vol. 37, 391-403.

CHECKEL, Jeff (1998): *Ideas and International Political Change: Soviet/Russian Behavior and the End of the Cold War*. Yale University Press, New Haven.

CHIPMAN, John (1992): "The Future of Strategic Studies: Beyond Grand Strategy." *Survival*, Vol. 34, 109-131.

CLARK, William C.; Paul J. CRUTZEN and Hans Joachim SCHELLNHUBER (2005): "Science for Global Sustainability: Toward a New Paradigm." *KSG Working Paper* No. RWP05-032. Harvard University, Cambridge, MA. At: *http://ssrn.com/abstract=702501*.

— (2004): "Science and Global Sustainability: Toward a New Paradigm." Ed. Hans Joachim SCHELLNHUBER; Paul J. CRUTZEN; William C. CLARK; Martin CLAUSSEN and Hermann HELD: Earth System Analysis for Sustainability. MIT Press, Cambridge, MA. 1-28.

COHEN, Richard and Michael MIHALKA (2001): Cooperative Security: New Horizons for International Order. The Marshall Center, Garmisch-Partenkirchen.

COLLOMB, Philippe (2003): "Population Growth and Food Security in the Countries of the Middle East and North Africa." Ed. Hans Günter BRAUCH: Security and Environment in the Mediterranean. Springer, Berlin, 777-811.

COMMISSION ON HUMAN SECURITY (2003): Human Security Now. Commission on Human Security, New York.

CONZE, Werner (1984): "Sicherheit, Schutz." Ed. Otto BRUNNER; Werner CONZE and Rienhart KOSELLECK: Geschichtliche Grundbegriffe. Historische Lexikon zur politisch-sozialen Sprache in Deutschland, Vol 5. Ernst Klett Verlag, Stuttgart, 831-862.

CRAWFORD, Beverly (1993): Economic Vulnerability in International Relations —The Case of East-West Trade. Investment and Finance. Columbia University Press, New York.

— (1995): "Hawks, Doves, But no Owls: International Economic Interdependence and Con-struction of the New Security Dilemma." Ed. Ronnie D. LIPSCHUTZ: On Security. Columbia University Press, New York, 149-186.

CRAWFORD, Robert M.A. and Darryl S.L. JARVIS (ed.) (2001): International Relations —Still an American Social Science? Toward Diversity in International Thought. State University of New York Press, Albany.

CRUTZEN, Paul J. (2002): "Geology of Mankind." Nature, Vol. 415 (January), 23.

— and Eugene F. STOERMER (2000): "The Anthropocene." IGBP Newsletter, Vol. 41, 17-18.

CZEMPIEL, Ernst-Otto (1966): Das amerikanische Sicherheitssystem 1945-1949. Walter de Gruyter, Berlin.

DALBY, Simon (2002): "Security and Ecology in the Age of Globalization." Ed. WOODROW WILSON INTERNATIONAL CENTER FOR SCHOLARS: Environmental Change & Security Project Report, Vol. 8 (Summer), 95-108.

— (2002a): Environmental Security. University of Minneapolis Press, Minneapolis.

— (2008): "Security and Environment Limkages Revisited." Ed. Hans Günter BRAUCH et al.: Globalization and Environmental Challenges. Springer, Berlin, 165-172.

—; Hans Günter BRAUCH and Úrsula Oswald SPRING (2009): "Environmental Security Concepts Revisited During the First Three Phases (1983-2006)." Ed. Hans Günter BRAUCH et al.: Facing Global Environmental Change. Springer, Berlin, 781-790.

DEDRING, Jürgen (2008): "Human Security and the UN Security Council." Ed. Hans Günter BRAUCH et al.: Globalization and Environmental Challenges. Springer, Berlin, 605-619.

DELBRÜCK, Jobst (1982): "Collective Security." Ed. Rudolf Bernhardt. Encyclopedia of Public International Law. Elsevier, Oxford, 104-114.

DEUTSCH, Karl (1957): *Political Community and the North Atlantic Area. International Organization in the Light of Historical Experience.* Princeton University Press, Princeton.

— (1991): "Kollektive Sicherheit." Ed. Rüdiger WOLFRUM: *Handbuch Vereinte Nationen.* C.H. Beck, München, 405-410.

DORFF, Robert H. (1994): "A Commentary on Security Studies for the 1990s as a Model Curriculum Core." *International Studies Notes,* Vol. 19, 23-31.

DUNAY, Pal (2008): "From Obsession to Oblivion: Reconceptualization of Security in NATO since 1990." Ed. Hans Günter BRAUCH *et al.: Globalization and Environmental Challenges.* Springer, Berlin, 713-723.

EISENHOWER, Dwight D. (1972): "Farewell Address." Ed. Carroll W. PURSELL: *The Military Industrial Complex.* Harper & Row, New York, 204-208.

FAO (1996): *The State of Food and Agriculture 1996. Food Security: Some Macroeconomic Dimensions.* FAO, Rome.

FEARON, James and Alexander WENDT (2002): "Rationalism v. Constructivism: A Skeptical View." Ed. Walter CARLSNAES; Thomas RISSE; Beth A. SIMMONS: *Handbook of International Relations.* Sage, London, 52-72,

FUENTES, Claudia (2002): "La Red de Seguridad Humana: Desde Lysoen a Santiago." Ed. Moufida GOUCHA and Francisco ARAVENA ROJAS: *Seguridad Humana, Prevención de Conflictos y Paz en América Latina y El Caribe.* UNESCO, FLACSO-Chile. 89-110.

— and Hans Günter BRAUCH (2009): "The Human Security Network: A Global North-South Coalition." Ed. Hans Günter BRAUCH *et al.: Facing Global Environmental Change.* Springer, Berlin, 991-1002.

GILPIN, Robert (1981): *War and Change in World Politics.* Cambridge University Press, Cambridge.

GOUREVITCH, Peter (2002): "Domestic Politics and International Relations." Ed. Walter CARLSNAES; Thomas RISSE; Beth A. SIMMONS: *Handbook of International Relations.* Sage, London, 309-328.

GOWA, Oanne S. (1994): *Allies Adversary and International Trade.* Princeton University Press, Princeton.

GRAY, Colin S. (1992): "New Dimensions of Strategic Studies: How Can Theory Help Practice." *Security Studies,* Vol. 1, 610-635.

— (1994): *Villians, Victims and Sheriffs: Strategic Studies and Security for an Inter-War Period.* University of Hull Press, Hull.

GROOM, John and Peter MANDAVILLE (2001): "Hegemony and Autonomy in International Relations: The Continental Experience." Ed. Robert M.A. CRAWFORD and Darryl S.L. JARVIS: *International Relations —Still an American Social Science?* State University of New York Press, Albany, 151-166.

GROTIUS, Hugo (1625, 1646): *De Jure Belli ac Pacis.* Iohanem Blaeu, Amsterdam.

— (1975): *Prolegomena to the Law of War and Peace.* Bobbs-Merril, Indianapolis.

HAFTENDORN, Helga (1991): "The Security Puzzle: Theory-Building and Discipline-Building in International Security." *International Studies Quarterly,* Vol. 35, 3-17.

HERRMANN, Richard K. (2002): "Linking Theory to Evidence in International Relations." Ed. Walter CARLSNAES; Thomas RISSE; Beth A. SIMMONS: *Handbook of International Relations*. Sage, London, 119-136.

HERZ, John H. (1959, 1962, 1966): *International Politics in the Atomic Age*. Columbia University Press, New York.

HINTERMEIER, Stefan (2008): "Reconceptualization of External Security in the European Union since 1990." Ed. Hans Günter BRAUCH et al.: *Globalization and Environmental Challenges*. Springer, Berlin, 659-676.

HOBBES, Thomas [1651] (1965): *Leviathan oder Wesen, Form und Gewalt des kirchlichen und bürgerlichen Staates*. Rowohlt, Reinbek.

HOFFMANN, Stanley (2001): "An American Social Science. International Relations." Ed. Robert M.A. CRAWFORD and Darryl S.L. JARVIS: *International Relations —Still an American Social Science?* State University of New York Press, Albany, 27-51.

HUNTINGTON, Samuel P. (1993): "The Clash of Civilizations?" *Foreign Affairs*, Vol. 72, 22-49.

— (1996): *The Clash of Civilizations and the Remaking of World Order*. Simon & Schuster, New York.

JACOBY, Klaus-Dietmar (2009): "Energy Security: Conceptualization of the International Energy Agency (IEA)." Ed. Hans Günter BRAUCH et al.: *Facing Global Environmental Change* Springer, Berlin, 345-354.

JAHN, Egbert; Pierre LEMAITRE and Ole WAEVER (1987): *European Security —Problems of Research on Non-Military Aspects*. COPRI, Copenhagen.

JONES, Richard Wyn (1999): *Security, Strategy, and Critical Theory*. Lynne Rienner, Boulder.

KAM, Ephraim (2003): "Conceptualising Security in Israel." Ed. Hans Günter BRAUCH et al.: *Security and Environment in the Mediterranean*. Springer, Berlin, 357-365.

KANT, Immanuel (1795, 1965): *Zum Ewigen Frieden. Ein Philosophischer Entwurf*. Reclam, Stuttgart.

— (1795, 1992): *Perpetual Peace and Other Essays*. Transl. Ted Humphrey. Hackett Publishing Co, Indianapolis.

KAPUR, Selim; Burcak KAPUR; Erhan AKCA; Hari ESWARAN and Mustafa AYDIN (2009): "A Research Strategy to Secure Energy, Water, and Food via Developing Sustainable Land and Water Management in Turkey." Ed. Hans Günter BRAUCH et al.: *Facing Global Environmental Change*. Springer, Berlin, 509-518.

KATZENSTEIN, Peter J. (ed.) (1996): *The Culture of National Security: Norms and Identity in World Politics*. Columbia University Press, New York.

KAUFMAN, Franz-Xaver (1970, 1973): *Sicherheit als soziologisches und sozialpolitisches Problem: Untersuchungen zu einer Wertidee hochdifferenzierter Gesellschaften*. Ferdinand Enke, Stuttgart.

KLARE, Michael T. (1994): *Peace and World Security Studies: A Curriculum Guide*, 6th ed. Lynne Rienner, Boulder.

— (1996): "Redefining Security: The New Global Schisms." *Current History*, Vol. 95, 353-358.

— and Daniel C. Thomas (1991): *World Security: Trends and Challenges at Century's End*. St. Martin's Press, New York.
— (1994, 1998): *World Security: Challenges for a New Century*. St. Martin's Press, New York.
Klein, Bradley S. (1994): *Strategic Studies and World Order. The Global Politics of Deterrence*. Cambridge University Press, Cambridge.
Kolodziej, Edward A. (2005): *Security and International Relations*. Cambridge University Press, Cambridge.
Koselleck, Reinhart (1979): *Vergangene Zukunft: Zur Semantik geschichtlicher Zeiten*. Suhrkamp, Frankfurt.
— (1989): "Linguistic Change and the History of Events." *The Journal of Modern History*, Vol. 61, 649-666.
— (1994): "Some Reflections on the Temporal Structure of Conceptual Change." Ed. Willem Melchung: *Main Trends and Cultural History*. Wyger Velen, Amsterdam, 7-16.
— (1996): "A Response to Comments on the Geschichtliche Grundbegriffe." Ed. Harmut Lehmann and Melvin Richter: *The Meaning of Historical Terms and Concepts*. German Historical Institute, Washington D.C., 59-70.
— (2000): *Zeitschichten: Studien zur Historik*. Suhrkamp, Frankfurt.
— (2002): *The Practice of Conceptual History: Timing History, Spacing Concepts*. Stanford University Press, Palo Alto.
— (2006): *Begriffsgeschichten*. Suhrkamp, Frankfurt.
Kostecki, Wojciech (1996): *Europe After the Cold War: The Security Complex Theory*. Instytut Studiów Politycznych PAN, Warsaw.
Krell, Gert (1981): "The Development of the Concept of Security." Ed. Egbert Jahn and Yoshikazu Sakamoto: *Elements of World Instability: Armaments, Communication, Food, International Division of Labour*. Campus, Frankfurt, 238-254.
— (2000): *Weltbilder und Weltordnung. Einführung in die Theorie der internationalen Beziehungen*. Nomos, Baden-Baden.
Leaning, Jennifer (2009): "Health and Human Security in the 21st Century." Ed. Hans Günter Brauch et al.: *Facing Global Environmental Change*. Springer, Berlin, 541-552.
Luciani, Giacomo (1989): "The Economic Content of Security." *Journal of Public Policy*, Vol. 8, 151-173.
Makropoulos, Michael (1995): "Sicherheit." Ed. Joachim Ritter; Karlfried Gründer and Gottfried Gabriel: *Historisches Wörterbuch der Philosophie*, Vol. 9. Wissenschaftliche Buchgesellschaft, Darmstadt, 745-750.
Mansfield, Edward D. (1994): *Power, Trade and War*. Princeton University Press, Princeton.
Mathews, Jessica Tuchman (1989): "Redefining Security." *Foreign Affairs*, Vol. 68 (Spring), 162-177.
— (1991): "The Environment and International Security." Ed. Michael Klare and Daniel Thomas: *World Security: Trends and Challenges at Century's End*. St Martin's Press, New York.

— (1992): "Preserving the Global Environment: Implications for U.S. Policy." Ed. C.W.J. KEGLEY and E.R. WITTKOPF: *The Future of American Foreign Policy*. St. Martin's Press, New York, 85-94.

— (1997): "Power Shift." *Foreign Affairs*, Vol. 76, 50-66.

McGWIRE, Michael (1988): "A Mutual Security Regime for Europe?" *International Affairs*, Vol. 64 (Summer), 361-379.

MESJASZ, Czeslaw (2003): "Economic and Financial Globalisation: Its Consequences for Security in the Early 21st Century." Ed. Hans Günter BRAUCH et al.: *Security and Environment in the Mediterranean*. Springer, Berlin, 289-300.

— (2008): "Economic Security." Ed. Hans Günter BRAUCH et al.: *Globalization and Environmental Challenges: Reconceptualizing Security in the 21st Century*. Springer, Berlin, 569-580.

MØLLER, Bjørn (1991): *Resolving the Security Dilemma in Europe. The German Debate on Non-Offensive Defence*. Brassey's, London.

— (1992): *Common Security and Non-Offensive Defense. A Neorealist Perspective*. Lynne Rienner, Boulder.

— (1995): *Dictionary of Alternative Defense*. Lynne Rienner, Boulder.

— (2001): "National, Societal and Human Security: General Discussion with a Case Study from the Balkans." Ed. UNESCO: *First International Meeting of Directors of Peace Research and Training Institutions. What Agenda for Human Security in the Twenty-first Century*. UNESCO, Paris, 41-62.

— (2003): "National, Societal and Human Security: Discussion —A Case Study of the Israeli-Palestine Conflict." Ed. Hans Günter BRAUCH et al.: *Security and Environment in the Mediterranean*. Springer, Berlin, 277-288.

MOURITZEN, Hans (1997): "Kenneth Waltz: A Critical Rationalist Between International Politics and Foreign Policy." Ed. Iver B. NEUMANN and Ole WÆVER: *The Future of International Relations: Masters on the Making*. Routledge, London.

MÜLLER, Harald (1994a): "Internationale Beziehungen als kommunikatives Handeln. Zur Kritik der utilitaristischen Handlungstheorien." *Zeitschrift für Internationale Beziehungen*, Vol. 1 (June), 15-44.

— (1994): "Institutionen und internationale Ordnung." Ed. Gert KRELL and Harald MÜLLER: *Frieden und Konflikt in den internationalen Beziehungen. Festschrift für Ernst-Otto Czempiel*. Campus, Frankfurt, 190-224.

— (2002): "Security Cooperation." Ed. Walter CARLSNAES; Thomas RISSE and Beth A. SIMMONS: *Handbook of International Relations*. Sage, London, 369-391.

MÜNKLER, Herfried (2005): *The New Wars*. Polity, Cambridge.

MURSHEED, S. Mansoob (2008): "Human Security from the Standpoint of an Economist." Ed. Hans Günter BRAUCH et al.: *Globalization and Environmental Challenges*. Springer, Berlin, 487-493.

MYERS, Norman (1989): "Environment and Security." *Foreign Policy*, Vol. 74 (Spring), 23-41.

— (1994): *Ultimate Security. The Environmental Basis of Political Stability*. W.W. Norton, New York.

NATO (1999): "The Alliance's Strategic Concept. Approved by the Heads of State and Government Participating in the Meeting of the North Atlantic Council in Washington D.C. on 23rd and 24th April 1999." At: http://www.nato.int/docu/pr/1999/p99-065e.htm.

NEWMAN, Edward (2001): "Human Security and Constructivism." *International Studies Perspectives,* Vol. 2 (August), 239-251.

NOLAN, Janne (ed.) (1994): *Global Engagement. Cooperation and Security in the 21st Century.* The Brookings Institution, Washington, D.C.

NOSSAL, Kim Richard (2001): "Tales that Textbooks Tell: Ethnocentricity and Diversity in American Introductions to International Relations." Ed. Robert M.A. CRAWFORD and Darryl S.L. JARVIS: *International Relations —Still an American Social Science? Toward Diversity in International Thought.* State University of New York Press, Albany, 167-186.

NYE, Joseph E. and Sean M. LYNN-JONES (1988): "International Security Studies: A Report of a Conference on the State of the Field." *International Security,* Vol. 12 (Spring), 5-27.

NYE, Joseph S. Jr. (1989): "The Contribution of Strategic Studies: Future Challenges." *Adelphi Paper, No. 235.* International Institute for Strategic Studies, London.

OECD (2002): *Agricultural Policies in OECD Countries: A Positive Reform Agenda* (COM/AGR/TD/WP(2002)19/FINAL). OECD Directorate for Food Agriculture and Fisheries, Paris (6 November).

OSWALD SPRING, Úrsula (2001): "Sustainable Development with Peace Building and Human Security." Ed. M.K. TOLBA: *Our Fragile World. Challenges and Opportunities for Sustainable Development. Forerunner to the Encyclopedia of Life Support Systems,* Vol. 1. Eolss Publishers, Oxford, 873-916.

— (2007): "Human, Gender and Environmental Security." Ed. Úrsula Oswald SPRING: *International Security, Peace, Development and Environment.* EOLSS/UNESCO, Oxford.

— (2008): "Oriental, European, and Indigenous Thinking on Peace in Latin America." Ed. Hans Günter BRAUCH et al.: *Globalization and Environmental Challenges.* Springer, Berlin, 175-193.

— (2009): "A HUGE Gender Security Approach: Towards Human, Gender and Environmental Security." Ed. Hans Günter BRAUCH et al.: *Facing Global Environmental Change.* Springer, Berlin, 1157-1182.

— (2009[a]): "Food as a New Human and Livelihood Security Challenge." Ed. Hans Günter BRAUCH et al.: *Facing Global Environmental Change.* Springer, Berlin, 471-500.

— and Hans Günter BRAUCH (2009): "Securitizing Water." Ed. Hans Günter BRAUCH et al.: *Facing Global Environmental Change.* Springer, Berlin, 175-202.

—; Hans Günter BRAUCH and Simon DALBY (2009): "Linking Anthropocene, HUGE and HESP: Fourth Phase of Environmental Security Research." Ed. Hans Günter BRAUCH et al.: *Facing Global Environmental Change.* Springer, Berlin, 1277-1294.

Ó TUATHAIL, Gearóid (1996): *Critical Geopolotics. The Politics of Writing Global Space.* Routledge, London.

— (2000): "Borderless Worlds? Problematising Discourses of Deterritoriali-
sation." Ed. Nurit KLIOT and David NEWMAN: Geopolitics at the End of the
Twentieth Century. The Changing World Political Map. Frank Cass, London,
139-154.
— (2004): "Geopolitical Structures and Cultures: Towards Conceptual Clarity
in the Critical Study of Geopolitics." Ed. Lasha TCHANTOURIDZE: Geopolitics:
Global Problems and Regional Concerns. CDSS, Winnipeg, 75-102.
PALME, Olof (1982): Common Security: A Blueprint for Survival. Simon & Schus-
ter, New York and Pan Books, London.
PRINS, Gwyn (1998): "The Four-Stroke Cycle in Security Studies." International
Affairs, Vol. 74, 781-808.
RALPH, Jason G. (2001): Beyond the Security Dilemma. Ending America's Cold
War. Ashgate, Aldershot.
RENNER, Michael (1997): Fighting for Survival. Environmental Decline, Social
Conflict and the New Age of Insecurity. Earthscan, London.
RITTBERGER, Volker and Peter MAYER (1993): Regime Theory and International Re-
lations. Clarendon Press, Oxford.
RODIER, Guénaël and Mary Kay KINDHAUSER (2009): "Global Health Security: The
WHO Response to Outbreaks Past and Future." Ed. Hans Günter BRAUCH et
al.: Globalization and Environmental Challenges. Springer, Berlin, 529-540.
ROJAS ARAVENA, Francisco (2008): "Security on the American Continent: Chal-
lenges, Perceptions and Concepts." Ed. Hans Günter BRAUCH et al.: Globali-
zation and Environmental Challenges. Springer, Berlin, 867-878.
RUGGIE, John Gerard (1998): Constructing the World Polity. Essays on Interna-
tional Institutionalization. Routledge, London.
SALIH, M.A. Mohamed (2009): "Governance of Food Security in the 21st Cen-
tury." Ed. Hans Günter BRAUCH et al.: Facing Global Environmental Change.
Springer, Berlin, 501-508.
SELIM, Mohammad El-Sayed (2003): "Conceptualisation of Security by Arab
Mashrek Countries." Ed. Hans Günter BRAUCH et al.: Security and Environ-
ment in the Mediterranean. Springer, Berlin, 333-344.
SHAW, Martin (1994): Global Society and International Relations. Polity Press,
Cambridge.
SMOKE, Richard and Andrei KORTUNOV (ed.) (1991): Mutual Security: A New Ap-
proach to Soviet-American Relations. St. Martin's Press, New York.
STEINBRUNER, John D. (2000): Principles of Global Security. Brookings, Washing-
ton, D.C.
SAS [Studiengruppe für Alternative Sicherheitspolitik] (1984): Strukturwandel
der Verteidigung. Entwurfe für eine konsequente Defensive. Westdeutscher
Verlag, Opladen.
— (1989): Vertrauensbildende Verteidigung. Reform deutscher Sicherheitspoli-
tik. Bleicher, Gerlingen.
SUHRKE, Astri (1999): "Human Security and the Interest of States." Security Dialogue, Vol. 30 (September), 265-276.
SUNSTEIN, Cass R. (2007): Worst Case Scenarios. Harvard University Press, Cam-
brdige, MA.

TICKNER, J. Ann (1995): "Re-visioning Security." Ed. Ken BOOTH; Ken SMITH and Steve SMITH: *International Relations Theory Today*. Polity, Oxford, 175-198.

ULLMAN, Richard (1983): "Redefining Security." *International Security*, Vol. 8 (Summer), 129-153.

UNITED NATIONS (1986): *Concepts of Security* (Disarmament Study Series 14). United Nations, New York.

— (2004): *Report of the Secretary General's High-Level Panel on Threats, Challenges and Change. A More Secure World: Our Shared Responsibility*. United Nations, New York.

UNDP (1994): *Human Development Report 1994*. Oxford University Press, New York.

UNESCO (2008): *Human Security —Approaches and Challenges*. UNESCO, Paris.

VÄYRYNEN, Raimo (ed.) (1985): *Policies for Common Security*. Taylor & Francis, London.

VON EINSIEDEL, Sebastion; Heiko NITSCHKE and Tarun CHHABRA (2008): "Evolution of the United Nations Security Concept: Role of the High-Level Panel on Threats, Challenges, and Change." Ed. Hans Günter BRAUCH et al.: *Globalization and Environmental Challenges*. Springer, Berlin, 621-636.

VON WEIZSÄCKER, Carl Friedrich (ed.) (1972): *Kriegsfolgen und Kriegsverhütung*. Hanser, Munich.

WÆVER, Ole (1995): "Securitization and Desecuritization." Ed. Ronnie D. LIPSCHUTZ: *On Security*. Columbia University Press, New York, 46-86.

— (1997): *Concepts of Security*. Department of Political Science, Copenhagen.

— (2004): "Aberystwyth, Paris, Copenhagen: New Schools in Security Theory and their Origins between Core and Periphery." Paper for 45th International Studies Association Convention, Montreal (17-20 March).

— (2006): *Security: A Conceptual History for International Relations*. Department of Political Science, Copenhagen.

— (2008): "Peace and Security: Two Evolving Concepts and Their Changing Relationship." Ed. Hans Günter BRAUCH et al.: *Globalization and Environmental Challenges*. Springer, Berlin, 99-111.

— (2008a): "The Changing Agenda of Societal Security." Ed. Hans Günter BRAUCH et al.: *Globalization and Environmental Challenges*. Springer, Berlin, 581-593.

—; Barry BUZAN; Morten KELSTRUP and Pierre LEMAITRE (1993): *Identity, Migration and the New Security Agenda in Europe*. Pinter, London.

—; Pierre LEMAITRE and Elzbieta TROMER (ed.) (1989): *European Polyphony: Perspectives Beyond East-West Confrontation*. Macmillan, London.

WALKER, R.B.J. (1988): *One World, Many Worlds: Struggles For A Just World Peace*. Lynne Rienner, Boulder and Zed Books, London.

— (1990): *Sovereignty, Security and the Challenge of World Politics* (Working Paper No 87). Australian National University Peace Research Centre, Canberra.

— (1993): *Inside/Outside: International Relations as Political Theory*. Cambridge University Press, Cambridge.

WALT, Stephen (1991): "The Renaissance of Security Studies." *International Studies Quarterly,* Vol. 35 (June), 211-239.

WALTZ, Kenneth (1959, 2001): *Man, the State and War. A Theoretical Analysis.* Columbia University Press, New York.

WENDT, Alexander (1992): "Anarchy is What States Make of It: The Social Construction of Power Politics." *International Organization,* Vol. 46 (Spring), 391-425.

— (1999): *Social Theory and International Politics.* Cambridge University Press, Cambridge.

WESTING, Arthur H. (1986): "An Expanded Concept of International Security." Ed. Arthur H. WESTING: *Global Resources and International Conflict: Environmental Factors in Strategic Policy and Action.* Oxford University Press, Oxford, 183-200.

— (ed.) (1989): *Comprehensive Security for the Baltic: An Environmental Approach.* Sage, London.

— (1989): "The Environmental Component of Comprehensive Security." *Bulletin of Peace Proposals,* Vol. 20, 129-134.

WORLD HEALTH ORGANIZATION (2002): *Global Crisis —Global Solutions. Managing Public Health Emergencies of International Concern through the Revised International Health Regulations* (WHO/CDS/CSR/GAR/2002.4). World Health Organization, Geneva.

WIBERG, Håkan (1987): "The Security of Small Nations: Challenges and Defences." *Journal of Peace Research,* Vol. 24, 339-363.

— (1988): "Concepts of Security. A Logical and Analytical Framework." Ed. Narindart SINGH: *Peace and Development.* Gower Publishing Company, New Delhi, 31-53.

WIGHT, Martin (1991): *International Theory. The Three Traditions.* Ed. Gabriele Wight and Brian Porter. Leicester University Press, Leicester.

WOLFERS, Arnold (1952): "National Security as an Ambiguous Symbol." *Political Science Quarterly,* Vol. 67, 481-502.

— (1962): "National Security as an Ambiguous Symbol." Ed. Arnold WOLFERS: *Discord and Collaboration. Essays on International Politics.* John Hopkins University Press, Baltimore, 147-165.

WOLFRUM, Rüdiger (ed.) (1995): *United Nations: Law, Policies and Practice,* Vol. 1. C.H. Beck, Munich and Martinus Nijhoff, Dordrecht.

— (1994): "Chapter 1. Purposes and Principles, Art. 1." Ed. Bruno SIMMA: *The Charter of the United Nations. A Commentary.* Oxford University Press Oxford, 49-56.

YERGIN, Daniel (1977): *Shattered Peace. The Origins of the Cold War and the National Security State.* Houghton Mifflin Co., Boston.

ZARTMAN, William I. and Victor A. KREMENUNK (ed.) (1995): *Cooperative Security. Reducing Third World Wars.* Syracuse University Press, Syracuse.

ZÜRN, Michael (2003): "Die Entwicklung der Internationalen Beziehungen im deutschsprachigen Raum nach 1989." Ed. Gunther HELLMANN, Klaus Dieter WOLF and Michael ZÜRN: *Die neuen Internationalen Beziehungen. Forschungsstand und Perspektiven in Deutschland.* Nomos, Syracuse. 21-46.

List of Abbreviations

CFSP	European Foreign and Security Policy
CHS	Commission on Human Security
Diversitas	international science programme on biodiversity
ECPR	Pan-European Conferences on International Relations
ESDP	Security and Defence Policy
ESSP	The Earth System Science Partnership
EU	European Union
FAO	Food and Agricultural Organization, Rome
GEC	global environmental change
HUGE	human, gender and environmental security concept (by Ursula Oswald Spring)
IEA	International Energy Agency
IGBP	International Geosphere-Biosphere Programme
IGO	international governmental organization
IHDP	International Human Dimensions Programme
IR	international relations
NATO	North Atlantic Treaty Organization
OECD	Organization of Economic Cooperation and Development
OSCE	Organization for Security and Co-operation in Europe
SAS	Study group on alternative security policy
UN	United Nations
UNDP	United Nations Development Programme
UNEP	UN Environment Programme
UNESCO	United Nations Educational, Scientific and Cultural Organisation
UNSC	United Nations Security Council
US	United States of America
USSR	Union of Socialist Soviet Republics
WCRP	World Climate Research Programme
WFP	World Food Programme
WHO	World Health Organisation

Celebrating the Founders
of Peace Research

A Short Tribute to the On-going Work of Elise Boulding

Linda M. Johnston

Kennesaw State University

Elise Boulding could not join us at the 2008 IPRA conference in Leuven, Belgium. I had several email and phone conversations with her daughter, Christine, prior to the conference and obtained film clips of interviews, photographs, and materials Elise had written to share with the assembled group. One of the most comprehensive books written about Elise's life and work is by Mary Lee Morrison, entitled: *Elise Boulding: A Life in the Cause of Peace* (2005).[1] Much of the biographical material for this tribute comes from that excellent research by Morrison.

I first got to know Elise when she was handling the Senesh Scholarship for the International Peace Research Association (IPRA) Foundation. She wanted to hand the administration of the scholarship off to someone new. I volunteered. One of the many things Elise did well was to start up projects, make sure they were well established, and then hand them off to people whom she thought would carry them on well. I have had many wonderful conversations with her about how she ran the scholarship program, how she managed to always select scholarship participants who went on to do such wonderful work in the field of peace studies, and what was important to her about the scholarship and its recipients. I have administered the scholarship for many years now and I always keep in mind the things Elise told me. I am not alone in saying that Elise was a major influence on me as I got into the field of peace research. In fact, many people I have met over the years consider her to be the guiding influence for their entry into the field and one of their advocates for their continued work. What I remember

---

[1] Many of the facts in this presentation were derived from the excellent biographical research done by Morrison, 2005.

most was the encouragement she gave me in every aspect of my work and the field. Just as Elise learned from and respected the people who mentored her, I had long ago learned to do so also.

Elise was born in 1920 in Oslo, Norway. Her family immigrated to the United States in 1923 and settled in New Jersey. Elise grew up surrounded by extended family. In 1941, Elise married Kenneth Boulding and moved to Princeton, New Jersey. Within four short years, she and Kenneth moved to Nashville so that Kenneth could teach at Fisk University, and then Ames, Iowa. The couple began their family and had five children over the next eight years, between 1947 and 1955: Russell, Mark, Christine, Philip, and William. During the first couple years of child raising, Elise received her master's degree in sociology from Iowa State University in 1949. She went back to school again at the age of forty-five and completed her doctorate in sociology at the University of Michigan in 1969. During the child raising years, the family lived and worked in Michigan, Jamaica, Stanford University, Japan, Colorado, Dartmouth, and back to Colorado. When Kenneth passed away in 1993, the couple had been married over fifty years. Elise moved back to Wayland, Massachusetts, in 1996, to be near Christine, and finally to retire in Needham, Massachusetts, in 2000.

Among Elise's many accomplishments are: beginning the IPRA Newsletter; helping to found IPRA; running for US Congress on the Peace Party platform; being appointed the International Chair of the Women's International League for Peace and Freedom; helping to found the Consortium on Peace Research, Education, and Development (COPRED); working for the American Association for the Advancement of Science; editing *The American Sociologist* and *The International Nonviolent Peace Teams Services*; researching sex roles and society for the International Sociological Association; serving on the Board of Directors of the Institute for World Order (later the World Policy Institute), the National Peace Institute Foundation, the Boulder Parenting Center, and the Exploratory Project on Conditions for a Just World Peace; publishing *The Underside of History: A View of Women Through Time*; consulting with the United Nations University and the United Nations Educational, Scientific, and Cultural Organization (UNESCO); teaching at Dartmouth College, the University of Colorado, and George Mason University; helping to found the IPRA Foundation; and serving as the Senior Fellow of the Dickey Center for International Understanding at Dartmouth. She was also appointed to the American Friends Service Committee Corporation, the Secretary General of IPRA, Congressional Commission on Proposals for the National Academy of Peace and Conflict Resolution (later the U.S. Institute for Peace), and the Committee for the Quaker UN Office. She has been awarded the IPRA UNESCO's annual peace prize, the Global Citizen's Award from the Boston Research Center for the 21st Century, and the World Futures Studies Federation Award. It is almost laughable to comprehend the many accomplishments Elise made after she officially "retired." One thing that is very clear about Elise's work is that she struck that difficult balance between academic and practitioner. She recognized the contributions that activists and advocates made to the peace movement and valued their contributions. She has continued to be an activist and advocate throughout her life, and combined that work with her academic pursuits. Her work with COPRED exemplified this connection, as that organization strived to bring these two groups of people together.

Elise's doctoral dissertation work was on the role of women and was entitled: "The Effect of Industrialization on the Participation of Women in Society." She was able to follow that theme throughout much of her career. Elise's research, teaching and writing interests were very broad and included the contributions of women especially in the role of peacemaker, the impact of gender, children's rights, the personhood of children, the Earth Charter, the role of the family in children's lives, the promotion of a culture of peace, conflict and security, Quaker life, peace studies and peacebuilding. She wrote prolifically, especially after taking the position at Dartmouth. Elise's early interest in the role of women seemed to be at the core of and the foundation for the rest of her work in the field of peace studies.

Elise had many turning points in her life. She was very aware of these and reflected upon them. In an interview, Elise described how she idealized Norway as the perfect place; this was the way her mother had described it to her. That all changed for Elise when Norway was invaded by the Nazis in 1940. She described in an interview with Nancy Wrenn that this was a major turning point for her; it forced her no longer to idealize Norway as the perfect place and also led her to become very involved with the Quakers and the Peace movement. A second turning point for her was when she started taking on more public roles. When she was busy raising children, she seemed to put her emphasis more on local projects, especially in her own community and those which involved children. As her own children grew up, moved out on their own, and became independent, Elise began taking on even much more of a public, national and then global role. During this time, she still maintained an amazing number of roles in local projects. Another turning point for Elise was when she moved to teach at Dartmouth. This represented the start of a long distance relationship for her and Kenneth, and the beginning of her very fruitful academic career. It is at this point that her research and writing projects really seemed to blossom.

In this field of peace studies, we are indebted to her research pursuits and also to the many younger people she influenced and encouraged to enter the field.

References

MORRISON, Mary Lee (2005): *Elise Boulding: A Life in the Cause of Peace*. McFarland, Jefferson, NC.

The Escalating Peacebuilding Potential of Global Governance

Chadwick F. Alger
Ohio State University

The purpose of this paper is to motivate more peace researchers to illuminate the widespread peacebuilding potential of escalating global governance. I will approach this issue primarily in the context of the threefold research and teaching agenda that I have pursued for many years: (1) the UN System (Alger, 2006), (2) the worldwide links of people and organizations in local communities (Alger, 1990, 1999) and (3) peace research (Alger, 2007[a]).

The Emergence of Global Governance

Practitioners in global governance today have important roots in the League of Nations Covenant that focused on the reduction of armaments, prevention of aggression and submitting disputes to arbitration; but the League was broadening its agenda and developing an economic and social council as World War I approached. Building on League experience, those writing the UN Charter included an Economic and Social Council (ECOSOC), seven references to human rights, and a Declaration Regarding Non-Self-Governing Territories (Chapter XI). The UN now has a Human Rights Council, and most of the territories that were colonies of UN member states when the UN was founded are now UN member states. In addition, the expanding UN System has added economic development, economic equity, communications equity and ecological balance. All of these elements of a broadening agenda are now dimensions of what is often referred to as post-conflict peacebuilding and long-term peacebuilding.

A "culture of peace" movement has emerged that reflects Galtung's broad view of the peace process (Galtung, 1980). In pursuit of this goal UNESCO published *UNESCO and a Culture of Peace: Promoting a Global Movement* in 1995, with a second edition in 1997, that declares that "every aspect of social relations can be affected by a culture of peace movement" (121). Another volume that has emerged out of UNESCO's campaign is *From a Culture of Violence to a Culture of Peace* (1996), with contributions from fifteen scholars, including one by Johan Galtung on "Cultural Peace: Some Characteristics" (1996, 75-92).

The emerging and very diverse peacebuilding agenda of the UN System is also reflected in the Millennium Declaration of the General Assembly in 2000 that called for eight Millennium Development Goals: (1) eradicate *extreme poverty*, (2) achieve universal *primary education*, (3) promote *gender equality* and *empower women*, (4) reduce *child mortality*, (5) improve *maternal health*, (6) combat *HIV/AIDS, malaria and other diseases*, (7) ensure *environmental sustainability* and (8) develop a *global partnership for development*.

Obviously the Culture of Peace Movement, and the Millennium Development Goals reveal that visions of emerging and future global governance reach beyond relations between governments of states and includes aspects of the everyday lives of people living within states that are on the agendas of various governmental authorities within states. Of course, this raises very challenging questions about when and how they should be involved.

Those advocating for the Culture of Peace Movement and the Millennium Development Goals obviously have a vastly expanding vision of the responsibilities of the UN System. Of course, it must be recognized that there are very important limitations that the UN System experiences in its efforts to carry out the goals of the Culture of Peace, and Millennium Development. First, even before the Iraq war, the total budget of the UN System was only 3% of the military budget of one UN member state, the United States. Second, frequently numerous UN member states are not prepared to vote in support of multilateral efforts to develop a Culture of Peace and attain the Millennium Development goals. Nevertheless, those who are developing strategies for overcoming these limitations are making very significant contributions to peacebuilding.

It will be the purpose of the remainder of this paper to illuminate the fact that the UN System has been evolving toward acquiring the capacity of carrying out these visions of global governance. We will first provide an overview of the expanding array of UN System agencies that now carry out sixty-four functions. We will then provide an overview of the escalating involvement in global governance of parliamentarians of states, civil society/NGOs, local governments and business.

The UN System Now Involves People from Most Professions and Disciplines

Sixty-three years of experience in the United Nations "laboratory" has led to an ever broader UN System for performing peacebuilding roles. The organization chart of the UN System *(www.un.org/aboutun/chart.html)* now includes sixty-six agencies, commissions, programs, funds and other entities. The array of functions that appear in the names of these agencies are listed in Table 1.

Table 1

Functions appearing in names of UN System units

Units Created by the General Assembly (27)

Capital development fund	Children's fund
Crime and justice research institute	Democracy fund
Development program	Disarmament research
Drug control program	Environment program
Fund for international partnerships	HIV/AIDS program
Human rights, council	Human settlements program
Peacekeeping commission	Population fund
Project services, office for	Refugees, High Commissioner
Refugees, Palestine	Research for social development
Staff college	Trade & development conference
Trade, international center	Training & research institute
University	Volunteers
Women development Fund	Women, research and training institute
World food program	

UN Specialized Agencies (19)

Agricultural development fund	Civil aviation
Education, science, culture	Food and agriculture
Health, world	Development, international association
Finance, international corporation	Industrial development
Investment, multilateral guarantee agency	Investment disputes, international settlement
Intellectual property, world	Labor, international
Maritime, international	Monetary fund, international
Meteorological, world	Postal union
Reconstruction and development bank	Telecommunications, international
Tourism, world	

ECOSOC Functional Commissions (8)

Crime prevention	Human rights
Narcotic drugs	Population
Science and technology for development	Statistics
Sustainable development	Status of women

ECOSOC, Other Bodies (2)

Forests forum   Indigenous issues forum

Security Council (4)

Military staff	Criminal tribunals, Yugoslavia & Rwanda
Peacekeeping operations and missions	Counter terrorism committee

Related Organizations (4)

Atomic energy agency	Chemical weapons prohibition
Nuclear test-ban treaty	World trade organization

Other Trust Funds (2)

International partnership fund   Democracy fund

The sixty-six UN System functions in Table 1 reflect the growing reach of global governance in response to the ever widening geographic borders of governance problems. This perspective very usefully reveals that it is essential that we ponder the possible impact of all global governance decisions on peacebuilding. Of course, all of these functions are also performed by regional organizations of states, by departments of the governments of states and by departments in many provincial and local governments. Obviously, those aspiring to be peacebuilders face very complex challenges. On the other hand, simplification that ignores the complexity of reality ignores the full array of peacebuilding opportunities. This quick overview challenges those involved in all professions to ponder the roles that their profession plays in the UN System and their personal options for involvement. It also challenges researchers in all academic disciplines to ponder how they might more adequately illuminate these involvements.

This overview also provides an overwhelming challenge to peace researchers. What is the potential impact of all of these functions on peacebuilding? How can the array of peace functions in the UN System be coordinated? Because most of these functions are also performed by governments that range in geographic space from local to global, how can the array of governments involved in each function be coordinated? How can the peacebuilding potential of most professions and disciplines become an explicit part of their education and practice?

As the UN peacebuilding agenda has broadened, there has been growing awareness of the need to collaborate with other institutions that have the same issues on their agenda (Alger, 2007[b]). We will provide brief overviews of the growing involvement of the UN System with parliamentarians of state governments, NGOs/civil society, business and local governments. We will also provide evidence of the relevance of NGOs/civil society, business and local governments to global governance with brief overviews of their involvement in world affairs outside the UN System.

Participation of Parliamentarians of States in the UN System

In 2004 the Panel of Eminent Persons on United Nations-Civil Society Relations (Cardoso Report) took a broader perspective of participation in peacebuilding when it emphasized that all constituencies relevant to an issue should be included in global governance, including parliamentarians and local authorities, because it "is not only essential for effective action on global priorities but is also a protection against further erosion of multilateralism" (UN General Assembly, 2004).

The Inter-Parliamentary Union (IPU), an organization of members of parliaments of states, was founded in 1889 in Paris. With the goal of "Promoting the concepts of peace and international arbitration, the IPU provided the origins for today's form of institutionalized multilateral co-operation and advocated the establishment of corresponding institutions ... which eventually came into being as the United Nations" (www.ipu.org).

Parliamentarians of states have long been members of General Assembly delegations of some member states. For some years there have been meetings of these parliamentarians. The IPU signed a cooperation agreement with the UN in 1996 that calls for "Parliamentary Hearings to be held every year during the fall session of the General Assembly. The meeting is usually opened by the UN Secretary General and the President of the IPU. Hundreds of parliamentarians from every region of the world participate" (www.ipu.org/un-e/un-hearings.htm). In 1997, the IPU adopted a Universal Declaration on Democracy that affirms that democracy is an international principle applicable to international organizations and states in their international relations, and that "the principles of democracy must be applied to the international management of issues of global interest" (Johnsson, 2003: 22).

In 1995, on the eve of the UN 50th anniversary celebration, the IPU convened a special session of its governing body (the Inter-Parliamentary Council) in the UN General Assembly Hall. After a three-day debate, the Council adopted a declaration calling for close cooperation between the UN and National Parliaments, and for the IPU to facilitate this process. The Secretary General of the IPU states that it also called for a formal agreement between the IPU and the UN that would provide a framework for cooperation "mirroring at the international level the relationship which exists at the national level between government and the parliament" (Johnsson, 2003: 23).

In pursuit of this agreement, the IPU signed a cooperation agreement with the UN in 1996 that calls for Parliamentary Hearings to be held every year during the fall session of the General Assembly. The Parliamentary Hearing at the 61st UN General Assembly, in 2006, focused on "Conflict Prevention and Peace-Building: Reinforcing the Key Role of the United Nations." The discussions centered on the main findings of the Secretary General's Report on Conflict Prevention, and the new UN Peace-Building Commission.

At the UN Millennium Summit, on 30 August and 1 September 2000, a conference of some 150 speakers, Presidents or Presiding Officers of National Parliaments gave an important impetus to increased cooperation between the UN and the IPU. Their declaration

> outlines a strategy for providing a parliamentary dimension to international cooperation. ... globalization demands that greater attention be paid to the wishes of the people. That, in turn, means reinforcing the role of parliament and its members as intermediaries between the complexities of international decision-making and the day-to-day existence of the individual (Johnsson, 2003: 24).

They pledged their support to the IPU as the "world organization for inter-parliamentary cooperation and for relaying the vision and will of its members to intergovernmental organizations" (Johnsson, 2003: 25).

After the UN and IPU concluded a formal agreement of cooperation in 1996, the IPU remained an organization with ECOSOC Category I Consultative Status, but in November 2002 the General Assembly granted IPU observer status, with the right to distribute its official documents in the General Assembly. Some refer to it as a "super-observer" status (Johnsson, 2003).

The overall mandate of the Office of [the IPU] Permanent Observer (OPO) has three main components: representation and outreach, information and communications, and project support. In particular, the Office represents the IPU at meetings of United Nations bodies in New York, monitors relevant United Nations debates and initiatives, and facilitates the presentation of IPU substantive positions before the United Nations General Assembly and its subsidiary organs (www.ipu.org/un-e/un-opo.htm).

The IPU website reports that these are the "leading IPU partners within the United Nations system": UN Development Program (UNDP), UN Conference on Trade and Development (UNCTAD), UN Children's Fund (UNICEF), Office of the UN High Commissioner for Human Rights (OHCHR), Joint UN Program on HIV/AIDS (UNAIDS), UN Educational, Scientific and Cultural Organization (UNESCO), UN Division for the Advancement of Women (UNDAW), UN Institute for Training and Research (UNITAR), UN Institute for Disarmament Research (UNIDIR) and UN Democracy Fund (UNDEF).

These developments challenge the long established practice that only the executive branches of states should represent themselves in inter-state organizations. Should the present, largely IPU-defined parliamentary relationship with the UN be permitted to evolve? Should a more explicit future vision of an IPU-led parliamentarian-UN relationship be developed? Instead, would the best peacebuilding strategy call for a directly elected UN Parliamentary Assembly?

Participation of NGOs/Civil Society in the UN System

The UN Charter says that ECOSOC "may make suitable arrangements for consultation with non-governmental organizations (NGOs) which are concerned with matters within its competence." Based on this phrase, NGO participation in the UN System has widely expanded through practice (Alger, 2002b, 1997). Four hundred NGOs are accredited to the Commission on Sustainable Development (a subsidiary body of ECOSOC), and 1500 NGOs are associated with the Department of Public Information (DPI). DPI helps these NGOs gain access to, and disseminate information about issues in which the United Nations is involved, so that the public can better understand the aims and objectives of the UN and support its work.

NGO involvement in public decision-making bodies at UN headquarters has now spread beyond observation. Opportunities for NGOs to address public sessions has spread beyond ECOSOC to include committees of the General Assembly. They have also participated in what have been labeled as "formal panels" and "informal panels" of General Assembly committees. It is very significant that NGOs have acquired access to a broad range of private meetings of committees and sub-committees of the General Assembly. Particularly significant is that a "Consultative Group" of the NGO Working Group on the Security Council, composed of members of several NGOs, has met informally with Presidents of the UN Security Council.

NGOs have also developed an array of relations with UN Secretariats. The diversity of modes for NGO contact with members of the Secretariat are impressive. They include regularly scheduled meetings with NGOs, representation of NGOs on committees, Annual Consultation meetings with NGOs, symposia for NGOs, and NGO participation on national steering committees. Policy papers are posted on the web for NGO comment. Support for NGOs is provided through training and financial support and NGO creation. NGOs support secretariats financially and serve as their stand-ins. Secretariats and NGOs collaborate through joint research and joint implementation and monitoring of programs. There are NGO Liaison Offices at the headquarters of UN agencies throughout the UN System. It is particularly significant that the growing involvement of NGOs with UN decision-making bodies and secretariats has come with very little change in formal rules that were established for NGO access to the UN in 1950 (Alger, 2003: 90-92).

Special UN conferences have had a significant impact on the styles of NGO participation in the UN System. The holding of UN conferences focused on specific global issues at various sites around the world builds on a tradition that reaches back to the 1932 World Disarmament Conference (Spiro, 1995: 49). These conferences have had an impact on evolving NGO involvement in the UN System in at least four respects. First, NGO conferences that run parallel to these governmental conferences has spurred the development of NGO collaboration in the development of policies on specific issues and in presenting them to assemblies composed of government representatives. Second, NGOs have become increasingly involved in the preparatory phases of UN conferences, thereby offering NGOs experience in the pre-public phases of parliamentary diplomacy. Third, because these conferences have been held around the world, they have been accessible to a growing number of NGOs, particularly those in the Third World. Fourth, ad hoc procedures employed for NGO participation at these conferences have led to demands for wider NGO access at permanent headquarters (Alger, 2003: 93-94).

NGO gatherings at UN conferences away from UN headquarters has spurred four other NGO conference formats. First, a number of NGO conferences have convened as a follow-up to UN world conferences with an issue focus. Second, building on NGO conferences linked with UN conferences focused on a single global issue, broad-agenda free standing NGO conferences, often referred to as "people's assemblies," have emerged. As the proposal for a Millennium UN General Assembly emerged, Secretary General Kofi Annan joined the call for a companion Peoples Millennium Assembly. This proposed assembly met during 22-26 May 2000 under the name "Peoples Millennium Forum." Participating in the Forum were 1350 representatives of over 1000 NGOs from more than 100 countries. Fourth, for several decades there have been proposals for a second General Assembly that have included differing proposals for the nature of its members, including members of state legislatures, representatives of non-governmental organizations and directly elected members. More recent proposals include the International Network for a UN Second Assembly (1996), Childers and Urquhart's proposal for a UN Parliamentary Assembly (1994) and a proposal for an annual Forum of Civil Society in the Report of the Commission on Global Governance (1995). Many working for the Peoples Millennium Forum, but certainly not all, saw it as a building block toward a permanent second assembly (Alger, 2002[b]: 112-114).

These proposals raise very significant questions about how NGOs might most effectively contribute to UN peacebuilding. Should their participation primarily be permitted to evolve, as it has since the founding of the UN? Or would their contribution to peacebuilding be more effective if they were part of a permanent second assembly? This leads to another important question. Should NGOs select the members of this assembly, or should they be directly elected by the people of the world?

NGOs/Civil Society in World Politics

Although there is no doubt that the number of NGOs involved in world politics has increased in recent years, it is essential that we recognize that this is not a new phenomenon. At a commemoration of the 50th anniversary of the Universal Declaration of Human Rights, Secretary General Kofi Annan reminded his audience:

> Before the founding of the United Nations, NGOs led the charge in the adoption of some of the Declaration's forerunners. The Geneva

conventions of 1864; multilateral labor conventions adopted in 1906; and the International Slavery Convention of 1926; all stemmed from the world of NGOs who infused the international community with a spirit of reform (UN Secretary General, 1998).

Research in the last decade has provided ever more comprehensive knowledge of the wide ranging peacebuilding roles in which NGO/civil society are engaged. These works reveal that NGO/civil society activities can be placed in a fourfold framework. First, it is necessary for those involved in peacebuilding to create and mobilize global networks. Second, in organizing these networks, and acquiring support for their operations, they must enhance public participation. Third, they must become involved with, and endeavor to influence International Governmental Organizations (IGOs) and other multilateral political arenas. Fourth, they must become involved in a diverse array of field activities.

It is important to recognize that those focusing on the roles of NGOs in world politics are concerned with only a small percentage of the total NGO population. Two volumes applying terminology from sociology make this fact very clear. Jackie Smith, et al., in *Transnational Social Movements and Global Politics*, define this category of NGOs as "clusters of relatively marginalized actors [that] promote some form of social or political change" and identify them as "social movements" (1997: 59). Their volume focuses on transnational social movements (TSMOs), i.e., those active across state borders.

Keck and Sikkink, in *Activists Beyond Borders*, prefer the term "transnational network" with this explanation:

> By importing the network concept from sociology and applying it transnationally, we bridge the increasingly artificial divide between international and national realms. ... The networks we describe in this book participate in domestic and international politics simultaneously, drawing on a variety of resources, as if they were part of an international society (1998: 4).

The complexity of the political processes in which NGOs that are the focus of this volume are involved is not only a result of the "sheer diversity" of those NGOs working for social and political change, but also a result of the array of other actors with whom they must interact. They list seven major actors in "transnational advocacy networks": (1) international and domestic nongovernmental research and advocacy organizations, (2) local social movements, (3) foundations, (4) the media, (5) churches, trade unions, consumer organizations, and intellectuals, (6) parts of regional and international intergovernmental organizations and (7) parts of the executive and/or parliamentary branches of governments (Keck and Sikkink, 1998: 9).

NGOs engaged in a diversity of field activities are increasingly informed about the ways in which their activities can impact peacebuilding (Bock and Anderson, 1999). For example, in *Do No Harm: How Aid Can Support Peace—or War* (1996), Mary Anderson asserts that the impact of aid is not neutral. She asks how humanitarian or development assistance can be offered in conflict situations in ways that do not exacerbate the conflict, but help local people to establish alternative systems to deal with problems that underlie conflict. John Prendergast concludes that humanitarian aid is the most important avenue of contact among the international community and conflicting parties, thereby aid offers one of the best policy instruments for preventing escalation of conflict and promoting long-term peacebuilding (1996: 143).

In the light of the prominent use of religious differences by leaders as a basis for waging conflict and war, research illuminating how religion can be employed as a peace tool is extending visions of roles that religious organizations can play in peacebuilding (Alger, 2002). Appleby, in *The Ambivalence of the Sacred: Religion, Violence and Reconciliation* (1999), asserts that religion's ability to inspire violence is intimately related to its equally impressive power as a force for peace. Cynthia Sampson informs us of the institutional moves within some religious communities toward developing "an increasingly intentional and systematic approach to peacebuilding" (1997: 304).

Recent research has been very informative on the peacebuilding relevance of roles played by NGOs in humanitarian field activities. *Peacebuilding: A Field Guide*, by Reychler and Paffenholz (2001) is a 543 page handbook for members of NGOs active in peacebuilding in the field. A quick overview of the fifty-five contributions to this volume, by fifty-seven scholars and participants in NGOs, usefully illuminates the diversity of challenges confronted by NGOs engaged in peacebuilding in the field. Seventeen aspects of field activity are divided into three sections: (1) preparing for the field, (2) working in the field, and (3) surviving in the field. Preparing for the field also involves selecting people, training people and creating awareness of multicultural environments and gender issues.

Discussion of training people opens with a listing of peacebuilding activities in which NGOs are involved: mediation and confidence building, humanitarian assistance, reintegration, rehabilitation, reconstruction, stabilization of economic structures, monitoring and improving human rights, interim administration, information and education.

It concludes with concern that "at best civilians are introduced to their mission tasks through short-term courses". Instead, it is advocated that "there is a need for comprehensive training programs that fit the needs of field operations" (Reychler and Paffenholtz, 2001: 36).

The concluding section of the volume, surviving in the field (Reychler and Paffenholtz, 2001: 443-533), offers essential insights on the survival challenges confronted by members of NGOs attempting to achieve their goals in strange, challenging, disruptive and often violent conditions. High Risk Job (HRJ) NGOs, such as the International Red Cross and Doctors Without Borders, have developed stress-prevention structures within their organizations.

Finally, it is very significant that learning, through both practice and research, about peacebuilding tasks for civil society has had an impact on peace agreements. Bell and O'Rourke (2007) have analyzed 389 peace agreements addressing 48 intra-state conflicts. They found that 139 of these agreements, addressing 41 intra-state conflicts, make explicit provisions for civil society involvement.

In conclusion, it is likely that virtually all readers of this article will be able to identify a role that they are playing, or could play, in a NGO/ civil society organization of which they are a member that is involved in peacebuilding. Also, peace researchers are challenged to bear in mind the simultaneous involvement of NGO/civil society organizations in a vast array of roles in transnational advocacy networks, humanitarian assistance roles, development assistance roles, religious roles, a diversity of peacebuilding roles in the field and tasks assigned in peace agreements. How can analysis of these activities by peace researchers help those involved to more adequately evaluate the interdependence of this vast array of peacebuilding roles and their impact?

Participation of Business in the UN System

The UN website states: "The business community has played an active role in the United Nations since its inception in 1945. A number of UN organizations have a successful history of co-operating with business. Recent political and economic changes have fostered and intensified the search for collaborative arrangements" (www.un.org/partners/ business). A detailed account of these developments is provided by Jane Nelson in *Building Partnerships: Cooperation Between the United Nations System and the Private Sector* (2002). The United Nations Fund for International Partnerships (UNFIP) was established in 1998 by Secretary General Kofi Annan. UNFIP is responsible for administering and developing partnerships between the agencies, departments, and programs of the UN and the private sector. UNFIP works with UN web foundations and corporations to identify opportunities for partnership and collaboration.

There is a vast literature that reveals the widespread influence of transnational business corporations on world affairs (Macleod and Lewis, 2004: 77-98). Recently there have been efforts to involve these corporations in standards that conform to UN declarations and covenants on human rights, labor and environment. Toward this end Secretary General Kofi Annan proposed the Global Compact in an address to the World Economic Forum in Davos, Switzerland in January 1999. He urged business corporations to join an international initiative involving UN agencies, labor and civil society. In July 2000 more than 50 corporation heads met with the Secretary General at United Nations Headquarters for the launch of the Global Compact.

Now, hundreds of companies from all regions of the world, international labor and civil society organizations are engaged in the Global Compact, working to advance ten universal principles in the areas of human rights, labor, the environment and anti-corruption that are derived from these four documents: (1) Universal Declaration of Human Rights, (2) the International Labor Organization's Declaration on Fundamental Principles and Rights at Work, (3) the Rio Declaration on Environment and Development and (4) the UN Convention Against Corruption. The Global Compact now involves over 2000 business, civil society, academic and city organizations. There are Global Compact Offices in six UN agencies: UN High Commissioner for Human rights (UNHCHR), UN Environment Program (UNEP), UN Development Program (UNDP), UN Industrial Development Organization (UNIDO), International Labor Organization (ILO) and the UN Office on Drugs and Crime (UNODC). In April 2004, Secretary General Kofi Annan addressed an open debate of the Security Council on the role of business in conflict prevention, peacekeeping and post-conflict peacebuilding.

The peace mission of the Global Compact, defined by the UN Global Compact Office in 2005 in *Enabling Economies of Peace: Public Policy for Conflict-Sensitive Business*, identifies a range of actions that governments and international organizations can undertake to assist private-sector efforts to promote conflict-sensitive business practices. The Global Compact Office has also created a *Business Guide for Conflict Impact Assessment and Risk Management* (2002, www.unglobalcompact.org). The UN website reminds business of the "contributions of the UN System to commercial order and openness" and informs them of the contributions of specific organizations in the UN system to worldwide business, including the International Maritime Organization, International Civil Aviation Organization, World Health Organization, International Telecommunications Union and World Meterological Organization (www.un.org/partners/business/otherpages/ factsheets).

> The Global Compact is not a regulatory instrument —it does not "police," enforce or measure the behavior or actions of companies. Rather, the Global Compact relies on public accountability, transparency and the enlightened self-interest of companies, labor and civil society to initiate and share substantive action in pursuing the principles upon which the Global Compact is based (www.unglobalcompact.org).

In conclusion, there is no doubt that UN efforts, through the Global Compact to involve business corporations in efforts to conform to UN standards on human rights, labor and environment, and to support the development of economies of peace is a significant innovation. This development creates a great need for peace researchers to illuminate exactly what strategies might most effectively induce business leaders to comply with these standards.

Business in World Politics

The brief overview of business in the UN System reflected diverse dimensions of business involvement in world politics that have been largely ignored by the mainstream of international relations research; but the international economic roots of peacelesness has received growing attention in peace research (Jeong, 2000, 87-93). Significant is the recent emergence of literature on the potential roles of business in "conflict prevention" (Wenger and Mockli, 2003) and "conflict management" (Haufler, 2001). The volume by Wenger and Mockli, *Conflict Prevention: The Untapped Potential of the Business Sector*, lays out a broad conceptual framework that incites this reader to ponder not only the "untapped potential," but also the "uninvestigated impact" of business on international conflict. They begin by a three-fold typology of "roles of corporate enabling" of the preventive role of other actors (Wenger and Mockli, 2003: 137-143):

> Role 1: Funding (e.g. any kind of corporation can fund NGO peace conferences, mediation processes, democracy programs and health measures)

Role 2: In-kind support (e.g. selected industries can provide modern communications equipment to peace builders, and education programs, and drugs to AIDS programs)
Role 3: Strategic philanthropy (e.g. any kind of corporation can enhance the management capacity of NGOs and make conflict prevention a strategic issue of social investment)

Wenger and Mockli also present a typology of three more roles that focus on "corporate economic peace building":

Role 4: Commercial (e.g., contractural agreements with the UN for supplying equipment, relief products and many other services to local or international actors involved in conflict prevention) (16)
Role 5: Semicommercial: "This role requires business operators with the willingness to take on additional risk in the cause of conflict prevention" (149); "semicommercial corporate peacebuilders are required to carefully coordinate their actions with other actors engaged in conflict prevention if they want to make sure that their involvement creates preventive value rather than harm" (151)
Role 6: Noncommercial: "Companies that take this role offer their extensive economic experience and know-how to any actor seeking to create economic opportunity in conflict-prone countries" (153); "The corporate community can, for instance, advise the local government in creating incentives (such as reduced import duties, tax exemptions, and the right to repatriate profits) that encourage business activities" (154)

Christopher L. Avery has written a report on *Business and Human Rights in a Time of Change* (2000) that "identifies sources of pressure on business to act responsibly, how this pressure is intensifying and how business is responding" *(www.amnesty.org.uk/business).* This hundred page report opens with a section on "changes in business thinking" (10-21) that is followed by enumerating fourteen sources of pressure on business to take human rights seriously (22-42). Of particular significance for our brief overview are the following four "steps towards change" (43-61).

1. *Business Groups Putting Human Rights on Their Agenda*

Examples are the Caux Round Table Principles for Business (adopted by a group of US, Japanese and European business leaders, and the US Business for Social Responsibility (an alliance of over 1400 companies and affiliated companies). Its Business and Human Rights Program helps companies to develop human rights policies and monitoring systems; to engage in dialogue with human rights organizations, labor unions and governments; and to address human rights issues that arise as a result of sourcing and manufacturing in developing countries.

2. Companies Adopting Human Rights Principles

Avery reports: "Until the late 1990s only a few companies had adopted policies that seriously addressed international human rights issues. Those in the forefront included Levi Strauss, Reebok and The Body Shop" (Avery, 2000, 46). By 2000 many more companies had adopted human rights policies, including Royal Dutch Shell, BP Amoco, Nokia, Statoil, Norsk Hydro, and Rio Tinto. One example is Royal Dutch Shell's *Business and Human Rights: A Management Primer* (1998).

3. Human Rights Training for Employees

BP Amoco has internet sites providing employees with guidance on human rights issues and contact information on international human rights and development organizations (BP Amoco, 1999: 38).

4. Independent Monitoring

In 1999 nine major US retailers agreed to help fund an independent monitoring of their factories in the Northern Marianas Islands (Sweatshop Watch, 1999).

It is not surprising that Avery follows this section of his analysis with a section on "A slow response to the new realities." He concludes:

> The trends discussed above ... mean that companies will increasingly find human rights issues coming onto their agenda whether they like it or not. ...But as the millennium approaches, most companies have still not come to terms with the new reality that they are to be held accountable for their human rights-related record (Avery, 2000: 62).

In conclusion, this brief view of literature on potential for enhancing corporate economic peacebuilding reveals this to be a subject that deserves enhanced attention by peace researchers. In addition, it causes us to note that all people live their daily lives in communication, transportation, housing, shopping, recreation, investment and other activities that involve them in the impact of business on human rights and other peacebuilding issues. How can peace researchers help people to make their business involvements more supportive of a peaceful world?

Participation of Local Governments in the UN System

There is now increasing involvement of local governments in the UN System. Cities were on the agenda of Secretary General Kofi Annan, who said that local governments should be given more authority to deal with the growing number of problems that are emerging as the world enters the "urban millennium." UN-Habitat (UN Human Settlements Program), established in 1977,

> is mandated by the UN General Assembly to promote socially and environmentally sustainable towns and cities with the goal of providing adequate shelter for all. ... It has a special relationship with local authorities, including Mayors, Councillors, and their municipalities in countries around the world to strengthen and maintain dialogue with central and local governments (www.unhabitat.org).

Table 5 lists examples of local government involvement in the UN System, beginning with UN-Habitat. A UN Advisory Committee of Local Authorities (UNACLA) was established in Venice in January 2000, at a meeting called by the Executive Director of UN-Habitat, and attended by mayors from all over the world and presidents of inter-state associations of local authorities. UNACLA held its fifth anniversary meeting in Washington, D.C. in February 2006. A sub-committee of UNACLA, an Advisory Group of Experts on Decentralisation (AGRED), held its first meeting in Gatineau, Canada in March 2004. Its membership includes experts from twelve countries around the world and representatives of Metropolis and United Cities and Local Governments (UCLG). Its function is "to guide the international dialogue on decentralisation and provide advice on strengthening local authorities around the world" *(www.unhabitat.org/unacla).*

In 2004 UN-Habitat and United Cities and Local Governments (UCLG) held a meeting in Barcelona on the theme of "Local Governments, Partners for Development." At this meeting the Executive Director of UN-Habitat and six mayors selected by UCLG signed an "Agreement of Cooperation" aimed at expanding their collaboration on issues such as: (1) the Global Campaign on Urban Governance, (2) the Global Observatory of Local Democracy and Decentralization, (3) localizing the Millennium Development Goals, (4) the international dialogue on decentralization and (5) UNACLA (ww2.unhabitat.org/unacla/agreement_of_cooperation.asp). The Best Practices and Local Leadership Program (BLP) was established in 1997. "It is a global network of government agencies of states, local authorities and their associations, professional and academic institutions and grassroots organisations dedicated to the identification and exchange of successful solutions for sustainable development" (www.unhabitat.org).

Table 2

Examples of local governments in the UN System

UN-Habitat	UN Advisory Committee on Local Auth. *(www.unchs.org/Committee)*
	Advisory Group of Experts on Decentralization (AGRED)
	Best Practices and Local Leadership Program (BLP) *(www.unchs.org)*
	Global Urban Observatory (GUO)
	World Urban Forum
	Sustainable Cities Program (SCP)
	Municipal Development Program (MDP)
	Global Campaign on Urban Governance
	Urban Sanitation and Solid Waste Management
	Millennium Development Goal 11, improve the lives of slum dwellers
World Bank	Municipal Development Program *(www.worldbank.org)*
	Local Economic Development Specialists (LED) in Urban Dev. Sector
UNDP	Urban Management Program *(www.undp.org)*
	World Alliance of Cities Against Poverty *(www.undp.org/hivmayors/worldallianc)*
	Colloquiums of Mayors, 1995 and 1997
UNESCO	The City: Network of Cultures
UNICEF	Mayors Defenders of Children Initiative, periodical meetings *(www.unicef.org)*
	International Child Friendly Cities *(www.childfriendly cities.org)*
WHO	Healthy Cities Program
UNEP	Environmental Management Systems (EMS) for Local Authorities
UNAIDS	Alliance of Mayors Initiative for Community Action on AIDS at Local Level *(www.amicaall.org)*
UNCDF	Local Development Program
UNITAR	Decentralized Cooperation Program (DCP)
UN Interim Administration Mission in Kosovo (UNMIK) *(www.un.org/Kosovo)*	
UN-Habitat/World Bank Cities Alliance: Cities Without Slums *(www.citiesalliance.org)*	
UN-HABITAT/UNDP Urban Management Programme (UMP)	
UN-HABITAT/UNEP Sustainable Cities Programme (SCP)	

Together with UN-Habitat's Urban Indicators Program, the BLP forms the Global Urban Observatory (GUO), UN-Habitat's facility for monitoring global trends in sustainable urban development and evaluating progress in the implementation of the Habitat Agenda. The

GUO helps governments of states, local authorities and civil society organizations develop and apply policy-oriented urban indicators, statistics and other urban information. The GUO Network (GUONet) is a worldwide information and capacity-building network established by UN-Habitat to help implement the Habitat Agenda at state and local levels. The local and national Urban Observatories in the network are governmental agencies, research centers and educational institutions that are designated as the "workshops" where monitoring tools are developed and used for policy-making. A Local Urban Observatory for a city or town is the focal point for urban policy development and planning.

Two years after UNACLA was formed, a World Urban Forum met "to examine one of the most pressing issues facing the world today: rapid urbanisation and its impact on communities, cities, economies and policies. It is projected that in the next fifty years, two-thirds of humanity will be living in towns and cities" (www.unhabitat.org). It is now a biennial gathering that involves non-governmental organizations, community-based organizations, urban professionals, academics, local authorities and national and international associations of local governments.

UN-Habitat has been charged by the UN General Assembly to help governments meet the Millennium Development Goal, target 11, of improving the lives of 100 million slum dwellers by 2020. The General Assembly mandated UN-Habitat to monitor the implementation of this goal, including designing innovations to collect, manage and analyze urban indicators and to assist local authorities with policy formulation programs.

In conclusion, examples involving ten other agencies in the UN System are listed in Table 5. This broad array of examples of involvement of local authorities in eleven agencies in the UN System clearly reveals the growing understanding that efforts to cope with a wide range of issues on the broadening agenda of the UN System requires collaboration with not only the governments of states, but also with the governments of local communities. At the same time it reveals growing appreciation by local governments of the roles that they must play in global governance. This development is clearly revealed in documents and web sites of both the UN System and organizations of local governments. But there is almost no recognition of it in public media and scholarship. This should be an important subject on the peace research agenda.

Local Governments, Organizations in World Politics

Local governments have joined together to create both global and regional organizations, some with general purposes and some with more limited agendas. The International Union of Local Authorities (IULA) was founded in 1913 in Ghent, seven years before the founding of the League of Nations. Later based in The Hague, it recently merged with the Federation Mondial des Cities Unies (FMCU), based in Paris, to form United Cities and Local Governments, with headquarters in Barcelona. With membership that includes both individual cities and national associations of local governments, it is "dedicated to promoting the values, objectives and interests of cities and local governments across the globe." With members from 127 countries, it aspires "to be the united voice and world advocate of democratic local self-government, promoting its values, objectives and interests, through cooperation between local governments, and within the wider international community" (www.cities-localgovernments.org).

There are also organizations of cities with global membership that have a specific focus. Organizations of larger cities include the Summit Conference of Major Cities of the World (SUMMIT) and METROPOLIS. The International Council for Local Environmental Initiatives (ICLEI) is dedicated to the prevention and solution of local, regional and global environmental problems through local action. The World Council of Mayors for Peace Through Inter-city Solidarity was initiated by the cities of Hiroshima and Nagasaki.

There are many regional organizations of municipalities, such as Arab Towns Organizations (ATO), CITYNET (Asia and Pacific), Eurocities, Red de Associationes de municipios de America Latina, Union des Villes Africaines (UVA), and Union of the Baltic Cities.

Finally, the direct participation of local and region authorities in governance of the European region is a quite surprising development. In fulfillment of its support of democracy, the Council of Europe (COE) created The Congress of Local and Regional Authorities of Europe (CLRAE) in 1994. Although only having an advisory role, it does establish the CLRAE as a third component, along with the Parliamentary Assembly and the Committee of Ministers, in the Council of Europe. Its responsibilities include helping new member states to make progress in establishing effective local and regional self-government. CLRAE has two chambers, the Chamber of Local Authorities and the Chamber of Regions, comprised of 291 members and 291 substitute members that represent more than 200,000 European local and regional authorities. The members of CLRAE, composed of only elected local and regional authority representatives, are representative of the various types of local and regional authority in each member state. Projects developed by CLRAE in fulfillment of its goals include efforts to establish and strengthen local democracy that include training local officials and transfrontier cooperation. Included in its projects are three conventions. The European Outline Convention on Transfrontier Co-operation recognizes the right of local and regional authorities to co-operate across frontiers in providing public services and environmental protection. Rights of foreigners are protected by The European Convention on the Participation of Foreigners in Public Life at the Local Level. There is also a Charter for Participation of Young People in Municipal and Regional Affairs.

The European Union (EU) has a somewhat similar body. The Committee of the Regions (CoR) was created in 1994 to address two main issues. First, because three quarters of EU legislation is implemented at a local or regional level, it is considered useful for local and regional representatives to have a say in the development of new EU laws. Second is concern that the public was being left behind as the EU developed. Involving the elected level of government closest to the citizens was one way of closing the gap. The Commission and Council of the European Union are required to consult CoR whenever new proposals are made in areas that have regional or local impacts.

CoR has 317 members and the same number of alternate members, appointed for a four-year term by the European Union Council, based on recommendations from member states. Each state chooses its members in its own way, but delegations from each state are supposed to reflect the political, geographical and regional/local balance in their state. All are elected members of or key players in local or regional authorities in their home region *(www.cor.eu.int/en)*.

This brief overview of the involvement of local governments in world politics has revealed that there are a number of worldwide and regional organizations of local governments focused on peace, the environment, local self-government and other global issues. This illuminates the fact that it is not just that local communities are affected by global forces, but that local economies, cultures and politics also affect global patterns. How might peace researchers assist local governments and their citizens in developing local policies that affect global patterns supportive of peacebuilding? Furthermore, the development of a Congress of Local and Regional Authorities in the Council of Europe and a Committee of the Regions in the European Union challenges peace researchers and peace activists to ponder possible future options for the participation of local governments in the governance of world regions and in global governance.

Conclusion

In conclusion, the UN peacebuilding agenda now includes an array of issues that are also on the agendas of government, civil society and business organizations that range from local to global. As a result, emerging global governance has become ever more complicated. Certainly this is a severe challenge to those involved in efforts to build a peaceful world. On the other hand, it also has informed them that there are a larger array of allies than they had realized until quite recently. Obviously Galtung was correct when he declared many years ago that "there are tasks for everybody" in the pursuit of peace. At the same time, to use a more recent term: in efforts to create a "culture of peace," all can contribute.

Thus peace researchers are now challenged to offer insight on the activities and potential of a very broad range of people involved in peacebuilding. A greater challenge is the need to offer knowledge of how this vast array of peacebuilding roles is linked. But an even greater challenge is for peace researchers to provide those involved with a vision of what the world would be like if all involved were attaining their maximum peacebuilding potential.

References

ALGER, Chadwick F. (1990): "The World Relations of Cities: Closing the Gap Between Social Science Paradigms and Everyday Human Experience." *International Studies Quarterly,* Vol. 34, 493-518.

— (1997): "Transnational Social Movements, World Politics, and Global Governance." Ed. Jackie SMITH; Charles CHATFIELD and Ron PAGNUCCO: *Transnational Social Movements and Global Politics.* Syracuse University Press, Syracuse, 260-278.

— (1999): "The Future of Democracy and Global Governance Depends on Widespread Public knowledge About Local Links to the World." *Cities,* Vol. 16, 195-206.

— (2002[a]): "Religion as a Peace Tool." *Ethnopolitics,* Vol. 1, 294-109.

— (2002[b]): "The Emerging Roles of NGOs in the UN System: From Article 71 to a People's Millennium Assembly." *Global Governance,* Vol. 8, 93-118.

— (2003): "Searching for Democratic Potential in Emerging Global Governance." Ed. Bruce MORRISON: *Transnational Democracy in Critical and Comparative Perspective.* Ashgate, Aldershot, UK, 88-105.

— (2006): *The United Nations System: A Reference Handbook.* ABC-CLIO, Santa Barbara.

— (2007[a]): "There are Peacebuilding Tasks for Everybody." *International Studies Review,* Vol. 9, 534-554.

— (2007ᵇ): "Widening Participation." Thomas G. Weiss and Sam Daws: *The Oxford Handbook on the United Nations.* Oxford University Press, Oxford, 701-715.

Anderson, Mary B. (1996): *Do No Harm: How Aid Can Support Peace —Or War.* Lynne Rienner, Boulder.

Appleby, R. Scott (1999): *The Ambivalence of the Sacred: Religion, Violence and Reconciliation.* Rowman and Littlefield, Lanham, MD.

Avery, Christopher L. (2000): *Business and Human Rights in a Time of Change.* Amnesty International, London.

Bell, Christine and Catherine O'Rourke (2007): "The People's Peace? Peace Agreements, Civil Society, and Participatory Democracy." *International Political Science Review,* Vol. 28, 293-324.

Bock, Joseph and Mary B. Anderson (1999): "Dynamite Under the Intercommunal Bridge: How Can Aid Agencies Help Defuse It?" *Journal of Peace Research,* Vol. 36, 325-338.

BP Amoco (1999): *Amoco Environmental and Social Report 1998.* At: http://bp.com/liveassets/bp_internet/globalbp/STAGING/global_assets/downloads/E/Environmental_and_social_report_1998.pdf.

Cardoso Report (2004): Report of the Panel of Eminent Persons on United Nations-Civil Society Relations (A/58/817 and A/58/817/Corr. 1). At: http://www.un.org/reform/civilsociety/panel.shtm/.

Childers, E. and Brian Urquhart (1994): *Renewing the United Nations System.* Dag Hammarskjold Foundation, Uppsala.

Galtung, Johan (1980): *The True Worlds: A Transnational Perspective.* The Free Press, New York.

— (1996): "Cultural Peace: Some Characteristics." UNESCO. *From a Culture of Violence to a Culture of Peace.* UNESCO, Paris, 75-92.

Haufler, Virginia (2001): "Is There a Role for Business in Conflict Management?" Ed. Chester A. Crocker; Fen Osler Hampson and Pamela Aall: *Turbulent Peace: The Challenges of Managing International Conflict.* US Institute of Peace Press, Washington, D.C.

Held, David and Anthony McGrew (2002): *Governing Globalization: Power, Authority and Global Governance.* Polity Press, Cambridge.

Hettne, Bjorn and Bertil Oden (2002): *Global Governance in the 21ˢᵗ Century Alternative Perspectives on World Order.* Almkvist & Wiksell International, Stockholm.

Hewson, Martin and Timothy J. Sinclair (1999): *Approaches to Global Governance Theory.* State University of New York Press, Albany.

International Commission on Intervention and State Sovereignty (ICISS) (2001): *Responsibility to Protect.* At: http://www.iciss.ca/menu-en.asp.

Johnsson, Anders B. (2003): "A Parliamentary Dimension to International Cooperation." Ed. Saul H. Mendlovitz and Barbara Walker: *A Reader on Second Assembly and Parliamentary Proposals* (Center for UN Reform). At: http://www.uno-komitte.de/en/documents/unpa-reader-2003.pdf. 20-29.

Jeong, Ho-Won (2000): *Peace and Conflict Studies: An Introduction.* Ashgate, Aldershot, UK.

KECK, Margaret E. and Kathryn SIKKINK (1998): *Activists Beyond Borders: Advocacy Networks in International Politics*. Cornell University Press, Ithaca.

MACLEOD, Sorcha and Douglas LEWIS (2004): "Transnational Corporations: Power, Influence, and Responsibility." *Global Social Policy*, Vol. 4, 77-98.

NELSON, Jane (2002): *Building Partnerships: Cooperation Between the United Nations System and the Private Sector*. UN Department of Public Information, New York.

PRENDERGAST, John (1996): *Frontline Diplomacy: Humanitarian Aid and Conflict in Africa*. Lynne Rienner, Boulder.

REYCHLER, Luc and Thania PAFFENHOLZ (ed.) (2001) *Peacebuilding: A Field Guide*. Lynne Rienner, Boulder.

ROYAL DUTCH SHELL (1998): *Business and Human Rights: A Management Primer*. At: http://www.shell.com/download/3359/index.

SAMPSON, Cynthia (1997): "Religion and Peacebuilding." Ed. I. William ZARTMAN and J. Lewis RASMUSSEN: *Peacemaking in International Conflict*. United States Institute of Peace Press, Washington D.C., 273-318.

SMITH, Jackie; Ron PAGNUCCO and Charles CHATFIELD (1997): "Social Movements and World Politics: A Theoretical Framework." Ed. Jackie SMITH; Charles CHATFIELD and Ron PAGNUCCO: *Transnational Social Movements and Global Politics*. Syracuse University, Syracuse, 59-77.

SPIRO, P.J. (1995): "New Global Communities: Non-Governmental Organizations in International Decision-making Institutions." *Washington Quarterly*, Vol. 18, 45-56.

SWEATSHOP WATCH (1999): "Retailers Agree to Join Settlement of Class Action Lawsuit Requiring Independent Monitoring of Factory Conditions." At: http://www.sweatshopwatch.org/swatch/marianas/settlement.html.

UN CAPITAL DEVELOPMENT FUND (2006): *Delivering the Goods: Building Local Government Capacity to Achieve the Millennium Development Goal*. UNCDF.

UN GENERAL ASSEMBLY (2004): A/58/58/817. At: http://www.unog.ch/80256ED D006B8954(httpAssets)/09916F545454357BC1256F5C005D4352/$file/A-58-817.pdf.

UN GLOBAL COMPACT OFFICE (2002): *A Business Guide for Conflict Impact Assessment and Risk Management*. United Nations, New York.

— (2005): *Enabling Economies of Peace: Public Policy for Conflict-Sensitive Business*. United Nations, New York.

UN-HABITAT (2004a): *Habitat Debate*, Vol. 10. At: http://ww2.unhabitat.org/hd/.

— (2004b): *The State of the World's Cities, 2004/2005: Globalization and Urban Culture*. Earthscan, London.

UN SECRETARY GENERAL (1998): "Arrangements and Practices for the Interaction of Non-governmental Organizations in all Activities of the United Nation System." UN General Assembly A/53/170 (10 July 1998). United Nations, New York.

UNESCO (1996): *From a Culture of Violence to a Culture of Peace*. UNESCO, Paris.

— (1997): *UNESCO and a Culture of Peace: Promoting a Global Movement*. 2nd ed. UNESCO, Paris.

VAN DER VYVER, Johan (2003): "Civil Society and the International Criminal Court." *Journal of Human Rights,* Vol. 2, 425-439.
WARAH, Rasna (2001): "The Emerging 'Urban Archipelago'." *United Nations Chronicle: On Line Edition,* Vol. 38.
WENGER, Andreas and Daniel MOCKLI (2003): *Conflict Prevention: The Untapped Potential of the Business Sector.* Lynne Reinner, Boulder.
WEST, Katrina (2001): *Agents of Altruism: The Expansion of Humanitarian NGOs in Rwanda and Afghanistan.* Ashgate, Aldershot, UK.

Remarks Presented at the Session Honoring the Founders of Peace Research

Herbert C. Kelman
Harvard University

A Historical Look at Peace Research

The beginnings of peace research —as a movement and a defined discipline (or inter-discipline, to be more exact)— are usually set in the 1950s. Exactly when in the 1950s peace research is said to have begun depends on whom you talk to.

There were, of course, important forerunners who carried out what we would now call peace research before the 1950s and who provided models and insights for this emerging and developing field. Most observers mention Quincy Wright, Lewis Richardson and Pitirim Sorokin, who pioneered the interdisciplinary, empirical and quantitative study of problems of war and peace. I would add to the list Mary Parker Follett, whose work on creative problem solving anticipated much of the recent work on conflict resolution. There were also scholars in the 1940s who defined peace research as a distinct domain of study and established programs to pursue it, notably Ted Lentz, an early advocate of the concept of a science of peace, and Bert Roling, who used the term polemology to designate the field (and who later became one of the founders of IPRA).

As an organized effort and intellectual movement, however, peace research began in the 1950s. I would like to offer some remarks about those beginnings of peace research as I experienced them and personally participated in them.

I chose social psychology as my field of graduate study because I saw it as a discipline in which I would be able to pursue my interests in issues of peace, justice and social change. I started my graduate work at Yale University in 1947. In 1951, while I was still a graduate student, completing my doctoral dissertation, Arthur Gladstone —a colleague at Yale and, like myself, a conscientious objector to the Korean War— and I published a letter in the *American Psychologist* in which we pointed out that pacifist theory rests on a number of psychological assumptions that could be put to empirical test, and proposed that psychologists and other social scientists might fruitfully place such efforts on their research agenda.

Our letter elicited a number of responses, some in the pages of the *American Psychologist* and others in private correspondence. Some of the responses were negative, reflecting the mood of the McCarthy era in which the U.S. found itself at the time. Many, however, were supportive. Among the more positive respondents, incidentally, was Harold Guetzkow, another pioneer of peace research, who started out as a social psychologist but transformed himself into an International Relations specialist and later —along with Chad Alger and other colleagues— developed the Inter-Nation Simulation (INS), which became a major tool for research and training in international relations.

The positive responses to Art Gladstone's and my letter identified a community of scholars interested in pursuing a peace research agenda. The respondents were mostly, but not entirely, young (Ted Lentz was part of the initial group) and mostly, but not entirely, psychologists. We called a meeting at one of the psychological conventions in 1951, at which we decided to establish an organization devoted to the promotion of research on issues of war and peace. The group took final shape in 1952, when we adopted the name Research Exchange on the Prevention of War. During that year, we began publishing the *Bulletin of the Research Exchange on the Prevention of War,* with Art Gladstone as editor and myself as book review editor. Over the next few years, the Research Exchange organized discussion groups at academic conventions, as well as symposia that included Quincy Wright and Pitirim Sorokin among other speakers. Two of these symposia (including papers by Wright and Sorokin) were published in professional journals in 1954 and 1955, respectively. The Research Exchange also organized two summer workshops to explore theoretical approaches and research ideas in the field of peace research.

In retrospect, the Research Exchange accomplished quite a bit during the few years of its operation. At the time, however, I lacked the historical perspective that I have today: after all, I did not realize that our efforts marked the beginnings of the peace research movement! I was frustrated about my own failure to start an active research program in peace research —to go beyond writing about what needs to be done and actually starting to do it. At the organizational level, I was disappointed in our failure to attract International Relations specialists to the Research Exchange.

I had the opportunity to act on this organizational concern in 1954-55, when I had the good fortune of being among the first group of Fellows to be invited to the newly established Center for Advanced Study in the Behavioral Sciences at Stanford, California. Even though I was one of the youngest members of the group, I was able —in the collegial, egalitarian atmosphere of the Center— to convene a sub-group of Fellows to inform them about the Research Exchange and to solicit their advice on how to broaden its base and move the enterprise forward. The group included, among others, the economist Kenneth Boulding, the mathematical biologist Anatol Rapoport, and a young sociologist named Stephen Richardson, who had brought with him the manuscripts of two unpublished books by his late father, Lewis Richardson: *The Statistics of Deadly Quarrels* and *Arms and Insecurity.* Boulding and Rapoport, incidentally, were greatly impressed with these two manuscripts and, indeed, helped to get them published. Lewis Richardson's work persuaded them of the possibility of applying mathematical models and quantitative methods in the study of issues of war and peace.

In discussing the early history of peace research, it is important to mention that Elise Boulding was also at Stanford in 1954-55 —not as a Fellow at the new Center, but as the very engaged wife of Kenneth Boulding. I am reminded of one of my favorite anecdotes about Elise Boulding dating back to that period. She had become very interested in the ideas of Fred Polak, one of the Fellows at the Center who had written a book —in Dutch— about the impact of the image of the future held by individuals and societies on the reality of the future itself. She felt that it was important to make Polak's book accessible to a wider audience. She therefore proceeded to learn Dutch in order to be able to translate the book. Later, of course, Elise Boulding acquired a PhD in sociology and went on to become a leading figure in the peace research movement. It is not surprising that one of her important contributions to the field was the workshop on envisioning the future as a tool in peacebuilding. Kenneth Boulding, by the way, spent the final months of his stay at the Center —the summer of 1955— dictating a short book on *The Image.*

Let me return now to the working group that I convened to discuss the Research Exchange on the Prevention of War. Our meetings led to the decision to start a new interdisciplinary journal that would replace and expand on the *Bulletin of the Research Exchange.* We named the new publication *Journal of Conflict Resolution: A Quarterly for Re-*

search Related to War and Peace. We decided to base the JCR at the University of Michigan because Kenneth Boulding was on the faculty there, Anatol Rapoport was about to join the Michigan faculty, and two energetic graduate students at Michigan —William Barth and Robert Hefner— were already handling the technical work of producing the *Bulletin of the Research Exchange* there.

The Journal began publication in 1957 as the first journal in the newly emerging field of peace research. It was guided by an interdisciplinary editorial board, chaired by Kenneth Boulding. The majority of the original board members were drawn from the Michigan faculty. The historical origins of the enterprise are reflected in the fact that the long list of names (including editorial board, managing editors, associate editors and sponsoring committee) that can be found on the cover page of the early issues of JCR includes 17 (out of a total of 36) members of the 1954-55 class of the Center for Advanced Study in the Behavioral Sciences, as well as the founding director of the Center, Ralph Tyler. The list also includes 10 of the active members of the Research Exchange. JCR was based at the University of Michigan until it moved to Yale University in 1972, where it continues to be published under the editorship of Bruce Russett. The Journal has changed over the years, reflecting changes in the field, but until recently some continuity with its origins was maintained by the presence of two of the founders of the Journal —the late Anatol Rapoport and myself— on the editorial board.

With the establishment of the new journal, the *Bulletin of the Research Exchange* ceased publication and the members of the organization decided that many of its other activities could be carried out by a new committee of the Society for the Psychological Study of Social Issues (SPSSI), chaired by Morton Deutsch —a pioneer in the study of conflict and cooperation. SPSSI, which is a division of the American Psychological Association, had an active Committee on the Psychology of War and Peace in the early 1940s. In 1945, it published a yearbook, entitled *Human Nature and Enduring Peace*, edited by Gardner Murphy. In the decade or so after World War II, however, it paid relatively little attention —as an organization— to issues of war and peace. This began to change around the middle 1950s. One of the symposia organized by the Research Exchange was held at a joint meeting of SPSSI and the Society for the Study of Social Problems and was published as a special issue of SPSSI's journal, *The Journal of Social Issues* ("Research Approaches to the Study of War and Peace," edited by Herbert C. Kelman, William Barth and Robert Hefner) in 1955. In 1959, SPSSI sponsored preparation of a book, which was eventually published in 1965 under the title *International Behavior: A Social-Psychological Analysis*, edited by myself. So SPSSI again became the address for research on issues of war and peace. I might mention here that, over the years, the engagement of psychologists with these issues has grown, along with the development of the field of peace research as a whole —much of it stimulated by the threat of nuclear war. By the 1990s, a separate Division of Peace Psychology was established within the American Psychological Association, which has published its own journal, *Peace and Conflict: Journal of Peace Psychology*, since 1995.

To return to the beginnings of the *Journal of Conflict Resolution:* The editorial work on the Journal created an interdisciplinary community of scholars at the University of Michigan interested in issues of war and peace —including, significantly, several International Relations specialists. This development led to the establishment of the Center for Research on Conflict Resolution at the University (which, to add a personal note, I joined in 1962, when I came to the University of Michigan on a joint appointment between the Department of Psychology and the Center). In some accounts of the history, the Journal is described as a product of the Center. What actually happened, however, was the reverse: The Journal was established first and the Center was created around the Journal —a product of the community of scholars engaged in putting out the Journal.

To provide a context for my description of the beginnings of peace research in the 1950s, I propose that a major impetus to the development of the movement in those years came from the convergence of two strands, loosely corresponding to two groups of scholars that recognized their interdependence: scholars from fields outside of international relations —such as economists, psychologists, anthropologists, as well as occasional physicists, biologists, or mathematicians— who were interested in applying the concepts and methods of their fields to the study of war and peace because of their strong commitment to peace (as well as, of course, the intellectual challenge of the enterprise); and scholars of international relations (many of whom, of course, also had strong commitments to peace), who felt the need to go beyond the traditional approaches of international law, international organization and diplomatic history, and develop a scientific basis for the study of war and peace.

Among the forerunners of peace research, Lewis Richardson —a physicist/ astronomer, as well as a Quaker— epitomizes the first strand. In the early 1950s, the founding of the Research Exchange on the Prevention of War and the establishment of the *Journal of Conflict Resolution* clearly represent the first strand: they emerged largely from the community of peace-oriented scholars who were not specialists in International Relations. The same can be said for some of the developments in the later 1950s and the early 1960s, including the establishment of the Canadian Peace Research Institute (founded by Hannah and David Newcombe in 1959), the Peace Research Institute in Oslo (conceived by the philosopher Arne Naess and originally established in 1959, under the direction of Johan Galtung, as a unit within the Institute for Social Research), the Polemological Institute at the University of Groningen (founded by Bert Roling in 1961), as well as the Peace Science Society (founded through the efforts of Walter Isard —like Kenneth Boulding, an economist and a Quaker).

The forerunner who epitomized the second strand was Quincy Wright. This strand was represented, in the United States, by research and training programs established in the 1950s by Richard Snyder (at Northwestern University), Robert North (at Stanford University) and Karl Deutsch (at Yale University and later at Harvard). At Northwestern, Snyder was joined by Harold Guetzkow, who —as already mentioned— had started out as a social psychologist (and, incidentally, also came from a pacifist background). Chadwick Alger began his academic career in that Northwestern program in the late 1950s, as did a number of other major contributors to peace research. Several important projects reflecting the new approach to the study of international relations —such as the work of Snyder and colleagues applying a decision-making model to the study of international politics, the work of North and colleagues using content analysis in the study of international crises, the development of the Inter-Nation Simulation by Guetzkow and colleagues, and the "Correlates of War" project of J. David Singer and colleagues —had their origins in the late 1950s and early 1960s.

The two strands needed each other in order to fulfill their potential. The non-specialists needed the specialists in order to legitimize their forays into areas in which they had not been trained, to fill in the substantive knowledge they lacked, and to provide reality testing for their conceptual models. The International Relations specialists, in turn, needed their colleagues from other disciplines as sources of concepts and methods, as well as of the validation and encouragement that they did not always receive in those days from their more traditional colleagues. The two groups thus formed a mutually beneficial coalition that provided stimulation and legitimization to both.

It is important not to exaggerate the distinctiveness of the two paths that led to the development of the peace research movement. Both the International Relations specialists and the non-specialists shared a normative commitment to the prevention of war and to the creation of a peaceful world order. And both shared the belief that the theories and empirical research methods of the behavioral sciences can be applied to the analysis of war and peace. Over time, the different origins of the two groups of scholars became relatively unimportant as they became partners in the new interdisciplinary field of peace research. It is not surprising, in this connection, that the *Journal of Conflict Resolution* was hatched at the Center for Advanced Study in the Behavioral Sciences, which was dedicated to the development of an interdisciplinary, multilevel, methodologically diverse approach to the study of social behavior. The interweaving of the two strands in a new field of peace research shared by International Relations specialists and scholars from various other disciplines was already evident in the establishment of the Center for Research in Conflict Resolution at the University of Michigan. It was institutionalized in the formation of the International Peace Research Association in 1964. It was reflected in the publication, under my editorship, of *International Behavior* in 1965. And it was fully operational in the establishment of John Burton's Centre for the Analysis of Conflict at University College, London, in 1966.

To conclude my remarks about the beginnings of the peace research movement, let me point out that back in the 1950s we could not even dream of the progress that the field has made over the decades, as reflected in IPRA and in this conference —a field represented (albeit not equally) in all parts of the world, ranging over many disciplines, using a wide variety of methods and effectively integrating theory, research and practice.

My Research

My own research within the broad domain of peace research over the years has focused on several topics, which I shall review briefly.

In the 1950s and 1960s, a central focus of my work was the effort to define the contributions of social psychology to the interdisciplinary study of war and peace. The major product of this effort was the book mentioned above, *International Behavior: A Social-Psychological Analysis*, published in 1965. The contributors to the volume were mostly social psychologists and political scientists; I edited it and wrote the introductory and concluding chapters. The volume brought together much of the theory and research on the social-psychological dimensions of international behavior available at the time and became a major text for students in international relations. A second focus of my work was the study of nationalism, national identity and the relationship of individuals to the national political system. Much of this work was carried out during the 1960s in collaboration with Daniel Katz and colleagues at the University of Michigan. A third focus of my work during the late 1950s and the 1960s was research on international educational and cultural exchanges —work that in a way reflects the functionalist approach to international relations pioneered by David Mitrany. A major product of this research was a book published in 1970, *Cross-National Encounters: The Personal Impact of an Exchange Program for Broadcasters* (by Herbert C. Kelman and Raphael S. Ezekiel, with the collaboration of Rose B. Kelman).

In the 1970s and 1980s, a major focus of my work was on international crimes —genocide, torture, war crimes. Our research— carried out in collaboration with V. Lee Hamilton —began with a national survey in the U.S. on public reactions to the trial and conviction of Lt. Calley for the My Lai massacre in Vietnam. It continued with a subsequent survey on people's conceptions of personal responsibility for actions in response to superior orders. One of our interests was the effect of political orientation —the nature of an individual's relationship to the state— to his or her view of personal responsibility. The work culminated in the publication in 1989 of *Crimes of Obedience: Toward a Social Psychology of Authority and Responsibility* (by Herbert C. Kelman and V. Lee Hamilton).

A significant turning point in my work occurred in 1966, when I met John Burton and learned about the unofficial third-party approach to conflict resolution that he was developing and beginning to apply. I was excited about his project, which I saw —from my parochial point of view— as a way of putting into practice the social-psychological approach to international conflict that I had been thinking about theoretically. I enthusiastically accepted his invitation to participate —along with Chadwick Alger and Robert North— on the third-party team in an exercise on the Cyprus conflict that he organized in London in the fall of that year.

Since then, I have increasingly devoted my efforts to developing and applying the approach that John Burton pioneered. I have come to use the term interactive problem solving to describe the approach and I have applied it over the years primarily —though not exclusively— to the Israeli-Palestinian conflict. This work has involved extensive travel in the Middle East, conversations with political leaders, dozens of problem-solving workshops with political influentials from the conflicting communities and three Israeli-Palestinian working groups that have met over a period of several years (including a group that is currently meeting at periodic intervals) to explore the two sides' perspectives on the conflict and jointly develop ideas for resolving it (or specific issues within it). These experiences, which can be described as some combination of field research and action research, have informed my writings about international conflict and conflict resolution in general, as well as the Israeli-Palestinian conflict and the possibilities for resolving it in particular. The writings in the last category constitute my particular version of policy analysis, drawing on my background as a social psychologist and peace researcher and on my experiences as a scholar-practitioner.

Scholar-practitioner is the term that my colleagues and I have come to use in describing our role in conflict analysis and resolution. One of the most satisfying aspects of my career has been the opportunity to contribute to the development of a cadre of scholar-practitioners through my work with my students across the years. My students have gone on to elaborate the model that I have helped to develop, to apply it to various conflicts around the world, and to undertake research to evaluate it. I am very proud to be able to count Luc Reychler as one of the scholar-practitioners that I have helped to train, who has continued to make major innovative contributions to the field.

Challenges for Peace Research

I conclude with some comments about the challenges for peace research today and in the future. To this end, I shall comment briefly on four dichotomies that have marked the field over the years, each characterized by tension between what are seen as two opposing elements: quantitative vs. qualitative methods, theory vs. practice, micro vs. macro levels of analysis and peace vs. justice (or negative vs. positive peace). The challenge to the field, as I see it, is to bridge the gap and maintain the balance between these seemingly opposing elements. It would be a setback for the field to come down on either side of any these dichotomies at the expense of the other. The continuing attention to both sides —and perhaps even the continuing tension between them— are necessary to the vitality of the field.

Thus, with respect to the question of quantitative vs. qualitative methods, we must remember that the application of quantitative methods and mathematical models to the study of war and peace was one of the most important innovations of the field of peace research, going back to the work of people like Richardson, Rapoport, Boulding, Isard and many others of the forerunners and founders of the peace research movement. The use of quantitative methods was a critical step in establishing war and peace as a legitimate topic for scientific research and it remains critical to the continuing claim of the field to the attention of policy makers, political analysts and wider publics. At the same time, it would be a mistake to fetishize quantitative methods and to treat them as the exclusive approach to the systematic study of war and peace. A vital field of peace research must be hospitable to the entire range of qualitative methods, including historical, ethnographic, literary and narrative approaches, and such methods as participant observation, discourse analysis and action research.

The question of theory vs. practice brings to mind Kurt Lewin's well-known view that there is nothing so conducive to theoretical insight as reflective application and practice and "nothing so practical as a good theory" (1951: 169). Although there is no need for every theoretician and researcher to be a practitioner (or for every practitioner to be a researcher), the inclusion of applied researchers and reflective practitioners within the peace research enterprise is likely to enhance the quality and relevance of the research, the effectiveness of the practice and the vitality of the shared enterprise.

As for the issue of the appropriate level of analysis, peace research is, of course, ultimately concerned with macro-level phenomena —with societal, intersocietal, and global processes. But from its inception, one of the important contributions of the field has been the exploration of micro-level processes —such as decision-making behavior, leadership, public opinion, or the formation of national identity— that can help to explain the functioning of national or international systems. Analysis of micro-processes is particularly useful for the understanding —and the promotion— of change in macro-systems. Micro-level research may also provide useful analogs for the analysis of the behavior of larger systems, as in the use of simulation or gaming experiments. Finally, the study of conflicts and of the resolution of conflicts between individuals or small groups is itself a legitimate focus for peace research, broadly defined. For all of these reasons, micro-level research is a legitimate and useful component of peace research, as long as we are careful to avoid the pitfalls of reductionism.

Finally, the issue of peace vs. justice has been debated within the peace research movement for a long time and continues to arise again and again. When peace and justice are framed in terms of negative peace —i.e., the absence of systematic collective violence, accompanied by a sense of security that such violence is improbable— and positive peace —i.e., the prevalence of conditions conducive to meeting the needs and interests of the population— two conclusions stand out. First, both negative and positive peace are high-order values and significant foci for research in their own right. Second, negative and positive peace are highly interdependent, in that negative peace is a vital condition for the fulfillment of human needs and positive peace enhances people's sense of security and reduces the probability of large-scale violence. Nevertheless, the pursuit of justice, especially in the form of holding perpetrators accountable for human rights violations in a conflict zone, may at times be an obstacle to conflict resolution. Peace research must be alert to the possible tension between human rights and conflict resolution, while maintaining its commitment to both values.

References

LEWIN, Kurt (1951): *Field Theory in Social Science: Selected Theoretical Papers.* Harper. New York.

What Does Professionalization Mean in Peace Research?[1]

Johan Galtung
TRANSCEND

On Professionalization in General

Generally, the sociology of professions identifies three characteristics of a profession:

1. There is a range of skills with which a range of professionals will handle a range of problems for a range of clients with proven competence. The clients have an idea of what to expect from the professional, and the professional has an idea of what to expect from a client.
2. There is a professional code of conduct, defining the relation of a professional to the clients, other professionals and others. The code of conduct may be supported by an oath.
3. There is a pattern of accountability of the professional to the clients, to other professionals and to others.

Professionalization of peace work moves us beyond peace research and studies, both indispensable for skills of peace work. The purpose of peace research is to produce intersubjectively communicable and verifiable knowledge according to the general rules of research. Thus, research is incompatible with secrecy, as research has to take place in public space. And one purpose of peace studies is the communication of the findings of peace research, in line with general rules for education, another public space activity. The free access of the rest of society to what happens is

---

[1] This paper was presented as a keynote speech at the 2006 IPRA conference "Patterns of Conflict, Paths to Peace" held in Calgary, Canada. For more on this and most of the topics mentioned in this paper see Galtung, 2004 (published in many translations).

of the essence. As the peace worker plans to not hurt or harm, in other words to not exercise violence, s/he has nothing to conceal.

In the following, a person exercising the peace profession will be referred to as a "peace worker," like a "social worker," or a "peace professional" like a "health professional." Others may find "peace specialist" more dignified. "Manager" must be avoided since the active participation of the clients, those seeking professional advice, is of the essence. "Facilitator" is much better.

Government Realism vs. Peace Movement Idealism: Tertium Non Datur?

To understand better where peace research may be heading, let me juxtapose governments and one special non-government, the peace movement. The governments of the state system of the 1648 Peace of Westphalia, to take a Eurocentric view of history, were successors to feudal lords, kings, emperors. They entered into violence-war-peace with *ultima ratio Regis* —the King's last argument, the gun, was frequently used— to he who has a hammer the world looks like a waiting nail. This also holds for the negation of the government, the peace movement: to he who has a mouth the world looks like an attentive ear.

Realism as a doctrine is based on the "*ultima*" above —force, not persuasion from basic principles, nor bargaining offering incentives, nor decision-making by authoritative bodies. A derivative of this thesis would be that the final word belongs to whoever has superior force, the big sticks of the big powers. In the present world this is Anglo-America; a peace proposal unacceptable to them is not "realistic."

The supreme goal of the realist will be security, meaning a low probability of being hurt/harmed by the violence of any Other. The underlying philosophy is that Evil exists, ready to turn violent for violence's own sake, and that the only counter-measure is sufficient strength to deter and/or crush Evil, thereby producing security.

Idealism as a doctrine is based on persuasion from basic principles, particularly principles held to be universally valid, even self-evident. Such principles tend to be of the ought —rather than the is— variety, like the sacredness of (human) life, meaning (human) life should be considered sacred. But what if the Other does not share that noble view? Or what if the Other considers that "in a war there are only losers." However, what if winning can be defined as losing least? This is an endless debate, with strong statements about human nature. Words, words, words.

Let us try to present the two positions along some dimensions, in no way claiming that the juxtaposition is complete, nor that there is not a solid range of variation. What we are looking for is, of course, a way of bridging the gap, even the contradiction bolstered by solid hatred on both sides, and the use of violence, or nonviolence.

Table 1

The government movement and the peace movement

1. Actors	*Government Movement* Foreign office, military	*Peace Movement* Permanent, conjunctural
2. Basic mode	Realism based on *ultima* ratio	Idealism based on ratio
3. Epistem-ology	Empiricism fact-based pragmatism	Criticism value-based moralism
4. Theory	Security paradigm based on strength Humans tend toward evil	Persuasion paradigm based on moral strength Humans tend toward good
5. Method I	Elite conferences	People's meetings
6. Method II	Negotiating harmonized national interests	Resolutions, advocacy
7. Method III	Demonstrations of — incentive power — threats of force	Demonstrations of — moral power — people power
8. Method IV	Violent action like bombing	Nonviolent action like economic boycott (A gandhian boycott of the USA might work, mass demonstrations not)

This is a clear case of thesis versus antithesis, at least as presented in this table, not denying that reality is more complex. It does not follow that the alternative, a *tertium*, has to be a synthesis. Dialectics offers three non-exclusive possibilities: (1) a positive transcendence, synthesis, accepting basic features of both, (2) a negative transcendence denying the validity of both and (3) a compromise picking some of this and some of that (Galtung, 2009, 2004).

We are talking about two world views, both of them found within the same societies, and not only in the West, although we sense the contradiction between carry-overs from feudal faith in force and enlightenment faith in human *ratio* and appeals to reason.

Realism, as spelt out above, would make allies of the carrier of Anglo-American dominance in today's world, the United States of America: say Yes-Yes-Yes to Washington D.C. And idealism would make the peace movements in the same countries say No-No-No to whatever comes out of their foreign offices. The world views are so contradictory that they become each other's antithesis.

And yet we see in the concrete case of the "US-led Coalition" in the war in and over Iraq one government after the other defecting. Without necessarily saying so, they actually do what their peace movements have demanded, they pull out. But this is more an act of protest than an alternative peace policy.

The best way of exploring these two peace discourses further is probably not by elaborating them, but by asking the question: how can this contradiction be transcended, if at all? There are eight jobs according to the table, so let us look at all eight.

But first permit me a little note from my own autobiography. I refused military service and became a conscientious objector in 1951 because I found the governmental approach unacceptable; and in 1954 refused the alternative "civilian service" because it was only a way of saying "No", not a way of serving peace. The outcome was half a year in prison during the winter of 1954-55 for a more extreme "No". I have lived this contradiction, at one time (early 1960s) being both some kind of consultant to the Norwegian foreign office, a member of the board of War Resisters International (in London) and president of its branch in Norway. And I was unhappy with them all; one is essentially built on bullets and bombs, the others on words.

So I will try to guide the reader toward a peace profession as something arising from this contradiction because that is how it came about in my case: as an effort to bridge the gap.

Obviously we are looking for an actor, the peace professional, who could transcend this government-peace movement dichotomy. The idea that governments are somehow on Track 1 and non-governments are on Track 2 freezes this dichotomy into its present form. And it begs the question whether governments are not often on Track 1 hoping that non-governments will compensate and bring about Track 2 as a result. Given the damage governmental diplomacy is capable of doing, this is a highly optimistic view. We need a better answer.

Some features of that answer are clear.

First, a peace professional will have governments and non-governments as clients and dispense advice to both. Like the health profession the skills would be available not only to friend and foe alike, but also to those uniformed (government) and civilian (non-government). The peace professional would not think of friend-foe or uniformed-civilian, but of actors desperately in need of any advice that might move the actor system closer to peace. Peace is a relation among actors, a system, not a property of one actor alone. The peace professional would engage in dialogues with the actors, but have the actor system at the top of his or her mind.

Second, the peace professional rejects violence as does the peace movement, based on the idealism of the heart, but combines that with the realism of the brain. Concretely, this leads to peace by peaceful means, rejecting violence less on moral grounds than on pragmatic grounds. Violence does not work. Shedding blood in a battle-field is like leeches sucking blood: not only does it not work, it may even make matters worse. While not denying some preventive and curative effects of minimum (threat of) violence, the approach would exclude violence from the peace-creating repertory, building more on *ratio*, less on *ultima*.

Third, the basic difference is here. Without rejecting empiricism linking theory and data, and criticism linking data and values as basic modes of intellectual activity, the focus will be on the third possibility: constructivism, linking values and theory. The values emerge from the legitimate goals of the parties to a conflict, and the theory from viable realities. The idea would be to search for a new reality where the parties might feel that their goals can be sufficiently comfortably accommodated.

Imagine a child busily adding and subtracting integers, establishing that $5 + 7 = 7 + 5 = 12$, moving on to $7 - 5 = 2$, and then running up against a wall when trying to tackle $5 - 7$. The contradiction between being mathematically correct and handling $5 - 7$ dissolves the moment negative numbers, a new mathematical reality, has been introduced. And then the child is no longer stuck.

The task is not to be stuck between the pragmatism of linking data to theories and the moralism of linking data to values. The peace professional will look for something new, like a physician who has realized that if the "system" had sufficient self-healing capacity then it would already have produced health. Neither single-minded empiricism, nor single-minded moralism will help although neither should be disregarded. An intervention bringing in something new is needed, for peace as well as for health.

Fourth, both the security and the persuasion paradigms fall short of the desirable. The former fails because efforts to deter by violence may stimulate an arms race, and efforts to crush by violence may produce trauma and stimulate a violence race with a vicious cycle of retaliation. And the latter fails, being based neither on ideas, nor incentives, nor threats. Neither facts nor values are sufficient guides for action. The parties get stuck.

A government confronted with insecurity —a risk of violence— derives an action agenda from the security paradigm. Neither the most brilliant analysis á la Noam Chomsky, nor the most stinging moral admonitions á la Pope John Paul II provide guides for action beyond the status quo of "No, No, No." This is where the peace professional enters, focusing on unresolved present conflicts, unconciliated trauma from past violence, and unresolved conflicts in the past, for constructive action. A rich action agenda.

This calls for mediation for the conflicts of the present, and conciliation for the conflicts of the past, dropping the "re" as it has a connotation of restoring a not necessarily desirable past. This is the essence of the peace paradigm. Deep conflicts exist. They may lead to violence. There is a way out: solve the conflicts, present and past. If done well, we get peace and with it security.

But these are only two of the tools in the tool chest of the peace professional. Here is a longer list of remedies (Galtung, 2009):

1. peace research and peace studies;
2. basic needs satisfaction, peace culture, peace structure;
3. goal restraint and consequence analysis;
4. mediation for conflict transformation by peaceful means;
5. anger control;
6. peacebuilding, with peace education and peace journalism;
7. nonviolence and soft peace-keeping;
8. conciliation for the removal of past traumas from the agenda;
9. creating virtuous peace cycles.

This article is not the place to spell them all out. The challenge is to stick to "peace by peaceful means," neither succumbing to violent governmental pragmatism nor to the status quo of "not in my name" peace movement moralism. Points 1-4 above are preventive therapy, points 5-8 curative therapy, and point 9 builds positive peace into the system, releasing the creative and constructive potential of conflicts rather than the potential for violence and destruction. All are based on diagnosis and prognosis of social ills. Therefore, there is much to do.

What, then, corresponds to Methods I, II, III, IV, given the general idea that direct violence is the smoke that comes out of the fire of unresolved conflicts, or from past violence with no conciliation? Generally speaking, this comes through the power of the word, *dia logos*, by helping the parties to deeper insights rather than by bribing them, threatening them or telling them how bad they are.

This, of course, is very similar to one basic assumption of psychotherapy: the talking method. Or sociotherapy rather, since violence, like conflict and peace, is a relation. A system of actors, not only single actors, is in need of change. The peace professional has to talk with all actors. There are schools of approach, here as elsewhere, all with some valid points.

Like the Table, the TRANSCEND approach has four phases:

— Method I: Meeting all parties, one-on-one.
— Method II: Empathic dialogues to elicit creativity.
— Method III: Demonstrations of

- transcending goals, positively or negatively;
- creating a new system capable of accommodating the legitimate goals of all parties.

— Method IV: Joint action to transform the conflict, always checking whether it works. If not, Methods I, II, III and IV can be followed again.

This approach differs substantially from both conventional, mainstream government approaches and peace movement action. The moral impulse, the (almost absolute) "No" to violence, is shared with the peace movement, but the pragmatism of step IV is shared with governments. There is no apodictic position, no a priori truth. Everything is tested for its validity and everything has to pass that test.

The focus is no longer on one party winning, like ETA or Madrid; nor on all parties winning, the famous win-win. The focus is on the relation, the system, on Spain moving forward into new and better realities. *Those who rest on carpets of gold, carpet bombing, or who fly on moral carpets are often short on ideas.* Peace professionals have the opposite profile. *Tertium datur.*

There is a Demand Out There: A Trip Around the World

Half a century after the tiny beginnings of peace research after World War II —including the founding of the International Peace Research Association (IPRA), 42 years ago, those foggy autumn days in London— some of us think we have a solid supply to offer. But there is always the nagging question: is there a demand out there?

There is, and the reader will pardon me for giving as cases what I know best: what I myself was asked to do in spring 2006, from mid-February to mid-June. Twelve cases, twelve processes to be more precise, some more, some less successful, all with a certain promise. The initiative often came from a go-between capable of organizing a direct encounter with one or more of the parties in the conflict. In no case did any of the parties cover any travel expenses. There was no honorarium. But the trip was combined with workshops on mediation, conciliation etc., and that balanced the budget. Perhaps this is one formula, among several?

Before delving into the cases, however, from which domain might we not expect any such demand, directly or indirectly, via a go-between? Obviously from actors to whom "winning is not everything, but the only thing": hegemons, perhaps and their challengers? Or actors who think they have mastered the necessary and sufficient skills themselves, with no need of an outsider's advice, even if softly offered under four eyes, or eight if both come with a colleague, using the one-on-one formula? Whatever the reason, the present author has not been approached, directly or indirectly, by the USA or by Norway; but by many other countries, including the UK.

The description of the cases will be the minimum necessary and sufficient to identify the issue and the nature of the demand (more details on www.transcend.org):

1. *Denmark vs Islam* in Geneva. In addition to the cartoons came the Danish refusal to dialogue and the newspaper's earlier refusal to print cartoons about the ascent of Jesus Christ to heaven, as it might hurt Christian sensitivities, *and* the burning of Danish flags and embassies, with economic boycott. The demand was for mediation.

2. *Germany vs the Herero people* in Windhoek. The issue was apology and compensation for the 1904 massacre, compounded by a court case against Germany ("apologizing is admitting"), other EU members fearing the consequences of apology and compensation, and the nature of any compensation. The demand was for conciliation.

3. *Sri Lanka* in Vienna. The issue was the breakdown of the cease fire agreement with the warring parties still hoping to force their solution. Of the five scenarios —unitary state, devolution, federation, confederation, independence— an asymmetric, bi-

cameral federation still seems preferable. The demand was for mediation.

4. *Israel-Palestine* in Berlin. The issue was to build a peace structure around a Middle East Community of Israel and its five Arab neighbors (Palestine fully recognized according to the UN resolutions), like the European Community for Western Europe after the Second World War. The demand was for new approaches.

5. *Turkey-Armenia* in Istanbul. "Something happened" in 1915, with high complexity, and involved many more than just those two parties. The search is also for a discourse to articulate what happened so that this major issue can be removed from the political agenda for the region can move forward. The demand was for conciliation.

6. *The Kashmir issue* in New Delhi. TRANSCEND took the initiative, with a former Pakistani foreign minister, a member of the Indian National Security Commission and myself proposing a "new reality" to accommodate India, Pakistan and Kashmir; this was well received and discussed at the top levels. The demand was for mediation.

7. *Myanmar* in Yangon. A military dictatorship stands for Myanmar autonomy and integrity against secession, the opposition supported by the outside for democracy and human rights. An agenda with all four goals, removing past traumas in favour of cooperative futures, might work. The demand was for mediation and conciliation.

8. *Cambodia* in Phnom Penh. "Something happened," indeed, in 1975-79: the Khmer Rouge against Phnom Penh. But from 1961-89, much else also happened. To select one atrocity for a tribunal may serve punitive justice. But the problem of conciliation remains. The demand was for holistic conciliation.

9. *Korea* in Seoul. The Korean war (1950-53), which played a major role in the Cold War discourse, started in 1948 with the Cheju uprising against US occupation. North Korea's cause, to help South Korea against US aggression, was not unfounded. The demand was for conciliation, using a history commission to explore what happened.

10. *Japan-China/Korea* in Tokyo. The Prime Minister's visit to the Yasukuni shrine —that turns the dead uniformed Japanese into gods— deepens the war trauma. An alternative memorial dedicated to the uniformed and civilians from all countries was solicited by, and presented to, a major LDP faction. The demand was for conciliation.

11. *USA* in Washington D.C. The US Empire is on its way down and US foreign policy must change, but how? Workshops are being organized, the peace movement is unprepared as is the Democrat "opposition." The demand is for peace research and peace paradigms.
12. *Mexico* in Puebla. Latin American integration is coming and one problem will be foreign policy in general, and toward the USA in particular. Workshops are being organized, but most people seem unprepared. The demand is for peace research and peace paradigms.

The reader will have noticed that the demand can usually be formulated in terms of mediation and/or conciliation. But there is also a demand for more basic services, like building peace structures, and for peace research to explore what is needed. All the other offers in a peace professional's chest, which contains nine remedies, are lurking in the background and will of course sooner or later be brought up by the peace worker.

Does this work? The first case (Denmark versus Islam) did. There have been dialogues and the burning has stopped. However, an apology, an exploration of the line between freedom of expression and respect for what is sacred to others and the lifting of the boycott are still to come.

Cases 2, 5 and 8 are complicated, and much work is needed. Case number three (Sri Lanka) looks bad right now (spring-summer 2006), but going to the brink again may possibly produce peace talks next time, and not only a discussion of a ceasefire. The fourth case is probably the only formula for Middle Eastern peace, but is a long term project even if more than ever is needed for its achievement. Case six (the Kashmir issue) may stand a good chance as long as the two leaders are in power, and that will not be forever. Myanmar, the seventh case, has slow dynamism on its side and is compatible with the idea of Myanmar being in control, not some "international community." Case nine (Korea) may become an important part in the North-South Korea process. Japan-China/Korea, case ten, will in one way or the other be on the agenda. Cases eleven (USA) and twelve (Mexico) are for a more conscious near future.

We are dealing with systems, not single actors. Peace workers have to become relations specialists, with maximum knowledge about all the actors' capacities for peace-making, -keeping and -building. Obviously, most such processes take time, as does the cure of complicated diseases for human beings. And no remedy comes with the guarantee that it will always work. It may even be counterproductive, so one must be watchful. But the demand is enormous and we have much to offer.

The Code of Conduct and the Problem of Accountability

TRANSCEND felt the need for some guidelines arising out of experience and their testing by yet more experience.

Mission Statement: Peace by Peaceful Means
— By *peace* we mean the capacity to transform conflicts with empathy and creativity, without violence; this is a never-ending process.
— By *transforming conflicts* we mean enabling the parties to go ahead in a self-reliant, acceptable and sustainable manner.
— By *with empathy* we mean the ability to understand the conflict as well as the ways the parties themselves understand the conflict.
— By *creativity* we mean channeling conflict energy toward new, innovative ways of satisfying basic human needs for all.
— By *without violence* we mean that this process should avoid:

  • any threat or use of direct violence that hurts and harms,
  • any use of structural violence that demobilizes the parties.

The Relation between the Conflict Worker and Him/Herself:

1. Your motivation should be to help the parties transform the conflict, not your own promotion, materially or non-materially.
2. You should possess skills/knowledge for the task and develop them further, but never use the conflicts only to acquire them.
3. Do not have a hidden agenda, for yourself or for others, beyond conflict transformation. Have nothing to conceal.
4. Your legitimacy is in your skills, knowledge, creativity, compassion and perseverance and ability to stimulate the same in the conflict parties; not in a mandate or organizational backing.

The Relation between the Conflict Worker and the Parties

5. Do not enter a conflict if you yourself have an unresolved conflict with any one of the parties or bear overly deep grudges.

6. Empathy/dialogue need be with *all* parties, including those you dislike.
7. Do not manipulate. Play with an open hand; say what you do.
8. Respect demands for confidentiality, do not attribute.
9. Do not receive honoraria, gifts, etc. from the parties beyond ordinary hospitality.
10. Communicate between the parties only with their permission.
11. Speak with one tongue, not one version for one party and another for the others, granted that the focus may be different.
12. Be open to new ideas, do not become a prisoner of any plan.
13. Never propose an outcome or process that cannot be undone. You may be wrong.

The Relation between the Conflict Worker and Society

14. Do not seek personal or organizational credit.
15. Disappear from the conflict formation when no longer needed.
16. Plans for conflict outcomes and conflict processes belong neither to you nor to the parties, but to the system at large.
17. Share your skills, knowledge and experience with others; try to contribute to a general conflict transformation culture.
18. Do not receive direct funding from past, present or future conflict parties who have used, use or may use your services.
19. Conflict work is a public service. The reward is to do it well.
20. All conflicts are born equal and have the same right to transformation. No conflict is at a "higher level" than any other.

Particularly important are points 4, 13 and 20. As mentioned, the code comes from experience. This is the kind of thing that has to be tested against the experience and moral philosophies of others, as a good dialogue that aims at an ever better code. And the essence of that code, the moral maxims in a Kantian sense, might one day provide a basis for the equivalent of an Hippocratic oath.

What, however, about accountability? This is a right and a duty between society and the profession, and between the profession and the individual professional. You give us/me the right to exercise the profession, and we/I assume the duty to do so according to a code of conduct. This is very different from the peace movement, protected as it is by the human right to the freedom of expression, with no clear duty ever defined. It is more similar to the governmental approach. There are the Vienna protocols for the exercise of the diplomatic profession, and the Geneva Conventions for the exercise of the military profession.

They set some limits even if the very essence of diplomacy —the skills of negotiation— seem to be exempt from any code of conduct and any accountability. There is an exception, however: as the saying goes, whoever pays the piper is hence entitled to call the tune. For example, the diplomat's foreign office or —if s/he is not simply seconded— the international governmental organization, the IGO, like the UN. The ultimate test remains the national interest, or the interest of the IGO, or the UN.

Not so for the peace profession. The ultimate test is the human interest and nature's interest, not the interest of systems at local levels, nations, states, regions, the world. The test of the pudding is in the eating. Is there a transformation heading for peace? Do people lead better lives, with less suffering, more fulfillment? Or less *dukkha*, more *sukha*, in age-old Buddhist terms.

Time Has Come, with Health Professionals as One Model

Health studies are highly inter- and trans-disciplinary, as even the most cursory look at the curriculum of any medical school will prove. But health studies are also inter- or trans-national. Ideally speaking, medical doctors have no father/mother-land. Not only can they practice anywhere, but they have a value overriding patriotism, sexism, racism and so on: *health*. The Hippocratic oath demands of them to treat friend, foe and the Other alike, as already mentioned.

We are moving in that direction also in the field of peace studies, promoting a value more important than national interests: *peace*. We are not there yet, nor is the task of inter/trans-disciplinarity carried as far as it merits. But conflict studies, or conflictology —as basic to peace studies as anatomy, physiology and pathology to health studies— spans the whole spectrum from micro, via meso and macro, to mega conflicts, from individual psychology into global psychology, not only inter-state and inter-nation studies, two sides of international relations. Increasingly, peace researchers feel at home at all these levels.

We need inter/trans-disciplinarity because traditional social sciences are so closely related to the growth of the now-waning Western state system, from the era of imperialism. Thus, world history is conceived of as parallel nation, state and regional histories. The social sciences' politicology, economics and sociology are clearly dedicated to the three pillars of the modern state, State, Capital and Civil Society, one at a time, endowed with a historicity not given to colonized peoples for whom anthropology was invented. And economics even explores only one economic system, capitalism ("capitalistics" would be a better word). This is not good enough. The social sciences are badly in need of globalization.

Transcending state borders is only one of these challenges, however. There are other fault-lines in the human construction: gender and generation, race and nation, class (political, economic, military, cultural, depending on the power involved), the environment. Peace studies need transcending paradigms for them all, with no built-in assumption favouring one fault-line side or the other.

A major task of peace studies is to come to grips with massive category killing, which is referred to as "genocide" when carried out against a nation. The killing of unborn and born women may be the most major form. Another is death by starvation, or by preventable or curable diseases. Health studies are focussed on avoidable diseases, including pandemics; peace studies focus on avoidable violence(s), including massive category killing. With more work on positive health and peace, not only to prevent disease and violence, these two can both serve as guidelights for higher levels of human self-realization.

Trans-disciplinary and trans-fault-line peace studies are around the corner. Security studies are the easy prey of upper class, white, old male patriotism from the Anglo-American countries producing settlers on the lands of others (like Israel). They have much to feel insecure about. Peace studies and "security through peace" would serve them much better than "peace through security."

With deep globalization comes professionalism, and with professionalism comes the dangers of self-righteous narrowness. Hence the need for pure academic peace studies able to analyze and critique practices emerging from within its own ranks.

But more challenges will line up. Whoever pushes in any direction, like peace researchers looking for more ways of turning theory into practice, and practice into theory, should not be surprised if counterforces appear. *Actio* always provokes *reactio*.

Other disciplines will try cooptation, like "the problem of peace is basically psychological" and hence Peace Psychology courses. This is excellent when combinable with respect for a broader view, for the forest, not only for a tree or two. Taken alone, it is a step backward.

The strong reactions, however, will come from the professions that feel threatened, like diplomacy. The Track 1/Track 2 formula —"governments do 1, NGOs do 2. Let us divide the turf"— is simply not good enough. Inter-state diplomacy —representation, information and negotiation— may in its present form be a dying institution, and not only because others do the job better. The problem goes deeper, into the notion of peace as harmonized national interests. Where is nature's interest? The human interest? The local level interest? The regional interest? The gender, generational, etc. interest? The global interest? The world is more complex today, demanding a very multi-layered approach. The peace workers of the future can be useful all over, but not if they are tied to national interests, the concern of a very few people.

A foreign office is not necessarily the obvious place to turn peace theory into peace practice, nor is a peace ministry for that matter. We are moving away from the world as an inter-state system, toward inter-regional, inter-local authorities, an inter-human, inter-gender/genera-tion/race/class world, all of which are dependent on the environment. Merely blowing fresh air into the Westphalia system is suboptimal. Train the diplomats to do a better job and move ahead in all the other systems, with nature's interest, and the human interest, as the ultimate test.

Conclusion

Research- and theory-guided peace work to produce more peace, not only more research, have come to stay, bridging the gap between foreign policy pragmatism and peace movement moralism.

References

GALTUNG, Johan (2009): "Conflict Transformation By Peaceful Means." Ed. Charles WEBEL and Johan GALTUNG: Handbook of Peace and Conflict Studies. Routledge, London.
— (2004): Transcend & Transform. Pluto, Paradigm Press, London.

Conference Highlights

Short Films and Moving Debates:
An Account of the IPRA Short Film Festival 2008

Wies De Graeve & Tomas Baum
Flemish Peace Institute

＊

> You know, I never could figure those varmints out. They was the orneriest, cussinest, most dag-blasted tribe of varmints you ever saw. They was always a-fightin' and a-feudin' and a-shootin' each other. If it wasn't one darn thing, it was another. No sooner did they settle one argument, than they find something else to fuss about. And when they couldn't find what else to fight over, the flat-footed people started shooting at the buck-tooth people, and the vegetarians started fighting the meat-eating people, and you couldn't make heads or tails of it.
>
> Grandpa Squirrel in the cartoon *Peace on Earth*, 1939

The IPRA Short Film Festival 2008

During an international conference such as the IPRA conference, scholars from all over the world meet to present papers, discuss their research and exchange ideas. The contribution of the Flemish Peace Institute —a local partner organisation— was to set up a festival of short films during the Conference "Building Sustainable Futures."[1] We believe that a social and informal event like a film festival stimulates contacts between participants, facilitates the building up of networks and provides new points of analysis and angles of approach. Moreover, a film festival combines leisure and entertainment while at the same time offering

[1] Our special thanks go to professor Cynthia Weber, who was very supportive of the project from its inception, to Guido Convents from the Leuven Africa Film Festival for valuable advice and to the staff of the Flemish Peace Institute.

a stimulating intellectual environment in which to consider issues of war and peace, thus supplementing the conference. The following text has the modest objective of giving a descriptive account of the event.

Films on war and conflict are abundant: from emotional drama to heroic action, from neutral documentary to burning critique. Traditionally the genre of short films gets less exposure than action blockbusters at movie theatres and the news items that bring conflicts from all over the world into our living rooms. However, short films are very condensed pieces of art, getting more and more attention and appreciation in the international scene. In addition, they are perceived as powerful media to bring across messages in an effective way. It does not take much time to engage with short films and due to their small size they can easily circulate in virtual space. As we formatted the festival for the convenience of conference participants, opting for short films was a natural choice. The shortened attention span after a day of conference lectures should not pose insurmountable problems. An added value was to invite the different filmmakers for a lively discussion after the screening and arrange for a cine-café afterwards. We were very happy to welcome filmmakers from Iran, the United Kingdom, Iraq, Zimbabwe, the United States and Belgium.

The programme was inspired by the programming of recent international film festivals and drawn up with the input of international experts. The virtual gateway called You Tube allowed us to scan the worldwide web and to dig up visual pearls and engaging imagery. Presenting an international mix was the programme's explicit aim. Different approaches to cinema and to film topics help to question clichés and assumptions not just about film and filmmaking but also about films as vehicles for promoting peace and sustainability. On the first night the topic was Disrupting Conflict. We focussed on three core protagonists of war: the gun, the victim and the soldier. The following night issues of identity were brought to the fore in Filming the Fear of Difference. The final night, Popular Film and Conflict considered the potential of popular film types as comedy, musical and cartoon.

Opening Scene

The so-called trailer for the festival —*It was a boring conversation anyway* by Jess De Gruyter— was screened at the plenary session on the first day of the conference. This montage is not a celebration of war, although the music could fool you into thinking so. It does, however, evoke a strange and uncanny feeling. Some people might even

IPRA
Short Film Festival

15, 16 and 17 July 2008 - 8 pm

Municipal Library 'Tweebronnen' I Rijschoolstraat 4 I Leuven (BE)

INTERNATIONAL SHORT FILMS ON PEACE AND CONFLICT
DEBATES WITH AWARD-WINNING FILM MAKERS
CINÉCAFÉ WITH FOOD AND DRINKS

www.flemishpeaceinstitute.eu

sense disgust, because the compilation rests upon a certain aesthetisa-
tion of violence. Colour scenes of a happy Eva Braun —Hitler's mistress,
as we know— are blended with shots from mobilizing troops and images of Stalin and Churchill. When the music reaches a first climax, one
minute into the movie, the action starts. And we as viewers are confronted with horrific scenes from World War II. All this enfolding before
our eyes is set to a happy tune that sings out in fascination "Can't take
my eyes off of you."

To academics dealing with theory and empirical issues of peace,
this movie does not make much sense. However, it does make one
think. An interview with the artist who compiled the material brought
some enlightenment:

> From my early childhood I have had this interest in World War II.
> This two-minute compilation has been based on a review of 50 hours
> of tape. Originally I was working with the Requiem by Wolfgang Mo-
> zart as the music for this short compilation. It worked quite well,
> but something seemed to be missing. The problem with violence did
> not come out enough, as the images I used are well known. The es-
> trangement that is introduced by using the tune "Can't take my eyes
> off of you" augments the wryness of the images. It makes the doc-
> umented violence at times unbearable. I felt that I had to do this as
> people in our society are so accustomed to seeing violence that they
> need to be triggered again by something else in order to see and feel
> the problem.[2]

What one learns from talking to the maker is that his work as a
poet revolves around three topics: his relation to women, World War II
and movies. His movies complement his written work as a poet. Dealing with World War II as an artist born in 1973 is not self-evident, but
his protracted interest in it is grounded in family stories about that war
he heard about as a child. Likewise, our aim in the plenary introduction
was to sensitise conference participants to the challenge of engaging
with short films and debating these with the makers.

Disrupting Conflict

On the first night of the festival, we left all context, narrative and
history aside and focused on three core protagonists of war: the gun,

---

[2] Interview with Jess De Gruyter on 18 June 2008.

the victim and the soldier. The complexity of this triangle and the disrupting results of their coming together were at the centre of the ensuing debate.

FAL by Hans van Nuffel (Belgium, 13′) presented a story about mutual fascination, tragic loss and automatic assault rifles. The son of a dead arms dealer takes shooting lessons from a Congolese man and former child soldier. The weapon of choice is the FAL, a product of the Belgian company FN. The gun is a glorified extension of his manhood for one, a brutal tool of destruction in the hands of the other. Filmed in a subtle style, this multilayered story describes how a gun is at the centre of very different lives, but with a disrupting impact for both.

Asylum by Rumbi Katedza (Zimbabwe, 5′) showed the audience the harrowing psychological effects of war on a Sudanese asylum seeker in the UK. *Asylum* is a very short and experimental film with horrifying flash backs, extreme sounds and hermetic storytelling. It shows the shocking human disaster caused by war crimes and makes these visible by confronting the psychological disruption with the indifference of red tape in border control.

In *Zero Degree* by Omid Khoshnazar (Iran, 8′) a soldier has his gun aimed at a handcuffed civilian captive. After a minute of suspense, the sound of shooting is heard. The man falls down on the ground while the camera is recording. The soldier is puzzled by fear and tries to escape but the camera stops him. He keeps on trying to run away from what he did, but the camera frame pushes him to a cliff. The soldier falls and keeps falling, until the camera stops him and starts to rewind. The camera keeps on rewinding to the moment of decision when he pulled the trigger. Although *Zero Degree* is an animated film, it confronts the audience with the psyche of a war protagonist, often seen as the figure of the soldier.

Concerning script, camera, soundtrack, etc., the three selected films could be labelled "experimental." Although not always easy to grasp and quite disrupting for the audience itself, it was clear that the three short films are powerful media to glimpse beyond the external and more physical aspects of conflict. The audience was forced to pay attention to the devastation that war and violence leave behind.

Directors Rumbi Katedza, Hans van Nuffel and Omid Koshnazar attended the screenings and debated their work. Afterwards the audience joined the debate. One of the central arguments in the discussion was that conflict is disruptive for everyone and that war makes victims. This fact was clearly illustrated by *FAL* and *Zero Degree*, as both films deconstruct the triangular relation between the gun, the soldier and the victim: the soldier is at times no more than an extension of the gun, while he is a victim as well. The three directors explicitly mentioned the psychological collapse caused by violence. Without a univocal and clear distinction between victim and perpetrator the protagonists of the short films —the son of the arms dealer, the ex child soldier, the Sudanese asylum seeker and the soldier shooting a defenceless captive— serve to illustrate this intangible but very real dimension of war. Although the narratives and images are confronting and at times shocking, the makers have injected sparks of hope. After the outburst of violence in *FAL*, some resolve is displayed. Both the son of the arms dealer and the ex child soldier can cope with their respective traumas. In *Asylum* we find that asylum is ultimately granted to the Sudanese refugee and she chooses to take up life. The finale of *Zero Degree* is the rewinding of the film to the beginning: it halts in the split second before the soldier pulls the trigger. One can always hope that a person decides otherwise.

Filming the Fear of Difference

Stereotypes, assumptions and generalisations are widely spread in the media and political discourse and can even be found in academia. Many of these are so common and seem so natural to us that we never question or even notice them. They block objective information, profound analyses and thinking about more structural aspects of shared life on a globe. Films often strengthen stereotypes and assumptions, but film can also be an instrument to deconstruct accepted identities of people and a means to start an open inquiry into identities and differences. The latter objective was at the heart of the programme of the second night of the IPRA Short Film Festival.

Filming the Fear of Difference involved narratives of two countries that are involved in one of the fiercest, complex and lasting battlefields in the world today. The makers inquire into the identity of individuals living in Iraq and the USA. The war on terror is a defining feature of the world that these portrayed individuals inhabit.

On 21 September 2001 —ten days after 9/11— the Advertising Council of the United States launched its "I am an American" campaign. The campaign "sought to celebrate the ideals that keep this country strong by highlighting the nation's extraordinary diversity." Cynthia Weber has taken a closer look at this ideal. In her series *I am an American* (US/UK 20″) she interviews a wide range of Americans about their experiences, from patriotic soldiers who have served in the Iraq war to patriotic Muslims who found themselves detained as enemy combatants. In these short films, the audience could observe how the rhetoric of the so-called war on terror is mobilised to combat other "threats" to the US, most notably undocumented immigrants and US citizens who dare to care for them; it also shows how US citizens are caught up in strikingly different ways in the post-9/11 US security crossfire.

On the other side of the world, thousands of Iraqis have been displaced by sectarian violence and have had to seek refuge in other parts of the country. A stranger in his own country by Hassanain al Hani (Iraq, 10") presents a portrait of Abu Ali, a refugee from Kirkuk living in a displaced person's camp on the outskirts of Kerbala. He is a peace-loving man with a keen sense of justice, trying to find a way to survive and provide for his family in the difficult circumstances in which they now find themselves.

These two films share the qualification "documentary." At first sight documentaries are less ambiguous than conceptualised fiction. However, these two eye-opening individual stories confront their audience with the complex opportunities and threats of (using) the identity of people living in a country at war.

Kasim Abid is the London-based director of the Independent Film & Television College Bagdad (FTCB), the college that coached the making of A stranger in his own country. Mister Abid highlighted the importance of films by people who are actually living through war; they truly know the impact of war on everyday life. The circumstances in Iraq make it very difficult to run a Film College: students and directors are wounded by attacks, they disappear, transport is often impossible due to check points and fuel and electricity is not always available. However, making these films and showing them in and outside Iraq is a way to re-introduce humanity to that setting. The ultimate message of all the films produced by the FTCB is that most of the Iraqi people want to live in peace, regardless of whether their neighbour is Shi'a, Sunni or Kurdish.

Cynthia Weber stressed that she wanted to deconstruct the myth of national identity by showing seven stories of Americans with very different backgrounds and very different ideas of their American identity. To strengthen this message, all seven stories end with the protagonist saying "I am an American." The motto "out of one, many" is used as an alternative to the classic "from many, one." Some in the audience questioned whether this message is effective and if repeating the motto "I am an American" is not strengthening the unreflective idea of a unique American identity. Other participants clearly understood and accepted the different appeal of this "I am an American" series.

Popular Film and Conflict

On the last evening of the IPRA Short Film Festival, the potential of popular film types, such as comedy, musical and cartoon, was explored. The programme balanced between good taste and pulp: Is mutual destruction not too serious for a funny cartoon? Is an ongoing brutal conflict mocked or made discussable in a foolish musical? Is such popular cinema a light in a dark world, or a tasteless provocation? Can humour give hope and offer a perspective on peace?

Peace on Earth is a 1939 Metro-Goldwyn-Mayer cartoon short subject directed by Hugh Harman (US, 8"26) about a post-apocalyptic world populated by animals. The cartoon presents the audience with a plot evolving around two young squirrels, asking their grandfather on Christmas Eve what are the "men" in the biblical lyric "Peace on Earth, good will to men." The grandfather squirrel then tells them a history of the human race, focusing on the never-ending wars men waged. Still the cartoon does indicate how wars have ultimately ended: with the death of the last man on Earth, a soldier.

West Bank Story by Ari Sandel (US, 21") is a musical comedy about David, an Israeli soldier, and Fatima, a Palestinian fast food cashier —an unlikely couple who fall in love amidst the animosity of their families' duelling falafel stands in the West Bank. Tensions mount when the Kosher King's new pastry machine juts onto Hummus Hut property. The Palestinians ruin the machine and the Israelis respond by building a wall between the two eating establishments. The couple professes their love for each other, triggering a chain of events that destroys both restaurants and forces all to find common ground in an effort to rebuild, planting a seed of hope.

The once very popular *Peace on Earth* was allegedly nominated for the Nobel Peace Prize in 1939, but the outbreak of World War II precluded peace prize awarding in that year. *West Bank Story* won an Oscar in 2006 for Best Short Film, but remains controversial.

The Popular Film and Conflict session turned out to be the most animated of the whole festival. The audience seemed to appreciate the efforts of the filmmakers to handle very serious issues in a refreshing way. After the screenings, Jonas Geirnaert —a Belgian comedian and director of *Flatlife* (Price of the Jury in Cannes in 2004)— and Amy Kim —producer of *West Bank Story*— started off the debate on comedy and conflict. They explained that such films are in the first place funny and pleasant to watch. Reaching an audience that is not familiar with a conflict, such as the Israeli-Palestinian one, they can make people think and make them sensitive to questions of peace and conflict resolution.

Moreover, it was stressed that humour is a powerful weapon to deconstruct assumptions, to cope with painful realities and to explore new angles.

It was clear that for a majority of the audience viewing the films, and especially *West Bank Story*, the experience was nothing less than a kind of release. *West Bank Story* presents some underlying dynamics of conflict in their naked truth and simplicity. This approach even bears the promise of unblocking the endless chain of violence, as soon as basic human relations get a chance. In the words of the director Ari Sandel (2005):

> I sometimes get remarks about the film being too simplistic and that it does not accurately show the suffering of any one side. I agree, it is simplistic because it has to be in order to be a comedy. This film is not meant to be a learning tool for the situation in the Middle East. It is not an historical explanation, or a political solution on screen. It is a movie about hope and peace and that is it. It is meant to counteract the multitudes of negative documentaries and news reports that, while very informative, usually seem to be skewed to one side and always leave the viewer feeling like this conflict will go on forever. I truly believe that peace between Israelis and Arabs will be achieved and don't believe it is a hopeless endeavour. We wanted to make a film that would convey that feeling.

That visual media have an enormous impact on people is now an established and widely accepted fact. Using visual media to critically engage with dominant paradigms or frames of reference is thus a meaningful undertaking. Scholarly engagement with movies and the image is often —but not exclusively— limited to verbal and explanatory exercises. In full awareness of the limits of the written word when images are concerned, we prefer to give the floor to the imaginaries to do their vital work. As the Russian writer Ivan Turgenev insightfully argued: "A picture shows me at a glance what it takes dozens of pages of a book to expound."

References

AL HANI, Hassain (2007): *A stranger in his own country.* Independent Film & Television College, Iraq.

DE GRUYTER, Jess (2007): *It was a boring conversation anyway.* Independent, Belgium.

GEIRNAERT, Jonas (2004): *Flatlife.* KASK, Belgium.

HARMAN, Hugh (1939): *Peace on Earth.* Metro-Goldwyn-Mayer, USA.
KATEDZA, Rumbi (2008): *Asylum.* Fides Fortuna Films, Zimbabwe/UK.
KHOSHNAZAR, Omid (2005): *Zero Degree.* Farhat Film, Iran.
SANDEL, Ari (2005): *West Bank Story.* Independent, USA.
— (2005): *Facts —West Bank Story.* At: http://www.westbankstory.com/new/
facts.htm.
VAN NUFFEL, Hans (2007): *FAL.* Caviar Productions, Belgium.
WEBER, Cynthia (2008): *I am an American.* PATO Productions, USA/UK.

Moral Report
of the International Peace Research Association
(July 2006-July 2008)

Luc Reychler
University of Leuven

Moral Report

Despite some good news reports regarding the state of conflict and peace in the world, there is still a high level of unarmed violence, which along with the confluence of a number of threats, if not responded to more effectively, can create havoc. The threats are: the growing competition over resources, the marginalization of the majority world, climate change, global militarization, competition between brutal and sophisticated capitalism and the pressure to democratize the international system. Conflict and peacebuilding has become part and parcel of national and international governmental and non governmental organizations. In addition, more universities provide M.A. and Ph.D. programs in conflict and peace studies. There are several international associations that meet at conferences to discuss the state of peace and conflict research. IPRA is the oldest peace research association and distinguishes itself by membership from all continents (it has five regional Peace Research Associations) and by the presence of researchers and reflecting practitioners. Every two years we can reckon on the support of donors and volunteers. IPRA is reorganizing itself to deal with the new challenges of researching conflict and peace and strengthening intellectual solidarity, which is essential in conflict transformation and peacebuilding processes.

Activities

Incorporation

For the second time, IPRA has been registered as an international non-profit organization. The first time was in the Netherlands in 1964; now in Brussels on 19 September 2007. This implies (1) that IPRA as a legal entity is registered in Belgium: the address is International Peace Research Association, c/o Luc Reychler Parkstraat 45, bus 3602, Leuven 3000, Belgium. New Secretary Generals will communicate its new *operational addresses*. IPRA (2) provides each year a financial report according to the generally accepted accounting practices for international non-profit organisations. IPRA (3) also should communicate all changes in the statutes and in its governing bodies.

Secretariat

The Secretariat has developed (1) a more functional website for communicating with members and advertising the association and (2) a method for paying membership fees; additionally, more people in the network are becoming lifetime members.

Conference Host Committee

The IPRA conference host committee in Leuven, together with the Secretariat took the responsibility to organize the 2008 conference. This implied organizing: a new conference website, processing paper proposals, fundraising, coordinating the plenary sessions, facilitating the distribution of the grants, enlarging the staff and engaging volunteers, designing the programme book and many other tasks.

UN and ISSC

IPRA has been more actively involved in the UN and the International Social Sciences Council-UNESCO. It has paid the ISSC membership fees of 2007 and 2008. With the aid of the IPRA Foundation, the SG paid 8000 US$ to the International Journal of Peace Studies for the period 2004-2008 and the delivery of 200 issues to (paid-up) IPRA members.

New Working Groups

New IPRA working groups have been created with the following specializations: sports and peace, negotiation and mediation and development and peace.

Quality Control

On the basis of the experiences during the last four years, a strategic note has been drafted that describes a series of challenges that need to be addressed (see next section).

Strategic Issues: On Deepening, Widening and Rejuvenating IPRA

IPRA was created in 1964 by a group of eminent scholars in order develop the study of peace research and to strengthen its impact on the decision-making related to conflict prevention and peacebuilding in the world. Since then, conflict prevention and peacebuilding have become incorporated into national and international governmental and non-governmental organizations and the research is growing and transforming in different ways. A great deal of today's peace research focuses on sustainable peacebuilding is transdisciplinary and tries to synergize the knowledge and know-how of researchers, practitioners and decision makers. All of this and more impacts the international research community. In order to improve its role as a facilitating and catalyzing agent, the IPRA Council decided to tackle some issues which need attention (below). Others ideas are welcome, especially actionable suggestions.

Positioning IPRA in an Expanding Field of Conflict Prevention and Peacebuilding

IPRA started as a scientific research association, later became a peace research movement, then became a place for exchanging knowledge and know-how from scientific researchers and practitioners. A great number of associations are now addressing conflict and peace issues. The International Studies Association (ISA), for example, has a large peace studies group, which organizes panels for discussing academic research papers at its mega conferences. Most other disciplinary associations have sections on, for example, psychology, anthropology, or economics of conflict and peace.

— How does IPRA position itself in the changing research land-scape?
— Are we a purely academic association or a hybrid association bringing together knowledge from different actors (researchers, practitioners, etc.)?
— Are we a transdisciplinary research community?
— Are we an inconvenient science that criticizes political claims, political correctness, diminishing academic freedom, etc.?
— Who do we consider a peace researcher? What are the academic and operational credentials expected?

SG opinion and suggestions:

— IPRA should remain an academic and hybrid association which tries to synergize the knowledge and know-how from peace re-searchers and practitioners. It should be a critical and creative association that analyzes and evaluates conflict behavior and searches for effective solutions.
— Since the majority of the members are academics, membership in IPRA should be perceived as asset in one's academic career. The association should therefore attract and select the best and most courageous scholars.
— A taskforce should be created to write a report on the qualities and credentials to expect from a peace researcher/ peace builder.

Regional Activities and Gaps

— How are IPRA's regional associations functioning? Some are active while others are in sleeping mode. What is needed to strengthen their activities?
— How can we get greater input from our weaker geographic re-gions like the Middle East, Francophone Africa, China, etc.? Should we promote the creation of national peace research associations?
— What is needed to create a new regional association for the Mid-dle East? Should we start at the national level?

SG opinion and suggestions:

— The less active regional associations should actively seek candi-dates which could rejuvenate the organization.
— Why not stimulate the creation of national or sub regional peace research associations?
— They could provide a more solid base for the regional associa-tions.

— Cooperation could be explored between, for example, EUPRA and the European Doctoral Enhancement Network for peace and conflict studies (EDEN).
— Create a Middle East Peace Research association (MEPRA) including researchers from all the stakeholders, including the excluded.
— Create a peace research association in the Great Lakes Region of Africa.

Periodicals on Conflict Transformation and Peace

Publish or perish is the reality for university students. Therefore it's important to map the periodical landscape and to understand how they are ranked.

— What are the main periodicals?
— How are the ranked?
— Who evaluates the periodicals and what criteria are used?
— Should IPRA research all and become part of the valuation process?

SG opinion and suggestions: A taskforce should be created to analyze and evaluate the current ranking process of the peace research journals.

The Role of IPRA Secretary General (SG) and the Functioning of the Secretariat

The Secretary General and the Secretariat team have spent most of their time on management issues such as: the registration of IPRA as a legal international body; setting up the website; promoting membership; fundraising for IPRA and the conferences; organizing the biennial conferences. There is practically no time for representation, critical thinking and strategizing. Luckily, the University of Leuven provided space for the Secretariat and the organization of the 2008 conference. The SG invested a great deal of his academic and spare time to IPRA business. A mobile Secretariat raises problems related to: (1) finding space, (2) raising money for paying the team, (3) transferring the know-how to and the steep learning-curve of the new Secretariat.

— What do we expect from the SG?
— How can we make the function of SG more bearable?
— What can be done do enhance the effectiveness of the SG?
— Should the administrative part be more well-defined and delegated to an executive director, as in ISA? ISA has a permanent

Secretariat: a paid executive director, a staff of more than 10 people, and a budget (dues and income from periodicals) that pays for an effective Secretariat. We are not an American-European based association, but nevertheless we should think about delegating and organizing the purely administrative functions of IPRA more effectively.

SG opinion and suggestions: The workload of the Secretariat needs to be shared by three groups: (1) the *conference host committee* should organize the conference and raise funds; (2) the administrative functions of the IPRA Secretariat —including paying staff, setting up a website, dealing with membership issues and dues, organizing the call for papers, and fundraising— could be done by creating the function of *director general* and a more stable Secretariat; (3) the *Secretary General* should represent, promote and steer IPRA. He/she should supervise and assist the working of IPRA and raise funds for its further development.

Commissions & Working Groups

The commissions are the pillars of IPRA. Some are functioning well and creatively; a few lead a passive life. There are old and new commissions, working groups aspiring to become commissions, and new working groups that should be created according to the evolution of peace research.

SG opinion and suggestions: Conveners of commissions should have a greater voice in IPRA. It would be useful to bring the conveners together at the conference and to discuss with them: (1) the function of their commissions, (2) the interaction with the Secretariat General in the preparation of the biennial conferences, (3) needs and expectations for the future, etc.

The Demography of IPRA

IPRA needs to make sure that all research generations are well represented in each of its bodies (Council, commissions, regional associations).

SG opinion and suggestions: In each of the IPRA bodies, active efforts should be made to identify and invite new and young researchers to the association. They could be asked to organize panels, become co-conveners, create new working groups, or set up national-level peace research associations.

The Financial Life of IPRA

IPRA rests a great deal on the voluntary efforts made by many members. This is very important, but it is not enough for an organization to function and respond effectively to the conflict and peace challenges we are confronted with. Therefore it's important we discuss what is minimally needed to keep a world organization alive and kicking. This implies making up a list of the fixed costs (such as personnel, space, communication, the journal, membership, ISSC fees, etc.) and the expected income from membership fees. To flourish, IPRA will need to raise funds in more committed and professional ways.

SG opinion and suggestions:

— The Secretariat will present a report on (1) what is financially needed to run IPRA, (2) the expected income from membership fees.
— One of the roles of the SG will be to raise money for the development of IPRA.
— The IPRA Foundation should generate a higher level of income and play a crucial role.

Thanks

Let me end by thanking all those who made this conference possible: the University of Leuven, the Faculty of Social Sciences, the Institute for International and European Policy and its Center for Peace Research and Strategic Studies; the conference host committee, the mayor of Leuven, Louis Tobback, the conveners of the IPRA commissions —they are the pillars of IPRA— and the IPRA Council. Our sincere thanks goes also to the Norwegian Ministry of Foreign Affairs, the Swiss Government, The German Ministry for Economic Cooperation and Development, the Belgian Ministry of Foreign Affairs, the Flemish Government, the Plowshares Collaboration and Manchester College, the Toda Institute, and the IPRA Foundation, all of whom provided financial means for organizing the conference and flying participants in from far away. Special thanks go to the Flemish Peace Institute who provided the conference bags and organized the short film festival. The conference also benefited from the support of the InBev brewery for beer, which in some European and African cultures is symbol of peace, and Lee Cooper Jeans for designing a new T-shirt. The concept is brilliant:

"Feel the peace"

is written in braille and in crimson. In addition to its elegance, it reminds us that *people who are not in touch with peace may turn to senseless war*. I also would like to recognize Wouter Mullier, an artist from Leuven, who designed the IPRA peace award to commemorate the 2008 conference.

Last but not least, there is the hard work of the IPRA Secretariat and our transnational conference team, consisting of Julianne, Natallia, Katharine, Erica, Greet, Peter, Chelley, Parmjeet, Ingrid, and many others who did everything to make this conference possible.